RELIGION AND
SOCIAL ORGANIZATION IN
CENTRAL POLYNESIA

AMS PRESS
NEW YORK

RELIGION AND SOCIAL ORGANIZATION IN CENTRAL POLYNESIA

BY

ROBERT W. WILLIAMSON, M.Sc.

Author of *The Mafulu Mountain People of British New Guinea,*
The Social and Political Systems of Central Polynesia,
Religious and Cosmic Beliefs of Central Polynesia

Edited by

RALPH PIDDINGTON, M.A., Ph.D.

With a Preface by

RAYMOND FIRTH, M.A., Ph.D.

Reader in Anthropology in the
University of London

CAMBRIDGE
AT THE UNIVERSITY PRESS
1937

Library of Congress Cataloging in Publication Data

BL
2600
W52
1977

Williamson, Robert Wood, 1856-1932.
    Religion and social organization in central
Polynesia.

    Reprint of the 1937 ed. published at the Uni-
versity Press, Cambridge, Eng.
    Includes index.
    1. Polynesia—Religion. 2. Ethnology—
Polynesia. 3. Polynesia—Social life and customs.
4. Mythology, Polynesian. I. Title.
BL2600.W52 1977   301.5'8   75-35218
ISBN 0-404-14241-9

Reprinted from the edition of 1937, Cambridge
First AMS edition published in 1977
Manufactured in the United States of America

AMS PRESS INC.
NEW YORK, N.Y.

CONTENTS

FOREWORD

THE work of the late ROBERT W. WILLIAMSON in social anthropology began in 1908, when he set out to do field-work in Oceania, the outcome of which was his book *The Mafulu Mountain People of British New Guinea*. How great were the difficulties with which he had to contend in obtaining the material for this work emerges very clearly from the following extract from the Introduction contributed to it by Dr A. C. Haddon:

Mr Williamson was formerly a solicitor, and always had a great longing to see something of savage life, but it was not until about four years ago [written in 1912] that he saw his way to attempting the realization of his desire by an expedition to Melanesia. He made my acquaintance in the summer of 1908, and seeing that he was so keenly interested, I lent him my MS. notes on Melanesia; by the help of these and by the study of other books he gained a good knowledge of the ethnology of that area. In November, 1908, he started for Oceania for the first time and reached Fiji, from which place he had intended to start on his expedition. Circumstances over which he had no control, however, prevented the carrying out of his original programme; so he went to Sydney, and there arranged modified plans. He was on the point of executing these, when he was again frustrated by a telegram from England which necessitated his immediate return. It was a sad blow to him to have his long-cherished schemes thus thwarted and rendered abortive, but, undaunted, he set about to plan another expedition. Accordingly, in January, 1910, he once more set sail for Australia as a starting-place for the Solomon Islands and British New Guinea, and this time achieved success; the book which he now offers to the public is the result of this plucky enterprise. In justice to the author it should be known that, owing to climatic and other conditions, he was unwell during the whole of his time in New Guinea, and had an injured foot and leg that hurt him every step he took. The only wonder is that he was able to accomplish so large and so thorough a piece of work as he has done.[1]

In spite of the difficulties and discomforts under which he laboured, it is noteworthy that nowhere in the whole book does he refer to these, except in so far as they interfered with his scientific work.[2] The work itself was carried out at a time when anthropological field research was in the pioneering stage, and Mr Williamson's legal training in the collection and sifting of evidence contributed very materially to the value of his

[1] Introduction to *The Mafulu Mountain People of British New Guinea*, pp. xvii–xviii.

[2] We learn, however, something of his personal experiences in his less strictly scientific and more autobiographical book, *The Ways of the South Sea Savage* (1914). Dangers, difficulties and physical discomforts alike were faced with fortitude and recorded with cheerful good humour, while throughout runs the continuous thread of scientific interest in native peoples.

researches. In particular, the description of "the big feast...the greatest and most important social function of a Mafulu community of villages" (Chapter VIII) gives a vivid picture of a series of significant ceremonies, and indicates their importance as factors of social integration.

After this, Williamson turned his attention from Melanesia to Polynesia, or more correctly to Central Polynesia, for time did not allow him to include Hawaii and New Zealand in his studies. He collected from literary sources an enormous amount of material, which is well known to students of Polynesian ethnology from his published works. The three volumes of *The Social and Political Systems of Central Polynesia* provide the only comprehensive account of social organization throughout this area, while his *Religious and Cosmic Beliefs of Central Polynesia*, in two volumes, gives a survey of a number of beliefs relating to the cosmogony, to the sky and celestial phenomena, and to the fate of the soul after death. Both of these works are remarkable for the thoroughness with which the ethnographic observations are collated and documented. The material embodied in the present volume concludes the study of religious beliefs and practices inaugurated in the second of the two works mentioned.

In January 1935 it was arranged with Mr Williamson's executors that I should undertake the task of editing, under the general supervision of Dr Raymond Firth, a body of Williamson's posthumous manuscripts. When these were first reviewed with a view to publication, certain problems presented themselves. In the first place, the subject was treated in a very detailed manner, and to a large extent duplicated material already published; for this reason it did not seem desirable to publish the manuscript *in extenso*, and it has accordingly been very greatly abridged. In doing this, however, I have retained, with a very few exceptions, the detailed references to the original authorities, in the hope that this work may serve not only to give a general description of Polynesian religion, but also to provide the specialist with references to the earlier and less well-known authorities. It was originally intended to incorporate in this work a body of manuscript dealing with the ceremonial surrounding the life of the individual—birth and pregnancy rites, marriage customs, and mortuary ritual, as well as a number of shorter sections dealing with specific phases of Polynesian ethnology. As the date of publication approached, however, it became clear that this material could not be incorporated, though I have drawn upon it in Part II, particularly in Chapter x where I have developed Mr Williamson's unpublished discussion of the religious functions of the *arioi* society of the Society Islands.

A further difficulty arose from the fact that the original manuscript was based almost exclusively upon the statements of earlier observers, and with a few exceptions did not go beyond material published up to the beginning of the war. It is common knowledge that since that time our appreciation of the ethnology of Central Polynesia has been very greatly augmented by the research of modern field-workers, in particular, of those working under the auspices of the Bernice P. Bishop Museum in Honolulu and of the Australian National Research Council. In dealing with the work of the earlier observers, Mr Williamson, with the assistance of Miss Muriel Campbell, collected, classified and collated a vast number of individual statements which were arranged in an elaborate filing system, involving some six hundred headings. This work occupied several years, and it would have been impossible, in the time at my disposal, to accord a similar treatment to the more recent material. I have, however, provided some general references to this in Part I, and have drawn upon it to a very large extent in Part II.

In addition to the amount of ethnographic material which has accumulated since the completion of Williamson's collection of references, the more recent researches have brought to light certain new principles of method and of presentation by drawing attention to the contextual relationships existing between groups of ethnographic facts. In Samoa, Dr Margaret Mead has studied kinship in relation to other forms of social grouping, while Dr P. H. Buck has drawn attention to a number of important factors in the social context of technological processes. Dr H. Ian Hogbin has made a functional study of law in Ontong Java, while Dr Raymond Firth has applied this method to the study of Maori economics, as well as to various phases of social organization in Tikopia.

Certain generalizations of this type are to be found in Mr Williamson's published works. To mention only two examples, in dealing with land tenure, he draws attention to the number of factors—legal, economic, and political—which must be taken into account in discussing this aspect of native life; and again, in considering chieftainship, he points out the importance of the

element of sanctity associated with this institution throughout Central Polynesia. But the task of treating Polynesian
religion in this way, of analysing it into its elements and of
indicating its relationship to other aspects of culture, had not
been attempted by him. In order, then, to bring this work into
line with modern tendencies in social anthropology, I have
tried, in Part II, to treat the material on Polynesian religion—
some of it collected by Williamson and some contributed by
recent field research—in this way. Though such a treatment
goes beyond the original scheme projected by the author, it is,
I believe, justified by the importance of a contextual study of
Polynesian religion, both for theoretical anthropology and for
actual observation in the field.

In presenting this work, I should like to express my indebted-
ness to those who have contributed towards its production. To
Miss Muriel Campbell, whose patient collection of references
and careful preparation of the original manuscript have considerably eased the work; to the President, Council and staff of
the Royal Anthropological Institute, in particular Miss K. M.
Martindell, for the many courtesies extended to me; to Professor C. G. Seligman, friend of the late R. W. Williamson, who
has taken a keen interest in the publication of his posthumous
manuscripts, and upon whose advice the present work was
undertaken; to the Executors of the estate, who have provided
the financial assistance necessary for the preparation of the
manuscript and its publication; and finally to Dr Raymond
Firth, whose scholarship and field research have contributed
so much to our understanding of Polynesian culture. It is
impossible to assess the debt which this work owes to his
wide knowledge of anthropological theory in general and of
Polynesian ethnology in particular.

RALPH PIDDINGTON

PREFACE

THE study of religion is always an attractive subject for the scholar and the layman. Whatever be our convictions as to the nature of the universe, whether or not we believe in the soul and a life after death, whether we regard God as the Creator or a social creation, we still cannot help but be moved by the struggles of humanity to solve these fundamental problems and to give a meaning and a stability to existence. Even to survey the life of a savage people has its interest—their battle with the forces of nature and their persistent attempts in the face of annihilation to forge and use the weapons of the supernatural to supplement their puny and in a sense fruitless efforts have a drama, a courage and a pathos which touch us closely. Here Polynesia offers a rich field for observation. Its people have a fascinating and intricate mythology personifying natural forces with a high degree of imagination and a beauty of narrative which stands comparison with the myths of Greece and Rome. (And like those of classical Europe the mythic tales of Polynesia have now been bowdlerized, emasculated, injected with foreign moral values to be used as reading material for school-children of the Antipodes.) The Polynesians have much else too: baffling concepts like *mana* and taboo; intriguing statuary and pseudo-pyramids of stone; atypical forms of totemism; curious fraternities like the *arioi*; seasonal cycles of worship; deification of ancestors; separation of spiritual from temporal rulers—all of which have been long subjected to scientific analysis and made the basis for anthropological theories.

In this field the position of R. W. Williamson was well established before his death; his three volumes of *The Social and Political Systems of Central Polynesia*, followed by his posthumous two volumes of *Religious and Cosmic Beliefs of Central Polynesia*, are standard works of their type. In them Williamson's indefatigable industry, care and accuracy, his wide range of scholarship and his sober speculations are already too well known to need further comment. This present volume is a continuation of the *Religious and Cosmic Beliefs*, taking up the unfinished study of "their great army of gods and spirits, beliefs and ideas relating to certain sacred places and objects, and other

matters ", as Professor C. G. Seligman said in his Preface to that
work, quoting Williamson's own words.

The Editor of this volume, Dr Piddington, has done a difficult task well. To take up the threads of another man's work,
interweave them with new strands spun since that work was
laid down, and yet present a fabric that preserves the rich
pattern of the original is an achievement. It has demanded not
only enthusiasm, industry and sound anthropological knowledge, but also a flair for seeing the relevance of new material
and new points of view and setting them in judicious perspective. He has thus been able to continue Williamson's plan
and to round off suitably the analysis of the esoteric aspects of
Polynesian culture.

There emerge from this book, as from Williamson's former
works, two important and related conclusions. The first is the
essential interpenetration of Polynesian religion into other
aspects of the native life and its supremely practical value.
Stories of the gods are not simple narratives, analogous to
literature, or merely primitive philosophy couched in allegoric
form; they appear as part of the dogmatic ideological background for the human affairs of daily life—the actions and
privileges of chiefs, titles to land, the maintenance of law and
order, the practice of carpentry and other crafts, fishing, dart-
throwing or dancing. Where variations of a tale are found they
are often to be explained not just as ignorant garblings of an
original "true" version, but as equally valid formulations, from
different angles, of present social status and privilege in terms
of the traditional past. The worship of the gods, again, is
directed to such practical and immediate ends as securing a
catch of bonito or other fish; a good taro harvest; or the recovery
of a patient from illness—not merely the vague amorphous
concept of "Life", as some writers would have it. In this
respect, as the present book shows, the vast and most valuable
collections of Fornander, Teuira Henry and Te Whatahoro are
most deficient. Consisting mainly of a body of traditional lore,
dogma verbally transmitted from one generation to another,
they contain but scanty records of how this dogma actually
worked in the life of the people, how individual fishermen or
gardeners made their appeals to the gods, what they thought
about them, and what they did when their appeals were not
successful. In particular, the social affiliations of the gods have
been neglected in the documentary accounts available to us.

Frequently the statement is given that a certain god was worshipped by the people of an island, but it is not said whether he was worshipped by all to the same degree. We know that in some cases this was not so. It has been ascertained, for instance, that in Tikopia each god was linked primarily with one only of the major kinship groups, but that the more important gods of each group were invoked in a secondary position by other kinship groups to perform specific duties. Hence in this island each group has its own "table of precedence" for worship of the gods which are in the main common to them all. This is not always the case in other Polynesian communities, but for many we have no adequate information. If we had, many conflicting statements as to the importance and functions of various deities might perhaps be resolved. But on this essential relation between dogma, rite and the practical affairs of specific social groups the Editor of this book rightly insists, and has done a great deal to collate what material there is and to present it in a unified account of religious worship. Arising out of this he shows too how the classical definitions of the relation between religion and magic, valuable as they are, do not cover the Polynesian situation exactly. He is moved to a re-formulation of the problem, treating religion as that which validates the supernatural and maintains it, and magic as that which uses the supernatural for practical ends, whether by appeal to the power of the gods or by formulae and acts believed to be self-sufficient. If this definitely novel idea in anthropology will not command general agreement, it should at least challenge attention and point to the need for a re-examination of the problem in the light of Polynesian data. Here as elsewhere the book is a meritorious contribution to the modern study of religion as well as a welcome addition to the literature of Polynesian anthropology.

The second conclusion which can be drawn is the importance of having anthropological field-work inspired by a systematic body of theory. Over and over again the Editor of this volume is impelled to point out, as Williamson did in his former works, that there are gaps in the data on even some of the fundamentals of Polynesian religion. Williamson noted the paucity of information about the soul, the distinction between human and non-human spirits, the fate and destination of the souls of the dead. Since he wrote some of these gaps have been filled, in part by the extensive and enterprising workers sponsored by

the Bernice Pauahi Bishop Museum, such as Dr Peter Buck (Te
Rangi Hiroa), Dr E. W. Gifford, Dr E. S. C. Handy, Mr J. F.
Stimson; in part by other investigators such as Mr D. G.
Kennedy, Dr H. I. Hogbin and the present writer. It is true
that in many islands there has been little opportunity for many
years for research into ancient beliefs and especially into ancient
practices. The conversion of the people to Christianity for
nearly a century has meant a loss of knowledge of the traditional
forms, and only in a few isolated islands, like Rennell and
Tikopia, do the old cults still hold sway. It is almost with a
shock that one realizes that only two present-day Polynesian
anthropologists have ever seen a religious ceremony actually
performed by people who hold and practise their ancient faith.
But in spite of the passing of the old faiths there is still much
that can be done. Culture-contact has produced specifically
Polynesian reactions to Christianity; adherence to the Church is
mingled with many active beliefs in *mana*, taboo and witchcraft;
and there are problems such as the relation of the new religion
to the social and economic order, or the inculcation of religious
ideology into children, which can be studied equally well under
modern conditions. This is quite apart from the investigation
of the special cults, such as the Ringa tu of the Urewera Maori,
originating in maladjustment to European contact and desire
for a brand of Christianity which will be in conformity with
native institutions. This book does not deal with the modern
situation at all, which lies outside its sphere, but in its emphasis
on the pragmatic aspect of the ancient religion it forms a most
useful background to such studies, and poses a number of
important problems which directly bear upon them. Even in
regard to the ancient Polynesian faith it may still be possible to
secure more data upon such questions as the validation of land
tenure and other property rights by religion, the attitude of individuals towards taboo places and things, or the operation of
ritual in fishing. Here the book gives a direct stimulus to new
research.

A great deal of the study of Polynesian anthropology hereto-
fore has been bound up with the hope of settling the problem
of origins, of tracing the migrations of the people, of setting the
history of one island group in perspective against that of others.
Attention to this problem is clearly dictated by the obvious
affinities in physical type, language and culture to be found
throughout the vast range of islands from Rennell and Ontong

Java in the west to Easter Island in the east, from Hawaii in the north to the Chatham Islands in the south. The problem has too a kind of detective interest, with tantalizing clues pointing in various directions—to Indonesia, to Indo-China, to China proper, to Japan, and even to the North-west coast of America. And the solution, if discovered, would be of the utmost importance for the understanding of that peculiar genius of the Polynesian people which is expressed in a combination of realism and practicality with a deep feeling for etiquette and ritual and a high artistic capacity. It would help us also to separate out in specific cultures the common heritage from local developments, to estimate more adequately the influence of particular environmental factors or the institutional effects of the clash of contending groups. The difficulty is that in dealing with the history of a non-literate people the investigator must rely so largely upon material culture and oral tradition. The evidence afforded by the first is fairly solid, but very limited, especially since the ephemeral nature of so many Polynesian artefacts leaves the archaeologist with only stone (and a few bone) objects for his reconstruction of the past, and tells him practically nothing of former social institutions. The evidence of tradition is much more far-reaching, but much less reliable. Only in a few instances, notably in that of the Maori, can we establish with any certainty the immediate antecedents of some elements in the present population. In other cases the reconstructions made have involved a great number of assumptions the validity of which is rarely considered, and too frequently inferences incorporating these assumptions are treated as generalizations of fact. The result has been the building of elaborate houses of traditional cards which are imposing for their height rather than for their substance.

But the most cogent criticism which can be made against such historical reconstructions is that, preoccupied with them, their authors have failed to realize the interest of the material for comparative generalizations on the one time-level—for studying the distribution of customs, different types and the variations from them, and the possible correlation of type and variation with specific social and geographical conditions. Some work of this kind has been done, notably by Dr Buck in technology. But in the field of religion there has been a tendency to concentrate attention on the common elements in the mythological material and set them in a time series, especially for the larger islands;

to seek to reconcile apparent discrepancies in the names and functions of the "major" gods; to look upon the less close resemblances in other, especially smaller, islands as attenuations, degeneration-products of an original cult; and to ignore the importance of the worship of gods with a limited distribution. A close study of the role of "local" gods in the various island groups would probably give more insight into the real character of Polynesian religion than does pursuit of the cult of Io or of Tangaroa, useful as that may be. Such thorough comparative study, in all branches of anthropology, must precede the building up of any scheme of Polynesian history, and will lay the foundations for it.

Some of this work has already been done by Mr Williamson, who in his scholarly fashion set himself to examine and compare all the records, including the earliest, and laid down clearly the fundamental premises upon which he based his conclusions. Though like all reconstructions of Polynesian history these conclusions are open to certain objections, they are stated as tentative hypotheses in a cautious form which might well have been imitáted by others in this field. This present book carries on and deepens the analysis of part of his field, in particular demonstrating the vitality of Polynesian religion and its specific cultural role in a number of island groups. As part of his plan Williamson envisaged a further comparative study of an integrative type which would take in traditional material and social institutions and consider their relevance to the problems of Polynesian history. A volume on this subject is now in preparation. When it is completed Polynesian scholars of the future will have still further reason to be grateful for the monumental research which Williamson carried out himself and caused to be sponsored when he had laid down his own pen.

RAYMOND FIRTH

1937

BIBLIOGRAPHY AND ABBREVIATIONS
(PART 1)

BIBLIOGRAPHY	ABBREVIATIONS USED IN NOTES
Agostini, Jules. Tahiti. Paris: 1905	Agostini
Aitken, R. T. Ethnology of Tubuai. Bishop Museum Bulletin 70. Honolulu: 1930	Aitken, *Tubuai*
Arbousset, M. Tahiti et les îles adjacentes... Paris: 1867	Arbousset
Ari'i Taimai (Mrs Salmon). The Memoirs of Ari'i Taimai. Paris: 1901	Ari'i Taimai
Baessler, Arthur. Neue Südsee Bilder. Berlin: 1900	Baessler, *N.S.B.*
—— Südsee Bilder. Berlin: 1895	„ *S.B.*
Baker, Shirley W. An English-Tongan Vocabulary... Auckland, N.Z.: 1897	Baker
Balfour, Marie C. *See* **Stevenson**, Mrs M. I.	
Banks, Sir Joseph. Journal of the Right Hon. Sir Joseph Banks, Bart.,...during Captain Cook's first voyage in H.M.S. *Endeavour* in 1768–71, etc. Edited by Sir Joseph D. Hooker. London: 1896	Banks
Bastian, Adolf. Die heilige Sage der Polynesier. Leipzig: 1881	Bastian, *H.S.P.*
—— Inselgruppen in Oceanien... Berlin: 1883	„ *I.O.*
Bays, Peter. A narrative of the wreck of the Minerva Whaler of Port Jackson, New South Wales... Cambridge: 1831	Bays
Beechey, F. W. Narrative of a voyage to the Pacific and Beering's Strait...in the years 1825, 26, 27, 28. 2 vol. London: 1831	Beechey
Behrens, Carl Friedrich. Reise durch die Süd-länder und um die Welt. Frankfurt und Leipzig: 1737	Behrens
Belcher, Sir Edward. Narrative of a voyage round the world, performed in His Majesty's ship Sulphur, during the years 1836–1842. 2 vol. London: 1843	Belcher
Bennet, George. Journal of voyages and travels by the Rev. Daniel Tyerman and George Bennet Esq....in the South Sea Islands...between the years 1821 and 1829. Compiled from the original documents by J. M. 2 vol. London: 1831	Tyerman
Bennett, Frederick D. Narrative of a whaling voyage round the globe, from the year 1833 to 1836... 2 vol. London: 1840	Bennett
Berchon, M. Le tatouage aux îles marquises. Bulletins de la Société d'Anthropologie de Paris, t. 1, p. 99. Paris: 1860	Berchon
Bille, Steen. Bericht über die Reise der Corvette Galathea um die Welt in den Jahren 1845, 46 und 47. Aus dem Dänischen übersetzt, und theilweise bearbeitet von W. v. Rosen, Mitarbeiter am Original. 2 Bd. Leipzig: 1852	Steen Bille
Bligh, William. A voyage to the South Sea. London: 1792	Bligh
Boisse, E. Les îles Samoa, Nukunono, Fakaafo, Wallis et Hoorn. Bulletin de la Société de Géographie, etc. Sixième série, t. x, Juillet-Décembre, 1875, p. 428. Paris: 1875	Boisse

BIBLIOGRAPHY	ABBREVIATIONS USED IN NOTES
Bougainville, L. A. de. A voyage round the world. Performed by order of His most Christian Majesty, in the years 1766, 1767, 1768 and 1769. Translated from the French by John Reinhold Forster, F.A.S. London: 1772	Bougainville
Bourdin, J. A. Vie du vénérable P. M. L. Chanel, prêtre de la Société de Marie. Paris: Lyon: 1867	Bourdin
Bovis, Lieut. de. État de la Société Taitienne, à l'arrivée des Européens. Annuaire des établissements français de l'Océanie...pour l'année commune 1863, p. 217. Papeete: 1863	de Bovis
Brenchley, Julius L. Jottings during the Cruise of H.M.S. Curaçoa among the South Sea Islands in 1865. London: 1873	Brenchley
Brigham, William T. An Index to the Islands of the Pacific Ocean. Memoirs of the B. P. Bishop Museum, vol. 1, No. 2. Honolulu: 1900	Brigham
Brodie, Walter. Pitcairn's Island, and the Islanders, in 1850. London: 1851	Brodie
Brosses, Ch. de. Histoire des Navigations aux Terres Australes. 2 t. Paris: 1756	de Brosses
Brown, George. Melanesians and Polynesians... London: 1910	Brown
Buck, P. H. *See* **Te Rangi Hiroa**	
Burney, James. A chronological history of the voyages and discoveries in the South Sea... 5 vol. London: 1817	Burney
Buzacott, Aaron. Mission life in the islands of the Pacific. Being a narrative of the life and labours of the Rev. A. Buzacott....Edited by the Rev. J. P. Sunderland and the Rev. A. Buzacott, B.A. London: 1866	Buzacott
Byron, Hon. John. An account of a voyage round the world, in the years 1764, 1765 and 1766. By the Honourable Commodore Byron, in his Majesty's Ship the Dolphin. (Hawkesworth, vol. 1.) *See* **Hawkesworth**, John	Hawkesworth
C., le Père A., Société de Marie. Dictionnaire Toga-Français. Paris: 1890	Père A. C.
Caillot, A. C. Eugène. Mythes, Légendes et Traditions des Polynésiens. Paris: 1914	Caillot, *Mythes*
—— Les Polynésiens orientaux au contact de la civilisation. Paris: 1909	„ *L.P.O.*
Calvert, James and **Williams**, Thomas. Fiji and the Fijians. 2 vol. London: 1858	Williams and Calvert
Campbell, F. A. A year in the New Hebrides, Loyalty Islands and New Caledonia. Geelong: Melbourne: 1873	Campbell
Carteret, Philip. An account of a voyage round the world, in the years 1766, 1767, 1768 and 1769. By Philip Carteret, Esquire, Commander of his Majesty's sloop the Swallow. (Hawkesworth, vol. 1.) *See* **Hawkesworth**, John	Hawkesworth
Chalmers, James. Journal of a missionary voyage among the out-stations of the Hervey Group, South Pacific, during the months of June and July, 1875. London: 1876	Chalmers
Chamisso, Adelbert von. Reise um die Welt mit der romanzoffischen Entdeckungs-Expedition in den Jahren 1815–18 auf der Brigg Rurik, Kapitän Otto v. Kotzebue. 2 Bd. Leipzig: 1842	Chamisso

BIBLIOGRAPHY AND ABBREVIATIONS xix

BIBLIOGRAPHY	ABBREVIATIONS USED IN NOTES
Cheyne, Andrew. A description of Islands in the Western Pacific Ocean... London: 1852	Cheyne
Christian, F. W. The Caroline Islands. London: 1899	Christian
Churchill, William. Easter Island. Publications of the Carnegie Institution, No. 174. Washington: 1912	Churchill, *E.I.*
—— The Polynesian Wanderings. Publications of the Carnegie Institution, No. 134. Washington: 1911	„ *P.W.*
—— Sissano. Movements of Migration within and through Melanesia. Publications of the Carnegie Institution, No. 244. Washington: 1916	„ *S.*
Churchward, William B. My Consulate in Samoa. London: 1887	Churchward
Claret de Fleurieu, C. P. *See* **Marchand**, Étienne	
Codrington, R. H. The Melanesians. Oxford: 1891	Codrington
Collocott, E. E. V. Tales and Poems of Tonga. Bishop Museum Bulletin 46. Honolulu: 1928	Collocott, *T.P.T.*
Colvin, Sir Sidney. *See* **Stevenson**, Robert Louis	
Cook, James. The voyages of Captain James Cook round the world. Printed verbatim from the original editions. 7 vol. London: 1813	Cook
Cooper, H. Stonehewer. Coral Lands. 2 vol. London: 1880	Cooper
Coppinger, R. W. Cruise of the "Alert"... London: 1883	Coppinger
Corney, Bolton Glanvill. The Quest and Occupation of Tahiti by the Emissaries of Spain during the years 1772–1776.... Translated into English and compiled with notes and an introduction by Bolton Glanvill Corney Vol. I. London: 1913. (Hakluyt Society, series II, vol. XXXII) Vol. II. London: 1915. (Hakluyt Society, series II, vol. XXXVI) Vol. III. London: 1919. (Hakluyt Society, series II, vol. XLIII)	Corney, *Tahiti*
—— The voyage of Captain Don Felipe Gonzalez in the Ship of the Line San Lorenzo, with the Frigate Santa Rosalia in company, to Easter Island in 1770–1: Preceded by an Extract from Mynheer Jacob Roggeveen's Official Log of his discovery of and visit to Easter Island in 1722. Transcribed, translated, and edited by Bolton Glanvill Corney. Cambridge: 1908. (Hakluyt Society, series II, vol. XIII)	„ *Easter*
Coulter, John. Adventures in the Pacific. Dublin: 1845	Coulter
Crook, W. MS. Journal. (London Missionary Society Library)	Crook
Cuzent, Gilbert. O'Taiti. Paris: 1860	Cuzent, *O.T.*
—— Voyage aux îles Gambier (Archipel de Mangareva). Paris: 1872	„ *V.I.G.*
Dalrymple, Alexander. An historical collection of the several voyages and discoveries in the South Pacific Ocean. 2 vol. London: 1770	Dalrymple
Darwin, Chas. Journal of researches into the natural history and geology of the countries visited during the voyage of H.M.S. "Beagle" round the world. London: 1884	Darwin, *Journal*
David, Mrs Edgeworth. Funafuti... London: 1899	Mrs David

*b*2

xx BIBLIOGRAPHY AND ABBREVIATIONS

BIBLIOGRAPHY — ABBREVIATIONS USED IN NOTES

[Davies, John.] A grammar of the Tahitian Dialect of the Polynesian Language. Tahiti: 1823 (B.M. C 33 b 45. This copy contains MS. notes apparently by Orsmond, whose name is written on the title page) — Davies, *Grammar*

—— A Tahitian and English Dictionary, with introductory remarks... Tahiti: 1851 — „ *Dict.*

Davin, Albert. 50,000 miles dans l'Océan Pacifique. Paris: [1886] — Davin

Deschamps, Émile. Les îles Wallis. Le Tour du Monde 1885. Premier semestre, t. XLIX, p. 273. Paris: 1885 — Deschamps

Desgraz, C. and Vincendon-Dumoulin, C. A. Les Îles Marquises... Paris: 1843 — Vincendon-Dumoulin, *I.M.*

—— —— Les Îles Taïti. Paris: 1844 — Vincendon-Dumoulin, *Taïti*

Dewar, J. Cumming. Voyage of the Nyanza R.N.Y.C.... Edinburgh: London: 1892 — Dewar

D'Ewes, J. China, Australia, and the Pacific Islands, in the years 1855–56. London: 1857 — D'Ewes

Dillon, Peter. Narrative and successful result of a voyage in the South Seas... to ascertain the actual fate of La Pérouse's expedition, etc. 2 vol. London: 1829 — Dillon

Dumont d'Urville, J. S. C. Voyage de la Corvette l'Astrolabe... pendant les années 1826, 1827, 1828, 1829. Histoire du Voyage (t. I–v). Paris: 1830–4 — d'Urville, *Astro.*

—— Voyage pittoresque autour du monde. 2 t. Paris: 1834 — „ *Voy. pitt.*

—— Voyage au Pôle Sud et dans l'Océanie sur les corvettes l'Astrolabe et la Zélée... pendant les années 1837, 1838, 1839, 1840. Histoire du Voyage (t. I–v). Paris: 1841, etc. — „ *V.P.S.*

Duperrey, L. I. Voyage autour du monde pendant les années 1822, 1823, 1824 and 1825. [No date] — Duperrey

Edwards, Edward. Voyage of H.M.S. "Pandora" despatched to arrest the mutineers of the "Bounty" in the South Seas 1790–1. Being the narratives of Capt. Edward Edwards, R.N., the Commander, and George Hamilton the Surgeon. With introduction and notes by Basil Thomson. London: 1915 — Edwards

Ellis, W. An authentic narrative of a voyage performed by Captain Cook and Captain Clerke, in His Majesty's ships Resolution and Discovery during the years 1776, 1777, 1778, 1779 and 1780... by W. Ellis, assistant surgeon to both vessels. 2 vol. London: 1783 — Ellis (Cook)

Ellis, William. Polynesian Researches. 4 vol. 2nd edition. London: 1839 — Ellis

Entrecasteaux, J. A. Bruni d'. Voyage de d'Entrecasteaux, envoyé à la recherche de La Pérouse... Rédigé par M. de Rossel, ancien capitaine de vaisseau. 2 t. Paris: 1808 — d'Entrecasteaux

Erskine, John E. Journal of a cruise among the Islands of the Western Pacific. London: 1853 — Erskine

Fanning, Edmund. Voyages round the world; with selected sketches of voyages to the South Seas... New York: 1833 — Fanning

Farmer, Sarah S. Tonga and the Friendly Islands... London: 1854 — S. Farmer

BIBLIOGRAPHY	ABBREVIATIONS USED IN NOTES
Firth, Raymond. Primitive Economics of the New Zealand Maori. London: 1929	Firth, *Maori Economics*
—— We, The Tikopia. London: 1936	Firth, *Tikopia*
Fitzroy, Robert. Narrative of the surveying voyages of His Majesty's ships Adventure and Beagle, between the years 1826 and 1836. 3 vol. London: 1839	Fitzroy
[Foljambe.] Three years on the Australian Station. London: 1868	Foljambe
Fornander, Abraham. An account of the Polynesian Race. 3 vol. London: 1878	Fornander
Forster, George. A Voyage round the world in His Britannic Majesty's sloop Resolution, commanded by Capt. James Cook, during the years 1772, 3, 4 and 5. 2 vol. London: 1777	Forster, *Voy.*
Forster, J. Reinhold. Observations made during a voyage round the world... London: 1778	Forster, *Obs.*
—— See also **Bougainville**, L. A. de	
Frazer, Sir James George. The Belief in Immortality. Vols. I and II. London: 1913, 1922	Frazer, *B.I.*
—— The Golden Bough. 3rd edition. London: 1914–17	„ *G.B.*
—— Lectures on the early history of kinship. London: 1905	„ *E.H.K.*
—— Psyche's Task... 2nd edition. London: 1913	„ *P.T.*
—— Totemism and Exogamy. 4 vol. London: 1910	„ *T. & E.*
Freycinet, L. C. Desaulses de. Voyage autour du monde... exécuté sur les corvettes...l'Uranie et la Physicienne, pendant les années 1817, 1818, 1819 et 1820, t. I–II. Paris: 1827–39	de Freycinet
Friederici, Georg. Wissenschaftliche Beihefte zum Deutschen Kolonialblatte. Mittheilungen aus den Deutschen Schutzgebieten, Ergänzungsheft Nr. 5 Wissenschaftliche Ergebnisse einer amtlichen Forschungsreise nach dem Bismarck-Archipel im Jahre 1908. II. Beiträge zur Völker- und Sprachenkunde von Deutsch-Neuguinea. Berlin: 1912	Friederici (1)
—— Wissenschaftliche Beihefte zum Deutschen Kolonialblatte. Mittheilungen aus den Deutschen Schutzgebieten, Ergänzungsheft Nr. 7 Wissenschaftliche Ergebnisse einer amtlichen Forschungsreise nach dem Bismarck-Archipel in Jahre 1908. III. Untersuchungen über eine melanesische Wanderstrasse. Berlin: 1913	, (2)
Garnier, Jules. Excursion autour de l'île de Tahiti. Bulletin de la Société de Géographie... Cinquième série, t. XVI, 'Juillet-Décembre, 1868, p. 447. Paris: 1868	Garnier, *E.A.T.*
—— Océanie. Paris: 1871	„ *Océanie*
Gaussin, P. L. J. B. Du dialecte de Tahiti, de celui des îles marquises, et, en général, de la langue polynésienne. Paris: 1853	Gaussin
Geiseler, Kapitänlieutenant (Kommandant S.M.Kbt. "Hyane"). Die Oster-Insel... Berlin: 1883	Geiseler
Gerland, Geo. See **Waitz-Gerland**	
Gifford, E. W. Tongan Myths and Tales. Bishop Museum Bulletin 8. Honolulu: 1924	Gifford, *T.M.T.*

BIBLIOGRAPHY	ABBREVIATIONS USED IN NOTES
Gifford, E. W. Tongan Society. Bishop Museum Bulletin 61. Honolulu: 1929	Gifford, *Tonga*
Gill, William. Gems from the Coral Islands. 2 vol. London: 1855	W. Gill, *Gems*
Gill, William Wyatt. From Darkness to Light in Polynesia... London: 1894	Gill, *D.L.P.*
—— Historical sketches of Savage Life in Polynesia. Wellington: 1880	„ *S.L.P.*
—— Jottings from the Pacific. London: 1885	„ *Jottings*
—— Life in the Southern Isles... London: [1876]	„ *L.S.I.*
—— Myths and songs from the South Pacific. London: 1876	„ *Myths*
—— The South Pacific and New Guinea... Sydney: 1892. Published by N.S.W. Commissioners for World's Columbian Exposition, 1893, Chicago	„ *S.P.N.G.*
Ginoux, Edmond de. La Reine Pomare. Les femmes de Taïti et des Marquises. Nouvelles Annales des Voyages, t. IV, p. 356. Paris: 1844	de Ginoux, vol. IV
Le Gobien, Chas. Histoire des Îles Marianes. Paris: 1700	le Gobien
Gonzalez, Felipe. The Voyage of Captain Don Felipe Gonzalez in the Ship of the Line San Lorenzo, with the Frigate Santa Rosalia in company, to Easter Island in 1770–1. (*See* **Corney,** Bolton Glanvill)	Corney, *Easter*
Goodenough, James G. Journal of Commodore Goodenough. Edited, with a memoir, by his widow. London: 1876	Goodenough
Grey, Sir Geo. Polynesian Mythology. London: 1855	Grey
Grézel, le Père. Dictionnaire Futunien-Français. Paris: 1878	Grézel
Gunn, William. The Gospel in Futuna. London: [1914]	Gunn
Haddon, A. C. Evolution in Art. London: 1895	Haddon
Hadfield, E. Among the natives of the Loyalty Group. London: 1920	Mrs Hadfield
Hale, Horatio. United States Exploring Expedition during the years 1838–1842. Ethnology and Philology. Philadelphia: 1846	Hale
Hamilton, George. A Voyage round the world in His Majesty's frigate Pandora. Performed under the direction of Captain Edwards 1790, 1791 and 1792. Berwick: 1793	Hamilton
—— *See also* **Edwards,** Edward	
Handy, E. S. C. History and Culture in the Society Islands. Bishop Museum Bulletin 79. Honolulu: 1930	Handy, *H.C.S.I.*
—— Marquesan Legends. Bishop Museum Bulletin 69. Honolulu: 1930	„ *M.L.*
—— The Native Culture of the Marquesas. Bishop Museum Bulletin 9. Honolulu: 1923	„ *N.C.M.*
—— Polynesian Religion. Bishop Museum Bulletin 34. Honolulu: 1927	„ *P.R.*
—— and **Handy,** W. C. Samoan Housebuilding, Cooking and Tattooing. Bishop Museum Bulletin 15. Honolulu: 1924	„ *S.H.C.T.*
Handy, W. C. String Figures from the Marquesas and Society Islands. Bishop Museum Bulletin 18. Honolulu: 1925	Handy, *S.F.M.S.I.*

BIBLIOGRAPHY	ABBREVIATIONS USED IN NOTES
Harlez, C. de. L'Île de Pâques et ses monuments graphiques. Le Muséon, t. xiv, p. 415; t. xv, p. 68. Louvain: 1895, 1896	de Harlez, vol. xiv, vol. xv
Hawkesworth, John. An account of the voyages undertaken by the order of His Present Majesty for making discoveries in the Southern Hemisphere... 3 vol. London: 1773	Hawkesworth
Hedley, Charles. The Atoll of Funafuti, Ellice Group... Memoirs of the Australian Museum, iii, part 3:	Hedley
—— The Ethnology of Funafuti. Memoirs of the Australian Museum, iii, part 4. Sydney: 1896–7	„
Henry, Teuira. Ancient Tahiti. Bishop Museum Bulletin 48. Honolulu: 1928	Henry, A.T.
Hesse-Wartegg, Ernst von. Samoa, Bismarckarchipel und Neuguinea... Leipzig: 1902	von Hesse-Wartegg
Hogbin, H. Ian. Law and Order in Polynesia. London: 1934	Hogbin, L.O.P.
Home, Sir E. Notes among the Islands of the Pacific. The Nautical Magazine and Naval Chronicle for 1849. London: 1849	Home
Hood, T. H. Notes of a cruise in H.M.S. "Fawn" in the Western Pacific in the year 1862. Edinburgh: 1863	Hood
Hooker, Sir Joseph D. See **Banks**, Sir Joseph	
Hoole, Elijah. See **Lawry**, Walter	
Hoppner, Richard Belgrave. See **Krusenstern**, Adam Johann von	
Hort, Dora. Tahiti, the Garden of the Pacific. London: 1891	Mrs Hort
Hübner, J. A. von. Through the British Empire. 2 vol. London: 1886	von Hübner
Jardin, Edelstan. Notice sur l'archipel de Mendana ou des Marquises 1853–1854. Mémoires de la Société Impériale Académique de Cherbourg 1856, p. 173. Cherbourg: 1856	Jardin
Jaussen, F. E. L'Île de Pâques. Paris: 1893	Jaussen
Kennedy, D. G. Culture of Vaitupu, Ellice Islands; Memoirs of the Polynesian Society, Vol. 9. New Plymouth: 1931	Kennedy, C.V.
Kotzebue, Otto von. A new voyage round the world in the years 1823, 24, 25 and 26. 2 vol. London: 1830	von Kotzebue
Krämer, Augustin. Hawaii, Ostmikronesien und Samoa... Stuttgart: 1906	Krämer, H.O.S.
—— Die Samoa-Inseln. 2 Bd. Stuttgart: 1901–2	„ S.I.
Krusenstern, Adam Johann von. Voyage round the world in the years 1803, 1804, 1805 and 1806. Translated from the original German by Richard Belgrave Hoppner. 2 vol. London: 1813	Krusenstern
Labillardière, J. J. Houtou de. Voyage in search of La Pérouse. 2 vol. London: 1802	Labillardière
Lambert, C. and S. The voyage of the "Wanderer". From the journals and letters of C. and S. Lambert. Edited by Gerald Young. London: 1883	Lambert
Lamont, E. H. Wild life among the Pacific Islanders. London: 1867	Lamont

BIBLIOGRAPHY	ABBREVIATIONS USED IN NOTES
Langley, S. P. The Fire Walk Ceremony in Tahiti. From the Smithsonian Report for 1901, p. 539. Washington: 1902	Langley
Langsdorff, G. H. von. Bemerkungen auf einer Reise um die Welt in den Jahren 1803 bis 1807. 2 Bd. Frankfurt: 1813	Langsdorff
La Pérouse, Jean F. Galaup de. Voyage de La Pérouse autour du monde. 4 t. Paris: 1798	La Pérouse
La Rochefoucauld-Liancourt, F. A. F. de. Voyage dans les États-Unis d'Amérique fait en 1795, 1796 et 1797. 8 t. Paris: 1799	La Rochefoucauld-Liancourt
Lawry, Walter. The Friendly and Feejee Islands: a missionary visit...in the year 1847. Edited by Rev. Elijah Hoole. London: 1850	Lawry, *F.F.I.* (1)
—— A second missionary visit to the Friendly and Feejee Islands in the year 1850. Edited by Rev. Elijah Hoole. London: 1851	„ *F.F.I.* (2)
Lesson, Pierre Adolf. Les Polynésiens. 4 t. Paris: 1880–4	Lesson, *Poly.*
Lesson, René Primevère. Voyage autour du monde...sur la corvette La Coquille. Paris: 1839	Lesson, *Voy.*
Lisiansky, Urey. A voyage round the world in the years 1803, 4, 5 and 6...in the ship Neva. London: 1814	Lisiansky
Loeb, E. M. History and Traditions of Niue. Bishop Museum Bulletin 32. Honolulu: 1926	Loeb, *Niue*
London Missionary Society. The Quarterly Chronicle of the Transactions of the London Missionary Society in the years 1815–19. Vol. i. London: 1821	L.M.S. *Q.C.* vol. i
—— The Quarterly Chronicle of the Transactions of the London Missionary Society in the years 1820, 1821, 1822, 1823 and 1824. Vol. ii. London: 1825	„ *Q.C.* vol. ii
—— Reports of the Missionary Society. London: 1814	„ *Rep.*
—— Transactions of the Missionary Society. Vols. i–iv. 2nd edition. London: 1804–18	„ *Trans.*
Lundie, George Archibald. Missionary Life in Samoa, as exhibited in the Journals of the late George Archibald Lundie during the revival in Tutuila in 1840–41. Edinburgh: 1846	Lundie
Macdonald, D. Oceania: Linguistic and Anthropological. Melbourne: 1889	Macdonald
Mangeret, le R. P. Mgr Bataillon et les Missions de l'Océanie Centrale. 2 t. Lyon: 1895	Mangeret
Marchand, Étienne. A voyage round the World, performed during the years 1790, 1791 and 1792, by Étienne Marchand.... Translated from the French of C. P. Claret Fleurieu. 2 vol. London: 1801	Marchand
Mariner, William. An account of the natives of the Tonga Islands, in the South Pacific Ocean. Compiled and arranged from the extensive communications of Mr William Mariner, several years resident in those islands. By John Martin, M.D. 2 vol. [3rd edition.] Edinburgh: 1827	Mariner
Markham, Sir Clements Robert. *See* **Quiros**, Pedro Fernandez de	
Marquardt, Carl. Die Tätowirung beider Geschlechter in Samoa. Berlin: 1899	Marquardt

BIBLIOGRAPHY	ABBREVIATIONS USED IN NOTES
Martin, Aylic. Promenades en Océanie. Le Tour du Monde 1885. Deuxième semestre, t. L. Paris: 1885	Martin
Martin, John. *See* **Mariner**, William	
Massachusetts Historical Society. Collections of the Massachusetts Historical Society, vols. I–IV. Reprinted. Boston: 1806–35	Mass. Hist. Soc.
Mathias, G. Lettres sur les îles marquises. Paris: 1843	Mathias
Mead, Margaret. Coming of Age in Samoa. New York: 1928	Mead, *C.A.S.*
—— Social Organization of Manua. Bishop Museum Bulletin 76. Honolulu: 1930	,, *Manua*
Meade, Hon. Herbert. A ride through the disturbed districts of New Zealand; together with some account of the South Sea Islands. London: 1870	Meade
Meinicke, Carl E. Die Inseln des Stillen Oceans. 2 Thle. Leipzig: 1875, 1876	Meinicke
Melville, Herman. Typee... New edition. London: 1893	Melville
Moerenhout, J. A. Voyages aux îles du Grand Océan. 2 t. Paris: 1837	Moerenhout
Monfat, A. Le Missionnaire des Samoa. Mgr L. Elloy de la Société de Marie. Lyon: 1890	Monfat, *M.S.*
—— Les Tonga, ou Archipel des Amis et le R. P. Joseph Chevron de la Société de Marie. Lyon: 1893	,, *Tonga*
Montgomery, James. Journal of voyages and travels by the Rev. Daniel Tyerman and George Bennet Esq....in the South Sea Islands...between the years 1821 and 1829. Compiled from the original documents by J. M. 2 vol. London: 1831	Tyerman
Montiton, Albert. Les Paumotous. Les Missions catholiques, t. VI, Jan.–Déc. 1874. Lyon: 1874	Montiton, vol. VI
Moseley, H. N. Notes by a Naturalist on the "Challenger", being an account of various observations made during the voyage of H.M.S. "Challenger"...in the years 1872–1876. London: 1879	Moseley
Moss, Frederick J. Through Atolls and Islands in the great South Sea. London: 1889	Moss
Moss, Rosalind. The Life after Death in Oceania and the Malay Archipelago. Oxford: 1925	R. Moss
Murray, A. W. Forty Years' Mission Work in Polynesia and New Guinea from 1835 to 1875. London: 1876	Murray, 40 *years*
—— The Martyrs of Polynesia. London: 1885	,, *Martyrs*
—— Missions in Western Polynesia... London: 1863	,, *M.W.P.*
Nicoll, M. J. Three voyages of a naturalist. 2nd edition. London: 1909	Nicoll
Parkinson, R. Dreißig Jahre in der Südsee... Stuttgart: 1907	R. Parkinson
Parkinson, Sydney. A journal of a voyage to the South Seas, in His Majesty's ship The Endeavour. London: 1784	Parkinson (1)
[——?] A journal of a voyage round the world, in His Majesty's ship Endeavour, in the years 1768, 1769, 1770 and 1771. London: 1771	,, (2)
Paton, John G. John G. Paton, missionary to the New Hebrides. An autobiography. Edited by his brother. Second Part. London: 1890	Paton

BIBLIOGRAPHY	ABBREVIATIONS USED IN NOTES

Paton, Maggie Whitecross. Letters and sketches from the New Hebrides. London: 1894 — Mrs Paton

Petit-Thouars, A. N. G. H. Bergasse du. Voyage autour du monde sur la frégate La Vénus, pendant les années 1836–1839. 4 t. Paris: 1840–5 — du Petit-Thouars

Pigeard, Ch. Voyage dans l'Océanie centrale sur la corvette française Le Bucéphale. Nouvelles Annales des Voyages... Nouvelle série, année 1845, t. IV, p. 141. Paris: 1845 — Pigeard, *N.A.V.*, vol. IV

—— Voyage dans l'Océanie centrale. Nouvelles Annales des Voyages... Nouvelle série, année 1846, t. I, p. 181. Paris: 1846 — Pigeard, *N.A.V.*, vol. I

Pinart, Alphonse. Voyage à l'île de Pâques. Le Tour du Monde 1878. Deuxième semestre, t. XXXVI, p. 255. Paris: 1878 — Pinart

Porter, David. Journal of a cruise made to the Pacific Ocean ...in the United States Frigate Essex, in the years 1812, 1813 and 1814. 2 vol. 2nd edition. New York: 1822 — Porter

[**Pratt**, Geo.] A Samoan Dictionary...Samoa: 1862 — Pratt

Pritchard, W. T. Notes on certain anthropological matters respecting the South Sea Islanders. Memoirs read before the Anthropological Society of London, vol. I, 1863–4 — Pritchard, *A.S.* vol. I,

—— Polynesian Reminiscences. London: 1866 — Pritchard

Quatrefages, A. de. Les Polynésiens et leurs migrations. Paris. [No date] — Quatrefages

Quiros, Pedro Fernandez de. The Voyages of Pedro Fernandez de Quiros, 1595 to 1606. Translated and edited by Sir Clements Markham. 2 vol. London: 1904. (Hakluyt Society, series II, vols. XIV, XV) — Quiros

Radiguet, Max. La Reine-Blanche dans les îles marquises... Revue des Deux Mondes, t. XXII, p. 431; t. XXIII, p. 607. Paris: 1859 — Radiguet, vol. XXII ,, vol. XXIII

Reeves, Edward. Brown Men and Women... London: 1895 — Reeves

Ribourt, P. État de l'île Tahiti, pendant les années 1847, 1848. Annuaire des établissements français de l'Océanie..., p. 302. Papeete: 1863 — Ribourt

Rivers, W. H. R. The History of Melanesian Society. 2 vol. Cambridge: 1914 — Rivers, *H.M.S.*

—— Sun-cult and megaliths in Oceania. American Anthropologist (N.S.), vol. XVII, No. 3, p. 431 — ,, *S.C. & M.*

Roggeveen, Jacob. (Official log of his discovery of Easter Island in 1722. *See* **Corney**, Bolton Glanvill)

Rosen, W. von. *See* **Bille**, Steen

Rossel, M. de. *See* **Entrecasteaux**, J. A. Bruni d'

Routledge, Mrs Scoresby. The Mystery of Easter Island. London: 1919 — Mrs Routledge

Rovings in the Pacific, from 1837 to 1849... By a merchant long resident at Tahiti. 2 vol. London: 1851 — *Rovings*

Rowe, G. Stringer. A Pioneer. A Memoir of the Rev. John Thomas, missionary to the Friendly Islands. London: 1885 — Rowe

Saffre, Dr. Archipel des Tonga, des Samoa, des Wallis, île Futuna, des Fidji. Archives de Médecine Navale..., t. XLI, p. 433. Paris: 1884 — Saffre

BIBLIOGRAPHY	ABBREVIATIONS USED IN NOTES
St Johnston, Alfred. Camping among cannibals. London: 1883	St Johnston
Salmon, Mrs. *See* **Ari'i Taimai**	
Scherzer, Carl von. Narrative of the circumnavigation of the globe by the Austrian frigate Novara... in the years 1857, 1858 and 1859. 3 vol. London: 1861–3	von Scherzer
Schmeltz, J. D. E. Die ethnographisch-anthropologische Abteilung des Museums Godeffroy in Hamburg. Ein Beitrag zur Kunde der Südsee-Völker. Hamburg: 1881	Schmeltz
Seligman, C. G. The Melanesians of British New Guinea. Cambridge: 1910	Seligman
Shillibeer, John. A narrative of the Briton's voyage to Pitcairn Island... 3rd edition. London: 1818	Shillibeer
Smith, S. Percy. Hawaiki. 3rd edition. Christchurch: 1910	Smith
—— The Lore of the Whare-wananga... Translated by S. Percy Smith. Part I. Memoirs of the Polynesian Society, vol. III. New Plymouth: 1913	,, *Lore of the Whare-wananga*
Speiser, Felix. Two years with the natives in the Western Pacific. London: [1913]	Speiser
Stair, John B. Old Samoa... [London]: 1897	Stair
Steinen, Karl von den. Ein marquesanischer Sarg. Ethnologisches Notizblatt. Herausgegeben von der Direktion des königlichen Museums für Völkerkunde in Berlin, Bd II, Heft I, p. 22. Berlin: 1899	von den Steinen
Stevenson, Mrs M. I. From Saranac to the Marquesas and beyond. Being letters written by Mrs M. I. Stevenson during 1887–88... Edited by Marie Clothilde Balfour. London: 1903	Mrs Stevenson
Stevenson, Robert Louis. Ballads. London: 1902	Stevenson, *Ballads*
—— A Footnote to History. London: 1892	,, *Footnote*
—— The letters of Robert Louis Stevenson... Selected with notes and introduction by Sidney Colvin. 2 vol. London: 1901	,, *Letters*
—— In the South Seas... London: 1900	,, *S.S.*
—— Vailima Letters. London: 1899	,, *V. Letters*
Stevenson, Mrs R. L. The Cruise of the "Janet Nichol" among the South Sea Islands. London: 1915	Mrs R. L. Stevenson
Stewart, C. S. A visit to the South Seas, in the United States' ship Vincennes, during the years 1829 and 1830... 2 vol. London: 1832	Stewart
Stimson, J. F. The Cult of Kiho-Tumu. Bishop Museum Bulletin 111. Honolulu: 1933	Stimson, *Kiho-Tumu*
—— The Legends of Maui and Tahaki. Bishop Museum Bulletin 127. Honolulu: 1934	,, *M. & T.*
—— Tuamotuan Religion. Bishop Museum Bulletin 103. Honolulu: 1933	,, *T.R.*
Stuebel, O. Samoanische Texte. Unter Beihülfe von Eingeborenen gesammelt und übersetzt. Herausgegeben von F. W. K. Müller. Veröffentlichungen aus dem königlichen Museum für Völkerkunde, Bd IV, Hefte 2–4, p. 59. Berlin: 1896	Stuebel
Sunderland, J. P. *See* **Buzacott**, Aaron	

BIBLIOGRAPHY	ABBREVIATIONS USED IN NOTES
"Sundowner" [Tichborne, Herbert]. Rambles in Polynesia. London: 1897	"Sundowner"
Taylor, Richard. Te ika a Maui; or New Zealand and its Inhabitants... London and Wanganui, New Zealand: 1870	Taylor
Te Rangi Hiroa (P. H. Buck). Ethnology of Tongareva. Bishop Museum Bulletin 92. Honolulu: 1932	Te Rangi Hiroa, E.T.
—— Ethnology of Manihiki and Rakahanga. Bishop Museum Bulletin 99. Honolulu: 1932	„ M. & R.
—— Mangaian Society. Bishop Museum Bulletin 122. Honolulu: 1934	„ M.S.
—— Samoan Material Culture. Bishop Museum Bulletin 75. Honolulu: 1930	„ S.M.C.
Thomas, Julian. Cannibals and Convicts. London: 1886	Thomas
Thomson, Sir Basil H. The Diversions of a Prime Minister. Edinburgh and London: 1894	Thomson, D.P.M.
—— The Fijians... London: 1908	„ Fijians
—— Savage Island. London: 1902	„ S.I.
—— See also Edwards, Edward	
Thomson, Wm J. Te Pito te Henua, or Easter Island. Report of the U.S. National Museum, under the direction of the Smithsonian Institution for the year ending June 30, 1889. Washington: 1891	W. J. Thomson
[Tichborne, Herbert.] See "Sundowner"	
Tregear, Edward. The Maori-Polynesian Comparative Dictionary. Wellington, N.Z.: 1891	Tregear
—— The Maori Race. Wanganui, N.Z.: 1914	„ Maori
Turnbull, John. A voyage round the world, in the years 1800, 1801, 1802, 1803 and 1804... 2nd edition. London: 1813	Turnbull
Turner, Geo. Nineteen years in Polynesia... London: 1861	Turner, 19 years
—— Samoa. London: 1884	Turner
Tyerman, Daniel. Journal of voyages and travels by the Rev. Daniel Tyerman and George Bennet Esq....in the South Sea Islands...between the years 1821 and 1829. Compiled from the original documents by J. M. 2 vol. London: 1831	Tyerman
Vancouver, Geo. A voyage of discovery to the North Pacific Ocean...performed in the years 1790, 1791, 1792, 1793, 1794 and 1795, in the Discovery...and...Chatham. 3 vol. London: 1798	Vancouver
Veeson, George. Authentic narrative of a four years' residence at Tongataboo. London: 1810	Veeson
Vincendon-Dumoulin, C. A. and Desgraz, C. Les îles marquises... Paris: 1843	Vincendon-Dumoulin, I.M.
—— —— Les îles Taïti. Paris: 1844	Vincendon-Dumoulin, Taïti
Waitz-Gerland. Waitz, Theodor. Anthropologie der Naturvölker. Bd v. Leipzig: 1865	Waitz-Gerland
—— Gerland, Geo. Anthropologie der Naturvölker. Bd VI. Mit Benutzung der Vorarbeiten des Verfassers fortgesetzt von Dr Geo. Gerland. Leipzig: 1872	Gerland

BIBLIOGRAPHY

ABBREVIATIONS
USED IN NOTES

Wallis, Samuel. An account of a voyage round the world, in the years 1766, 1767, 1768. By Samuel Wallis, Esq., Commander of His Majesty's Ship the Dolphin. (Hawkesworth, vol. I.) *See* **Hawkesworth**, John — Hawkesworth

Walpole, Hon. Fred. Four years in the Pacific in Her Majesty's Ship "Collingwood". From 1844 to 1848. 2 vol. London: 1849 — Walpole

Waterhouse, Joseph. The King and People of Fiji... London: 1866 — Waterhouse

Wesleyan Missionary Society. Notices, vol. IV. For the years 1823, 1824, 1825. London. [No date] — *Miss. Notices*, vol. IV

—— Notices, New Series, vol. I. For the years 1839, 1840, 1841. London: 1842 — ,, ,, N.S., vol. I

—— Notices, New Series, vol. II. For the years 1842, 1843, 1844. London: 1845 — ,, ,, N.S., vol. II

West, Thomas. Ten years in South-Central Polynesia. London: 1865 — West

Westervelt, W. D. Legends of Ma-ui... Honolulu: 1910 — Westervelt

Wheeler, Daniel. Extracts from the letters and journal of Daniel Wheeler... London: 1839 — Wheeler

Whitmee, S. J. A missionary cruise in the S. Pacific... in the barque "John Williams", during 1870. 2nd edition. Sydney: 1871 — Whitmee

Wilkes, Charles. Narrative of the U.S. Exploring Expedition during the years 1838, 1839, 1840, 1841, 1842. 5 vol. Philadelphia: 1845 — Wilkes

Williams, John. A narrative of missionary enterprises in the South Sea Islands. London: 1837 — Williams

Williams, Thomas and **Calvert**, James. Fiji and the Fijians. 2 vol. London: 1858 — Williams and Calvert

Williamson, Robert W. The Social and Political Systems of Central Polynesia. 3 vol. Cambridge: 1924 — *Systems*

—— Religious and Cosmic Beliefs of Central Polynesia. 2 vol. Cambridge: 1933 — *Beliefs*

Wilson, William. A missionary visit to the Southern Pacific Ocean, performed in the years 1796, 1797, 1798, in the ship Duff, commanded by Captain James Wilson. Compiled from journals of the officers and the missionaries... London: 1799 — Wilson

Wragge, Clement L. The romance of the South Seas. London: 1906 — Wragge

Young, Gerald. *See* **Lambert**, C. and S.

Young, J. L. Remarks on Phallic Stones from Rapanui. Occasional papers of the Bernice Pauahi Bishop Museum of Polynesian Ethnology and Natural History, vol. II, No. 2, p. 31. Director's Report for 1903. Honolulu: 1904 — Young, *P.S.*

Young, Robert. The Southern World... London: 1854 — Young, *S.W.*

BIBLIOGRAPHY AND ABBREVIATIONS

(Part II)

(Articles from Journals, etc., which are seldom quoted from are included in Part I of the Bibliography under the names of the Authors.)

List of Journals, Publications of Societies, etc.	Abbreviations
Annales hydrographiques. Paris	*Ann. hydro.*
L'Anthropologie. Paris	*L'Anthro.*
Anthropos. Wien, Salzburg	*Anthrop.*
Association de la Propagation de la Foi, Annales. Lyon	*A.P.F.*
Das Ausland. Augsburg	*Ausland*
Australian Association for the Advancement of Science	*A.A.A.S.*
Australian National Research Council, *see* Oceania	
Berliner Gesellschaft für Anthropologie, Ethnologie und Urgeschichte, Zeitschrift für Ethnologie. Berlin	*Z.f.E.*
Ethnological Society of London, Journal. London	*J.E.S.*
Folk-Lore Society, Folk-lore. London	*Folk-lore*
Die geographische Gesellschaft in Hamburg, Mittheilungen. Hamburg	*M.G.G. Hamburg*
Die Gesellschaft für Erdkunde zu Berlin.	
Verhandlungen. Berlin	*V.G.E.*
Zeitschrift. Berlin	*Z.G.E.*
Globus. Braunschweig	*Globus*
Internationales Archiv für Ethnographie. Leiden	*I.A.E.*
Man. *See* Royal Anthropological Institute *below*	
Museum Godeffroy, Journal. Hamburg	*J.M.G.*
Nature. London	*Nature*
New Zealand Institute, Transactions and Proceedings. Wellington, London	*N.Z.I.*
Oceania, Sydney	*Oceania*
Polynesian Society, Journal. Wellington, New Plymouth, N.Z.	*J.P.S.*
Revue d'Ethnographie. Paris	*Rev. d'Eth.*
Revue Maritime et Coloniale. Paris	*R.M.C.*
Royal Anthropological Institute of Great Britain and Ireland.	
Journal. London	*J.R.A.I.*
Man. London	*Man*
Royal Geographical Society of London, Journal. London	*J.R.G.S.*
Royal Society of New South Wales, Journal and Proceedings. Sydney, London	*R.S.N.S.W.*
Das Verein für wissenschaftliche Unterhaltung zu Hamburg, Verhandlungen. Hamburg	*V.V.U.*
Victoria Institute, or Philosophical Society of Great Britain, Journal of Transactions. London	*J.V.I.*
Zeitschrift für Ethnologie. *See* Berliner Gesellschaft für Anthropologie, etc. *above*	

Part I

GODS & WORSHIP

CHAPTER I

THE CREATION AND THE GODS

THE COSMOGONY

THE study of Polynesian cosmogonies[1] is complicated by several factors. In the first place the beliefs connected with the origin of the world varied from one island group to another; and even within the one group[2] several variants of the same myth were sometimes found, giving an impression of that inconsistency which is a feature of Polynesian legendary history, and, indeed, of primitive mythology generally. Secondly, there is the specific difficulty arising from the danger of translating concrete native terms into the abstract concepts embodied in a European language. Thirdly, in regard to the more esoteric parts of the cosmogony, there was a reluctance on the part of informants to reveal to white investigators the more intimate secrets of their religion. Finally, there is evidence that original legends have been altered by the jealousies of rival cults and similar factors.

There are, however, certain general features of Polynesian cosmogonies to which we may draw attention. They generally start with a condition of void or nothingness, and from this there emerge by a series of acts or processes of genesis various natural phenomena, human and animal species, and social institutions. These legends, because of their heterogeneous and disparate character, should not be thought of as a philosophy, if by this term it is intended to imply an attempt to construct a unified body of knowledge designed to explain the phenomena of nature. The real significance of cosmogonies will emerge from a treatment of their social functions, and of the role which they play in institutional activities. For the moment we shall content ourselves with mentioning the more important processes of genesis employed in Polynesian cosmogonies.

The first emergence of things from the initial state of nothingness is sometimes conceived as due to the *fiat* of some

[1] Myths of the cosmogony have been dealt with elsewhere (*Beliefs*, vol. I, chaps. I and II) and for this reason we shall merely attempt briefly to indicate the general configuration of this body of belief.

[2] For example, Mead (*Manua*, p. 156 *n.*) cites five different legends concerning Manono and Apolima, two small islands in western Samoa.

supreme being, such as Io in New Zealand[1] or Ta'aroa in the Society Islands,[2] and sometimes simply as a process of evolution. In Samoa the two types co-existed—thus Turner gives an evolutionary legend[3] in which a series of qualities and natural objects emerged from Nothing; first came Fragrance, then Dust, then Perceivable, and so on. From a series of inter-marriages between the objects so produced came ultimately Tangaroa-the-originator-of-men. But in another myth, cited by Dr Margaret Mead,[4] Tangaloa existed first in the illimitable void, and from him sprang all things. Handy[5] considers that the conception of a "World Soul" or supreme creator was universal in Polynesia, and that where the cosmogony is de-scribed without reference to such a being, the omission is due either to ignorance or reticence on the part of informants. This view, however, appears to be an inference from his theory of nature as a "psychic dynamism" to the Polynesian, in which everything was conscious and animate, rather than an induction from the ethnographic material. Polynesian creation chants contain so much poetic imagery and so many allusive references, that, when translated into abstract and metaphysical terms in the English language, they readily lead to misunderstanding. Probably many of the terms, if their meaning were sought in their social contexts rather than in facile dictionary equivalents, would be found to be far more concrete and intelligible than many of the translations would lead us to believe. For example, it would seem to be unnecessary to assume, as does Handy, that such figures of speech as the use of the word *tumu* (the base of a tree) for the foundation of the world make it "logical to conclude that these people, who described the universe and nature as evolving through propagation or growth, should regard all elements therein as conscious and animate",[6] any more than we would regard our own use of the word "root" in linguistic science as implying an analogous conception of language.

The evolutionary processes described in Polynesian cosmo-gonies are of various kinds, examples of which have been given in another work.[7] In addition to these there are the acts of creation and procreation by gods, the raising of the sky, the fishing up or disposition of islands, or the ordering of the daily

[1] See Handy, *P.R.* pp. 9–11.   [2] See below, p. 226.
[3] Summarized in *Beliefs*, vol. I, p. 3.
[4] *Manua*, pp. 149–51.   [5] Handy, *P.R.* p. 9.
[6] *Ibid.* pp. 19, 25.   [7] *Beliefs*, vol. I, chap. I.

course of the sun. As examples of these have already been given elsewhere,[1] as well as in other parts of the present work, we may pass on to a consideration of the general question of Polynesian deities.

CLASSES OF GODS

The difficulties which we have mentioned in connection with the legends of the cosmogony (local variations, the difficulty of translating Polynesian concepts into European terms, the reticence or ignorance of informants, and the distortion of original legends) are also found in the more general myths concerning the gods. Here, however, more specific sources of confusion occur. In the first place evidence concerning the relationships of the gods is often contradictory, for example god *A* may appear in one story as the son or descendant of god *B*, whereas in another legend, perhaps found in the same island, it is *B* who is the son or descendant of *A*. Secondly, confusion exists as to the relative importance of certain individual gods. Finally, the duplication of names of gods or demigods in the mythologies is apt to lead to misunderstanding.

From the functional point of view, however, these sources of confusion are not as serious as would at first sight appear. The impression of insurmountable difficulty arises from the tendency, all too common in writings on Polynesia, to assume that there must be "true versions" of all Polynesian myths, and that the synthesis of these would give us a consistent system of religious ideology, of which the various conflicting versions are unfortunate distortions. If, on the other hand, the local variations are conceived as existing in their own right, each playing a definite part in the culture of an autonomous social group, a strictly empirical approach is made possible, and from being sources of confusion, the local variants become valuable scientific data, which shed light on the role played by dogma in the dynamics of religion.

The number of Polynesian gods was enormous. There were the great gods whose worship was spread widely over the Pacific; minor gods, also more or less widely known; gods whose worship was confined to one island or group of islands, but who were of high importance within the spheres of their own dominions; minor and local gods within those dominions, such as district or village gods, who, again, were often worshipped

---

[1] *Beliefs*, vol. I, chaps. I and II.

in more than one district or village, and some of whom were of importance; and tutelar gods of domestic or other small families. There were also gods of individuals.

Thus the Samoans had gods who were reverenced throughout the entire group and others whose worshippers were only the people of large districts.[1] The former of these are probably what Stair calls national gods.[2] There were also gods of villages and gods of households or families,[3] and the latter included gods who became tutelar deities of individual members of the family.[4] Krämer says that every district had its own special god, and gives the names, Su, 'Aufua and Saolevao as the gods of Aana, Atua, and Tuamasanga respectively, saying that the last-mentioned god had been brought over from Savai'i. He also says Fe'e (the cuttle-fish) lived inland from Apia, and was revered by the village of Vaimaunga.[5] Again in the Society Islands, we shall see that gods of various degrees of importance were associated with the various orders of *marae*.

The gods may be divided into classes in several other ways also. Some of them were supposed to live in the distant heavens above, or in places at all events on or above the earth; the homes of others were believed to be in the regions below, these being in some cases conceived as being below the islands in which they were worshipped; again other gods were believed to reside in the region of *Po*; or in *Havaiki*, sometimes conceived as being a distant place, perhaps an island, situated away to the west (or in some islands in some other direction), or a place in the skies, or a region also below the earth, in some cases reached by plunging into the ocean.[6] *Po*, either in the heavens above, or down below, was a home of the gods, and especially the great original gods, born of night; but in some of the islands the people believed that there was a beautiful spot, distinguished from *Po*, also a residence of the gods, which was also the home of such departed souls as had the good fortune to get there instead of being destined for the miseries or discomforts of *Po*. A special feature of the Polynesian ideas as to these places was the belief, prevailing in

---

[1] Brown, pp. 227, 245. See also Wilkes, vol. II, p. 131.
[2] Stair, p. 216.
[3] Turner, p. 18. Stair, p. 216 (see *Systems*, vol. I, pp. 40–1 for the grounds for identifying Stair's "settlement" with Turner's "village", and Stair's "village" with Turner's "family"). Krämer, *S.I.* vol. I, p. 23.
[4] Turner, p. 17.   [5] Krämer, *S.I.* vol. I, p. 23.
[6] On the relation between *Po* and *Havaiki*, and the tendency to identify them, see *Beliefs*, vol. I, pp. 316–18; vol. II, pp. 260–1.

many of the islands, that the journey thither involved travelling in a westward direction.[1]

Such a belief was found in the Pulotu (or Bulotu) of Samoa and Tonga, an island or region under the sea situated in the west, which was the destination of the souls of the dead.[2]

In Tonga the journey to this region seems to have been either by sea or underground[3] and we shall see that a similar belief existed in the Society Islands.[4] In both Samoa and Tonga writers also speak of gods living in the heavens, of which there were believed to be several,[5] while certain gods were also said to reside on earth,[6] or in the sea.[7]

We shall see, in dealing with the Society Islands, that various deities were believed to live in different regions. Thus in Henry's account of the pa'i-atua ceremony occurs the chant[8] whereby the gods were summoned from their abodes to attend the ceremony, various messengers being sent off to fetch them. The following table gives the names of the gods summoned, the messengers which were sent for them, and the destination to which the latter were directed to go:

God	Messenger	Place from which god was to be summoned
Tane	Ti'a-o-atea	'Uporu (Taha'a)
Tu and Te-mehara	Rei-tu	Tai-nuna
Ro'o-te-ro'oro'o	Rei-tu	"To the east"
Rua-hatu and Hau	Nevaneva	Fare-papa-hauriuri (in the ocean)
Hiva	Nevaneva	Papa-uri and Papa-tea (Ma'atea)
Ra'a	Irinau	Papa-roa
To'a-hiti	Irinau	"Great cliff of the inland recess"
Punua-moe-vai	Irinau	"The river bank"
Ta'aroa and Rua-tupua-nui	Ti'a-o-uri	Po
Ta'ere-maopo'opo	Ti'a-o-uri	Rua-papa-nui
Roma-tane	Ti'a-o-uri	Rohutu-no'ano'a
Kind ghosts and malignant ghosts	Ti'a-o-uri	"The wall of skulls"

The general conclusion in regard to the homes of Polynesian deities is that these varied with the specific gods under con-

[1] This belief is associated by some writers with the idea that their ancestors had come from the west, which was therefore the original home of their race.
[2] Stair, p. 211; Wilkes, vol. II, p. 132; Hale, p. 27; Turner, p. 16; Gill, *Myths*, p. 168; Pritchard, p. 401; Krämer, *S.I.* vol. I, p. 23; Wilkes, vol. III, p. 22; Mariner, vol. II, pp. 102 *sq.*; cf. Veeson, p. 151; Wilson, p. 273; Cook, vol. v, p. 423.   [3] S. Farmer, p. 132; Gifford, *Tonga*, p. 287.
[4] See below, p. 275.
[5] Powell, *J.P.S.* vol. I, p. 177; Krämer, *S.I.* vol. I, pp. 22, 25, 392; Cook, vol. v, pp. 422 *sq.*; Wilkes, vol. III, p. 23; Wilson, p. 272; S. Farmer, p. 126; cf. Mariner, vol. I, pp. 206 *sq.*   [6] Wilkes, vol. II, p. 98; Mariner, pp. 206 *sq.*
[7] Cook, vol. v, pp. 422 *sq.*
[8] Henry, *A.T.* pp. 162–4; for a description of the ceremony see below, p. 222.

sideration, and were determined by the social context in which the particular legends occurred. The context might relate to local associations, for example the summoning of Tane from 'Uporu (Taha'a) depended on the existence there of a national *marae* dedicated to him;[1] again the reference to Ta'aroa coming from *Po* and Roma-tane from *Rohutu-no'ano'a* can be understood in the light of the Tahitian theory of the fate of the soul after death, while the oceanic residence of Rua-hatu is explained by the role which he played as the "Tahitian Neptune".[2] The common characteristic of the various regions in which the gods were supposed to reside—in the sky, under the earth, beneath the sea, or on a distant island—is their inaccessibility, the function of which will be referred to later. In conclusion we may draw attention to the association of certain deities with the destination of the souls of the dead. This should be considered from the point of view of the deification of certain souls and also as a validation of the belief in immortality by its mythological charter.

Some of the deities were what may be called departmental gods, these including gods of the sea, of the various forces and phenomena of nature and of the various trades, occupations and practices—including even amusements—of the people; and beliefs as to the attributes and functions of a god were not always the same with different groups of people.

Some of the great gods were not believed to concern themselves with the affairs of men, except perhaps on special and important occasions; but they were commonly believed to have wide and varied ranges of power, and sometimes they also were conceived as being departmental gods, or as performing departmental work.

There was also a vast array of supernatural beings who may, broadly speaking, be described as being of an inferior order, as compared with those whom writers call "gods", and who are often spoken of as "spirits"; but it would be difficult—indeed often impossible—to draw a line of distinction between them and the so-called "gods", especially as the terminology of different writers in this respect is sometimes conflicting or inconsistent, and we do not know what was the Polynesian term which was translated either as "god" or "spirit".

There are references by writers to beliefs that the gods were in many respects similar to human beings, except in so far as

---

[1] Henry, *A.T.* p. 99.   [2] See below, p. 247.

they were differentiated by their superior knowledge and super-natural power; and that the lives of the gods were also similar, in that they ate and drank, married and indulged in sexual gratifications, and quarrelled and fought among themselves.

In regard to the general attitude—beneficent or malignant—of the gods towards mankind, we shall see that there were in some islands certain classes of supernatural beings who were regarded as being, generally at all events, either one or the other of these; and when we consider the individual gods separately we shall perhaps sometimes find references to their personal characters in this respect. Most of the gods and supernatural beings, however, were believed, on the one hand, to look after the well-being of their worshippers or to regulate the affairs of nature and mankind, whilst, on the other hand, their anger was recognized and they were feared accordingly. It should be noted that it was mainly neglect of worship and of giving of offerings to themselves that more especially excited their wrath. Too much reliance must not therefore be placed upon the sweeping state-ments of some writers in regard to the punitive functions of Polynesian deities.

SAMOA

Turner does not provide any systematized scheme of classifica-tion of the gods of Samoa, but he gives two lists of them, calling the gods mentioned in the first list "Gods superior—War and General Village Gods",[1] and those in the second "Gods in-ferior, or Household Gods".[2] He applies to them the Polynesian name *aitu*.[3] He includes in the first list Tangaloa and Tu, some well-known and important Samoan gods, and a number of other deities many of whom are not mentioned by other writers; his gods inferior are probably quite local gods, perhaps of domestic families.

Stair refers to the following classes or orders of spiritual beings recognized in Samoa:

1. *Atua*, the original gods, who dwelt in *Pulotu* and in the *langi* or heavens. These were believed to have been the pro-genitors of the other deities, and to have formed the earth and its inhabitants. They were not invoked like their descendants, and were not represented by any priests or temples. The chief

---

[1] Turner, pp. 23–66.   [2] *Ibid.* pp. 67–77.
[3] *Ibid.* p. 17.

place among these was assigned to Tangaloa. But Turner[1] says that Tangaloa was worshipped and had temples.

2. *Tupua*, the deified spirits of chiefs, who were also supposed to dwell in *Pulotu*, and certain objects "into which they were supposed to have been changed" were also called *tupua* and believed to personate them. The more exalted of them were supposed to become posts in the house or temple of the gods in *Pulotu*.

3. *Aitu*, a class which included the descendants of the original gods, whose aid was invoked by the different orders of priests. They comprised war gods, family gods, those invoked by prophets and sorcerers, as well as the tutelar deities of the various trades and employments. As every settlement had its local god of war in addition to the national war gods, so every family had its own particular *aitu* or tutelar deity, who was usually believed to inhabit some familiar object, animate or inanimate, which was regarded with superstitious reverence; but it often happened that if the gods were not propitious to their supplicants torrents of abuse were heaped upon them, though as a rule they were much dreaded.

4. *O Sauali'i*, which term Stair thought might be said to include ghosts or apparitions. These seem to have been regarded as an inferior class of spirits, ever ready for mischief or frolic, but who do not appear to have been represented by any class of priesthood, or to have had any dwellings sacred to them. The term was also used respectfully for an *aitu* or god.[2]

Brown says that the word *tupua* was "supposed by some" to mean the deified spirits of chiefs, indicating that they constituted a separate order from the *atua*, who were the original gods.[3] Wilkes, on the other hand, says that the *atua* were the gods of human origin;[4] but he says elsewhere that many inferior gods watched over particular districts, and refers to the custom of worshipping as *aitu*, or inferior gods, dead chiefs to whose memories they erected monuments of wood or stone.[5] According to Hale, some people thought that the souls of chiefs went to *Pulotu*, and became inferior deities.[6] Pritchard says there were national gods, in which term he includes original gods, who were the great gods that created the islands and man and ruled the

[1] Turner, pp. 52 *sqq.*
[2] Stair, pp. 211 *sq.*, 215 *sqq.*, 228–32; cf. Stair, *J.P.S.* vol. v, p. 34.
[3] Brown, p. 223.   [4] Wilkes, vol. III, p. 22.
[5] *Ibid.* vol. II, pp. 131 *sq.*   [6] Hale, p. 27.

universe, as well as deified men; and that there were also gods of districts, villages, families, and individuals.[1] According to von Bülow, the Samoans believed in one god, Tangaloa-a-langi, who had human feelings and desires. He had several sons, who with their posterity were *aitu*, that is supernatural beings. Men became *aitu* after death, they enjoyed themselves with kava-drinking and other pleasures, and received the power of doing good or evil to the survivors. The *aitu* were the tools of Tangaloa by whom his commands were carried out. They generally appeared after sunset, avoided the light, and caused evil; so that the people were afraid, even on moonlight nights, to go alone on a lonely path.[2] Krämer speaks of Tangaloa as the highest god, or *atua*, who had no beginning. He distinguishes between the *atua*, or true gods of heaven, and the supernatural beings called *aitu*, whose number was unlimited, and their origin very various; to these the great gods handed over the government of men, who feared and worshipped them. He says they were all village gods, and that each family also had its own special guardian spirit, and every district had also its special god. The more powerful of these supernatural beings had assistants and servants called *tautangata* or 'auao.[3] Krämer also speaks of the *tupua* as being the spirits of dead relations and being reverenced.[4] Each of the three main divisions of the island of Upolu (Aana, Atua, and Tuamasanga) had its own special god.[5] Graeffe speaks of the chief gods who personified the powers of nature, and then says the Samoans worshipped and feared a great number of lesser deities called *aitu*, and that they had house gods, district gods, and grove gods, most of which were worshipped in animal forms.[6] According to Ella the Samoans had some idea of a supreme being, but there were many tutelar deities and subordinate spirits, represented in natural objects, to whom much deference was paid and worship offered.[7] They believed in the existence of *aitu* (spirits), superior and inferior, and thought that the air, the sea, and the bush were inhabited by these beings, of whom some were wandering about seeking rest and finding none.[8] Each district in Samoa had its tutelar deity, and each

---

[1] Pritchard, pp. 112 *sq.*; cf. p. 109.
[2] Von Bülow, *Globus*, vol. LXVIII, pp. 366 *sqq.*
[3] Krämer, *S.I.* vol. I, pp. 22 *sqq.*, 104–7.
[4] *Ibid.* vol. II, p. 108; cf. Wilkes, vol. II, p. 131.
[5] Krämer, *S.I.* vol. I, p. 23; cf. Ella's statement that in each of the three great divisions of Upolu different sets of traditions were found (*J.P.S.* vol. IV, p. 53).
[6] Graeffe, *M.G.G. Hamburg*, p. 71.   [7] Ella, *A.A.A.S.* vol. I, p. 493.
[8] *Ibid.* vol. IV, p. 643.

family its totem. Some were more especially respected as national deities in different districts.[1] Hood says that they lived in the greatest fear of their deities, whose name was legion; so much so that they appeared to be afraid of rendering too particular service to one, lest they should offend another.[2] According to Fraser every family had its own tutelar animal, called an *aitu*, which was specially reverenced by the members of the family from generation to generation.[3]

In Pratt's *Dictionary* we find the word *atua* given as meaning "a god", *tupu* defined as having the meanings of "to grow", and "a chief of the highest rank"; *tupua* is the term applied to "an image", *aitu* means "a spirit", "a god"; and *sauali'i* is given as meaning "a god (the respectful term for an *aitu*)".

The consideration of the evidence provided by the various authorities is largely a matter of terminology, and in spite of the confusion as to the native conceptions of the different classes of gods, it is desirable that some attempt should be made to summarize the evidence.

The term *atua* is used widely in Polynesia with the general meaning of "a god"; but it was apparently applied in Samoa only or mainly to the deities of the highest order, according to Stair, Brown, Pritchard, and Krämer. Wilkes is the only writer who says the *atua* were supposed to have been of human origin.

The term *aitu* evidently included a great number of gods, varying largely in character, attributes and importance. Turner applies it to all the gods, including Tangaloa himself, on the one hand, and to mere household gods on the other; and Pratt gives it as meaning both "a god" and "a spirit", while Stair and Krämer include among the *aitu* some of the most important of the Samoan gods. Wilkes speaks of them as being dead chiefs.

The *tupua* are mentioned by Stair, Brown and Krämer; and the use of the word, as indicated by Pratt, for an image might point to it as referring to gods of whom the images were symbols. Stair says they were deified spirits of chiefs; Brown says they were "supposed by some" to be so; according to Krämer they were the spirits of dead relations.

Concerning the class, referred to by Stair, of *sauali'i*, it may be noticed that he says that it was also used respectfully for an *aitu*, and that this is confirmed by Pratt; and if these beings were, as Stair indicates, a separate class, inferior to the *aitu*, it is strange

[1] Ella, *J.P.S.* vol. VI, p. 155.   [2] Hood, p. 141.
[3] Fraser, *R.S.N.S.W.* vol. XXIV, p. 213 *n.* 2.

that it should be an act of respect to call the latter by their name.

We may draw attention, with reference to the general characteristics attributed to the gods, and the lives they were supposed to live, to von Bülow's statement that Tangaloa-of-the-skies was believed to have human feelings such as love and hate and to his jealousy of any attainment by his subjects to too high a position. He also says that the *aitu* of human origin drank kava, had games, banquets, and practised polygyny. We have also seen Pritchard's statement that the gods held communion with each other. Von Bülow also describes Tangaloa-of-the-skies as being thought of as a human chief, who shared all the impulses of his fellows in rank on earth, being fond of chiefly sport (such as pigeon-catching, duelling with clubs, fishing and war), living in luxury, and marrying as he pleased.[1] Probably this might be said of the gods generally, for it is indicated in the numerous traditions concerning them, including stories of their loves and conflicts among themselves, which might be accounts of the doings of human beings but for the attribution to them of supernatural powers.

Concerning beliefs as to the aloofness of the greater gods from human day-to-day affairs, we may refer to Stair's statement that the *atua* were not invoked like their descendants; to Krämer's statement that the great gods handed over to the *aitu* the government of men, and to his reference to the employment by the more powerful *aitu* of assistants and servants. Von Bülow, speaking of Tangaloa, says that his duties as a ruler did not give him much trouble, as he had servants who fulfilled his commands, and that he himself was conceived as being a great chief, who, like his earthly prototypes, considered all work as being dishonouring.[2]

TONGA

Mariner says that in Tonga the hotooas, or supernatural intelligent beings, might be divided into classes.[3] These classes were:

(1) The original gods.
(2) The souls of nobles, having all attributes in common with the first, but inferior in degree.

---

[1] Von Bülow, *I.A.E.* vol. XII, p. 64.
[2] *Ibid.* pp. 64 *sq.*; cf. Pratt, *R.S.N.S.W.* vol. XXVI, p. 295.
[3] Mariner, vol. II, p. 103; by this term he evidently means *otua*, which is the Tongan pronunciation of *atua*, and is given in Baker's *Dictionary* as meaning "a god", and in Père A.C.'s *Dictionary* as meaning "god", "divinity", "spirit". In quoting Mariner the spelling "*otua*" will be adopted.

(3) The souls of *matabule*, which were still [more?] inferior, and had not the power, as the two first had, of coming back to Tonga to inspire the priests, though they were supposed to have the power of appearing to their relatives.

(4) The original attendants, or servants, as it were, of the gods, who, although they had their origin, and had ever since existed, in *Bulotu*, were still inferior to the third class.

(5) The *otua pow*, or mischievous gods.

(6) Moooi [Maui], the god who supported the earth, and did not belong to *Bulotu*.[1]

Baker gives in his *Dictionary* the word *faahikehe* as being " the name for all the Tonga gods; an evil spirit ",[2] and several other writers refer to this word, or to others which are perhaps the same or have a more or less similar basis.[3]

Cook says that in Tongatabu the supreme author of most things was a goddess Kallafootonga; but the same religious system did not extend all over the Tongan Islands.[4] The *Duff* missionaries say that each family of note had a god considered as being its peculiar patron.[5] According to Veeson each district called upon its appropriate god.[6] Also they thought every man had an *atua* or particular spirit attending him;[7] Sarah Farmer refers to two uncreated gods living in the sky, who were held in profound reverence, but not worshipped, and to whom no offerings were made; she says their names were too sacred for utterance, and that only a few persons of the highest rank knew them.[8] According to Lawry the four principal gods of the Tongan Islands were Maui, Hikuleo, Tangaloa, and Heu-moana-uli-uli, all of whom were brothers.[9] West says that the spirits of chiefs and persons of rank became servants of the gods and as such were often worshipped and had offerings made to them so as to secure their interposition with the gods.[10] Bastian says that every *fahinga* or clan had a protecting god in the sea; and that, besides the *otua* or gods of the sky, each clan had its protector god, and that besides the gods who had " their fixed seat " [were incarnate or immanent] in certain objects, there were gods who came when called, entering into the priest.[11]

---

[1] Mariner, vol. II, pp. 103–10.   [2] Baker, p. 30.
[3] Wilson, p. 273; Lawry, *F.F.I.* (2), p. 37; Bastian, *I.O.* p. 33; Reiter, *Anthrop.* vol. II, pp. 230, 747 *n.* 1.   [4] Cook, vol. V, p. 422.
[5] Wilson, p. 271.   [6] Veeson, p. 152.
[7] *Ibid.* p. 153.   [8] S. Farmer, pp. 125 *sq.*
[9] Lawry, *F.F.I.* (1), p. 248.   [10] West, p. 255.
[11] Bastian, *I.O.* p. 34.

According to Reiter, each country [*pays*] and each village had its special deities. It was they who conquered, or were conquered, as the tribe or village conquered or was conquered; and each deity had a special individual in whom he appeared from time to time.[1] Tafakula was the goddess worshipped by the people of the island of Eua.[2]

Concerning the general characteristics of the gods, and the lives they led, we may refer to Mariner's description of the lofty and peaceful character of the souls of the *eiki*. Against this there is Reiter's reference to the gods conquering or being conquered [evidently by one another]; but this is only in accord with a widespread Polynesian belief that the opposing parties in war were helped by their respective deities.

Mariner tells us something about the beliefs of the people as to the general attitude of the gods towards mankind. He refers to the *otua pow*, as never dispensing good, but inducing petty evils and troubles, not as a punishment, but indiscriminately, from a purely mischievous disposition;[3] but apparently the attitude of these beings was supposed to be only mischievous, and not what we can call malignant. He says, concerning the gods generally, that all human evil was inflicted by them on mankind on account of some neglect of religious duty; and tells us that the primitive gods and souls of nobles [*eiki*] sometimes appeared visibly to mankind to warn them, or to afford comfort or advice, and that omens [which must be regarded as intended for their guidance] were believed to be direct indications sent by the gods.[4] On the other hand Mariner refers to a curious belief that every man had some deep-seated evil, in either his mental or bodily constitution, sent him by the gods, and for which the people could assign no other reason than the delight they took in punishing mankind; but Mariner adds that this belief was by no means universal, that most of the people did not pretend to assign any reason, and that upon mature consideration he is convinced that the malignity of the gods was not a Tongan doctrine, except so far as it applied to the *otua pow*.[5] Young says that the gods, who possessed power of life and death, were feared by all and loved by none;[6] and similar statements are made by other writers.[7] In regard to the latter we must emphasize

---

[1] Reiter, *Anthrop.* vol. II, p. 747 *n.* I.   [2] *Ibid.* p. 753.
[3] Mariner, vol. II, p. 99.   [4] *Ibid.* pp. 100 *sq.*
[5] *Ibid.* vol. I, p. 334 *n.*   [6] Young, *S.W.* p. 225.
[7] *A.P.F.* vol. XVII, p. 11; Père A.C., pp. x, xx.

the caution with which we must regard general statements of this character.

As regards the aloofness from human affairs of the great gods, we may refer to Mariner's statement concerning the original *otua*; to Sarah Farmer's reference to two gods who were held in profound reverence, but not worshipped; and to West's reference to the practice of appealing to the souls of chiefs and persons of rank to secure their interposition with the gods. Lawry says that human crimes, such as lying, theft, adultery, and murder, were not considered by the higher gods, because of their more elevated natures, and were left to the inferior gods to deal with; the higher gods were concerned only with such crimes as sacrilege committed in the temples, or an improper use of the offerings.[1]

For a full account of the gods of Tonga, including the great gods, and minor local deities, as well as the beliefs concerning ghosts, further reference should be made to the more recent work of Gifford.[2]

SOCIETY ISLANDS

Ellis says that *atua* or *akua* was the term for what may most appropriately be translated "god", and that the word had a meaning totally different from that of *varua*, "a spirit", although that term was sometimes applied to the gods.[3] He supplies a good deal of information about the ranks or orders of the gods but his evidence is full of confusion and inconsistencies. The investigation of the matter is, moreover, complicated by his way of speaking sometimes of Tahiti and the other south-eastern islands (called by him the Georgian or Windward Islands) and sometimes of the north-western islands (called by him the Society or Leeward Islands), and passing backwards and forwards between these two groups in a way that leaves us uncertain sometimes as to which of them he is dealing with, or indeed whether he is referring to both the groups. We may try, however, to present what seems to be the probable explanation of what Ellis tells us. The following classification seems to apply to the Society Islands generally:

(1) Ellis says that Tangaroa, Oro, and Tane, with other deities of the highest order were said to be *fanau po*, born of night; but

[1] Lawry, *F.F.I.* (1), p. 251; cf. Wilkes, vol. III, pp. 22 *sq.*
[2] Gifford, *Tonga*, pp. 287–332.   [3] Ellis, vol. I, pp. 333 *sq.*

that the origin of the gods, and the priority of their existence in comparison with the formation of the earth were involved in obscurity, being a matter of uncertainty even among the priests. Tangaroa was generally spoken of by the Tahitians as the first and principal god, uncreated, and existing from the beginning, or from the time when he emerged from the *Po*, or world of darkness.[1]

(2) Ellis also refers to an intermediate class of gods whose origin was veiled in obscurity. They were not supposed to have existed from the beginning, or to have been born of night; and they were often described as having been renowned men who after death had been deified by their descendants. He includes among these gods Roo and other gods of greater or less importance.[2]

(3) The next class to which Ellis refers were the gods of particular localities or professions.[3]

As regards the beliefs in the north-westerly islands, Ellis commences with a reference to Tangaroa, who had existed from eternity and had not had parents; and tells us of his creation of Hina, spoken of as his daughter, and of their joint creation of the heavens, earth and sea. Then follows a classification of the other gods:

(1) The first order of deities was a number of Society Island gods (some of them well known) whom Ellis mentions by name, and who had been created by Tangaroa. They do not include Raa.

(2) The second class, also created by him, were inferior to the first class; they were employed as heralds between the gods and men. Their names are not given.

(3) The third class "seems to have been" the descendants of Raa. These gods were numerous and varied in their character, some being gods of war, and others, apparently, of the healing art. The names of these gods are not mentioned.

(4) Oro, the son of Tangaroa, was the first of the fourth class, and "seems to have been" the medium of connection between celestial and terrestrial beings. Tangaroa then created a wife for Oro, and the children of this marriage also were gods. Tangaroa had also other divine sons, who were apparently included in this class, but their names are not given.[4]

---

[1] Ellis, vol. I, pp. 322 *sq*. But cf. the remarks on the cult of Tane in *Systems* vol. I, chap. VI.   [2] Ellis, vol. I, p. 327.   [3] *Ibid*.
[4] *Ibid*. pp. 325 *sqq*.

It does not appear to be possible to co-ordinate these two classifications. One point of difference between them is that the north-western orders of gods, other than Tangaroa, are all represented as having been created by or descended from other gods, whereas the general Society Island system includes gods who were often described as having been of human origin. Looked at very broadly, however, the general Society Island classification gives us something more or less definite in that it begins with the original gods born of *Po* or night, of the highest order, after which comes a lower class, not believed to have been original gods or born of night, and thought by some to have been of human origin; who are themselves followed by local gods and tutelar gods of human occupations.

Ellis is apparently speaking of the Society Islands generally when he refers to the gods of the sea. He says there were many of these sea gods, and suggests that they were probably men who had excelled their contemporaries in nautical adventure or exploit and had been deified by their descendants.[1] He tells us that "next in number and importance" to the gods of the sea were those of the air, sometimes worshipped in the form of a bird. Hurricanes, tempests, and all destructive winds were believed to be sent by them to punish those who neglected the worship of the gods. Ellis tells us of the way in which the people tried to appease these gods in stormy weather by liberal presents, and to induce them to cause storms to destroy hostile fleets.[2] There were also gods of the villages, the mountains, the precipices, and the dells or ravines.[3]

As regards the gods of professions, the following information, supplied by Ellis, will give an idea of the wide range of departmental deities presiding over the various activities of men. We are given the names of some "beneficent" gods, among whom are included Tane and Roo, who were invoked by the "expelling priests", and were supposed to be able to restrain the effects of sorcery, or expel evil spirits which had, through the incantations of sorcerers, entered into people; also the names of patron deities of the healing art, including medicine and surgery, these two branches of the profession having separate gods.[4]

Among, presumably, the gods of the sea there were numerous deities whose favour was essential to success in fishing;[5] and

[1] Ellis, vol. I, pp. 327 *sq.*
[2] *Ibid.* pp. 329 *sq.*
[3] *Ibid.* p. 330.
[4] *Ibid.* p. 333.
[5] *Ibid.* p. 140.

gods whose help had to be invoked and to whom offerings had to be made on the laying of the keel, the completion, and again on the launching of a newly built canoe.[1] So also prayers and offerings had to be made on the first wetting of a new fishing-net.[2] There was a god of husbandry; a god of carpenters, builders (including canoe-wrights) and of all those who wrought in wood; gods of those who thatched houses, and especially of those who finished the angles where the thatch on each side joined.[3] The hairdressers invoked the god of their profession.[4] Several gods were supposed to have presided over the *upaupa* or games;[5] and there was a god of thieves.[6] A curious conception, of a somewhat different character, is found in the belief that there was a god of ghosts and apparitions.[7] Davies refers to Tuete, the god of adultery and fornication.[8]

Moerenhout refers to Tangaroa as the supreme being, the creator of the world, and the source from which all beings had emanated, and of whom all the other gods were merely creatures, agents, or attributes, representing the god in his diverse functions.[9] All the gods were begotten or created by him.[10]

Starting on this basis, Moerenhout tells us something of the other *atua* or first class of gods. He says that this class was composed of all those who were the object of the public cult; they were the national gods, and were divisible into two classes, namely (a) the superior *atua* and (b) the inferior *atua*.

He then gives a list of the progeny of Tangaroa by his wife Feu-feu-maiterai, all of whom are evidently included among the superior *atua* [class (a)]. He says there were a great many gods of the first class, amongst whom were, according to some people, several of their deified chiefs. He is not certain as to this latter point, because a very careful research regarding the ancient customs of the people in this respect made him realize that deification, even if it existed at all, was very rare, and it was proved that the most celebrated chiefs of a period of at least four or five generations back did not figure in the list of gods though they all connected their origin with the gods. He then gives a list of the most notable of the beings included among the superior gods.[11]

[1] Ellis, vol. I, p. 164. [2] *Ibid.* p. 142.
[3] *Ibid.* p. 333. [4] *Ibid.* p. 136.
[5] *Ibid.* p. 332. According to Davies's *Dictionary* this word included plays, music, dancing, and all other games and amusements (Davies, *Dict.* p. 302).
[6] Ellis, vol. I, p. 333. [7] *Ibid.*
[8] Davies, *Dict.* p. 285.
[9] Moerenhout, vol. I, p. 559; cf. pp. 437, 440.
[10] *Ibid.* p. 439; cf. p. 442. [11] *Ibid.* pp. 442–6.

Moerenhout gives us some information about the inferior members [class (b)] of the atua. He says there was an infinite number of local deities, some dwelling in the waters, some in woods, some on the tops of mountains. Every object, substance, and place had a spiritual being or guardian, and every situation, state, and work of man had its tutelar and protecting deity. Echo was a god, thunder was Oro in anger, lightning was the flash of his eyes, and so on. Each of these deities fulfilled a special function, some watching over the development of plants, and others over the maturity of fruits, and there were gods of professions. Moerenhout gives the names of a number of these gods, classifying them as follows: (1) *Atua maho*: shark gods, patrons of navigators, invoked before going on a voyage; he mentions twelve of these. (2) *Atua pe'ho*: deities of the valleys, presiding over agriculture; he names thirteen of these. (3) *Atua note oupaoupa*: patron gods of actors and singers, who presided over the *paoupa* or scenic games—a sort of opera, with words, music and dancing; he gives four of these. (4) *Atua note ravavi*: who presided over fishing and fishermen; he names five of them. (5) *Atua raaou paou mai*: the gods of medicine, of whom he mentions four. (6) *Atua no apa*: gods to whom offerings were made to guarantee oneself from enchantment and sorcery; he mentions five. (7) The god of labourers and planters. (8) The patron of carpenters, house-builders and canoe-makers. (9) Two gods, patrons of thatchers. (10) The patron of net-makers.[1]

Moerenhout also says that there were in the Society Islands two distinct cults, of which one was public and related to the atua or national gods, and the other was private or individual and related to the *oromatua* or domestic gods. The atua had *marae* or temples which contained their images, and in which lived those who officiated at their altars; but the *oromatua* had no temple other than the house of its worshippers, and its priest was the father of the family.[2] Public worship was rendered in the name of all to the gods of the whole nation in cases concerning the welfare of the larger majority or of all the people, such as war, peace, famine, the birth of a chief, or his accession to power; and it was rendered to all the gods, more particularly to certain gods whom Moerenhout mentions, including Roo, Tane, Oro, and other well-known Society Island gods.[3] Domestic worship was the principal cult; it permitted every father of a family to

[1] Moerenhout, vol. I, pp. 451 sqq.   [2] Ibid. p. 463.
[3] Ibid. pp. 465 sq.

have his temple near his dwelling, attendances at the public temples being only occasional.[1]

There are scattered references to the classes of gods in the works of other writers,[2] but they are so heterogeneous and unsystematic as not to be worth summarizing.

We may now refer to the subject of the *oromatua* and *ti'i*, who undoubtedly occupied a very important place in the religious beliefs of the Society Islands. There seems to have been some confusion between these two classes of supernatural beings. Thus Ellis speaks of them as though they were identical[3] while Moerenhout distinguishes between them.[4] One or both of these classes of spirits is also referred to by J. R. Forster,[5] Cook,[6] the *Duff* missionaries,[7] the London missionaries[8] and de Bovis.[9] Probably much of the confusion in the evidence is due to the fact that the two words were used with a number of qualifications, and in several contexts.

Taking the material as a whole, it appears that there was a recognized difference between the *oromatua* and the *ti'i*, the *oromatua* being the spirits of dead men, and the *ti'i* beings of non-human origin; nevertheless some of the *ti'i* were also believed to have been the spirits of dead men. Apparently the *oromatua* were regarded as being more sacred than the *ti'i*. Both of them were, or might be, vindictive; but this belief applied more especially to the *ti'i*, the *oromatua* being recognized also as the guardian spirits of their surviving relatives or descendants. We must remember as to this view of the *oromatua* what we are told of their punishment of family quarrels, which, if correct, would perhaps account, at all events to some extent, for the fear with which they were regarded; and it must also be borne in mind that the gods themselves were believed to punish severely those who did not treat them with sufficient respect and give them the customary offerings.

We may now turn to the final question of the general character of the gods and other supernatural beings. Ellis says that the

---

[1] Moerenhout, vol. I, p. 283.

[2] Wilson, pp. 333 *sq.*; Bougainville, p. 255; G. Forster, *Voy.* vol. II, pp. 149 *sq.*, 153 *sq.*; J. R. Forster, *Obs.* p. 539; Cook, vol. VI, p. 148; vol. I, pp. 321 *sq.*; Banks, p. 173; Corney, *Tahiti*, vol. II, pp. 259, 472; Lesson, *Voy.* vol. I, p. 399; de Bovis, p. 267; Davies, *Dict.* pp. 19, 45.

[3] Ellis, vol. I, pp. 334 *sq.*; cf. also pp. 396 *sq.*

[4] Moerenhout, vol. I, pp. 433 *sqq.*, 454, 458 *sqq.*, 473, 480 *sq.*

[5] J. R. Forster, *Obs.* pp. 541 *sq.*; cf. G. Forster, *Voy.* vol. II, p. 151.

[6] Cook, vol. VI, p. 149.   [7] Wilson, pp. 333 *sq.*

[8] L.M.S. *Trans.* vol. IV, p. 433.   [9] De Bovis, pp. 266 *sq.*, 289.

people imagined them to be such as they (the people) were themselves, only endowed with greater powers. It was supposed that in all their actions they were influenced by motives exactly corresponding with those that operated upon the minds of men; and it was therefore thought that even spirits could be diverted from their purpose by the offer of a larger bribe than had been received to carry it into effect; or that the efforts of one *ti'i* could be neutralized or counteracted by those of another more powerful.[1] Ellis refers elsewhere to the belief that it was the spiritual part of the sacrifices that was eaten by the god or being to whom they were offered.[2]

Concerning the aloofness of the great gods, the missionaries of the *Duff* say that Tangaroa and Tane were only prayed to in times of great distress, being supposed to be too exalted to be troubled with matters of less moment than the illness of a chief, storms, devastations, war, or any great calamity.[3] Banks says that though Tangaroa, the chief of all gods, was not actively concerned with mankind, his son Tane was much more generally invoked, as he was supposed to be the more active deity.[4] Moerenhout says that Tangaroa was too far above the things of this world to concern himself with them, or to interest himself in the fate of men. Therefore they did not dedicate any temples or altars to him, and few worshipped him, although all were zealous in celebrating his glory, power, and works;[5] and he was the only *atua* to whom victims were not offered.[6] De Bovis says that no worship was offered to Tangaroa, and it was to the god Oro that almost all the *marae* were consecrated.[7]

With reference to the question of the supposed general attitude of the gods towards human beings, Ellis says that it was believed that the gods were powerful spiritual beings, acquainted, in some degree, with the events of this world, and generally governing its affairs; never exercising anything like benevolence towards even the most devoted followers, but requiring homage and obedience, with constant offerings, and dispensing destruction on all who either refused or hesitated to comply.[8] According to Cook, though they had no notion that their god must always be conferring benefits, without sometimes forgetting the people, or suffering evil to befall them, they seemed to regard this less than the attempts of some more inauspicious being to hurt them;

[1] Ellis, vol. I, p. 369.
[2] *Ibid.* p. 358; cf. Cook, vol. VI, p. 40.
[3] Wilson, p. 333.
[4] Banks, p. 173.
[5] Moerenhout, vol. I, pp. 439, 462.
[6] *Ibid.* p. 509.
[7] De Bovis, p. 271.
[8] Ellis, vol. I, p. 336.

and, as regards the latter, he refers to the *etee* [*ti'i*] as an evil spirit who sometimes did them mischief, and to whom, as well as to their god, they made offerings.[1] Banks refers to the humble regard shown to the deity, whose assistance was asked on all occasions with much ceremony and some sacrifice.[2] Moerenhout says that the gods were not merely concerned with the important events of life, for there was not a single action, enterprise, or event, which was not attributed to them, submitted to their inspection, or done under their auspices; and he says as to this, by way of example, that the people did not receive a stranger without the consent of the gods, and that no public or private dances, exercises, pleasures, or rejoicings were celebrated without their approbation.[3] They punished severely any act committed without their being informed beforehand, being so jealous of their privileges that the most trivial occurrences called for their intervention, and must take place under their auspices.[4] The observance of ritual was imperiously exacted by them, and non-observance of the sacred rites, or neglect or contempt for gods and altars, was a crime.[5]

MARQUESAS

There are a number of references to the character of Marquesan gods in the works of various writers.[6] The information that approaches most closely to what we may call a classification is that given by Radiguet. In this he distinguishes between the superior gods presiding over the elements; the secondary gods who haunted places on earth, and were perhaps the respective presiding gods of mountains, valleys, woods and streams (though he does not say so), and were tutelar deities of various human occupations; and gods of human origin which he places in a separate category, though he does not say they were regarded as being inferior in rank to the other two. So also von den Steinen distinguishes between the gods living in the mythical *Havaiki*, and the numerous minor gods, all apparently of human origin. Concerning terminology, Shillibeer confines the term *atua* to

---

[1] Cook, vol. VI, p. 149.   [2] Banks, p. 173.
[3] Moerenhout, vol. I, pp. 438 *sq*.   [4] *Ibid*. pp. 441 *sq*.
[5] *Ibid*. p. 440; cf. p. 433.
[6] Shillibeer, p. 39; Radiguet, vol. XXIII, p. 626; Jardin, p. 186; Stewart, vol. I, p. 243; d'Urville, *Voy. pitt.* vol. I, p. 503; cf. p. 481; Wilson, p. 143; des Vergnes, *R.M.C.* vol. LII, pp. 722 *sqq.*; von den Steinen, *V.G.E.* vol. XXV, pp. 509 *sq.*; Porter, vol. II, p. 114; Tautain, *L'Anthro.* vol. VIII, p. 677; Christian, *J.P.S.* vol. IV, pp. 187 *sqq.*

one superior god; but the rest of the evidence points to its having been a general term for the different classes of gods. Jardin says that each valley had its own god and did not recognize a superior god, and the *Duff* missionaries say that none of the gods seemed to be superior to the rest. It may be mentioned that in Nukuhiva the different main groups of the people seem to have been greatly separated from one another by the mountains between their deeply secluded valleys, and indeed we have seen that there were beliefs that these groups had different skies. The most important gods seem to have been Tiki, Atea, and Maui. But we cannot say whether and to what extent the worship of these respective gods prevailed among the different groups in their separate valleys. Probably the geographical formation of the island would be unfavourable to any widely spread community of worship. Des Vergnes apparently regards Tiki and Tupa as having been two principal gods; but according to Tautain, Tupa, though sometimes described as a god of all the Marquesas, was really a deity peculiar to the Teii group of Taiohae (Anna Maria Bay), and he draws attention to the danger of assuming that, because a god was found in one locality, he was worshipped throughout the Marquesas.[1] As a large amount of our information concerning Nukuhiva has been obtained from Anna Maria Bay, it might well be that such a mistake as that to which Tautain refers might be made.

Handy classifies the gods of the Marquesas into " gods of myth and creation; departmental gods, including gods of nature and the elements, patrons of occupations, and gods of sickness; and tutelary deities, including personal, family, and tribal ancestral spirits. There was also what may be regarded as a class of demigods, including legendary heroes and other characters." These classes, however, were not mutually exclusive, and one god might belong to several of them. All of the above classes were ancestral and all were called *etua* or *atua* except the legendary characters which were generally referred to as men.[2]

Concerning the attitude of the gods towards mankind, Mathias says the gods were not concerned with the moral conduct of man, being angered only by actions inimical to themselves, such as the withholding of offerings and sacrifices, and the non-observance of taboo, which offences were punished by them with illness and death.[3]

---

[1] Tautain, *L'Anthro.* vol. VIII, p. 540 *n*. I.
[2] Handy, *N.C.M.* p. 244.   [3] Mathias, p. 39.

PAUMOTU

Montiton, whose information was probably collected mainly in the islands of Fangatau and Takoto, supplies some information as to religious beliefs and practices, some of which bears upon the present subject. He says that besides Tane, "who seems to have been the Oceanic Jupiter", and Tama his voice, the redeemer of men,[1] the Paumotu Olympus contained a great number of secondary and local deities. Generally speaking, the worship paid to these gods was inspired only by fear or the desire for abundant fishing. The ancestors were always associated with the honours paid to the gods, for it was supposed that they too, as well as the latter, could attract or send away at will the fish of the islands they had inhabited. This cult of the ancestors was public and consisted essentially in ceremonies and sacrifices at the *marae*. Montiton says that there were little cradles or coffins, in which were retained locks of hair and beard, and even nails and teeth, taken from the corpses of men before their inhumation; on occasions of religious or patriotic ceremony they were taken out of the house in which they were normally kept and placed in or near the *marae*, so that each warrior might venerate his ancestors, and offer food in sacrifice.[2] Montiton tells us something about the performances and sacrifices at the *marae*; and he says, with reference to the catching on the previous day of large fish to be offered in sacrifice, that a song was chanted by the successful fisherman. This song ends with an invocation addressed to Tangaroa.[3] He also gives an account of the subsequent ceremony at the *marae*, which begins with a prayer to "all the gods" of which he gives a list of names, and to the family gods, who were very numerous, but without interest, except for the locality. Montiton later refers to a chant in which a number of the gods are mentioned by name, and among them are deities described as "the god of polished mats", "the god of light breezes", "the god of ropes", "the god of hospitality", "the god of peace", and "the god who gives the finish to vessels".[4] Then, again, after the cooking of the food and its distribution, there was another invocation of all the gods and ancestors, who were called upon by their names.[5]

Caillot, speaking of the island cluster of Mangareva, says that

[1] Cf. *Beliefs*, vol. II, chap. XVIII.
[2] Montiton, vol. VI, p. 366; cf. pp. 491 *sq.*
[3] *Ibid.* p. 367.
[4] *Ibid.* pp. 368 *sq.*
[5] *Ibid.* p. 379.

the people had a considerable number of *atua* or gods, of whom the first were Atu-motua, Atu-moana, and Tangaroa, but that prayers were generally addressed, not to them, but to Tangaroa-Hurupapa, whom they regarded as being *par excellence* the true king of Mangareva; and he suggests that they were probably ancient chiefs deified. Below them came a class, also called *atua*, whose names and departmental duties are given. They were respectively the gods of the heavens; of night; of peace and breadfruit; of war; of pleasures; of evils; and a great many others of less importance such as the gods of stars; of thunder; of rain; of the souls of the dead; of births and wandering souls; and of captive souls. There were also the demigods; and finally a class called *ati-miru*, who were called by this name because they were descended from the god of night.[1] Caillot also refers to the practice of burying some of the Mangarevan kings in a certain cave, and adds that after this burial the honours of apotheosis were often bestowed upon them, and they then took their place among the ranks of the gods.[2] The prayers repeated at the cutting of the navel-string of a royal child were simply composed of invocations to departed kings and chiefs.[3]

The French missionaries, also speaking of Mangareva, say that the gods were innumerable, and were divided into two opposite classes of good and evil spirits, some of which they describe. All the principal phenomena of nature were deified as good or evil spirits, according as they inspired hope or fear.[4] The people called all their gods *aruaino* (malevolent spirits), only one or two of them being good, while all the others were evil and much feared.[5] These gods were imagined to have monstrous heads, horns, hideous skins, and sepulchral voices.[6] The gods were greatly feared and immense offerings had to be made to them, because whoever neglected them might expect all evils.[7] The missionaries also refer to the little boxes containing relics of ancestors.[8]

Both Beechey and d'Urville say that everyone had his peculiar deity.[9] Tregear gives the term *atua* as meaning a god, and *atiru* and *gatiru* as being applied to a good spirit.[10] Smith, whose

---

[1] Caillot, *Mythes*, pp. 153 sq.
[2] *Ibid.* p. 153; cf. p. 224.
[3] *Ibid.* p. 150 n. 1.
[4] *A.P.F.* vol. XIV, pp. 332 sq.
[5] *Ibid.* vol. IX, p. 36.
[6] *Ibid.* p. 38.
[7] *Ibid.* vol. X, pp. 187 sq.; cf. vol. XLIV, p. 130.
[8] *Ibid.* vol. XLIV, p. 130.
[9] Beechey, vol. I, p. 243; d'Urville, *Voy. pitt.* vol. I, p. 520.
[10] Tregear, *J.P.S.* vol. II, pp. 197, 201.

information was taken from materials provided by the French missionaries, refers to the deification of the souls of still-born children of kings.[1]

NIUE

Smith says that in the island of Niue Tangaloa held the supreme position among the gods.[2] Smith makes several references to the *tupua* class of gods,[3] but the whole account is somewhat confused and difficult to understand in detail. We may, however, gather from it that the supernatural *tupua* worshipped in Niue, or some of them, were believed to be the souls of dead men. Turner says they worshipped the spirits of their ancestors.[4] Hood refers to the worship of the spirits of their ancestors and the terrible gods of disease.[5] According to Thomson, every village had its *deus loci*, who protected its crops in peace, and its warriors in war; but there is no direct evidence to show that they were deified ancestors.[6] He says elsewhere that every tribe had its tutelar deity, who was probably a deified ancestor;[7] and that the gods to whom offerings were made were the spirits of dead ancestors.[8]

Loeb refers to the great gods of Niue, of whom the chief was Tagaloa, and he also gives a list of localized and lesser deities.[9]

ROTUMA

Gardiner apparently places Tangaloa by himself at the head of the gods of Rotuma, for he says that this deity was only prayed to about matters concerning the whole island.[10]

Before dealing with the other gods we must refer to a feature of the social and political systems there, which has been described in detail elsewhere.[11] The island was divided into a number of districts, and each of these districts was subdivided into a number of *hoang*, a term applied to all the houses of a family placed together, and forming, if the family was a large one, a small village; the term *hoang* was also applied to the family itself, and each *hoang* had a name.

Gardiner says that each *hoang* had its own *atua*, but several

[1] Smith, *J.P.S.* vol. xxvii, p. 125. [2] *Ibid.* vol. xi, pp. 195 *sq.*
[3] *Ibid.* p. 196; vol. ii, pp. 22–6; vol. xii, pp. 28 *sq.*
[4] Turner, p. 306. [5] Hood, p. 17.
[6] Thomson, *S.I.* p. 84. [7] *J.R.A.I.* vol. xxxi, p. 138.
[8] *S.I.* p. 96. [9] Loeb, *Niue*, pp. 158–62.
[10] Gardiner, *J.R.A.I.* vol. xxvii, p. 467.
[11] *Systems*, vol. i, pp. 355–62.

hoang might acknowledge a big *atua* over all of them, while each had its own *atua*. All these *atua* were ever ready to punish and prey upon anyone who did not propitiate them with plenty of food and kava. A *hoang* would suffer no great harm so long as it propitiated its own *atua*, unless a greater *atua* laid a curse on it and so caused misfortune; the power of these *atua* was confined, however, to the people themselves, and extended but little or not at all over their crops, and the elements, which seem to have been under the exclusive control of Tangaloa. Then, again, beneath the *hoang atua*, came an inferior class who, Gardiner says, might be called "devil spirits", their sole delight being to cause sickness and death, and only evil influences were ascribed to them. Below the devil spirits was a still lower class of *atua*, with little or no power of themselves alone, who, he says, would best be termed "the ghosts of men"; they could to some extent be called up at will by relatives to cure them of "sickness of a certain class supposed to be due to the influence of soul upon soul", or for assistance against enemies. The *hoang* gods were usually incarnate in some sort of animal.[1]

The French missionaries say that, besides Raho, who was the principal god, there were hundreds of lesser gods, including certain fish, certain birds, and in general all the great chiefs of the island to whom divine honours were accorded with burial. The natives had a great respect for the dead.[2]

There are two references to the use in Rotuma of the term *atua*. Gardiner says it was the generic name for all devils, spirits, and ghosts, and was also used for the soul, as we understand it.[3] Hocart says that it meant "a spirit", "a ghost", and tells of some children who were playing with human bones and told him they were "the bones of *atua*"; and he says that the words *atua* and *aitu* overlapped; but that not all the *aitu* were *atua*.[4]

FOTUNA

Bourdin divides the gods of the island of Fotuna into two classes —the first and the second. At the head of these was Maui-alonga, but the names and attributes of the other gods of the first class were not known, with the exception of Mafuikefulu, or the sleeping god. The gods of the second class (*atua muli*) were greatly feared, as their peculiar function was to inflict

---

[1] Gardiner, *J.R.A.I.* vol. xxvii, pp. 466 *sq.*
[2] *A.P.F.* vol. xx, p. 363.   [3] Gardiner, *J.R.A.I.* vol. xxvii, p. 466.
[4] Hocart, *Man*, 1915, No. 75, pp. 129 *sq.*

punishment; and wounds, ulcers, and all kinds of illnesses were thought to befall those who angered them. They were apparently family gods, for the presence of the *atua muli* was indicated in the domestic hearth by a pillar, called "the divine pillar", in the fields by a stone of conical shape, and in the forests by a little basket hung on a tree. All the gods were hideous, malevolent, and hidden in darkness, and had the necessities and weaknesses of men. The people did not ask the gods for benefits, but only implored them not to do evil, and tried to appease them by prayers, offerings and sacrifices.[1]

The French missionaries say that the greatest of all the gods was called Faka-Veli-Kele;[2] below him there was a swarm of inferior spirits called *atua-muli*. Like their king, they had as tabernacles certain natives—men or women—who transmitted from generation to generation the divinity which had become hereditary in their families. All the ills came from them, and when a man was ill, it was believed that one of these *atua-muli* was eating him, and the man in whom the *atua* dwelt had to be found, and the anger of the god appeased through him by presents.[3]

UVEA

The French missionaries say that the deities of the island of Uvea were all spirits, formerly united to bodies, with the exception of certain principal gods who had never been human and whose origin was a mystery to them. All these spirits dwelt in the region of the clouds or came from a distant land which they called *Poratu* and the generic name of their Olympus was *Epoouri* (night). There was a hierarchy there, like that on the island—that is, all these spirits recognized a king; and the first after him were the ministers of his desires. To one he confided the care of the sick; to another that of seeing that the taboos were observed; this one would decide in matters of peace or war; that one had charge of the waves, of the winds, of the protection of the fruits, and so on. Others—the greater number—simply composed the court of the great spirit, and never came to earth except by way of an excursion (*promenade*) and to drink kava; they entered the bodies of the priests of the god. There were more than sixty of these in Uvea; but of these the only ones that were much regarded were the priests of the superior spirits.

[1] Bourdin, pp. 440 *sqq.* [2] Cf. Bourdin, *loc. cit.*
[3] *A.P.F.* vol. xv, p. 39; cf. Smith, *J.P.S.* vol. i, pp. 44 *sq.*

Those who occupied a very secondary rank in the kingdom of night were only respected by the people lest they should denounce them to the great gods. Kings were much feared after death, and their spirits returned to their old subjects. The missionaries give as an example the case of the spirit of a great chief who had died, which entered the body of a relative, told his relations of the dignity with which he was invested in the kingdom of night, and became duly installed in the ranks of the gods of the island; and they say that this was pretty much the history of all its gods.[1] The cult consisted in offering kava, especially in case of illness; in invoking Kakau and Finas, the two powerful gods of the island; and in keeping up the sanctuaries sacred to them.[2] The beliefs of the people concerning the attitude towards themselves of the gods are illustrated by the missionaries' account of an annual feast in honour of the two great gods mentioned above, to whom offerings of food were made and prayer was addressed, the substance of which was a supplication that the deities would cease to be evil to them, and a complaint that they continued to make the people die, and to give false reports of them to the King [of spirit-land].[3]

Mangeret says that in Uvea they had no conception of a single deity superior to all the others, but he refers to the existence of two classes of gods. Firstly, superior gods, spirits which had no bodies, masters over the island, and, secondly, spirits which had lived in the body, and especially those of chiefs. Below these superior and middle-class gods came the *atua-muli*, as in Fotuna.[4]

ELLICE ISLANDS

There are several references to the worship of ancestors in the Ellice Islands,[5] particularly the original ones who had swum from Samoa. Murray tells us that in the island of Nanomea there were said to be ten principal deities and there were various objects which the people held sacred, the chief of which seemed to be the skull of one of their ancestors called Folasa, and the seat of one of the canoes in which their ancestors came from Samoa, both of which appeared to be held in great veneration.[6] Turner refers to two principal gods in the island of Nukufetau, one of whom went about at night in the form of a man; and he

[1] *A.P.F.* vol. XIII, pp. 12 *sq.*   [2] *Ibid.* p. 15.
[3] *Ibid.*   [4] Mangeret, vol. I, pp. 152–5.
[5] Whitmee, pp. 26 *sq.*; Hedley, p. 46 ; Sollas, *Nature*, 1897, pp. 353 *sq.*
[6] Murray, 40 *years*, p. 408.

says that household gods were incarnate in fishes.[1] He tells us that in the island of Nanomanga the soul after death went to the heavens, but came at a call to the place where the skull was, drove away disease, and spoke through the living. He refers to two principal gods in this island, and says that here also the household gods were incarnate in fish.[2]

Kennedy refers to a female deity, Tinai, and her two brothers as the chief guardian spirits of Vaitupu, but he also mentions "an un-named deity who dwelt in the heavens". In addition, there were minor tutelar deities connected with specific areas.[3]

MANIHIKI AND RAKAHANGA

According to the extracts taken from Gill's papers, the people of the islands of Manihiki and Rakahanga had no gods of their own, their deities having been stolen.[4] He refers to two gods, and another who had "drifted ashore". He says, however, that they had many minor gods, such as fish, his reason for so doing being apparently that there were certain animals which the people would not eat, and as examples he mentions shark, turtle, sea-snake, crayfish, and some species of birds. Another species of deities were stones, and they also had a custom of deifying dead men.[5] In one of the traditions as to the god Maui there is a reference to a house of *tupua*, which is translated as meaning "demons", "spirits".[6] Gill himself says that if a king, priest, or distinguished fisherman died, his head was cut off, deposited in a finely woven coconut-leaf basket, and placed in the forepart of a canoe as a sea god. If they were overtaken by unfavourable winds, the head was taken out of the basket, and held aloft by its hair, while prayers were offered to it for good weather. The hands and feet of dead chiefs, priests, and fishermen were used for the same purpose by people of inferior rank.[7]

TONGAREVA

We are told that in the island of Tongareva they had four great gods, of whom two were good and two were bad. The two good gods gave life and all that was necessary for its preservation;

[1] Turner, p. 285. [2] *Ibid.* pp. 288 *sq.*
[3] Kennedy, *C.V.* pp. 147–9.
[4] For an interpretation of the significance of this term, together with a general account of the religious system, see Te Rangi Hiroa, *M. & R.* pp. 205 *sqq.*
[5] Gill, *J.P.S.* vol. XXIV, pp. 150 *sq.* [6] *Ibid.* pp. 147 *sq.*
[7] Gill, *S.L.P.* p. 104.

while the other two were constantly trying to counteract this.[1] Dr P. H. Buck refers to four "functioning gods" as well as a number of legendary deities.[2]

AUSTRAL ISLANDS

According to Tyerman and Bennet, the great national god of the Austral island of Rurutu was Tangaroa. After him came Rooteabu, and they also had family gods.[3] Williams says that Aa was the national god of this island; and that he was said to be the ancestor by whom the island had been peopled, and who was deified after death.[4]

EASTER ISLAND

The French missionaries refer to the lack, or disappearance, of religious beliefs and practices in Easter Island.[5] Geiseler (1882) says that the chief gods were Meke-meke[6] (or Make-make) and Haua; and first-fruits of all products of the soil were offered to them. Meke-meke was the god most dreaded. He had power over the soul after death and was represented by the eggs of the sea birds of the island of Motu-nui.[7] He was a creator god and all the stone images of the island served in former days as secondary gods, by means of which he could be worshipped[8]— he was never worshipped directly.[9] Geiseler speaks of a stone which was supposed to be the representation of the god of bananas, and received worship at the time of the ripening of the bananas.[10] He refers also to a god of dancing.[11]

Thomson (1886) says that Meke-meke was the great spirit of the sea,[12] and was also connected with war.[13] In connection with the annual egg-gathering competition, which appears to have determined succession to chieftainship,[14] no special authority was vested in the victor; it was supposed that he had won the approval of Meke-meke.[15] Thomson provides a translation of one of the tablets which gives a list of forty-two gods and goddesses, and states what were the things ascribed to their respective marriages, which comprised a large number of species

---

[1] Lamont, pp. 180 sq.   [2] Te Rangi Hiroa, E.T. pp. 85–6.
[3] Tyerman, vol. I, p. 508.   [4] Williams, pp. 43 sq.
[5] Mrs Routledge, p. 236 n. 1 (quoting A.P.F. Jan. 1866); A.P.F. vol. xxxix, pp. 254 sq.; cf. Lapelin, R.M.C. vol. xxxv, p. 111; Geiseler, p. 31.
[6] Cf. Palmer, J.E.S. (N.S.), vol. I, p. 372.
[7] Geiseler, p. 31.   [8] Ibid. p. 33.   [9] Ibid. p. 31.   [10] Ibid. p. 53.
[11] Ibid. p. 48.   [12] W. J. Thomson, p. 482.   [13] Ibid. p. 519.
[14] Cf. Systems, vol. I, p. 394.   [15] W. J. Thomson, p. 482.

of the animal and vegetable kingdoms, and also rocks, medicine, and a large number of other natural phenomena.[1] A recent study (unpublished) by Stimson, however, indicates that Thomson's translation is of little value. Thomson does not intend to imply that the deities in question were afterwards the tutelar gods of the respective things which they produced, but the text illustrates a conception of detailed mythical association of various gods with different objects and conceptions. We are, however, told of some of the departmental gods. There was Era Nuku, a god of feathers, connected with war, who kept off evil spirits if feathers were placed over the burial places. He also protected the yam and potato plantations if feathers were tied upon a stick, and placed close together between the hills.[2] Mea Kahi was a bonito god, and by faithful worship of this deity abundance of fish was secured;[3] there was a tradition that when bone fish-hooks were substituted for those of stone a fisherman spent an entire night worshipping this god.[4] Mea Moa was the fowl god, to whom was ascribed the custody of chickens; and his beneficial influence was secured by putting a beach pebble that represented him under a sitting hen for a short time before the eggs were hatched.[5] Mea Ika was a fish god, whose stone was really worshipped.[6] There was a god of thieves, under whose patronage successful operations were believed to be accomplished, thefts only being detected when he had not sanctioned them.[7]

Thomson says that the small wooden and stone images known as "household gods" were made to represent certain spirits. They occupied a prominent place in every dwelling, and were regarded as the medium through which communication might be made with the spirits, but were never worshipped. Fishermen were always provided with the stone god that was supposed to be emblematic of the spirit having cognizance of the fish.[8] Similar figures, made to represent dead chiefs and persons of note, were given a place of honour at feasts and ceremonies.[9] After describing the stone representing Mea Ika, the fish god, he tells us that these gods were never common, and were possessed by communities or clans, and not by individuals; they were said to have been brought to the island by Hotu-matua (the traditional head chief of a party of immigrants, and first king of

---

[1] W. J. Thomson, pp. 521 sq. [2] Ibid. p. 519.
[3] Ibid. p. 539. [4] Ibid. p. 533. [5] Ibid. p. 537.
[6] Ibid. [7] Ibid. p. 465. [8] Ibid. p. 470.
[9] Ibid. pp. 534 sq.

Easter Island) and the first settlers.[1] He also says that deified spirits were believed to be constantly wandering about the earth, and to have some influence over human affairs.[2] There are other references to the small images of Easter Island.[3]

Mrs Routledge says that the religion of the islanders, employing the word in our sense, seems always to have been somewhat hazy, and the difficulty in grasping it is now increased by the fact that the people, since becoming Roman Catholics, dislike giving the name of *atua* or god to their old deities, and it only drops out occasionally. They term them *aku-aku*, or more often *tatane*. She then says that she would use both these terms with the meaning of "supernatural beings", without prejudice to their original character, or claims to divinity. Some of them were certainly spirits of the dead, but had probably become deified; and the ancestors of Hotu-matua were said to have come with him to the island. They existed in large numbers, being both male and female, and were connected with different parts of the island; and a list of about ninety was given, with their places of residence. No worship was paid, and the only notice taken of these supernatural persons was to mention before meals the names of those to whom a man owed a special duty, and invite them to partake; it was etiquette also to mention with your own the patron of any guest who was present. There was no sacrifice; the invitation to the supernatural power was purely formal, or restricted to the essence of the food only. Nevertheless the *aku-aku* were amiable or the reverse according to whether or not they were well fed. If they were hungry, they ate the women and children, and one of them was reported as having a proclivity for stealing potatoes. If, on the other hand, they were well disposed to a man, they would do work for him, and he would wake in the morning to find his potato field dug. The *aku-aku* appeared in human form, in which they were indistinguishable from ordinary persons. An example is given of one of them who was the wife of a man and bore him a child, he having no idea that she was really a *tatane*, until at a later date he disappeared like a whirlwind over the sea; and there is another story of the appearance as human beings and the conduct of *tatane* in Easter Island. Mrs Routledge says that *aku-aku* were not immortal; and she tells us a story as to a man killing a number

[1] W. J. Thomson, p. 537.　　　　[2] *Ibid.* p. 469.
[3] Geiseler, pp. 49, 53; *A.P.F.* vol. xxxviii, pp. 60, 69; Palmer, *J.R.G.S.* vol. xl, p. 174; W. J. Thomson, p. 486; cf. pp. 496, 538.

of them. She says that the *tatane* attacked human beings, particularly at night, and she refers to a class of persons called *ivi-atua*, of whom the most important held commune with *aku-aku*.[1] There are indications of god-worship in the book, for example a ceremony at which prayers for rain were addressed to Hiro,[2] chanting in connection with the egg-gathering performances,[3] and a reference to the intervention of the gods in the search for the eggs in order to secure success to the man who was destined to win.[4] The evidence from Easter Island, taken as a whole, indicates that worship was offered to the gods, although the missionaries did not observe it. It is possible that the partial lack of visible worship may have been due to the carrying off, in about the middle of last century, by the Peruvian slave-raiders of very large numbers of the population, including chiefs and priests, the effect of which would be that there would probably be but few left who were qualified to perform the ceremonies.

TIKOPIA

In Tikopia the word *atua* is a general term for supernatural objects, whether human or not. There are a number of varieties of *atua*:

(1) Spirits of the dead, ancestors, and important deities who have never been men. The latter are specifically termed *tupua*. (The word *tupua*, however, is sometimes used in a somewhat loose sense to designate ancestors in general.)

(2) *Atua vare* (common or foolish *atua*), wandering spirits of the bush and of the sea. They are not individually named—they are merely a class of spirits, which manifest themselves from time to time. They are generally malignant or mischievous, and include the *atua fakafua*, or bringers of disease.

(3) Special objects with supernatural powers—stones, trees, or weapons—are classed as *atua*.

It should be mentioned that, in addition to these usages, the word *atua* is also employed in what might be termed a secular sense to denote certain living things regarded by the natives as unfit for food. In these cases *atua* is used simply as the antithesis of *kai* (food), and there is no suggestion of a religious taboo.

Apart from the *atua vare* the attitude of most of the gods towards mankind is beneficent, subject to the correct

---

[1] Mrs Routledge, pp. 236 *sqq.*   [2] *Ibid.* p. 242.
[3] *Ibid.* p. 260.   [4] *Ibid.* p. 262.

performance of ritual obligations. There are, however, a few *atua pariki* (evil *atua*) who are particularly apt to exert a baneful influence, and are employed in hostile sorcery. It should be noted that such terms as *vare* and *pariki* are terms descriptive of the behaviour of the *atua* rather than names of distinct classes of supernatural beings.

Atua may become incarnate in living creatures—such as hermit crabs, bats or domestic cats—but the association here is of a temporary and occasional character, the presence of an *atua* in a particular living creature being inferred from any abnormal or striking behaviour which it may manifest. In this case the creature is spoken of as being the *ata* (shadow) of the god. In addition to this there is a permanent association between the four principal sources of vegetable food (taro, coconut, breadfruit and yam) and the four clans of the island. This is linked up with a complicated body of religious beliefs, involving the conception that each of the foodstuffs mentioned represents corporeally the clan god, whether in whole or in part, and this again is connected with religious observances and taboos.

The beliefs and linguistic usages connected with "incarnation", "manifestation" and the concept of living creatures as "shadows" of the *atua*, widespread throughout Polynesia, have been subjected to a sociological analysis by Dr Raymond Firth.[1]

ONTONG JAVA

According to information communicated by Dr H. Ian Hogbin, the spirits and gods of Ontong Java are termed *kipua* or *aitu*. They do not include any of the well-known Polynesian gods. With the exception of one or two spirits connected with the sea, invoked in connection with fishing, they are all ancestral. There is, however, a distinction between remote and immediate ancestors. The former were the culture heroes of the mythology, who had a cult with temples and priests, and to whom offerings were made daily and also in connection with the seasonal *sanga* festivals.

The spirits of immediate ancestors, generally called *kipua*, were not the object of any regular cult, though they played an important part in causing and curing illness. The sociological implications of this have been the subject of a detailed study by Dr Hogbin.[2]

[1] R. Firth, "Totemism in Polynesia", *Oceania*, vol. I, pp. 291–321, 377–98.
[2] Hogbin, *L.O.P.* chap. IV; cf. below, pp. 317 *sqq.*

CHAPTER II

MAJOR POLYNESIAN DEITIES

TANGAROA

THE cult of Tangaroa was more important and (with the possible exception of that of Maui[1]) more widely spread than that of any other Polynesian deity, and we may therefore commence our study of the pantheon by considering the beliefs and practices associated with him. Because of his special importance in Samoa we shall consider the evidence from that area in some detail, and then proceed to examine the material from other areas somewhat more briefly.

SAMOA

The traditional importance of Tangaloa in Samoa is shown by the genealogies of the kings, both in Manu'a and Upolu. A list of the *tuimanu'a* went back to the original god Tangaloa-of-the-skies, followed by his son, the god Tangaloa-a-Ui, who was followed by his son Tae-o-Tangaloa, who was supposed to have been the first divine earthly *tuimanu'a* or king of Manu'a.[2] Tangaloa also featured in the genealogies of the *tuiaana*,[3] of the Malietoa,[4] and, through a marriage with a daughter of a *tuiaana*, of the *tuiatua*.[5]

These genealogies represent, in their earlier parts, what probably were either old traditions or additions to traditions, made by the royal families to enhance their glory by claiming divine descent.[6] Probably all these royal families had become connected by intermarriages such as would enable one of them to

---

[1] The beliefs connected with Maui and Tiki, together with a hypothesis concerning their historical significance, have been presented elsewhere (*Beliefs*, vol. II, chaps. XXIV–XXVII; cf. also Stimson, *M. & T.*).

[2] Powell, *R.S.N.S.W.* vol. XXV, p. 138 (the actual list begins with Tae-o-Tangaloa, but his relationship to the two others forms part of the traditions).

[3] Krämer, *S.I.* vol. I, pp. 167 *sqq.*   [4] Von Bülow, *I.A.E.* vol. XI, p. 109.

[5] Krämer, *S.I.* vol. I, pp. 292–5.

[6] The suggestion of this practice of enhancing family glory is based on a study of Polynesian genealogies and traditions, including those of Samoa; but von Bülow, speaking of one of the Samoan stories of creation by Tangaloa, says that it was probably told by a Manu'an man in order to demonstrate the superiority of Manu'a over the other Samoan islands, and of the Manu'a chiefs over the other chiefs, the legend serving exclusively dynastic ends. (*Globus*, vol. LXXI, p. 376.)

share in the ancestry of another, and in fact the traditions and history show that they did so intermarry.

Beliefs as to the origin of Tangaloa have been dealt with elsewhere.[1] The following brief extracts may be given here: Tangaloa "the originator of men" was the son of Cloudless Heavens and Spread-out Heavens, the previous ancestry beginning with the High Rocks and the Earth Rocks, and their child, the earth, this being followed by a number of male and female ancestors whose names were those of phenomena of nature. He was the son of Cloudless Heavens and the Eighth (highest) Heavens. He existed in space, but it was not known how or whence he came. He dwelt in the expanse. The following beliefs also are mentioned by writers. He was born of the "Void of Heaven" and the "Vault of Heaven".[2] He was sometimes thought of as the begetter of original matter; sometimes as a human chief.[3] He always existed, and had no beginning.[4] He dwelt in the illimitable void, and at first he alone existed.[5]

In regard to the region inhabited by him, all the myths and traditions point to a region in the skies above as his home. This belief is disclosed in some of the myths of creation and other traditions and stories that have appeared in previous pages; so far, at all events, as the myths of creation are concerned, this would not necessarily indicate beliefs as to his home in later times, but there are other indications of it.[6]

Some writers refer to a number of Tangaloa gods with descriptive additions to their names; but whenever they do so, and one of the names is Tangaloa-langi (Tangaloa-of-the-skies), he always or almost always appears as the original or principal Tangaloa. The number of descriptive additions appended to the name of Tangaloa may be illustrated by the following further extracts from the myths of the creation: in one of them we find it said that Tangaloa-the-originator-of-men married the Great Heavens and his son was Tangaloa-of-the-heavens. Another begins with Tangaloa-the-dweller-in-lands, who was the son of Cloudless Heavens and the Eighth Heavens, and who had a son

---

[1] *Beliefs*, vol. I, chaps. I and II.
[2] Von Bülow, *I.A.E.* vol. XI, p. 109.   [3] *Ibid.* vol. XII, pp. 58, 64.
[4] Krämer, *S.I.* vol. I, p. 22.   [5] Powell, *J.V.I.* vol. XX, p. 148.
[6] Thus Pritchard says that Tangaloa lived in the highest heavens (Pritchard, p. 112). Turner speaks of him as Tangaloa-of-the-Eighth-Heaven (Turner, p. 52); Krämer says he lived in the sky (Krämer, *S.I.* vol. I, p. 22); Fraser says he was the chief god of the sky (Fraser, *J.P.S.* vol. VI, p. 35); Stuebel says he was in the tenth (highest) heaven (Stuebel, p. 143; cf. references to the eighth heaven above). The number of these heavens is stated differently by the various writers.

Tangaloa-the-explorer-of-lands. Another commences with Tangaloa and his son fishing. Then in the myths of creation by gods we find that, according to one of them, after the *fue* plant had been pulled up by the Tuli bird, by order of its father Tangaloa-in-the-heavens, and rotted, and produced two gods, the latter were operated upon by Tangaloa-the-marker and Tangaloa-the-seer who had been sent down by Tangaloa-in-the-heavens, and so produced two men. So also the long story of creation by Tangaloa-the-creator-of-lands, who was evidently Tangaloa-of-the-skies, after telling of various acts of creation by him and other matters, says that he created Tangaloa-the-immovable, Tangaloa-the-omnipresent, Tangaloa-the-extender-of-lands (or people), and Tangaloa-the-messenger; and there is a note suggesting that these other Tangaloa, dealers with men, were intermediary emanations from himself, but were all gods and all called Tangaloa. Turner in speaking of Tangaloa-langi, refers also to Tangaloa-the-creator-of-lands, Tangaloa-the-visitor-of-lands, and Tangaloa-the-abandoner-of-lands, and says that these were some of the names by which Tangaloa-of-the-heavens was known.[1] In addition von Bülow refers to Tangaloa-the-increaser-of-peoples, Tangaloa-the-unchange-able, Tangaloa-the-messenger-of-the-gods, and Tangaloa-the-prophet.[2] Krämer, again, says that the highest god, Tangaloa, had many descriptive names, for example, Tangaloa-the-creator, Tangaloa-the-infinite, and Tangaloa-the-worker-of-miracles; but he says that the Samoans regarded these less as descriptive names than as brothers, sons, or the posterity of Tangaloa-a-langi, the god of heaven, and classed them together under the name of *Satangaloa*, "the family of Tangaloa".[3] Powell refers to Tangaloa-the-creator, Tangaloa-the-unchange-able, Tangaloa-the-visitor-of-peoples, Tangaloa-the-prohibitor-of-peoples, and Tangaloa-the-messenger, and says that the creator Tangaloa produced other Tangaloa.[4]

The comments made by some of the writers as to the several Tangaloa gods raise the question whether they were really separate gods, or whether they were all the same god Tangaloa, the additions to his name being merely descriptive of the various attributes or departmental activities with which he was credited. A similar question arises with reference to Tangaloa in Niue and

---

[1] Turner, p. 52.   [2] Von Bülow, *Globus*, vol. LXXII, p. 376.
[3] Krämer, *S.I.* vol. I, p. 22. *Sa* is used as a prefix to names with the meaning of "family of".
[4] Powell, *J.V.I.* vol. XX, pp. 145, 150, 150 *n*.

to some of the other gods, notably the god Tane, as worshipped in the Hervey Island of Mangaia. Perhaps there was a general tendency for different attributes to be conceived as conferring separate identity under the influence of local and political factors. It may be added that, so far as Samoa is concerned, traditions disclose a belief in a Tangaloa family, living in the skies.[1] According to one of these the Tangaloa family came down from heaven to earth to bestow the chiefdom of Manu'a upon a newly born boy, and afterwards came down again to substitute for this title the superior title of *tuimanu'a*, and on this occasion dwelt in a house on earth which had been built for their reception. According to another, two of the people of Tangaloa-of-the-heavens stole the fowls of the god Lu and carried them off to the skies; Lu followed them there and fighting occurred between him and them, but Tangaloa (the great Tangaloa) forbade the continuance of the fight, and gave his daughter in marriage to Lu. According to another story, Losi and a number of other gods engaged in an expedition to the heavens, where they attacked and defeated the Tangaloa family. Another story refers to the courting by Tafa'a of Sina, the daughter of Tangaloa-of-the-skies, of the visits to her in the skies, first of his representatives, and then of himself and his brother, to press his suit, when they were lent a house in the skies in which to live, and finally of the marriage, which took place on earth, and which was attended by the Tangaloa family who came down from heaven to earth for the purpose. There is another story of the wanderings of three sons of Tangaloa-of-the-skies, in which they reached *Pulotu* (paradise) and remained and built a house there.[2] These sons were not also named Tangaloa, so this story may not point to a "Tangaloa family" such as we are considering.

Tradition and history alike bear witness to the highly important position held by Tangaloa in Samoa, though we cannot say whether his dominant position was recognized or admitted universally by all the people, including those who attached themselves to other gods. There are, however, many general statements as to his pre-eminence.[3] The statement of Wilkes[4] that the war gods were more worshipped than was Tangaloa is not inconsistent with his supremacy, as they would be approached in war as departmental deities, and the greatest gods,

[1] Cf. *Systems*, vol. I, chap. II.   [2] Stair, pp. 293 *sq.*
[3] Pritchard, p. 112; Brown, p. 227; Williams, p. 546; Krämer, *S.I.* vol. I, p. 22; Stair, p. 212.   [4] Wilkes, vol. II, p. 131.

such as Tangaloa, were sometimes or often conceived in Polynesia as being too great to interest themselves in the daily affairs of men, whose prayers were more usually addressed to minor or local gods.

There is evidence that Tangaloa was associated with celestial phenomena, the sun,[1] the moon,[2] and the rainbow,[3] while thunder was, according to Turner, associated with an answer to prayers offered to him. Though the accuracy of Turner's statement concerning the connection with the moon may be questioned, it may be pointed out that as Tangaloa was regarded as the great god of the skies, it would be natural that celestial phenomena should be associated with him, and that the beliefs as to the sun, the rainbow, and thunder, and perhaps the moon, may have been merely incidental to his dominion over the skies. One of the names given, according to Turner, to the month of January was Tangaloa-tele, or "Great Tangaloa" which referred to the worship of the god. The name given by Fraser is Tangaloa-fua, and he says that it was the season for great offerings to him.

Reference has been made elsewhere[4] to evidence connecting Tangaloa and some other gods with eels, snakes and lizards (animals with pointed tails); though as far as Tangaloa himself was concerned the connection was mainly indirect rather than direct. A statement of Turner suggests the incarnation of Tangaloa in the snipe (*tuli*).[5]

Turner says that in one place Tangaloa's image [*sic*] was a large wooden bowl, said to have come from Fiji, and he was supposed to be present in a hollow stone. A temple was built for him there, ánd called "The house of the gods"; it was carefully shut up all round, lest the gods should get in and out of it too easily, and so be all the more destructive. Offerings were presented to Tangaloa in war time; also offerings of gifts and prayers before going to fish or planting a fresh section of bushland, and in time of sickness or a special epidemic. It was firmly believed that if there was no prayer to Tangaloa there could be no blessing. Thunder was a sign that the prayer had been heard; but merely a slight tremulous reverberation indicated a rejected prayer and threatened punishment. In another district Tangaloa was said to have come along the ocean in a

---

[1] Krämer, *S.I.* vol. i, p. 24.   [2] Turner, p. 53.
[3] Von Bülow, *Globus*, vol. lxxi, p. 376.
[4] *Systems*, vol. ii, chap. xx.   [5] Turner, p. 53.

canoe, with a crew of seven, and to have taken up his abode in the bush inland from the settlement. Confused noises from the bush there were supposed to be the murmurs of the gods and a cause of death in the village. When war broke out two of the chiefs went inland to consult Tangaloa. One sat down in front of the grove of high trees, and the other went round behind. This man was covered from head to foot with leaves, and had only a hole left for the eyes. No creepers ran up the trees, and no leaves were allowed to be seen on the small stones under the trees, for it was supposed that the god was in the stones. If the stones appeared separated, and unusually far apart, that was a sign that the district was about to be broken up and the people killed or banished. But if the stones were huddled together, that was a good omen, as it indicated union, victory and strength.[1]

At the commencement of the fishing season the first bonito caught was brought to the title chief, and was called "the fish of Tangaloa",[2] which suggests that the chief received it as an offering to the god; this is Krämer's interpretation of its meaning.[3] The same custom prevailed with reference to the first bonito caught in a new boat, this fish also being associated with Tangaloa.[4] This practice is referred to in one of the versions of the Manu'an legend of creation by Tangaloa, where it is said that fishes must be at heaven's disposal, and that the offering to Tangaloa must be bonito;[5] and Fraser in commenting upon this interprets it as a claim by Tangaloa to his favourite fish, and adds that fishers, if they wished to secure Tangaloa's favour, and have prosperity, must show him respect by offering a bonito, as first-fruits, as soon as they came to land; and that any neglect in this matter would bring disaster.[6] Williams is probably speaking of Samoa when he says that at feasts, before food was distributed, an orator arose, and after enumerating each article, exclaimed "Thank you, great Tangaloa, for this!"[7]

Tangaloa was associated with the origin of the arts of building houses and canoes. These arts were, both technologically and sociologically, important elements in Samoan culture.[8] Reference has been made elsewhere[9] to Krämer's version of the

[1] Turner, pp. 53 sq.   [2] Krämer, S.I. vol. II, p. 195 n. 3.
[3] Ibid. vol. I, p. 398 n. 18.   [4] Ibid. vol. II, p. 198 n. 1.
[5] Powell, R.S.N.S.W. vol. XXIV, p. 211; cf. Krämer, S.I. vol. I, p. 398.
[6] Fraser, R.S.N.S.W. vol. XXIV, p. 216 n. 35. Cf. the importance of the bonito in Samoan life (Te Rangi Hiroa, S.M.C. p. 520).
[7] Williams, p. 547.
[8] Cf. Mead, Manua, p. 37; Te Rangi Hiroa, S.M.C. pp. 8 sqq., 370 sqq.
[9] Beliefs, vol. I, p. 54.

myth of creation by Tangaloa, and we may now mention a passage which follows it. Here the Tangaloa family is represented as being gathered together in a *fono* (council-meeting) in the skies, the great Tangaloa being there on his throne, and there is a reference to the carpenter, and to his laying the keel of his boat, and receiving the first kava, his leaving of the *fono*, and going down below (presumably to earth), and the gathering together of the carpenter people, of whom there were many thousand, under the leadership of this carpenter, and the building of the first canoe, which belonged to the *tuimanu'a*; after this we are told of the god (Tangaloa) coming down and destroying a house that had been erected.[1] Powell's version of the story of creation, also referred to in another work,[2] is followed by matter relating to this subject of building. There is a reference to the son of Tangaloa who was Manu'a's first chief, and to the summoning of Tangaloa-the-builder's council, described as being the circle of the chiefs on high, presumably the Tangaloa family in the skies, and to the offering of the first kava cup to him, so that the boat whose keel was laid would be perfect. Later on there are what seem to be references to the councils to be held on earth when they built a ship or a house, and to Tangaloa sitting in heaven, while the Builder and his workmen would come down; the question is asked, "Who was the first to begin so honoured a work?" and it is answered by saying that the first to own a ship was the great king of Manu'a, for which purpose the people of the Builder came down, a body of ten thousand of them, with the chief builder at their head. Then it is said that the workmen next went on to build a splendid house for the king of Manu'a, without first consulting Tangaloa; so he descended and destroyed it.[3] These two stories are apparently versions of the same tradition, and Krämer is probably referring to it when he associates the first house and boat builders with Tangaloa.[4] He also says (quoting Stuebel) that Mataiteite, a daughter of Tangaloa, was believed to have caused boatmakers to come from heaven in order to get a boat for her husband in the island of Savai'i, the people then being only able to gnaw wood with their teeth, and refers to another case of boat-building by supernatural means.[5] Caillot says that, according to traditions, the original immigrants to Samoa landed in Manu'a,

[1] Krämer, *S.I.* vol. i, p. 399.   [2] *Beliefs*, vol. i, pp. 53–4.
[3] Powell, *R.S.N.S.W.* vol. xxiv, p. 211; cf. Powell, *J.V.I.* vol. xx, pp. 160 *sq.*
Krämer, *S.I.* vol. ii, p. 203.   [5] *Ibid.*

and that from this group came the carpenters who built houses.[1]

The main story of which two versions have been given evidently refers to the mythical past, apparently to the period of the first semi-divine *tuimanu'a* or king of Manu'a who was a member of the divine Tangaloa family in the skies. It is presumably of Manu'an origin, and not unnaturally it attributes the origin of the highly honoured crafts of canoe and house building to Tangaloa and the Manu'ans. Powell's version refers also to an intention that in future years canoe or house building on earth should be helped by the Builder and his workmen, coming down from heaven; and this perhaps points to a belief among his worshippers that Tangaloa was the god of house and canoe builders, which would be consistent with the common Polynesian conceptions of tutelar gods of the various trades and occupations.

Von Bülow says that in Samoa incision was "a regulation of the Tangaloa cult",[2] though this does not necessarily mean that Tangaloa was the tutelar god either of the practice or of its operators.

Having completed our survey of the Samoan material, we may now turn to a consideration of that from other island groups.

TONGA

Nowhere did Tangaroa occupy such an important place as in Samoa. Elsewhere his claims to unique pre-eminence are disputed by rival deities, sometimes he is merely *primus inter pares* among the great gods, or a member of the pantheon sharing equality with them, while in still other places he is of distinctly minor importance. This will become clear in the following brief review of the evidence.

In Tonga only one statement, made by a chief to Lawry,[3] suggests that Tangaloa was the greatest of the gods, while all the others indicate that he shared equal rank with other deities, notably Hikuleo and Maui.[4]

In dealing with Samoa we have already pointed out the intimate association of Tangaloa with the cosmogony. Myths of the creation presented elsewhere[5] indicate that similar beliefs

---

[1] Caillot, *Mythes*, p. 253 *n.* 1.
[2] Von Bülow, *Globus*, vol. LXVII, p. 367.
[3] *Miss. Notices*, vol. IV, p. 101.
[4] Wilkes, vol. III, p. 23; Lawry, *op. cit.* vol. V, p. 339; *F.F.I.* (1), p. 248.
[5] *Beliefs*, vol. I, chap. II.

associating Tangaroa with the cosmogony also existed in other island groups. In Tonga, Tangaloa was associated with other deities in the creation of the world,[1] while one version of the story of the fishing up of the Tongan Islands attributes this feat to him.[2]

The Samoan beliefs concerning the descent of the high chiefs from Tangaloa are paralleled in Tonga, where the first *tuitonga* was believed to have sprung from Tangaloa.[3]

In regard to the home of Tangaloa, in both Reiter's and Caillot's versions[4] of the Tongan creation the original home of Tangaloa was in the sky, and there is further evidence that this was so in later times also,[5] though Hale says that his home was believed to be in the north-western region of *Bulotu*.[6]

As regards the titles of Tangaloa there were, in Tonga, according to Reiter's and Caillot's versions of the creation story, Tangaloa-the-chief, Tangaloa-the-artisan and Tangaloa-the-messenger; and Sarah Farmer also refers to three Tangaloa gods.[7]

In dealing with Samoa we have quoted Turner's statement in regard to the incarnation of Tangaloa in a snipe. Attention should also be drawn to Reiter's version of the Tongan creation story, in which Tangaloa-the-messenger was carried down to earth by a *kiu*, a bird which he believes to have been a snipe, and to Caillot's reference to Tangaloa-the-messenger transforming himself into a kingfisher.[8]

In regard to actual worship, Bastian states that the *tuitonga* was at times regarded as the priest of Tangaloa, whereas the ordinary priests acted for the *fahegehe*, or family gods (*Stammes-götter*).[9] Lawry says that Tangaloa and Maui were not repre-sented or approached, having no shrines or idols,[10] and according to Sarah Farmer the three Tangaloa of whom she speaks had no offerings made to them.[11] Mariner provides a list of what he calls the principal gods, nearly all of whom had temples and priests; and it is a curious fact that, according to him, Hikuleo had neither temple nor priest, and he doubted whether Tangaloa had a temple; he says that Tangaloa was the god of artificers and the arts and that his several priests were all carpenters.[12]

---

[1] *Beliefs*, vol. I, pp. 10, 55. [2] *Ibid.* p. 33.
[3] See *Systems*, vol. I, pp. 136 sq.; cf. below, chap. XI.
[4] See *Beliefs*, chaps. I and II.
[5] Wilkes, vol. III, p. 23; S. Farmer, p. 126; Wilson, p. 272.
[6] Hale, p. 22.   [7] S. Farmer, p. 126.   [8] *Beliefs*, vol. I, pp. 55, 56.
[9] Bastian, *I.O.* p. 33. [10] Lawry, *F.F.I.* (2), p. 37. [11] S. Farmer, p. 126.
[12] Mariner, vol. II, pp. 104-8.   Cf. the reference to Tangaloa-the-artisan in Reiter's and Caillot's version of the creation story.

Veeson says that Tangaloa was appealed to in times of drought or excessive rain, which signified his anger,[1] and there is also a statement in Lawry's book that Tangaloa sent thunder and lightning, and that when a thunderstorm occurred it was supposed that he was killing a chief.[2]

MARQUESAS

The first thing to be noted in connection with the worship of Tangaroa in the Marquesas is the long chant of the creation, reported by Fornander, telling of the defeat of Tangaroa[3] by Atea; and an interesting feature of this myth is that it represents Tangaroa, who in most parts of Polynesia was regarded as being a sky god, as lying afterwards in darkness beneath the feet of Atea's wife Atanua (the dawn), which would presumably refer to a region below the horizon.[4] Another less important legend tells of him and his wife settling in the small island of Fatuhuku.[5]

It has been suggested elsewhere[6] that Tangaroa did not appear to have been worshipped in the Marquesas, this statement being based on the fact that not one of the writers about this group referred to any such worship. Since the publication of the book, some fresh Marquesan material has been supplied by Handy, who says that of the gods of nature and the elements, Tangaroa's name was the most prominent, as he was god of the sea and the wind.[7] He mentions a stone platform on the island of Fatu Uku which was a favourite fishing place. Here, he says, fishermen made offerings to Tana-oa. He also mentions local gods invoked by fishers, including a deity who was the patron of fishers in general;[8] but these would be merely departmental gods, whose attributes might be quite distinct from those of Tangaroa as god of the sea and wind. Nevertheless, it is curious, if Tangaroa occupied so important a position, that none of the other writers about the Marquesas (except Fornander, as above) even mentions his name; one may question, seeing the Handy's material was collected in 1920–1, whether it really discloses an

---

[1] Veeson, p. 152. [2] Lawry, *F.F.I.* (1), pp. 249 *sq.*
[3] In the Marquesas his name would be pronounced Taka'oa in some parts of the group, and Tana'oa in others. [4] *Beliefs*, vol. I, pp. 20–1.
[5] Christian, *J.P.S.* vol. IV, p. 199. This and another story have been referred to in *Systems*, vol. I, chap. VIII, where it was suggested that the tiger-shark may have been the god Tane, and that the two stories, taken together, may have had their origin in a tradition that there had been in this island a race of worshippers of Atea, Tane, and other gods, and that at a subsequent period the Tangaroans landed and took possession of it. [6] *Systems*, vol. I, p. 308 *n.* I.
[7] Handy, *N.C.M.* p. 246; cf. p. 165. Elsewhere (*M.L.* pp. 85–102) he gives a long legend concerning Tana-oa. [8] Handy, *N.C.M.* p. 165.

old belief concerning Tangaroa, or whether this belief had not reached some part of the Marquesas from some other islands at a more recent period.

SOCIETY ISLANDS

Here there are many statements affirming the priority of Ta'aroa,[1] but these should be considered in the light of what we shall say concerning his worship. Nearly all the accounts of the creation, like that of Henry,[2] attribute it to Ta'aroa. The *Duff* missionaries, however, speak of Ta'aroa as having been the wife of Tane, whom they put at the head of the list of Tahitian gods. These variants of the creation story will be mentioned again when we come to deal with Tane. One of the stories of fishing up the islands attributes this feat to Ta'aroa.[3] According to one of the tales of the discovery of fire, it was Ta'aroa and not Maui who was the great god of the underworld of fire,[4] and consistently with this, earthquakes were attributed to him as well as to Maui.[5]

There was a belief that Ta'aroa dwelt in a shell at the beginning of time.[6] Concerning his home in later times, evidence has been cited elsewhere[7] indicating that he dwelt in the sun or in the underworld of *Po*.[8] In the Society Islands one of the ancestors of the Pomare family was, according to Henry, Ta'aroa-manahune (Plebeian Ta'aroa).[9] Tyerman and Bennet were told that Tamatoa, the king of Ra'iatea, traced his genealogy to Ta'aroa,[10] while Ari'i Taimai says that every chief family in the Society Islands traced descent from Ta'aroa or Oro or some other of the established deities.[11]

As regards the titles of Ta'aroa, Henry gives the following four: Ta'aroa-of-the-heavens, Ta'aroa-the-great-foundation, Ta'aroa-of-the-surface-of-the-earth, and Ta'aroa-of-the-nether-lands.[12]

We have seen that in Samoa the month corresponding to January was called after Tangaloa. In the Society Islands it is possible that the month equivalent to the end of March and beginning of April, called by Henry Ta'a-'oa,[13] derived its name

[1] Ellis, vol. I, p. 322; Cook, vol. I, pp. 221 *sq.*; Banks, p. 173; Forster, *Obs.* p. 539; Tyerman, vol. I, p. 523; Moerenhout, vol. I, p. 437; de Bovis, p. 270.
[2] See below, p. 226. [3] *Beliefs*, vol. I, p. 35.
[4] *Ibid.* vol. II, p. 191. [5] *Ibid.* p. 214.
[6] See below, p. 226. [7] *Beliefs*, vol. I, p. 59.
[8] *Ibid.* pp. 59, 290. [9] Henry, *A.T.* p. 265.
[10] Tyerman, vol. I, p. 523. [11] Ari'i Taimai, p. 77.
[12] Henry, *J.P.S.* vol. X, p. 51. Elsewhere she gives a number of his "attributes" (*A.T.* p. 336). [13] Henry, *A.T.* p. 333.

from the god, while three nights of the moon were also named after him.[1]

The evidence concerning the actual worship of Ta'aroa in the Society Islands is somewhat confusing, particularly when taken together with the many affirmations of his pre-eminence. We may therefore cite the statements of writers on this subject at some length.

Davies says that in Tahiti they presented to him the first-fruits of their lands.[2] Ellis, in describing the inauguration of a king, refers to the various ceremonies in the *marae* of Oro, who was evidently the god with whom the ceremonies were associated, and mentions one rite in which the priest of Oro struck the king on the back with a branch of the sacred *miro*, and offered up the prescribed invocation to Ta'aroa. He also states that the head of the first enemy warrior captured in war was taken to the temple and burned before Ta'aroa, and that human victims were sacrificed to Ta'aroa and other gods.[3] On the other hand Moerenhout says that victims were offered to all the gods except Ta'aroa.[4] Henry states that the Ra'iatean *marae* at Opoa was dedicated to Ta'aroa, who required no human sacrifices; but that afterwards he gave it to Oro, who delighted in them.[5] This statement may be compared with the legend which she gives of the origin of human sacrifice.[6] Cook says that Ta'aroa was the supreme god, but that prayers were generally addressed to Tane, as he was supposed to be more active.[7] The *Duff* missionaries say that Ta'aroa, Oro, and Tane were only prayed to in times of great distress, being too exalted to be troubled with small matters.[8] Moerenhout says that, as the people expected nothing from Ta'aroa, they did not dedicate any temples or altars to him, and few worshipped him, though all were zealous in celebrating his glory, power and works; he was believed to be too far above the things of this world to concern himself with them or with the affairs of men.[9] Similar statements are made by Cuzent and Davies.[10] Much additional information, some of which is summarized in another section,[11] concerning the importance of Ta'aroa in the Society Islands is given by Henry.[12]

[1] Henry, *A.T.* p. 331.   [2] Davies, *Dict.* p. iii.
[3] Ellis, vol. III, p. 110; vol. I, p. 289.
[4] Moerenhout, vol. I, p. 357.   [5] Henry, *J.P.S.* vol. XXXI, p. 77.
[6] See below, p. 229.   [7] Cook, vol. I, pp. 221 sq.
[8] Wilson, p. 333.   [9] Moerenhout, vol. I, pp. 439, 462.
[10] Cuzent, *O.T.* p. 44; Davies, *Dict.* p. 238.
[11] See below, chapter IX.
[12] See Henry, *A.T.* Index, *s.v.* Ta'aroa.

Paumotu

In the Tuamotus Moerenhout says that Tangaroa was one of the principal gods, and this is confirmed by Henry.[1] In creation myths, Tangaroa features in the lifting up of the sky, though not as protagonist.[2] The evidence in regard to the worship of Tangaroa in the Tuamotus is difficult to collate, as it is collected from different islands in this extensive archipelago. There are, however, statements which indicate that prayers were addressed and *marae* dedicated to him.[3]

Niue

According to Smith, Tangaloa was the principal god of Niue.[4] Thomson says that Tangaloa and Maui were the principal gods, but Tangaloa, the creator, was too august and remote to concern himself with human affairs.[5] In Niue Tangaloa had four titles, which are given by Smith.[6] He also states that Tangaloa was a rainbow.[7] Tangaloa was appealed to in Niue in time of war[8] and also after the birth of a child, to endow it with manly or womanly virtues.[9] Tregear mentions a chant glorifying Tangaloa.[10] Murray says that prayers were addressed to Tangaloa, but no sacrifices were offered to him.[11] Some of the confusion may arise from the fact that Tangaloa is not only the great god of Niue, but also appears several times, with descriptive additions to his name, in a list of the lesser gods.[12]

Rotuma

In Rotuma, according to Gardiner, Tangaroa was above all the other deities and, as the son of Langatea and Papatea, is stated to have raised the sky. He was prayed to for food, to make the trees fruitful, for rain, and in any great enterprise in which all were taking part. He could avert a hurricane or any other great calamity; all his attributes were great, and " he did not concern himself with the doings of the *atua* "—that is, the [other] gods. He was also invoked to direct the life of a newly born boy.

[1] Moerenhout, vol. I, p. 110; Henry, *A.T.* p. 109.
[2] *Beliefs*, vol. I, pp. 28, 44.
[3] Caillot, *Mythes*, pp. 149, 153, 174; Montiton, vol. VI, p. 379; Smith, *J.P.S.* vol. XII, p. 221; "French Missionaries", *J.P.S.* vol. XXVII, p. 124; Seurat, *L'Anthro.* vol. XVI, p. 476.
[4] Smith, *J.P.S.* vol. XI, p. 195; cf. Loeb, *Niue*, pp. 158 sqq.
[5] Thomson, *S.I.* p. 84. [6] Smith, *J.P.S.* vol. XII, pp. 104 sq.
[7] *Ibid.* vol. X, p. 181. [8] *Ibid.* vol. XI, pp. 175 sq.
[9] *Ibid.* pp. 204 sq. [10] Tregear, *J.P.S.* vol. IX, pp. 234 sq.
[11] Murray, *M.W.P.* p. 368. [12] Loeb, *Niue*, pp. 160, 162.

Gardiner states, however, that he was never addressed directly, but usually by the term *sonoiitu*, which seems to have been applied generally to all the gods.[1]

ELLICE ISLANDS

That Tangaloa was a god of the Ellice Islands is stated by Gill[2] and Graeffe.[3] The statement that there was a taboo on the utterance of his name[4] suggests that he might be identified with the "un-named deity who dwelt in the heavens", mentioned by Kennedy, to whom prayers for food were addressed.[5]

AUSTRAL ISLANDS

Tyerman and Bennet say that in the island of Rurutu, Tangaroa was the great national god[6] and Ellis also mentions him.[7] Aitken, citing his own material and an unpublished manuscript of J. F. G. Stokes, says that Taio Aia was the supreme god, and had a *marae*, near the modern village of Avera, where human sacrifices were offered.[8]

OTHER ISLANDS

Tangaroa was one of the clan gods of Tikopia, associated with the sea and with the *ono* fish.[9] He is mentioned as a god of secondary importance in Fotuna,[10] and the feat of lifting up the land with a fishing-net was attributed to him in Uvea.[11] As regards the Tokelau group, Hale refers to "Tangaloa-above-in-the-heavens"[12] though Lister says that he heard nothing about Tangaroa.[13] The name Tangaroa (Ariki) occurs at the beginning of a genealogy of one of the sub-groups of Easter Island; and it is followed by the name of his son Ko Rongo-Rong'a-Tangaroa[14] which may or may not indicate that he was a god there. In Tongareva, Tangaroa was one of the eleven offspring of Atea and Hakahotu[15] and he is also mentioned in the legendary history of Manihiki and Rakahanga.[16] In the Hervey Islands a somewhat unusual situation has arisen, which Dr Buck has discussed

[1] Gardiner, *J.R.A.I.* vol. xxvii, pp. 466 *sq.* Cf. the taboo on his name in the Ellice Islands (see below).
[2] *Jottings*, p. 12. [3] *Ausland*, vol. xl, pp. 1188 *sq.*
[4] Wilkes, vol. iii, p. 44; Hale, p. 116. [5] *C.V.* pp. 147–9.
[6] Tyerman, vol. i, p. 508. [7] Ellis, vol. iii, p. 394.
[8] Aitken, *Tubuai*, p. 115.
[9] R. Firth, "Totemism in Polynesia", *Oceania*, vol. i, No. 4, p. 379.
[10] Smith, *J.P.S.* vol. i, p. 44. [11] *Beliefs*, vol. i, p. 38.
[12] Hale, p. 156. [13] Lister, *J.R.A.I.* vol. xxi, p. 51.
[14] *Systems*, vol. ii, p. 57. [15] Te Rangi Hiroa, *E.T.* p. 85.
[16] Te Rangi Hiroa, *M. & R.* pp. 14, 205.

in detail. In Mangaia, Tangaroa occupied a minor position[1] though he was important in other islands of the group. He was the great god of Rarotonga, and features in legends of the creation.[2] He lived in the heavens,[3] and was actively worshipped by the people,[4] being invoked at feasts[5] and receiving the heads of those slain in battle.[6] Savage says that if a person was killed in time of peace for the purpose of a feast, the body had to be conveyed to the shrine of the god Tangaroa as an offering to him.[7] His worship seems to have had important political implications.[8] Tangaroa was also pre-eminent in Aitutaki[9] and in Atiu.[10]

TANE

Another god whose worship was widespread throughout Central Polynesia was Tane. There is no record of his having been worshipped in Samoa and Tonga, though certain evidence suggests that he may once have been a god of the Samoans. However, as this is of a speculative character we shall limit ourselves to a survey of his worship in other island groups.

SOCIETY ISLANDS

The worship of Tane in the Society Islands appears to have been more important in some areas (that is, where Tane was a tutelar deity) than in others. For example in Huahine he seems to have occupied an extremely important position. Tyerman and Bennet were told there that Tangaroa was the supreme god and the creator of all things, and that among the rest he made the first man and called him Tani, which word therefore did not primarily signify a husband, but was a generic term for the whole human race.[11] They were also told that Tane was regarded in Huahine as the father of the gods.[12] Ellis, speaking of this island, says that Tane was its tutelar idol. He was numbered among the uncreated gods, considered as having proceeded from the state of night or chaos (*Po*).[13] Henry was told that his principal *marae* in Huahine was built by Rua-hatu-Tinirau, the Tahitian Neptune,

---

[1] Te Rangi Hiroa, *M.S.* pp. 15–32.   [2] Cf. *Beliefs*, vol. I, pp. 66–7.
[3] Pratt-Fraser, *R.S.N.S.W.* vol. xxv, p. 76; Gill, *J.P.S.* vol. xx, p. 207.
[4] Gill, *Myths*, p. 47.   [5] Gill, *L.S.I.* p. 45.
[6] Gill, *Jottings*, p. 118; cf. Gill, *Myths*, p. 11 *n.* 1.
[7] Savage, *J.P.S.* vol. xx, pp. 201 *sq.*; cf. Gill, *A.A.A.S.* vol. II, p. 342.
[8] Gill, *J.P.S.* vol. xx, p. 205.   [9] Williams, p. 108.
[10] Gill, *S.L.P.* pp. 188 *sq.*; cf. Cook, vol. v, p. 247; Large, *J.P.S.* vol. xxII, pp. 69 *sq.*
[11] Tyerman, vol. I, pp. 312 *sq.*   [12] *Ibid.* p. 271.
[13] Ellis, vol. I, p. 325.

and was dedicated to the worship of Tane.[1] The dominating importance of Tane in this island is indicated by the statements that he was the god to whom an offering of first-fruits was made every year, and that his bearer [the priest who carried his image] had set apart for him a portion of this food, which even kings dared not take away or touch.[2] In fact this priest was so sacred that everything he touched became sacred; he might not climb a coconut tree, because if he did so it became taboo, and he might not marry.[3] According to a story told by Davies Tane was associated with the descent of the chiefs of the island.[4] A fragment of stone, believed to be a portion of Tane's canoe, and having the power of floating on water, was shown to Tyerman and Bennet, who were told that there were others like it on the island, attributed to the same canoe.[5] J. R. Forster also refers to Tane as the tutelar deity of Huahine.[6]

Tane seems to have been also at one time the god of the island of Tahaa. Anderson refers to him as the god of that island, meaning, presumably, that he was so when Cook visited it;[7] and Henry states that the national *marae* there was dedicated to him;[8] but Forster says Oro was their god,[9] and de Bovis (1855) says that Tane was the original god there, but that his *marae* had been consecrated at a later date to Oro.[10] Apparently Tane was also worshipped in Borabora, though the island was mainly connected with the Oro cult.[11]

We may now pass to some general evidence as to his worship in the Society Islands, the greater part of which has been collected in Tahiti.

We have seen that in nearly all the Society Island stories of creation by gods, Tangaroa appears as the one great creating deity. According to one of these, told by Cook, Tane was the son of Tangaroa but was not concerned in the process of creation; according to a version told by Gaussin, Tane was the son of Tangaroa, and apparently worked under his orders and helped him in the acts of creation; but the tale told by the *Duff* missionaries begins with Tane as a husband and Tangaroa as his wife, and points to them as the original parents of all things, including man.

[1] Henry, *J.P.S.* vol. XXII, p. 25.
[2] Tyerman, vol. I, pp. 284 sq.
[3] *Ibid.* p. 279.
[4] Davies, *Dict.* p. iv.
[5] Tyerman, vol. I, p. 285. It is stated that it was pumice stone.
[6] Forster, *Obs.* p. 541.
[7] Cook, vol. VI, p. 160.
[8] Henry, *A.T.* p. 99.
[9] Forster, *Voy.* vol. II, p. 151.
[10] De Bovis, p. 273.
[11] Tyerman, vol. I, p. 318.

Cook says that Tangaroa was the supreme deity, and that it was he who caused earthquakes; but that prayers were more generally addressed to Tane, who was supposed to take a greater part in the affairs of mankind;[1] and that the high priest Tupia[2] often prayed to Tane (when they were on the sea) for wind.[3] The *Duff* missionaries say that the people only prayed to Tane in times of greatest distress, as he was too exalted to be troubled with small matters.[4] Parkinson says that in Ra'iatea, Tahaa, and Bolabola, they worshipped the rainbow, which they called *Toomeitee no Tane*.[5]

Ellis, in speaking of the gods of the highest order, who were said to have been *fanau po*, or born of night, mentions the names of Tangaroa, Oro, and Tane.[6] In speaking of the ten heavens above he says that the tenth heaven (the highest) was called *te-rai-haamama-no-tane*, which may be associated with Tane.[7] Davies says that the firmament or heaven, called *Aoroa*, or *Moana-roa*, was believed to be Tane's residence.[8] Ellis shows that Tane was of considerable importance in times of war.[9] Tane was also one of the gods who were supposed to be able to restrain the effects of sorcery, or expel the evil spirits which, on the incantations of sorcerers, had entered people's bodies.[10] Marriages were supposed to require the sanction of the gods, and those of parties connected with the reigning family were solemnized in the temple of Oro or of Tane, the two principal national idols.[11]

Reference should be made to beliefs connecting Tane with sharks[12] and birds. Henry refers to a belief as to the *Vai-ora-a-Tane*, "the living water of Tane", which she says was the [celestial] Milky Way. The handsome shark Fa'aravi-i-te-ra'i (sky shade) was there in his pool, as also was a bird; there were also star fishes, and two trigger fishes, that dwelt in holes, vacant spots in the Milky Way, and ate mist.[13] This may be compared with Moerenhout's statement that there were one or two points in the Milky Way which they called *mao* and *ari*, the names of

[1] Cook, vol. I, p. 222. Banks (p. 173) makes a similar statement.
[2] Cf. *Systems*, vol. I, p. 238.
[3] Cook, vol. I, p. 231; cf. Banks, p. 111.
[4] Wilson, p. 333.   [5] Parkinson (1), p. 70.
[6] Ellis, vol. I, p. 322; cf. pp. 325, 327.
[7] *Ibid.* p. 169; cf. Moerenhout, vol. I, pp. 442 *sq.*
[8] Davies, *Dict.* p. 26.   [9] Ellis, vol. I, pp. 281, 285, 316.
[10] *Ibid.* p. 333.   [11] *Ibid.* p. 271.
[12] Cf. *Systems*, vol. I, pp. 238 *sq.*
[13] Henry, *J.P.S.* vol. XVI, p. 102.

sharks which were supposed to eat certain stars when they disappeared from the horizon.[1] According to Davies there was a bird called Taefeiaitu which was sacred to the god Tane;[2] though there is nothing to show that this bird, whatever it may have been, was supposed to have been the species that lived in the Milky Way. Ellis speaks of the gods Tane and Ru leading bands of warriors, spreading dismay among the enemy by waving their long tails, which the natives believed to resemble shooting stars or the tails of comets.[3]

We may refer in conclusion to this belief that Tane possessed a long tail. It was said that Tane often wanted to fly away from his *marae* at Huahine, but he had a long tail, like a boy's kite, and it always caught in the boughs of a sacred tree there, so that he was always dragged down to earth again,[4] and similar tales are told of other *marae* of Tane.[5]

Henry provides further evidence of the worship of Tane in the Society Islands, and in particular parts of this group.[6] He was apparently the tutelar deity of canoe builders and travellers,[7] and he appears prominently in the creation chants given by her.

MARQUESAS

Reference has been made elsewhere[8] to the tradition as to the pressure of the world above upon the world beneath, and the consequent imprisonment in darkness of their children, including Atea and Tane, and to Atea's urging upon Tane that they should try to get out, and Atea's success, on Tane's suggestion, in breaking through; also to another version of the story, according to which it was Tane who succeeded in forcing the separation, though Atea was the first to leap out and see the light. But Handy states that, apart from his place in legend and chants, Tane was of little importance in the Marquesas.[9]

PAUMOTU

The Paumotu Islands are very numerous, and cover an enormous area as compared with any of the other groups, the more north-westerly islands being in fact close to the Society Islands, and

---

[1] Moerenhout, vol. II, p. 181. [2] Davies, *Dict.* p. 239.
[3] Ellis, vol. I, p. 285; cf. Tyerman, vol. I, p. 283.
[4] Tyerman, vol. I, p. 266.
[5] *Ibid.* p. 283. This conception of gods' tails was found in Polynesia with reference to other gods also.
[6] Henry, *A.T.* pp. 128–9, 148, 189. [7] *Ibid.* pp. 146–8, 179–81.
[8] *Beliefs*, vol. I, pp. 25–6. [9] Handy, *N.C.M.* p. 245.

the group spreading from there in a south-easterly direction, Mangareva being one of the most south-easterly of them. It is from Mangareva that most of our information is obtained, but in some cases the source of it is only partially indicated, or not disclosed at all. It is therefore difficult and sometimes impossible to attempt the interpretation of the significance of the several religious cults with any confidence. It should be mentioned that Montiton seems to have obtained most of his information from the islands of Fangatau and Takoto, of which the latter was one of the central islands of the group. Paumotuan creation legends mentioning Tane have been given elsewhere.[1]

The fundamental feature of these stories, as affecting the worship of Tane, is their indication of confusion of beliefs as to the relative importance of Atea and Tane, including a possible conception in one of them of Atea as having once had a prior position which was afterwards taken by Tane; and of the relative unimportance of Tangaroa. It must be remembered that the stories have come from the central region of the Paumotu group.

Concerning the south-eastern island, or rather cluster of islands, called collectively Mangareva, there is a little evidence which may be interpreted as indicating the worship of Tane. Caillot refers to the principal *marae* in the Mangareva cluster of islands, and the name of one of these *marae* was Anga-o-Tane.[2]

Some evidence of the worship of Tane is provided by Montiton, whose information was probably obtained in the central islands of the archipelago. He says that as soon as a child was born the high priest prayed to Tane to preserve the nursling; after which he made the accustomed libation, and everyone took part in a feast. Tane was similarly invoked in connection with incision and wedding ceremonies.[3] Montiton tells us that Tane seems to have been the ocean Jupiter.[4] In one legend he is said to have performed a miraculous caesarean operation on a virgin who thus produced a child.[5] Caillot tells us that in Makemo [one of the more north-westerly of the central group of islands] it was said that "Vatea is our god, even as Tane and Tangaroa".[6] According to Audran, in the northerly island of Napuka, Tane

[1] *Beliefs*, vol. I, pp. 15, 27-8, 44. Cf. also Henry, *A.T.* pp. 347 *sqq.* She says that Tane was one of the chief gods of the Tuamotus (*ibid.* p. 109).
[2] Caillot, *Mythes*, pp. 174 *sq.* This *marae* is also mentioned by Smith (*J.P.S.* vol. XXVII, p. 124).
[3] Montiton, vol. VI, p. 491; cf. Mangareva, where on the birth of a child they prayed to Tangaroa (Caillot, *Mythes*, p. 149).
[4] Montiton, vol. VI, p. 366.   [5] *Ibid.* p. 354.
[6] Caillot, *Mythes*, p. 22.

was believed to have been the first man, whose descent was unknown, but who was said in one legend to have been descended from spirits or ancestors in Havaiki,[1] which means that it was in the distant past; but nothing is said here about his worship.

MANGAIA

Although Tane is mentioned in the creation myth of Mangaia he was not worshipped until immigrants brought his worship from Tahiti. He was subsequently the tribal god of the Ngati-Tane.[2] An interesting feature is the number of attributes attached to his name which in the course of time came to be regarded as one god.

RAROTONGA

Gill provides a mythical account of the origin of the family name (Makea) of the great royal Karika family of Rarotonga; and it begins with the marriage of the god Atea with Papa (the earth or a rock) and the names of their divine children, the latter including Rongo, Tane, Tangaroa and Tu.[3]

Savage narrates a long tradition concerning the god Iro [Hiro] in the earlier part of which Tane is mentioned occasionally, while later on he becomes one of the principal personages of the story.[4] There is another version of this legend, in which Tane is referred to as the god of sailors.[5] There are several other references to Tane in the legends of Rarotonga.[6]

ATEA

The question arises whether Atea, in Polynesian religion, can properly be described as a "god", in view of the comparative lack of evidence of an Atea cult, in the sense of actual worship. Further, Atea is less often anthropomorphically conceived than the other deities, and seems to correspond to an abstract conception, the nearest English translation of which is "space". The name of Atea was a word signifying, in different islands, the somewhat similar conceptions of "light", "day", "daylight", "noon", "clearness", "openness", "distinctness"; and,

---

[1] Audran, *J.P.S.* vol. XXVII, p. 132.   [2] Te Rangi Hiroa, *M.S.* pp. 163–4.
[3] Gill, *A.A.A.S.* vol. II, p. 629.
[4] Savage, *J.P.S.* vol. XXVI, pp. 14–18; cf. p. 88.
[5] *J.P.S.* vol. XXIX, p. 120.
[6] Smith, *J.P.S.* vol. XXX, pp. 201–11; Gill, *J.P.S.* vol. XX, pp. 212–15; Smith, *J.P.S.* vol. XXIX, p. 113; Savage, *J.P.S.* vol. XVIII, p. 217.

perhaps as derivative meanings, "width", "spaciousness", "freedom from obstruction". There were variations in the pronunciation of the name, such as Vatea and Oatea.

SOCIETY ISLANDS

The lack of reference to Atea by observers is curious, in view of later material supplied by Henry. According to her, Atea was invoked together with other deities in connection with canoe-launching rites and ceremonies for the royal heir,[1] and there are numerous references to Atea in the legends given by her.[2]

MARQUESAS

We must refer once more to the myths cited above in which Atea is mentioned, together with Tane, in stories of the creation.[3]

There were beliefs that Atea was the first man who reached the island of Nukuhiva, or perhaps in some cases another island of the group, and from whom the people were descended.[4] Concerning the subject of genealogies, it is fairly evident that Atea was regarded as an ancestor god in the Marquesas.[5]

Mathias says that Atea or Akea was the god or father of stones.[6] Christian tells us that his wives bore him respectively the kava plant, which was brought over the seas to the Marquesas, the shark, smooth rocks and reed-grass; and that he was the god of husbandry, who brought good seasons and rain, and the patron of agriculture and planting.[7] According to von den Steinen, Atea, the light of day, was the creative power of procreation, which had called all nature into being. He created—that is, begot—the ancestors of the Marquesans by Atanua, and all the stones, plants, and animals by numerous other wives; and von den Steinen gives examples of specific trees and of the fowls, with the names of their mothers, that were attributed to him. The sea was attributed to a miscarriage of Atanua, the embryo-envelope bursting and the sea coming out; and in it were born the fish, including molluscs, crabs, worms and corals. Von den Steinen also includes among the posterity of Atea the day, the moon, cloud, the shadow, the north wind, the wind, the rain,

---

[1] Henry, *A.T.* pp. 180, 184.   [2] *Op. cit.* Index, *s.v.* "Atea".
[3] See above, p. 54.
[4] D'Urville, *Voy. pitt.* vol. I, p. 501; Porter, vol. II, p. 30; Fornander, vol. I, p. 63.
[5] Handy, *N.C.M.* p. 341.
[6] Mathias, p. 44.
[7] Christian, *J.P.S.* vol. IV, p. 189; cf. Handy, *N.C.M.* p. 245.

and dampness—in short the personifications of natural phenomena which constitute the riddle of all cosmogonies.[1] According
to von den Steinen, the name of Atea occurs in chants associated
with human sacrifice.[2] Reference has been made elsewhere[3] to
a belief associating Atea with the planet Venus.

There is no information of actual acts of worship or supplication offered directly to Atea; if he was the god of husbandry, who
regulated the seasons and weather and supervised agriculture,
he would probably be invoked, unless he was believed to be too
distant to be approached, the actual prayers being offered to
some other god. But whether or not Atea was invoked directly,
he was the ancestral power in the background, recognized in
religious ceremonies.

PAUMOTU

In dealing with Tane, we have referred to myths associating
Atea and Tane with the cosmogony. According to a belief
reported from the island of Mangareva[4] it was Tea [Atea?] who
created the water, the wind and the sun; and there was a belief
in one of the central islands that Atea created the god Tiki and
his wife Hina, which is another example of confusion in beliefs.
Then in the story of creation by gods, obtained from two of the
central islands, we are told that Vatea, Tane, and Tangaroa were
their gods; but that it was Vatea who made the earth and sky,
and everything in them. On the other hand, we are told that in
Mangareva, to the extreme south-east of the Paumotu group,
Atu-Motua, Atu-Moana and Atea Tangaroa were the first three
gods, and that they created the universe.[5] Henry refers to Atea
as one of the great gods of the Tuamotus.[6] She speaks in several
places[7] of Atea being one of the major deities of the Tuamotus,
but neither she nor any other writer refers to any acts of worship.

TONGAREVA

In Tongareva, Atea and Hakahotu were the primary parents
from whom sprang other gods.[8]

HERVEY ISLANDS

Avatea (or Vatea) occupied an important place in the Mangaian
cosmogony.[9] The union of Avatea and Papa produced the

[1] Von den Steinen, V.G.E. vol. xxv, p. 505.
[2] Ibid. pp. 512 sq. [3] Beliefs, vol. 1, p. 134.
[4] Ibid. p. 151. [5] Ibid. pp. 68–9.
[6] Henry, A.T. p. 109. [7] Ibid. pp. 109, 112, 128.
[8] Te Rangi Hiroa, E.T. p. 85. [9] Te Rangi Hiroa, M.S. pp. 11 sqq.

Mangaian gods, and the legend of this union also occurs in Rarotonga.[1] There was also a Rarotongan tradition as to a dispute between Atea and Tangaroa as to the parentage of the son of Atea's wife, of which each god claimed to be the father. The child was cut into halves which were thrown into the sky; Tangaroa's half became the sun, and Atea's half became the moon.[2]

RONGO

The name of the god Rongo, as pronounced in the several groups, should be spelt Ro'o in the Society Islands, and Oko or Ono in the Marquesas; from this arises a source of confusion between him and Ru in the Society Islands, where the names of some of the gods referred to by writers are variously spelt Ru, Rou, Roo, Rua, Roua and Rooa, these being in many cases only the commencements of names, the rest of which may be merely descriptive in some cases, and in others may refer to separate deities. In the latter case again, it is possible that the names of these separate deities may be etymologically derived from the names of either Ro'o or Ru.[3] Specifically this may be the case with those compound names beginning with "Rua-", though there does seem to have been a separate god of this name.[4] In the later material of Henry and Handy the spellings Roo, Ro'o and Ru occur. The first two of these may be taken to apply to Rongo.

SOCIETY ISLANDS

In regard to the difficulty of distinguishing between Rongo and Ru, we may draw attention to the names given by three writers[5] to the sixteenth day of the month, this being called Otooroo by Forster, Oturu-tea by Ellis, and Otoutou-tea by Moerenhout, the letters "oo", "u", and "ou" being used to represent what was presumably the same sound. On the other hand, the story, told by Moerenhout, of the birth of winds, storm, anger and so on[6] begins with the birth of certain divine children of Tangaroa, first referring to the birth of Rouanoua[7] and two others (Tie'ri and Te'fatou), then speaking of Roo as being in his mother's

---

[1] Nicholas, *J.P.S.* vol. I, pp. 25 *sqq.*; Gill, *J.P.S.* vol. XXI, pp. 132 *sq.*
[2] Pratt-Fraser, *R.S.N.S.W.* vol. XXV, p. 76; cf. Buzacott, pp. 74 *sq.*
[3] Cf. the suggestion that Roma-tane, god of paradise, is really a corruption of Ro'o-ma-Tane.
[4] Henry, *A.T.* p. 344.   [5] See *Beliefs*, vol. I, p. 187.
[6] *Ibid.* p. 141.   [7] *Nua* means "above".

womb, and afterwards telling of the birth of Roo. It would seem
from this that Moerenhout understood Roua and Roo to be two
distinct gods. So also, Ellis repeats a song that was sung preparatory to war, which begins with references to Tane and Hiro;
the singer declares the war song "before the face of the armies of
Rai and Roo. And [before?] great Ru, who in Mauarahu lifted
the heavens"; after referring to what is probably the entry into
the war of the gods, and to the fighting, it says that Roo, the
first-born god, should cause destruction, and refers to the
shouting of the name of Ro on the right hand and the left.[1]

This song as repeated by Ellis refers, on the assumption here
adopted, to Ro'o, whom he distinguishes from Ru, as one of the
great gods who supported their worshippers in war; it is probable
that Ro is the same god—perhaps the difference in spelling is
due to a printer's error. We have also seen[2] that according to
a story told by Ellis, Tangaroa and Hina, having created the
heavens, earth, and sea, created a number of gods, these including Rootane (the god of peace) and Ruanuu[3] (said to have
a bald head). Ellis tells of a ceremony performed after war in
connection with the offering of the bodies of the slain to the
gods, and speaking of a prayer to them, he says that the burden
of it was "Let the god of war return to the world of night; let
Roo, the god of peace, preside in the world, or place of light."[4]
Ellis also tells us that Roo was one of the most benevolent of the
gods and that he was one of the gods who were able to restrain
the effects of sorcery.[5] Ellis also, speaking of the people's
prayers, gives as an example a morning prayer addressed to Roo
and other gods.[6]

Moerenhout says that Roo, though he was a god himself, was
only a messenger of the gods, travelling through the skies with
the speed of the wind. He tells us that Roo, Tie'ri, Te'fatou, and
Rouanoua were, according to one tale, found at the four corners
of the world. It has been suggested elsewhere that this belief
was connected with the winds.[7]

Anderson says that Oroo hadoo was a god of the island of
Eimeo;[8] as also does G. Forster, who spells his name O-Rooa-

[1] Ellis, vol. I, pp. 200 sqq.   [2] Beliefs, vol. I, p. 59.
[3] Nu'u is the verbal equivalent of the Maori nuku, which means (see Tregear's
Dictionary) "space", "wide extent", "far off".
[4] Ellis, vol. I, p. 311. The god of war here referred to was probably Oro. (See
Ellis, vol. I, pp. 276, 308.)
[5] Ibid. p. 333.   [6] Ibid. pp. 343 sq.
[7] Beliefs, vol. I, p. 141.   [8] Cook, vol. VI, p. 160.

hattoo,[1] but these are perhaps to be identified with the sea god Ruahatu.

Leverd tells what seems to be a series of Tahitian stories, the first part of which commences with Ro'o-nui,[2] who had come from *Po*, and his wife Haumea living on earth, and the birth of their son, a quarrel between them, and the consequent return of Ro'o-nui to *Po*, leaving his wife on earth.[3]

Henry gives a considerable amount of additional information concerning Ro'o. He was invoked in connection with *marae* ceremonies and before the birth of a royal heir[4] and, together with other gods, at the canoe-launching ceremony.[5] He is referred to in prayers and myths as the messenger of Tane.[6] A god called Ro'o-te-roro'o was invoked by disenchanters to remove curses,[7] and Henry's account suggests that this was Ro'o, though in a chant the two names are given separately, Ro'o-te-roro'o as a god and Ro'o as the messenger of Tane.[8]

MARQUESAS

Reference has been made elsewhere[9] to the Marquesan myth of the defeat by the god Atea (representing light) of the god Tangaroa, in which the name of Ono (representing sound) occurs. Mathias also refers to a god Oko who was supposed to eat men, but tells us nothing about him.[10] *Oko* is the dialectal form of *rongo* in the north-western Marquesas, and *ono* is the form in the south-eastern Marquesas, so possibly the difference between the two modes of spelling may be an indication of two sources of origin of the evidence; but this is not a point upon which we must be confident. Handy states that Ono was of no importance in actual worship, though his name occurs in the legends.[11]

PAUMOTU

We must refer to the Paumotuan myth[12] of the sleeping, face to face, of the sky and earth, in which Rongo was included, along with Atea, Tane, Tu, and others. Rongo is also mentioned in other Paumotuan chants.[13]

[1] Forster, *Voy.* vol. II, p. 150.
[2] *Nui* means "great".
[3] Leverd, *J.P.S.* vol. XXI, p. 1.
[4] Henry, *A.T.* pp. 151, 183.
[5] *Ibid.* p. 180.
[6] *Ibid.* pp. 164, 354, 369.
[7] *Ibid.* pp. 210, 213.
[8] *Ibid.* p. 164. This presents again the problem to which we have referred above.
[9] *Beliefs*, vol. I, pp. 20–1.
[10] Mathias, p. 43.
[11] Handy, *N.C.M.* p. 245; *M.L.* pp. 104 *sqq.*
[12] *Beliefs*, vol. I, pp. 27–8.
[13] *J.P.S.* vol. XII, pp. 231–42.

The French missionaries say that it was believed in the island of Mangareva that Rongo opened the clouds and poured rain on the thirsty fields.[1] Both Caillot and Tregear, speaking of the same island, say he was worshipped there.[2] Montiton, describing the proceedings at a solemn turtle feast (apparently in the island of Takoto), refers to the invocation offered by the high priest or king to all the gods, and among the gods so invoked the name Teati-Rongo occurs.[3]

This evidence shows that Rongo was known in Paumotuan traditions; we may infer from the statement of the French missionaries that he was believed to be an active deity, while Montiton indicates that he was actually invoked.

Caillot tells us of a dramatic entertainment given in the Paumotu, or one of the islands of that group—he does not say which—and Rongo-ma-tane was one of the characters that appeared in it.[4]

Austral Islands

Tyerman and Bennet say that in the island of Rurutu, of the Tubuai (Austral) group, Rooteabu was a god inferior to Tangaroa,[5] but this may refer not to Roo but to the god called by Aitken Rua Paauri.[6]

Tongareva

In Tongareva, Rongonui was one of the eleven offspring of Atea and Hakahotu.[7]

Hervey Islands

Nowhere was Rongo so important as in Mangaia, owing to the specific development of the religious system of that island.[8] In Mangaia Rongo was the dominant god, while Tangaroa, though known and referred to in traditions, received little or no worship. In Rarotonga, on the other hand, it is said by William Gill that the great Tangaroa was over all the other gods, and was regarded as the creator of all things, and the preserver of all things;[9] while, though Rongo's name appears in some of the traditions, he occupied a secondary place.

As regards the other Hervey Islands, Williams says that in

[1] A.P.F. vol. xiv, p. 332.
[2] Caillot, Mythes, pp. 153 sq.; Tregear, p. 425.
[3] Montiton, vol. vi, p. 379.　　[4] Caillot, Mythes, pp. 95–109.
[5] Tyerman, vol. i, p. 508.　　[6] Aitken, Tubuai, p. 115.
[7] Te Rangi Hiroa, E.T. p. 85.　　[8] Te Rangi Hiroa, M.S. pp. 15–34.
[9] W. Gill, Gems, vol. ii, pp. 13 sq.

Aitutaki Te-Rongo was one of the great deities. He was called the man-cater, and his priests were supposed to be inspired by a shark. But Tangaroa was the great national god of the island and almost all the adjacent islands.[1]

Gill says that in the island of Atiu Te-Rongo was said to be the son of Tangaroa;[2] and Large tells us that a very important focus of tribal activity in that island was the *marae* of the god Rongo (after Tangaroa the greatest deity there).[3] It would seem from this that the relative importance of these two gods was similar to that found in Aitutaki.

RU

SAMOA

The Samoan name of the god Ru would be Lu, and a being called Lu occupies a prominent position in some of the Samoan myths and traditions which have been referred to elsewhere.[4] These point to beliefs that Lu's father was the first man, derived from evolutionary processes of nature, that the great Tangaloa was his maternal grandfather, and that he was the founder of the Atuan dynasty of kings, a combination of facts which would cause him to be regarded as being of great antiquity and political importance.

There is, however, no indication of any actual worship of Lu in Samoa.

SOCIETY ISLANDS

In dealing with the statements of writers concerning the Society Islands we must bear in mind the possible confusion already referred to between Rongo and Ru.

We have seen that Ellis refers to the divine children of Tangaroa, including Rootane and the bald-headed Ruanuu and to the battle-song in which Roo and Ru are both mentioned. We have also seen that in one of the stories of the lifting-up of the sky reported by Ellis the feat was attributed to Ru.[5] Ellis tells a tradition concerning Ruahatu[6] which, he says, prevailed in the north-westerly islands of the Society group and which very closely resembles the story of the deluge given below.[7] Other

---

[1] Williams, p. 108.
[2] Gill, *Myths*, p. 14 *n.* 2.
[3] Large, *J.P.S.* vol. XXII, p. 70.
[4] *Systems*, vol. I, pp. 56, 96 *sq.*
[5] Cf. *Beliefs*, vol. I, p. 42. It should be noted that in the version given by Henry, Ru began the process of lifting but was unable to finish it (*A.T.* pp. 409–10).
[6] Ellis, vol. I, pp. 389 *sqq.*
[7] Pp. 247 *sqq.*

writers supply different versions of this story.[1] Ellis says elsewhere that Ruahatu, and another god, appear to have been the principal marine deities.[2] He also says that Ruaifaatoa was the god of cockfighters.[3] Moerenhout says that Roua, who presided over the birth of stars, was often credited with the creation of the universe, and confused with Tangaroa;[4] and that Roua was sometimes identified with the sun;[5] and perhaps we must associate with this belief the use, to which Moerenhout refers, of the term *roua roa* (great Roua) for the summer and *roua potu* (little Roua) for the winter solstice.[6]

There are several legends associating Ru with the cosmogony[7] and with the parentage or ancestorship of a great variety of celestial bodies.[8] According to Henry he was a great navigator.[9] Moerenhout says that Rou was the god of winds, principally of the east wind; and that the unbridled winds, the trembling earth, and the surging waves were Rou and Maui furious.[10] Rou made the waters of the ocean swell, broke up the earth, which was formerly *fenoua noui* (large earth), and only left the islands now existing.[11] According to another story, men ceasing to fulfil their duties to the gods, the latter decided to destroy them and the earth. Therefore Rou, the god of winds, unchained the tempests, and the sea arose and submerged the earth, though one family escaped in a canoe. When the sea sank these people landed on one of the Society Islands, constructed a *marae*, thanked the gods, and repeopled the earth.[12] These beliefs as to the trembling earth and surging waves, the swelling of the sea, and perhaps submerging of land may have had their origin in some great terrestrial upheaval; and it may be noticed that Maui, who was, it has been suggested elsewhere,[13] an earthquake and volcano god, is introduced in the belief and this may be compared with the statement that according to one belief it was Ru, and not Maui, who lifted up the sky. Some of the Polynesian traditions as to floods are suspiciously like the Biblical story of the deluge, and

[1] Moerenhout, vol. I, pp. 573 *sq.*; d'Urville, *Voy. pitt.* vol. I, p. 565; Tyerman, vol. I, p. 523; Gaussin, pp. 255–9.
[2] Ellis, vol. I, p. 328.   [3] *Ibid.* p. 223.
[4] Moerenhout, vol. I, pp. 561 *sqq.*; vol. II, p. 206 *n.*
[5] *Ibid.* vol. I, p. 562.
[6] *Ibid.* p. 178; cf. Davies, *Dict.* p. 234.
[7] *Beliefs*, vol. I, p. 64.   [8] *Ibid.* p. 120.
[9] Henry, *A.T.* pp. 459–64.   [10] Moerenhout, vol. I, p. 451.
[11] *Ibid.* p. 446.
[12] *Ibid.* pp. 571 *sq.* See also another story given by Ellis (vol. I, pp. 387 *sqq.*) which does not, however, refer to Ru; and again another story told by Agostini, p. 85.   [13] *Beliefs*, vol. I, chap. XXVI.

missionary writers are apt to assume that they were of Biblical origin. This may have been so—partly at all events—in some cases, the tales having perhaps been obtained from white men, and interwoven with native traditions; but probably some of them were Polynesian. In any case the introduction of Ru as the god who caused the disturbances would be based on the people's conception of him. Moerenhout also says that Rouanoua was believed to be a kind of monster, who was so ugly that he hid himself in the sea in the daytime, and only came out on dark nights to see his wife. He was so large that, without being able to kill him, they cut several pieces as large as rocks out of his head.[1]

De Bovis, after referring to the practice of addressing prayers and making offerings to many birds and fishes, as to gods (based on the belief that the gods dwelt in their bodies), gives as an example the case of the *otuu*, a sort of crab-eater (*crabier*) which was sanctified by the presence of Ruanuu.[2] The London missionaries speak of Ruahadu as the god of the island of Eimeo, and say he was a shark god.[3]

Paumotu

In one of the Paumotuan stories of fishing up islands it is said that this was done by Maui and Ru, working together. We have also seen that, according to Caillot, while apparently Maui's attributes were fire, those of Ru seem to have been the waters.[4] Ru features in the Paumotuan account of the lifting up of the sky.[5]

The name of Ru appears in some of the legends relating to Rongo. In one of the chants there are references, first to Rongo-nui and then to other gods, among whom are Ru-roa, Ru-poto, Ru-farara, and Ru-tuanoho.[6] Then Caillot speaks of Ruanoku as the god of heaven, and Ruterangi as the god of stars;[7] and among the gods invoked at the turtle feast and invited to partake of it, to which Montiton refers, are Roua, Rouanoukou and Rouafatou.[8]

Tregear says[9] that *ruapoto* was the name given to the north tropic, the winter solstice, and *ruaroa* was that of the south tropic, the summer solstice, which it will be noticed, they were also called in the Society Islands.

[1] Moerenhout, vol. I, pp. 446 *sq.*
[2] De Bovis, p. 284; cf. p. 273.
[3] L.M.S. *Trans.* vol. III, p. 171.
[4] *Beliefs*, vol. II, p. 198.
[5] Henry, *A.T.* p. 351.
[6] *J.P.S.* vol. XII, pp. 236–42.
[7] Caillot, *Mythes*, pp. 153 *sq.*
[8] Montiton, vol. VI, p. 379.
[9] See *Beliefs*, vol. I, p. 176.

There is some evidence as to the worship of Ru. Caillot refers to traditions concerning two persons Tupa and Noa who instituted the cult of the god Tu in the island of Mangareva; and he says that Tupa had several *marae* built for this god, but that there were also two *marae* of Ruanuku, one of Tangaroa, and one of Tane, and *marae* of other gods.[1] These *marae* are also referred to in material obtained by the French missionaries, who also attribute them to Tupa.[2] Then again, one of the missionaries says of the island of Napuka that, before the introduction of Christianity, there were in it three celebrated *marae*, and adds: "The *marae* was the sacred place of Polynesian paganism. It was formed from Ruahatu"; and the editor suggests in a note that the words in inverted commas mean that the *marae* was dedicated to the Tahitian god Ruahatu.[3] Though we may agree with this suggestion, we must point out that the missionary's meaning may be that the Napuka *marae*, or one of them, were or was founded with a stone taken from another *marae* of Ruahatu situated elsewhere—say in Tahiti—in accordance with the Polynesian custom. There is also an account of the ceremony of ordination of three young priests in Mangareva, one of the proceedings in which was a request to the god Tu and four "subordinate" deities, of whom one was Ruanuku, that they would deign to support these priests in the performance of their functions.[4] It seems clear, then, that Ru was actually worshipped in Mangareva and Napuka, and probably was so in some of the other islands also, although we have no specific evidence of this.

NIUE

Smith in referring to the *tupua* class of gods in Niue says that there was one of these for each of the four quarters of the island, and that Lua-tupua was the deity of the south end. Apparently, however, Smith thinks that this god was not the general Polynesian god Ru, but that he was named after that deity. He also refers to a family whose names begin with Lua, but it is not clear whether these were human beings or deities.[5]

TOKELAU

Reference has been made elsewhere[6] to a belief in the Tokelau island of Fakaofo that Lu [Ru] drew up some of the islands from

[1] Caillot, *Mythes*, pp. 173 *sqq.*   [2] *J.P.S.* vol. XXVII, p. 124.
[3] *Ibid.* p. 134 and *n.* 4.   [4] *Ibid.* p. 122.
[5] Smith, *J.P.S.* vol. XI, p. 196, vol. XII, pp. 104, 106.
[6] *Beliefs*, vol. I, p. 37.

the sea, and that he heaved up the heavens off the earth, with the help of the twelve corners of the earth, the winds, waterspouts, and hurricanes carrying the sky up to its present height; also[1] that he was supposed to have given the names to the winds of the twelve corners of the earth. It was also said that he drew the trees and other plants out of the ground, pulling them as though with a rope.[2]

HERVEY ISLANDS

We may refer to the genealogy, from Rarotonga, of the great Tangiia family, in which Ruanuku [Ru of space, or spacious Ru] Rongo, Tane, Tu and Tangaroa appear as the children of the original parents, Te Tumu, the root or foundation, and Papa, the earth. Another genealogy of the Tangiia [Pa] family begins with Atea and Papa as the original parents, and among the names of a number of gods which appear in it there are four Ru gods, of which three have additions to their names;[3] all these names of gods may refer to the deities themselves, or they may only have been supposed human beings.

In two legends from Mangaia Ru is associated with Maui in the feat of lifting up the sky.[4]

In relating Tahitian tales of the exploits of Ru as a navigator, Henry refers to a legend of Aitutaki, Hervey Islands, according to which Ru was the discoverer and first settler on the island.[5]

TU

In summarizing the evidence concerning the god Atea we drew attention to the fact that there was a word *atea* which had meanings related to "light" or of a similar character. In general, however, the identity of a god's name with a word may be accidental, and does not justify an assumption that the god himself was associated with the conception involved by the meaning of the word, unless the beliefs and traditions concerning the god indicate it. Thus a myth as to Atea (light) and Ono or Rongo (sound) might refer merely to these things as physical conceptions, and not to the gods whose names were identical unless there are reasons for thinking that the myth under discussion referred to the gods themselves. The interest of all this

---

[1] *Beliefs*, vol. I, p. 152.   [2] Lister, *J.R.A.I.* vol. XXI, p. 53.
[3] *J.P.S.* vol. I, pp. 25 *sqq.*   [4] *Beliefs*, vol. I, pp. 42–3.
[5] See Henry, *A.T.* p. 465; cf. Large, *J.P.S.* vol. XII, chart facing p. 144.

as affecting the god Tu is that the word *tu* had a general Poly-
nesian meaning of "to stand" and was associated with stability.
We shall perhaps have to refer to gods whose names begin with
Tu-, who may or may not have been the great Polynesian deity
Tu, and the references must be considered subject to the
possibility of error, and regarded with caution.

SAMOA

Turner includes, among his village and war gods, two deities
called Tu. One of these is Ali'i Tu, incarnate in the *ve'a* or rail.
The bird's flight was observed during war. If it flew before, the
omen was good, but otherwise it was bad.[1] The other reference
is to Tu, who was supposed never to sit down,[2] also incarnate
in the rail. If the bird appeared reddish and glossy, it was a sign
that the people were to go to war; if dark and dingy, the omen
was bad, and the warriors were ordered to stay.[3] According to
one of the Samoan stories of restraining or catching the sun,[4]
the feat was accomplished by the "great" Itu; he may have been
Tu, but it is possible that Itu was a misspelling of *aitu*, meaning
merely "a god".

We cannot, without more information about these beings, say
with confidence whether any of them was in fact the great
Polynesian god Tu; but as regards the two gods mentioned by
Turner, it is possible that, whoever they were, they were the
objects of some form of worship and not merely helpful guides
to their subjects when engaged in war. The name of Turner's
Tu may refer simply to a habit, attributed to the bird, of never
sitting down.

SOCIETY ISLANDS

We may first refer to the Tahitian myth[5] that Tangaroa, having
emerged from an egg, conjured forth the god Tu, who became
his companion and artisan in the work of creation; that after a
period of harmony war arose among the gods and men, and
Tangaroa and Tu cursed the stars, the sea, the rivers and the
trees, but that Hina saved them from the effects of the curse;
and that they also cursed mankind whom Hina was unable to

---

[1] Turner, p. 24. The name means literally "the chief who stands", but gods
were often spoken of as chiefs.
[2] Cf. the general meaning of *tu* mentioned above.
[3] Turner, p. 61.   [4] *Beliefs*, vol. I, p. 110.
[5] *Ibid.* p. 65. Cf. Henry's legend of the cosmogony summarized below,
p. 226.

save owing to the machinations of Ti'i, and who therefore lost eternal life. We shall refer at a later stage to Henry's account of how Tu guided the island of Tahiti when it broke away from Ra'iatea. She also tells of the chiefs dividing the land among themselves and their people, erecting *marae* to prove their titles to these respective possessions, their tutelar gods being Tangaroa, Tu, and Tane; and, in connection with this, she says that the boundaries of their districts were well defined, and finally became little independent kingdoms, over which self-made men ruled as *ari'i* [chiefs], but that gradually the blood of the people of Tahiti became ennobled by that of the aristocracy, and finally the royalty, of Opoa in Ra'iatea, from which all the high chiefs of the Society Islands had to prove their descent in order to be entitled to wear the *maro-ura*; and she says there were in Tahiti a few chiefs of this rank who were associated with *marae*, which obtained their greatest sacredness by obtaining a stone from one of the royal *marae* of Opoa, or its offshoots in the Leeward Islands.[1] Attention should be drawn to the alleged descent of the Pomare family from Tu, whose name they bore. This has been fully discussed elsewhere.[2]

Tu was worshipped in the Society Islands.[3] Ellis includes Roo, Tane, and Tuu (presumably Tu) among the gods to whom the people offered their morning prayers.[4] Anderson and Forster mention the worship of Otoo or O-Too in Eimoo,[5] and Gill refers to Tu as the tutelar goddess [*sic*] of Eimeo.[6] The *Duff* missionaries include him among what they believed to have been the great gods of Tahiti.[7] Ellis, in describing the proceedings on the fall of the first warrior on either side in battle, says that sometimes this first victim was called *Te-ivi-o-te-vai-o-Tu*.[8]

Gaussin gives a translation of fragments of a Tahitian song[9] which attributes thunder and lightning to the anger of Tu, and which had some connection with war, but we cannot say from his translation whether this referred to human warfare or warfare among the gods, or both.

We have seen elsewhere[10] that the sixteenth day of the month was variously spelt by three writers as "Otooroo", "Oturu-

---

[1] Henry, *J.P.S.* vol. xx, p. 5.
[2] *Systems*, vol. i, pp. 241 *sq.*
[3] Henry, *A.T.* pp. 163, 180.
[4] Ellis, vol. i, pp. 343 *sq.*
[5] Cook, vol. vi, p. 160; Forster, *Voy.* vol. ii, p. 151.
[6] Gill, *Myths*, p. 6.
[7] Wilson, p. 333.
[8] Ellis, vol. i, p. 289; cf. Henry, *A.T.* pp. 311, 317.
[9] Gaussin, pp. 260 *sq.*
[10] *Beliefs*, vol. i, p. 187.

tea", and "Otoutou-tea". The last of these suggests that this
day may have been dedicated to or named after the god Tu; but
the question is obviously uncertain.

MARQUESAS

Von den Steinen refers to the legends he was told concerning
the gods and heroes, including Tangaroa, Maui, Tiki, Tu, and
others; but he does not tell the legends.[1] Des Vergnes speaks
of a being called Tupa[2] as having been "certainly" the father
of the gods, the Jupiter of the country, from whom all the rest
were descended, including Tiki.[3] It would appear from his
account that Tupa was a god of traditional importance, recognized widely in the Marquesas, though there is no reference to
his being worshipped. Other writers tell us something more
about him, and Tautain speaks of him as having been a god;[4]
while Smith refers to him as a great hero whose special god seems
to have been Tu.[5] These references to him have been introduced
here in view of the possibility that he was the god Tu, or was
supposed to have been a worshipper of Tu.[6] Handy refers to
Tu as a legendary character and the patron of war.[7]

PAUMOTU

We must refer to the creation legend, mentioned above, of the
embrace of earth and sky, and the subsequent escape of their
children Atea, Rongo, Tu, and Tane. Henry refers to Tu as
one of the great gods of the Paumotus.[8]

We have the following information concerning the worship
of Tu in Mangareva. D'Urville was told that Tou [presumably
Tu] was believed to be the eldest son of Tangaroa; and was
shown a place where, a few years before, a man had been killed,
eaten, and offered to Tou, then the principal god of the place.[9]
Tu presided over the productions of the earth, and was therefore
most often prayed to by the natives.[10] The French missionaries
say that he was the originator of breadfruit.[11] Caillot says that
he was the god of peace and breadfruit.[12] He also tells a story
which says that the little grandson of King Anuamotua was

[1] Von den Steinen, *V.G.E.* vol. xxv, p. 500.
[2] Cf. Handy, *M.L.* pp. 81 *sqq.*
[3] Des Vergnes, *R.M.C.* vol. LII, pp. 722 *sq.*
[4] Tautain, *L'Anthro.* vol. VIII, p. 540 *n.* 1.
[5] Smith, *J.P.S.* vol. xxvii, pp. 125 *sq.*   [6] Cf. below, p. 71.
[7] Handy, *N.C.M.* p. 245; *M.L.* p. 110.   [8] Henry, *A.T.* p. 109.
[9] D'Urville, *V.P.S.* vol. II, Part I, pp. 156 *sq.*   [10] *Ibid.* p. 166.
[11] *A.P.F.* vol. XIV, p. 332.   [12] Caillot, *Mythes*, p. 154.

nearly drowned while playing in the sea. His father saved him, but a big fish called him, inviting him to come on its back, which he did; and the fish, named Tu, carried him to Hao Island, where it tore him to pieces.[1] Smith supplies the following information collected by the French missionaries. Tu was the supreme being among the Mangarevans, and was a sort of trinity. He was also Atu-motua, Atu-moana, and Atea-Tangaroa. In view of the source of this information, the influence of Christianity must be suspected here. It is, however, clear that prayers and sacrifices were made to Tu, who was associated with other less important deities. The ceremony on the birth of the eldest child of the king was performed at the place dedicated to Tu.[2]

Tupa—hero or god or both—who has been mentioned in connection with the worship of Tu in the Marquesas, appears also in the traditions of Mangareva according to a story given by Caillot.[3] But it does not appear from this evidence that in Mangareva Tupa was the deity Tu. He seems to have been regarded as a traditional or perhaps historical being, and there is no statement that he had been deified. But he was evidently believed to have brought the worship of Tu to the island, and his close association with that god is perhaps reflected in the statements as to his bringing breadfruit and fruit trees and teaching agriculture, and planting coconuts in another island, and comparing them with the conception of Tu as the god of peace and breadfruit, who presided over the productions of the earth.

The belief that Tu was the supreme being in Mangareva, embodying, as it were, Atu-motua, Atu-moana, and Atea-Tangaroa—that is, that he was supreme over and above Tangaroa—is not substantiated by what we know of the several cults of the island; and it seems probable that d'Urville and the French missionaries obtained this information from people who were devoted to the worship of Tu. We may quote, on the other side, Caillot, who says that Atu-motua, Atu-moana, and Atea-Tangaroa were the three greatest gods, and that Tangaroa-hurupapa was the most often prayed to, being regarded as *par excellence* the true king of Mangareva;[4] perhaps this statement was obtained from a Tangaroa-worshipper, but it is much more in accord with the broad indications of the traditions and history of the island. Another possible explanation of the discrepancy

[1] Caillot, *Mythes*, pp. 195 *sq.*   [2] Smith, *J.P.S.* vol. XXVII, pp. 120 *sqq.*
[3] Caillot, *Mythes*, p. 173.   [4] *Ibid.* p. 153.

is that Tangaroa was the great national god of the island, but that Tu was the family god of the reigning kings at the times when d'Urville and the missionaries obtained their information, and so acquired a special importance. Caillot, in describing the funerals of the two kings of Mangareva at a comparatively recent time, says that before the bodies were dried in the sun they were taken to Tu's *marae*, and offered to him;[1] and this, together with the ceremony connected with the king's eldest child, is consistent with a supposition that he was the tutelar god of the royal family.

One of the gods invoked at the solemn turtle feast, referred to above, was Tou (apparently Tu). We also find, in a genealogy of the chiefs of Hao Island, the names of a number of gods, including that of Tunui;[2] and though it is not clear that this referred to the god, and not to an ancestral chief who bore his name, it suggests the probability that the cult of Tu had reached that island.

NIUE

We have seen, in considering the gods of Niue, that according to Smith Tangaloa was the head of them. There were what he calls "greater" gods, though he does not say who they were, and there were gods of the *tupua* class, who would not, he thinks, be placed in the same rank as the greater gods. Elsewhere he speaks of five *tupua*, who were supposed to have reached the island, and whom, apparently, he regards as having been original *tupua*; but none of their names (which he gives) are those of any of the major Polynesian deities. He tells us of some of their doings in Niue, and of their descendants; and he refers to the increase in their numbers till they became numerous, and specifies by name eighteen of these descendants who, he says, "ascended to the kingdom above of day and night"; and among these occur the names Tu-tau and Tu-mote-kula.[3] These beings, or one of them, may or may not have been the god Tu, and that is all that can be said about the matter. Smith also says that Tu was an albino, that there were a few albinos among the people, that they were said to have been the offspring of the god Tu, who caught the original ones in a net at night, and that this was the reason why these people blinked their eyes in daylight.[4] Loeb heard nothing of Tu in Niue and does not think he was ever of any importance.[5]

---

[1] Caillot, *Mythes*, pp. 224 sq.   [2] *Ibid.* p. 11.
[3] Smith, *J.P.S.* vol. XII, pp. 22–8.   [4] *Ibid.* vol. XI, p. 166.
[5] Loeb, *Niue*, p. 159.

ELLICE ISLANDS

Hedley says that in the Ellice island of Funafuti one of the early gods was a spirit Tufokoula, who was worshipped also in the form of a sea bird.[1] But perhaps this was Tafakula, said to have been one of the gods of the islands of Vaitupu and Nanomanga.[2]

HERVEY ISLANDS

Although Rongo was the war god of Mangaia, Dr Buck considers that "the association of Tu with war is retained in the myth of the combat between Tu-tavake and Tu-kai-taua and references in songs".[3]

In a Rarotongan creation story Tu was one of the offspring of the union of Atea and Papa,[4] and there are references which may relate to Tu in Aitutaki and Atiu. The Aitutaki reference speaks of the time of old, the progress of earth, and sky, when the sky was embracing the earth below, the time of the gods Tu-te-arakura and Tu-te-akatere;[5] it evidently associates these gods with the mythical period of evolution, and they may have been conceptions of Tu. The Atiuan reference appears in a story of a wife who was beaten by her husband for suspected infidelity, and fled from him, with the help of her god Tu-te-rangi-marama. There was a lament by her for her husband, in which was an appeal to Tu that he would make the sea calm so that [her husband's] canoe might come to her; and Tu, hearing the lament, inspired a kingfisher bird to carry her message to her husband, which it did, whereupon he followed the bird back to where she was, and they were reunited.[6]

[1] Hedley, p. 46.
[3] Te Rangi Hiroa, *M.S.* p. 162.
[5] *J.P.S.* vol. XII, p. 135.
[2] Newell, *A.A.A.S.* vol. VI, p. 609.
[4] Cf. *Beliefs*, vol. I, p. 14.
[6] *Ibid.* vol. XXII, pp. 70 sq.

CHAPTER III

ISLAND GODS

HAVING considered the major deities whose worship was widespread throughout Central Polynesia, we may now turn our attention to the less important ones, whom we may conveniently refer to as "island gods", because their worship was confined to certain islands or small groups of islands. As there were a very large number of these, including village, family and individual gods, it will only be possible to mention the more important ones here.

SAMOA

Dealing first with Samoa, we may mention the references to Fe'e, the cuttle-fish, who was a god of the underworld, *Sa-le-Fe'e*. At Faleasao, at the north-western corner of Tau, there was a deep hole in the sea floor, with a strong eddy into which the souls of the dead plunged; this hole was (like that in Savai'i) called *fafa*, and a large block of stone standing out of the water was called Fe'e.[1] Fe'e is mentioned in the Tangaloa legends,[2] and was supposed to be one of the gods who fought against the Tangaloa family. Fe'e appears to have been a general Samoan god. He is mentioned in connection with the genealogy of the *tui-manu'a*,[3] and was connected with the island of Tau,[4] and with the district of Aana in Upolu, where he was a war god.[5] There was a village called Sa Fe'e in the western extremity of Savai'i and another in Safotu;[6] a coral island in the division of Atua, in Upolu, was dedicated to him.[7]

There was a legend that Fe'e, in the form of a cuttle-fish, was brought by a woman from Savai'i to the village of Apia, in Tuamasanga; but on reaching that place he made his escape from the basket in which he had been carried and, following the course of the mountain torrent-bed inland, he reached and took

---

[1] Krämer, *S.I.* vol. I, p. 369.
[2] Fraser, *J.P.S.* vol. VI, p. 111; cf. Krämer, *S.I.* vol. I, p. 45; Turner, p. 7.
[3] Krämer, *loc. cit.*
[4] Fraser, *R.S.N.S.W.* vol. XXIV, p. 201; vol. XXV, pp. 70–3.
[5] Fraser, *J.P.S.* vol. VI, p. 34; Stair, pp. 218, 235 *sq.*; *J.P.S.* vol. V, pp. 41, 54; Krämer, *S.I.* vol. I, p. 153; cf. Turner, p. 28.
[6] Krämer, *S.I.* vol. I, pp. 59, 80.   [7] *Ibid.* p. 290.

up his abode at the spot where was the famous *fale o le Fe'e* (the house of Fe'e).[1] Variant legends of the arrival of Fe'e are given by other writers.[2] It seems clear that the district with which Fe'e was particularly associated in Tuamasanga was Vaimaunga (in which was Apia).[3] He was a war god there, and if it thundered in the direction of the sea, the people went to war, because the cuttle-fish loved the white waves.[4] The harbour at Apia was believed to be a hole in the reef made by Fe'e that he might the more easily pass in and out to visit his wife, the daughter of a chief in Upolu.[5]

Some further information on the cult of Fe'e is given by Turner, though he does not specify the part of Samoa from which it was obtained. This material connects Fe'e particularly with war and with omens observed during war time; the special emblem of Fe'e was a piece of white cloth, which was worn by his worshippers when going into battle. In one place, where he was a village god, he was associated with certain seasonal festivals held during the month of May. In another district his priest had a death-bowl for the punishment of offenders in cases of injury and theft; it was said that the conscience-stricken thieves, when taken ill, were carried with presents of food to the priest's house that he might pray over the bowl for Fe'e's forgiveness.[6]

Moso was another important Samoan deity; Pritchard describes him as a national god[7] and Turner says that he was one of the great *land* gods, in opposition to Tangaloa, the god of the heavens.[8] In all the versions of the fighting of Losi and his supporters against the Tangaloa family[9] the name of Moso appears as one of the Losi party.

Pritchard describes him as a rapacious monster, who ate those who angered him, and sometimes those who did not. A form of oath was associated with Moso. A man, doubting the truth of a statement made by another, would say, "Shall Moso eat you?" and the reply "Moso may eat me" would satisfy the most incredulous. But if a man dared not say this it was presumed that he lied. The god was also invoked for the destruction of enemies; and in quarrels the bitterest imprecation a man could

---

[1] *J.P.S.* vol. III, p. 243.
[2] Turner, p. 28; Krämer, *S.I.* vol. I, p. 405 *n.* 9.
[3] Cf. Krämer, *S.I.* vol. I, pp. 23, 231.
[4] *Ibid.* p. 229; cf. Pritchard, pp. 117 *sqq.*; and a version of a Tuamasangan legend in *J.P.S.* vol. XXIV, p. 118.
[5] Turner, p. 31.
[6] *Ibid.* pp. 7, 28–32.
[7] Pritchard, p. 113.
[8] Turner, p. 36.
[9] Cf. *Beliefs*, p. 157.

hurl at another was: "May Moso eat you!"[1] Like Fe'e, he was employed in the punishment of personal injury and theft; his priest also had a bowl, over which he cursed the offender, who was thus often driven to confession and reparation.[2]

According to Krämer he was a war god of Sangafili, in the district of Aana in Upolu, and was also worshipped in Savai'i.[3] According to Turner, Moso was incarnate in or represented by a number of different animals or objects, one "family" seeing him in one thing, and another "family" in another. Among these objects associated with Moso, Turner mentions highly fragrant yellow flowers, a pigeon, a domestic fowl, a cuttle-fish, a creeper bird, a turtle, a mullet, a stinging ray-fish. Two families worshipped him as a god with human incarnation. In connection with Moso's animal and other incarnations food taboos and other ritual obligations were observed.[4]

Another Samoan god was Sepo, whose functions were similar to those of Moso—in fact Krämer says that Sepo was only another name for Moso,[5] though other writers seem to regard him as a separate god. Turner speaks of Sepo as being worshipped in Upolu and Savai'i, where he was a war god.[6] Pritchard says that he was invariably invoked when cursing children; and angry elders would say to children: "May Sepo eat you!"[7] and this may be compared with Brown's statement that sacrifices may have been offered to Sepo, children especially being the victims.[8] Sepo was believed to have animal incarnations similar to those of Moso.

A Samoan deity called Le Sa (the sacred one) is mentioned in the Losi-Tangaloa legends as one of the gods who fought against Tangaloa. According to one of the legends of the creation by Tangaloa, Le Sa was the son of Fatu and Ele'ele, who according to one version of the creation were the first man and woman to be created by Tangaloa.[9]

According to Pritchard Le Sa was the great god under whose supervision the plantations of the Samoans flourished or faded, and in times of scarcity special offerings were made to him, as failure was attributed to his displeasure.[10] Turner says that in several villages he was a war god, incarnate in the lizard, whose

[1] Pritchard, p. 113. [2] Turner, p. 36.
[3] Krämer, S.I. vol. I, pp. 70, 79 sq., 157; cf. p. 360 n. 3.
[4] Turner, pp. 36 sq. [5] Krämer, S.I. vol. I, p. 23.
[6] Turner, p. 51. [7] Pritchard, p. 113.
[8] Brown, p. 230.
[9] Powell, R.S.N.S.W. vol. XXVI, p. 275; J.P.S. vol. I, p. 176.
[10] Pritchard, p. 113.

movements were observed as omens of war, but he also refers to Le Sa as an agricultural god, who sent rain and an abundance of food, and was worshipped about the month of April. Offerings and prayers were made to induce him to remove from the plantations the caterpillars, supposed to be sent by him by way of punishment; and a sick man would go out and weed in the bush in order to placate him. He was also invoked to devour the bodies of thieves, to which he was supposed to be partial.[1]

The legendary tales of the Samoan deity Pava open in the island of Manu'a; Tangaloa-a-U'i once came to Pava's house there, but was inhospitably received, both Pava and his son being guilty of breaches of etiquette. Tangaloa was so enraged at this that he cut Pava's son in half, and then put the pieces together, bringing the boy back to life again, in order to show his power. This so terrified Pava that he and his wife fled, but wherever they went, they saw, whenever they looked back, the eye of Tangaloa following them; not till they reached Upolu did they escape it, and here they settled at a spot bearing the name of Pava in the district of Fale-alili in Atua, where Pava became a war god. This legend associates Pava specially with a *taro* leaf, which he used on one occasion to conceal himself from Tangaloa, and for this reason the war ensign of his worshippers was a *taro*-leaf cap.[2] In spite of his flight from there, Pava seems to have left descendants in Manu'a, for they are mentioned in the *fono* greetings of Fitiuta.[3] Turner says that Pava was seen in the rainbow, which was observed as an omen of war.[4]

According to one of the legends connecting the Tangaloa family with the *tuimanu'a*, a god called Le Fanonga was the turbulent son of Tangaloa-a-U'i, and was passed over in the granting of the title in favour of his brother Ta'e-o-Tangaloa;[5] but Stair includes Le Fanonga as one of the children of Pava.[6] He appears as one of the allies of Losi in his fight with the Tangaloa family.[7]

One legend of Le Fanonga relates an incident which occurred before he lost his title; he and La'a-mao-mao, another son of

[1] Turner, pp. 46 *sq.*
[2] Fraser-Powell, *R.S.N.S.W.* vol. xxv, pp. 105 *sq.* Variants of this legend are given by other writers: Turner, pp. 42 *sq.*; Krämer, *S.I.* vol. i, pp. 405–8; cf. p. 287; Stair, *J.P.S.* vol. iv, p. 49.
[3] Krämer, *S.I.* vol. i, p. 371. [4] Turner, p. 43.
[5] *R.S.N.S.W.* vol. xxv, pp. 107, 112; vol. xxvi, p. 294; *J.P.S.* vol. vi, pp. 67 *sqq.*; Krämer, *S.I.* vol. i, pp. 392 *sq.*, 416–20.
[6] *J.P.S.* vol. iv, p. 49.
[7] Cf. *R.S.N.S.W.* vol. xxvi, pp. 275 *sq.*; Krämer, *S.I.* vol. i, pp. 418 *sqq.*

Tangaloa-a-U'i, were cooking yams in an oven for their father; they went off to play on the beach, as a result of which the yams were all red-hot or black and spoiled. So Tangaloa in his anger flung a red-hot yam at Le Fanonga and a blackened yam at La'a-mao-mao. Le Fanonga's body was burned reddish in several places, and the blackened yam hit La'a-mao-mao on the neck, which was thus blackened and elongated. Le Fanonga assumed the form of an owl, and it was the red-hot yam which caused the Samoan owl to be so red; similarly the long black neck of the black heron is due to the yam thrown at La'a-mao-mao, who became a heron. Le Fanonga flew to Sale-i-moa, on the northern shore of Tuamasanga, and became its war god, the owl being his emblem; La'a-mao-mao flew to the little island of Manono, and became a war god there, with the black heron as his emblem.[1]

Turner refers to Fanonga as a war god, incarnate in the Samoan owl, and says that in war time food was offered to a pet owl, kept for the purpose, whose movements were regarded as omens; he also states that this god was connected with the annual fish festivals, at which the first fish was presented to him.[2] Fraser refers to a feast in Fanonga's honour in October.[3]

A deity called Tui-fiti was the god of two villages in Savai'i; in addition to human and animal incarnations, he was believed to inhabit a grove of trees, which, in spite of their economic value, were for this reason left untouched. In fact one legend tells of a party of men from Upolu, who attempted to cut down one of these trees; when they did so, blood flowed from it and all the sacrilegious strangers became ill and died. The name of the god is of some interest, as it might be translated "King of Fiji".[4]

Another Samoan god was Vave, who was known both in Upolu and Savai'i; he was a war god, said to be incarnate in

---

[1] Fraser-Powell, R.S.N.S.W. vol. xxv, p. 107; cf. a similar story told by Krämer (S.I. vol. I, pp. 191, 378) in which, however, Le Fanonga is the son of Ia Fotu, and not of Tangaloa-a-U'i, and his brother is called Matu'u. On La'a-mao-mao and Matu'u see also Wilkes, vol. II, p. 131; Stair, J.P.S. vol. v, p. 56; Krämer, op. cit. p. 160; Turner, pp. 35 sq.; Fraser, R.S.N.S.W. vol. xxv, p. 118 n. As well as being incarnate in the heron, La'a-mao-mao was also connected with the rainbow which was observed as an omen of war. The references just cited lead us to think that there was some confusion between La'a-mao-mao and Matu'u but it is also possible that they were merely two names for the same deity.
[2] Turner, pp. 25 sq.   [3] Fraser, R.S.N.S.W. vol. xxv, p. 146.
[4] Turner, pp. 62 sq.; Stair, J.P.S. vol. v, p. 41; Krämer, S.I. vol. I, p. 58; Fraser, R.S.N.S.W. vol. xxiv, p. 199 n. 5; Pratt, R.S.N.S.W. vol. xxiv, pp. 201, 203 n. 8.

various birds, whose movements were observed as omens of war. IIis power was apparently very great; there was a tale of the help he gave to his worshippers in repelling an attack by Tongan invaders, enabling them to kill a great Tongan hero who had been taking heavy toll of their warriors' lives. Again, when a number of gods had tried to raise a rocky precipice between one of his villages and the sea, he had driven them off into another district. Here they effected their purpose, the relics of which still remained.[1]

A Samoan god whose worship seems to have been widespread throughout the islands was Pili, incarnate in the lizard and eel. He was particularly associated with Manu'a[2] and with the early political organization of Upolu,[3] though he is also mentioned in connection with Savai'i and Tutuila.[4]

In the legends Pili is spoken of as the son of Tangaloa, and is associated particularly with net-fishing and taro-growing.[5] He may also have been connected with war, for Turner in his list of Samoan gods includes Pili-ma-le-maa (the lizard and the stone). They were twin gods and were worshipped in certain villages in times of war, famine and pestilence. The month of May was a specially fixed time for prayers and food offerings. He describes various ways by which the movements of the lizard were watched as omens in time of war.[6]

Tinilau (sometimes spelt Tingilau) is important, not on account of any evidence that he was worshipped extensively in Samoa, but because he was widely known throughout Polynesia as a god of the sea and of fishes. Several Samoan legends tell of his doings[7] but only two of these associate him particularly with fishes or things of the sea.[8]

There was an important group of gods, specially associated with the island of Savai'i, and as they were closely connected it seems desirable first to say something of the legends as to their origin. It was said that Papa (rock) and Maluapapa (hollow rock) were husband and wife, and had a daughter Popoto

---

[1] Turner, pp. 64 sq.; Pritchard, p. 110; Krämer, S.I. vol. I, p. 58.
[2] Pratt, R.S.N.S.W. vol. xxv, pp. 260 sq.; Stair, J.P.S. vol. IV, pp. 50 sq.
[3] Turner, p. 4; Pratt, loc. cit. pp. 254–7; Krämer, S.I. vol. I, pp. 24 sq.; cf. pp. 27, 156, 167, 438 n. 4.
[4] Krämer, op. cit. pp. 27, 63, 314; Thilenius, Globus, vol. LXXX, p. 169 n.
[5] Turner, pp. 4, 232 sqq.; Pratt, op. cit. pp. 254–7; Krämer, S.I. vol. II, p. 167.
[6] Turner, p. 44.
[7] Powell-Fraser, R.S.N.S.W. vol. XIV, pp. 197 sq.; Krämer, S.I. vol. I, pp. 131 sqq., 133–6, 139–42.
[8] Pritchard, pp. 387–90; Krämer, S.I. vol. I, pp. 128 sqq. For another version see Turner, pp. 110 sq.

(round, well-formed). She went to Upolu to seek a husband, and married Maungafolau (the name of a hill at the western end of Aana) but his efforts to deflower her were unavailing, as she had no vagina. She therefore left him, and went to Tofua-upolu (the name of another hill in Aana) but the same difficulty occurred again. She then went to Masa (a rock near the western end of Savai'i) and he met the difficulty by means of a shark's tooth, thus forming a vagina; she lived with him, and had a daughter called Taufa. She was married by Alao in Falealupo (the western end of Savai'i, where the souls of the dead made their final plunge in their journey to the unknown) and they had a son called Savea Si'uleo, who had a tail like that of a sea eel.[1]

Another legend, the earlier parts of which are rather confused, goes on to say that Papatea married a woman Papanga, and had children, among whom was a daughter Taufailematangi, who was married by Alao, and had two sons, Salevao and Savea Si'uleo; but because their two sons were cannibals, she and her husband ran away to Salafai, where they had a third son Ulufanuasese'e.[2] The latter married and had two daughters, Taema and Tilafainga, the latter of whom married her uncle Savea Si'uleo, and Nafanua was born of this marriage.[3] It is said that Alao and Taufa had other children, but Savea Si'uleo ate them all up; and Ulufanuasese'e had a narrow escape from being devoured also. But the three brothers, Savea Si'uleo, Salevao, and Ulufanuasese'e, met on the seashore and made "their testament", which provided that Savea Si'uleo should go to *Pulotu* and rule over it, that Ulufanuasese'e should make a good marriage, that the chiefs of the *alataua* (great divining orator-chiefs) might spring from it, and that Salevao should be the voice of the *alataua*, and only the voice of the *alataua*.[4]

Thus it came about that Savea Si'uleo, who was born near the place in Savai'i where the souls of the dead left this world for their ultimate destination, became a deity especially associated with them. It has been mentioned elsewhere that the souls of the dead did not all go to the same place;[5] some were destined for *Pulotu*, the abode of the blessed; but others went to Sa-le-Fe'e, the Samoan hades. The latter was ruled by the Fe'e family; but according to Krämer its government passed to Savea Si'uleo, so it would appear that he was a god of the dead in both regions.[6]

[1] Krämer, *S.I.* vol. I, pp. 104 sq. [2] *Ibid.* pp. 105 sq.
[3] *Ibid.* pp. 45, 107. [4] *Ibid.* pp. 106 sq. [5] Cf. *Beliefs*, vol. I, chap. XIII.
[6] Krämer, *S.I.* vol. I, p. 45; cf. Turner, pp. 259 sq.; Stair, p. 293.

In addition to this he was a fisherman's god, and was supposed to be able to walk on the sea; he had a fisherman's hut erected for him on the seashore, and was supposed to preside over certain divisions of the coast.[1] He is also said to have been a war god.[2]

According to the legend given above, Salevao was to be the voice of the *alataua*; these were the great divining orator-chiefs, of whose order there were members in different parts of the islands, but of whom there were a number collected together in the *alataua* district of Safata on the southern shore of Tuamasanga. Krämer states that Salevao was the special god of Tuamasanga, and that he was actually incarnate in the great *alataua* orator-chief Lio, who was specially consulted in connection with portentous decisions.[3]

Turner refers to Salevao as a war god and says that he was incarnate in a dog, whose movements were observed as omens of war. In one place he was incarnate in the eel and turtle. He was the god of a number of villages where thanks for past crops and prayers for more were offered to him at fixed times. Salevao was also the god of a Savai'i village, where he had a temple in which a priest constantly resided; the sick were taken there, and cured by him, and he was generous to travellers.[4]

Taema married in Savai'i, and Tilafainga, as already stated, married her uncle Savea Si'uleo.[5] They were twins, joined back to back, but were eventually separated by a stroke of a wave.[6] Turner, speaking of them as household gods only, says that their worshippers when going on a journey were supposed to have the goddesses with them as guardian angels. To these people everything double—such as a double yam or two adhering bananas—was sacred and might not be used under penalty of death; further, people were not allowed to sit back to back, as this might be regarded as mockery of the goddesses.[7]

The most interesting thing in connection with these deities was that they were the goddesses of tattooers. It was said that they had swum from Fiji to introduce the craft to Samoa, and on leaving Fiji were told to sing all the way: "Tattoo the women

---

[1] Turner, p. 52.   [2] Wilkes, vol. II, p. 131.
[3] Krämer, *S.I.* vol. I, pp. 23, 107 *n.* 2, 115 *n.* 7; cf. Powell-Fraser, *R.S.N.S.W.* vol. XXIV, pp. 203–6.
[4] Turner, pp. 49 *sq.*; Krämer (*S.I.* vol. I, pp. 22, 75, 77, 79) also associates Salevao with Savai'i, particularly with the western end of the island.
[5] Krämer, *S.I.* vol. I, p. 45.   [6] Turner, p. 56.
[7] *Ibid.* p. 36.

but not the men." Unfortunately on their long journey they got muddled over this song and arrived in Samoa singing: "Tattoo the men and not the women." From this mistake arose the universal exercise of the blackening art on the men rather than on the women.[1]

According to one legend Nafanua was the issue of Tilafainga by her uncle Savea Si'uleo.[2] She was an important war goddess of Savai'i.[3] A legend given by Turner describes how she gave help to her people suffering from oppressive rule. She led them in battle and defeated their oppressors. During the fight she concealed her sex by covering her breasts with coconut leaves; and a few of these, bound round the waist, formed the distinguishing mark of her troops. After the battle she had coconut leaves tied round the trees, thus marking them out as hers, and defied the enemy or anyone else to touch them. This incident is given as the origin of the fastening of coconut leaves round trees as taboo marks,[4] but the custom was a common one in the Pacific. The important part played by Nafanua in the legendary political history of Samoa has been dealt with elsewhere.[5]

Three other gods may be mentioned, which, though they do not appear to have been worshipped, are referred to in the legends. Such a one was Alo-alo, said to be a son of Tangaloa-of-the-skies, who may be regarded as important because there was a Tongan god of that name.[6] Another was Le Folasa, who was also a member of the Tangaloa family.[7] Finally we may mention Lata, because of his general importance in Polynesian history.[8]

In concluding our treatment of Samoan deities we may say that it is impossible to formulate definitions with which to distinguish between gods largely and widely worshipped in an island or group and those whose jurisdiction covers only a small

---

[1] Turner, pp. 55 sq.; Krämer, S.I. vol. I, p. 107; cf. Stair, p. 157; versions of another tale of the origin of these two goddesses are given by Brown (pp. 96 sqq.), Turner (pp. 55 sq.), and Fraser-Powell (J.P.S. vol. v, pp. 171–8). According to the last of these Tilafainga took the name of Nafanua, and remained in Savai'i as a war goddess; but Taema went to Tutuila as a tattooing goddess. Taema was, however, worshipped elsewhere in Samoa (ibid. p. 181 n. 7).

[2] Krämer, S.I. vol. I, p. 107; cf. preceding note.
[3] Krämer, S.I. vol. I, p. 45; Fraser, J.P.S. vol. v, p. 181 n. 7.
[4] Turner, pp. 38 sq.; cf. Krämer, S.I. vol. I, p. 107.
[5] Systems, vol. I, chap. II.
[6] Turner, pp. 67, 245 sqq.; Krämer, S.I. vol. I, pp. 393, 412–16; Pratt, R.S.N.S.W. vol. xxv, pp. 243–53.
[7] Powell, R.S.N.S.W. vol. xxv, pp. 107, 134.
[8] Turner, p. 264; Stair, pp. 272–86.

area, for example, district, village, family and personal gods. Indeed, some of the greater gods were probably not the subjects of universal worship; they had their principal seats and outlying habitations, and there seems to be little doubt that the connecting links between all these have been of a social or family character. A great god of a great family dominating a wide area would sometimes appear as a village god in one of that family's outlying settlements. Though Krämer's voluminous material offers glimpses of the family nature of the connections here and there, it is not sufficient for working the matter out effectively.

We can only now speak of district, village, and family gods in the general and undefined sense that they were gods whose worship was found to be only specially connected with relatively small social groups or areas. Turner's list of gods is divided into two categories, "gods superior—war and general village gods" and "gods inferior or household gods". Among the former are included most or all of the Samoan island gods who have been mentioned above, and a number of others of whom some were probably more local. His inferior or household gods would have still more restricted areas of worship. It appears extremely probable that if we only had copious and exact data we should be able to tabulate the gods, allocating great gods to large or important families, and finding their worship in the districts or villages occupied by those families, while beneath them we should place smaller gods, each having its jurisdiction over its own branch of a family; and again, beneath these we should place the tutelar gods of domestic households and even of individuals. All the writers speak of district gods and town or village gods, and some of personal gods, and there can be no doubt as to the general question; but detailed quotation and comparison of the authorities are useless because of the inexactitude of their terminology.

The Samoans had what may be called departmental gods; but it is impossible to say whether they were island, district, or village gods, or belonged to all these categories, though some of the gods discussed above were more or less departmental. Turner tells us of three gods, of whom one provided yams, breadfruit and coconuts, another sent fish to the nets, and the third provided rain or fine weather as was desired. They were all represented by stones.[1] Another god, incarnate in the cockle, was specially entreated to remove the coughs and other ailments

[1] Turner, p. 45.

prevalent during the period of transition from the wet to the dry season.[1] There was also an accoucheur god, whose priest was sent for and prayed for the safety of the mother in time of childbirth,[2] and Stair says that each principal trade or employment had its presiding god.[3]

TONGA

According to Cook, in Tongatabu, the sacred island of Tonga, the supreme author of most things was Kallafootonga, a goddess connected with the weather and the fertility of the earth.[4] But Gifford was unable to identify her[5] and apparently Cook did not think she was supreme all over the Tongan Islands. She is not even mentioned by Mariner.

Hikuleo must be regarded as having been the great island god of Tonga. His name was closely associated with those of Tangaloa and Maui. One belief was that he was one of two great gods, he the angry one, living in *Bulotu*, and the other—probably Tangaloa—a loving god, living in the sky.[6] It was said that he "proceeded" from Maui, who was from the beginning, and a female deity called Malikula.[7] He was believed to be the elder brother of Tangaloa, and the younger brother of Maui.[8] He was also credited with helping in the creation of the islands, having thrown down the high lands from heaven, while Maui fished up the low lands from the bottom of the sea.[9] A solution offered to the mystery of the origin of the *tuitonga* was that they were descended from Tangaloa, Hikuleo, and Maui.[10] Mariner speaks of Hikuleo as a very high god, regarded mainly by the *tuitonga* family.[11] Wilkes says he was the third god (Maui and Tangaloa being the first and the second) in order of time.[12] Wilkes was told that Hikuleo lived in a cave;[13] but abundant evidence has been cited elsewhere[14] to show that he lived in *Bulotu* and was a malevolent god of the dead, there being many legendary accounts of his doings in this connection. Gifford states that there is some doubt as to the sex of this deity, some informants describing Hikuleo as male and some as female, though the consensus of

[1] Turner, p. 41.   [2] *Ibid.* p. 24.   [3] Stair, p. 142.
[4] Cook, vol. v, p. 422; cf. Veeson, p. 152; Wilson, p. 272.
[5] Gifford, *Tonga*, pp. 289–90.   [6] Lawry, *Miss. Notices*, vol. IV, p. 339.
[7] Young, *S.W.* p. 256.   [8] Lawry, *F.F.I.* (1), pp. 249 sq.
[9] S. Farmer, p. 133.   [10] Thomson, *D.P.M.* pp. 293 sq.
[11] Mariner, vol. II, p. 106.   [12] Wilkes, vol. III, p. 23.
[13] *Ibid.*   [14] *Beliefs*, vol. I, chap. XIV.

opinion favours the former view. Gifford suggests that Hikuleo may have been bisexual.[1]

Mariner says that Hikuleo had neither priest nor house, and that the people were uncertain as to his attributes.[2] Wilkes, speaking of the god of *Bulotu*, whom we may identify with Hikuleo, says that he was invoked when the *tuitonga* was ill, but that otherwise the people never prayed to him, "except when some sacrilege had been committed to the offerings they made him" (whatever this may mean), and on this occasion they always made human sacrifice.[3] Sarah Farmer says that offerings were rarely made to Hikuleo, but she states that he was the god to whom offerings were presented at the great annual *inaji* ceremony.[4]

The names of the Samoan god Savea Si'uleo or Si'uleo and of Hikuleo of Tonga were identical (allowing for the rules of interchange of consonants), and it is clear that they were the same god.[5]

In dealing with the island gods of Samoa, reference has been made to the legends of the Taema-Tilafainga-Nafanua group of deities. A similar legend is recorded from Tonga.[6] When there was a drought Nafanua and her sister Topokulu were asked for rain; in time of dearth they were asked for abundance; in case of tempest they were asked for calm; they were supplicated for abundance of fish, fruits, and other food; but they were never approached in cases of illness.[7]

Alo Alo was, according to Cook, the supreme god of the island of Haapai.[8] The name means "to fan", and he was a Tongan god of wind, weather, rain, harvest, and vegetation in general. So long as the weather was seasonable, he was generally invoked about once a month, that it might remain so; but if unseasonable or destructive on shore by excessive wind or rain, he was applied

---

[1] Gifford, *Tonga*, p. 291.
[2] Mariner, vol. II, p. 106. The absence of a house or temple seems to have been consistent with the attitude of the Tongans towards their greatest and presumably most remote gods; it is doubtful, for instance, whether Tangaloa had a temple. *Ibid*. p. 108.
[3] Wilkes, vol. III, pp. 23 *sq*.   [4] S. Farmer, p. 129.
[5] Thus they were both gods of the dead, Hikuleo living in *Bulotu* and Si'uleo either there or in *Sa-le-Fe'e*. Hikuleo was celebrated for his long tail, and according to one tradition Si'uleo had a tail like a sea eel. Both gods were believed to use the souls of the dead in the construction of their houses. Si'uleo was a cannibal god; and the statements about Hikuleo point in the same direction. There were Samoan beliefs that Si'uleo came from Tonga.
[6] Reiter, *Anthrop*. vol. II, pp. 743–54.
[7] Reiter, *loc. cit*.   [8] Cook, vol. V, p. 423.

to every day. He was not concerned with thunder or lightning—indeed Mariner says these phenomena never did much mischief and had no god—nor was he connected with weather at sea. He was the special god to whom, among others, offerings of yams and other provisions were made when the yams were full grown. Alo Alo had two temples and two priests.[1]

Talletubu was the patron god of the secular king and his family—not of any one king, but of whoever should hold the office for the time being. He was also a god of war, and was invoked in time of war, and occasionally for the general good of the people in time of peace.[2] This god is mentioned by Cook.[3] He was one of five gods to whom Finau I, after victory in battle, offered the bodies of sixty slain enemies.[4]

Tui-fua-bulotu was, according to Cook, the god of clouds and fog.[5] The meaning of the name is "Chief-of-all-Bulotu", but Mariner says that, though he was the god of *Bulotu*, he was inferior in rank to Talletubu. He was, however, a very great deity. He was the god of people of rank in society, and in this character was often invoked by the heads of great families, such as the king and other great chiefs, in times of sickness or other family troubles. He had several houses dedicated to him, and several priests, whom he occasionally inspired.[6] To him was consecrated a sacred kava bowl, used in ceremonies devoted to his honour, and on which chiefs had to place their hands when taking an oath, swearing in the name of Tui-fua-bulotu.[7] The importance of this god is illustrated by the statement that the dying daughter of Finau I, and afterwards the dying Finau himself, were taken first to the temple of Talletubu, and next to that of Tui-fua-bulotu, with entreaties to those gods to spare the invalids' lives.[8] He was also one of the gods among whom Finau divided his sixty human beings referred to above.[9] There may possibly have been some confusion between Hikuleo and Tui-fua-bulotu. The former was the recognized god of *Bulotu*; but according to Mariner this was Tui-fua-bulotu.

Futtafaihe was, according to Cook, the chief god of the sea, having the government of it and its productions.[10] This was also the family name of the *tuitonga*, taken by them from the god, who, Cook thinks, was probably their tutelary patron, and

[1] Mariner, vol. II, p. 107.
[2] *Ibid.* vol. II, pp. 104 *sq.*
[3] Cook, vol. V, p. 422.
[4] Mariner, vol. I, p. 172.
[5] Cook, vol. V, p. 422.
[6] Mariner, vol. II, pp. 104 *sq.*
[7] *Ibid.* vol. I, p. 137.
[8] *Ibid.* pp. 288 *sq.*, 301.
[9] *Ibid.* p. 172.
[10] Cook, vol. V, pp. 422 *sq.*

perhaps their ancestor.[1] Cook does not think the sea gods lived
in the sky; apparently, according to him, they lived in the sea or
on the shore.[2] Mariner supplies information as to this and
connects the sea gods with the *tuitonga*.[3] Mariner does not
however appear to have known of the god Futtafaihe. He says
that Tubu Toutai (Tubu-the-mariner), the patron god of the
Finau family, was also the god of voyages. He was invoked by
chiefs when starting upon maritime expeditions and by all people
going to sea in canoes. He was not the god of the wind, but was
supposed to have great influence with that deity (Alo Alo). It
would seem, therefore, that the statement that Alo Alo was not
connected with weather at sea is not strictly correct; what is
probably meant is that this god was not appealed to at sea. Tubu
Toutai's chief power was extended to the protection of canoes.
He had several houses dedicated to him.[4] Another god of the
sea was Hea-moana-uli-uli, who, it is stated, was believed to be
the brother of Maui, Hikuleo, and Tangaloa. He was incarnate
in the sea serpent, controlled all fish, and was approached by
fishermen in their undertakings.[5]

A number of other Tongan gods are referred to by writers.[6]
A goddess Fyega was prayed to for a favourable season for
making cloth.[7] A goddess Finau-tau-iku was the daughter of
a past *tuihaatakalaua*, a guardian of the chiefs, and a city of
refuge from the power of the *tuikanokubolu*.[8] Another goddess,
Fakatoumafi, was also the daughter of a *tuihaatakalaua*, and was
represented by a whale's-tooth necklace. She must have been
important, as human sacrifice was offered to her.[9] Fenoulounga
was a god of rain.[10] Feaki, represented by a whale's tooth, is
spoken of by Lawry as the fountain-head of all the minor gods;
human sacrifice was offered to him, and it is even said that the
inaji or first-fruits were presented to him.[11]

Gifford mentions a bisexual god Fehuluni, who always appeared to men as a woman and to women as a man. In these
circumstances Fehuluni used to have intercourse with mortals,
with fatal results for the latter.[12] He mentions several other

[1] Cook, vol. v, p. 425; cf. Mariner, vol. II, p. 83.
[2] Cook, vol. v, p. 423. [3] Mariner, vol. I, pp. 206 *sq.*
[4] *Ibid.* vol. II, p. 106.
[5] Lawry, *F.F.I.* (1), pp. 248, 250. Cf. Pritchard, p. 401; Reiter, *Anthrop.*
vol. II, pp. 237 *n.* 4, 752 *sqq.*
[6] Mariner, vol. II, pp. 105–8; Cook, vol. v, p. 423.
[7] Wilson, p. 231. [8] Lawry, *F.F.I.* (2), p. 36.
[9] *Ibid.* p. 37. [10] Wilson, p. 272.
[11] Lawry, *F.F.I.* (2), pp. 35 *sq.* [12] Gifford, *Tonga*, pp. 292 *sqq.*

Tongan gods, as well as gods of specific islands in the Tongan group.[1]

In regard to district, village, household and personal gods, there seems to be hardly any specific information as far as Tonga is concerned. Veeson says that each district had its appropriate god,[2] and this is confirmed by the *Duff* missionaries.[3] Probably some of the gods mentioned by Mariner and other writers were only local. Some at all events of the families had their special gods and perhaps there were personal gods. For example, Futtafaihe was, as stated above, the god of the *tuitonga* family; Tubu Toutai is spoken of by Mariner as the patron of the Finau family[4] and as Finau's tutelary god,[5] and he refers to Alai Valu as being the patron god of Finau's aunt.[6]

SOCIETY ISLANDS

Oro was by far the most important of the island gods of the Society Islands. He was believed both in Tahiti and in the north-western islands to have been the son of Tangaroa,[7] and Ellis refers to his high rank among the gods.[8] There are statements that he was the great national idol of Ra'iatea, Tahiti, Eimeo, and some of the other islands;[9] that he was the national protector of Tahiti, Ra'iatea, Huahine, Tahaa, Borabora, and Mauroa,[10] and the principal national god of Tahiti, to whom alone human sacrifices were offered, at least in modern times;[11] that the gods of the islands adjacent to Ra'iatea were regarded as tributary to Oro, and the chiefs of these islands had to make gifts to the king of Ra'iatea, as his high priest;[12] and that he and Tane were the two principal national idols of Tahiti, in one or other of whose temples marriages of people connected with a reigning family had to be solemnized.[13] Ellis says that in the north-western islands he appears to have been the medium of connection between celestial and terrestrial beings, though a few lines above he speaks of a class of gods, two grades above him, who were employed as heralds between gods and men.[14] The

[1] Gifford, *Tonga*, pp. 290–315.   [2] Veeson, p. 152.
[3] Wilson, p. 271.   [4] Mariner, vol. II, p. 106.
[5] *Ibid.* vol. I, p. 290.   [6] *Ibid.* p. 294; vol. II, p. 107.
[7] Cf. Gill, *Myths*, p. 14 n. 2; Henry, *A.T.* p. 375.
[8] Ellis, vol. I, pp. 324, 326.   [9] *Ibid.* p. 324.
[10] L.M.S. *Trans.* vol. IV, p. 433.   [11] L.M.S. *Rep.* p. 57 n.
[12] Tyerman, vol. I, p. 530. On the special association of Oro with Ra'iatea, see Henry, *A.T.* pp. 119 *sqq.*
[13] Ellis, vol. I, p. 271.   [14] *Ibid.* p. 326.

sixth, seventh, twentieth, twenty-first and twenty-second days of the Tahitian lunar month were sacred to him. It is said that his image was a shapeless log.[1] He was the god to whom the bodies of those slain in battle were offered,[2] and was undoubtedly a great war god.[3]

Oro was specially connected with the *arioi* societies of the Society group, and there are several versions of the legendary role he played in the origin of this institution[4] of which he was the patron deity.

There were several natural species—the boar, a kind of parakeet, the man-of-war bird, and the pearl-oyster—which were specially associated with this god.[5] The southerly gale was Oro's, and brought forth war.[6]

The demigod Hiro was known in several of the Polynesian groups, but as he was admittedly only a deified man, he cannot be placed with Tane, Tangaroa, and Rongo among the major Polynesian gods; he is therefore introduced here as a Society Island god, and this is perhaps justifiable seeing that he is said to have been a head chief or king of Ra'iatea, and so was specially connected with the group.

He was contemporary with Tangiia and Karika and therefore lived, according to Percy Smith, about the middle or latter part of the thirteenth century.[7] Hiro and his brother Hua were persons of special importance, for one or other of them comes into the ancestral genealogies of Maori, Rarotongans, Tahitians, and Hawai'ians.[8] This applies in particular to the genealogical table of the ancestry of the Rarotongan chieftainess Pa, as given by Nicholas,[9] a table reaching back to a pre-Pacific period, and to the genealogy of the kings of Ra'iatea.[10] In both of these he appears as the son of Moeterauri,[11] and it is said that his mother was Akimano,[12] a woman of the Samoan island of Upolu.[13] He seems ultimately to have settled in Ra'iatea, for he was recognized as having been a Ra'iatean,[14] and indeed is said to have been

[1] Tyerman, vol. I, p. 243.
[2] Ellis, vol. I, p. 308; vol. II, p. 77; Moerenhout, vol. I, p. 524; vol. II, p. 48; Tyerman, vol. I, p. 549; vol. II, p. 14; d'Urville, *Voy. Pitt.* vol. I, p. 537.
[3] Henry, *A.T.* pp. 304 *sqq.*
[4] Moerenhout, vol. I, pp. 485–9; Ellis, vol. I, pp. 230–3; Henry, *A.T.* pp. 230 *sqq.*
[5] Henry, *A.T.* pp. 383, 385, 387–8, 390.   [6] *Ibid.* p. 393.
[7] Smith, p. 28.   [8] *Ibid.* pp. 27 *sqq.*
[9] Nicholas, *J.P.S.* vol. I, pp. 25 *sqq.*
[10] Quatrefages, p. 195.   [11] Cf. Smith, p. 32.
[12] *Ibid.* pp. 32 *sq.*   [13] Nicholas, *J.P.S.* vol. I, p. 25.
[14] Tyerman, vol. I, p. 254.

the head chief or king of the island.[1] He was a navigator and adventurer, and a great thief.[2] Tyerman and Bennet say that he was so subtle and audacious a robber that even the altars and *marae* of the gods were not safe from him; that to his skill in thieving were added the accomplishments of lying, debauchery, and murder; and that he was famous for his ability in managing a canoe and playing the pirate at sea.[3]

Hiro was a great navigator and legends of his journeys are given by various writers.[4] After Hiro's death his skull was preserved in the *marae* at Opoa in Ra'iatea, which he himself had built, and his hair was, it is said, put into the body of Oro's image there, and he was enrolled among the gods.[5] He became the god of thieves in the Society Islands[6] and in Mangaia;[7] and in the Society group he was also a god of the sea,[8] or at all events of sailors.[9] In the Society Islands his worship prevailed throughout the whole group;[10] and he was served with scarcely less devotion than Oro himself.[11] His devotees were not so much the common people as the chiefs, including the principal chiefs.[12] Great deeds were credited to him in this group. He fought with Oro, threw him down, and lay upon him.[13] He had a struggle with Tane in which he pursued this great god up to the vast regions beyond the ninth heaven, and conquered him.[14] Various natural features in the Society Islands were associated with the legends of Hiro.[15] Although Hiro was a sea god, his chief activities seem to have been connected with his office of god of thieves. In the Society Islands a prayer for success would be offered to him before a thieving expedition.[16] The operations of his votaries were conducted in darkness, at the change of the moon; and while the husband went forth to rob, the wife prayed for his success. If a hog were stolen, an inch or two of the end of the tail was thought a sufficient thank-offering for Hiro. The thief went to the *marae* and laid this on the ground, offering it

---

[1] Quatrefages, p. 186.   [2] *Ibid.* p. 195.
[3] Tyerman, vol. I, p. 255.
[4] Henry, *A.T.* pp. 537 *sqq.*; Smith, pp. 243 *sq.*; Nicholas, *J.P.S.* vol. I, pp. 25 *sq.*; cf. also Stair, chap. XXII.
[5] Tyerman, vol. I, p. 255.
[6] Ellis, vol. I, p. 333; Tyerman, vol. I, p. 91; Quatrefages, p. 186; Moerenhout, vol. I, p. 446.   [7] Gill, *L.S.I.* p. 49.
[8] Ellis, vol. I, p. 328.   [9] Quatrefages, p. 186.
[10] Tyerman, vol. I, p. 254.   [11] *Ibid.* vol. II, p. 11.
[12] *Ibid.* vol. I, pp. 91, 255.   [13] *Ibid.* p. 255.
[14] Quatrefages, p. 186.
[15] *Ibid.* p. 186; cf. Ellis, vol. I, p. 328; Tyerman, vol. I, pp. 253 *sq.*; *J.P.S.* vol. II, pp. 30 *sqq.*   [16] Quatrefages, p. 195.

to the god, and, it is said, begging him not to tell.[1] A band of robbers would sometimes sally forth under the leadership of a priest, and spread terror through the surrounding country.[2] Thieves carried with them a dragonfly, for this insect was the shadow of Hiro.[3]

It should be noted that Henry considers that Hiro the navigator was a being distinct from Hiro, the god of thieves, who was, she says, his patron.[4]

The names of a large number of Society Island deities, some perhaps island gods and others district or village gods, are given by writers. There is some confusion in these names, and identities can in some cases neither be assumed nor rejected; and so little is said about these gods that an attempt to introduce them all here would involve little more than a series of lists. Anderson, G. Forster, and J. R. Forster supply lists of islands with their respective tutelary gods;[5] the lists are similar to one another, but not identical, and most of the gods are well-known deities, the name of Oro being specially prominent. G. Forster says that in every island they had a different god.[6] As regards gods of districts and villages, the information at our disposal is vague and indefinite. There were what Ellis calls local and departmental gods. Anderson says that not only the several islands, but the several parts of those islands had their different gods, and that the inhabitants of each place "no doubt think they have chosen the most eminent". He also explains that if people were not pleased with the behaviour of their god they would choose another in his place, illustrating his statement by the example of the desertion by the Taiarabu people of their two tutelary deities, and adoption in their place of the victorious Oro.[7] Similarly Moerenhout says there were an infinite number of local deities, some dwelling in the waters, others in woods, others again on the tops of mountains, and so on; and that every object, substance, and place had a spiritual being as its guardian.[8] So, as regards what may be called departmental gods, Moerenhout says that every work of man had its tutelar and protecting deity, and he gives lists of a number of these.[9] Andia y Varela

[1] Tyerman, vol. I, p. 91. [2] Ellis, vol. III, p. 9.
[3] Henry, *A.T.* p. 391. [4] *Ibid.* p. 552.
[5] Cook, vol. VI, p. 160; G. Forster, *Voy.* vol. II, p. 151; J. R. Forster, *Obs.* p. 539.
[6] G. Forster, *Voy.* vol. II, p. 150; cf. J. R. Forster, *Obs.* p. 539.
[7] Cook, vol. VI, pp. 148 *sq.*
[8] Moerenhout, vol. I, p. 451; cf. Ellis, vol. I, p. 330.
[9] Moerenhout, vol. I, pp. 451 *sqq.*

says that the people had several different gods; if they were sailing they had one for the wind, another for the sea, and another for fishing, to whom they would dedicate their first catch by throwing a morsel of it back into the sea; and they had another god for their daily sustenance, for whom they set apart a little snack of each victual before beginning to eat.[1]

Hiro was a sea god but, according to Ellis, Tuaraatai and Ruahatu were their chief marine deities; they (and apparently other sea gods) were spoken of as *atua mao* or shark gods, because they were believed to employ the large blue shark as the agent of their vengeance.[2] Moerenhout gives the names of twelve gods, the patrons of navigators, invoked before going on voyages; the name of Ruahatu appears in this list, but not that of Tuaraatai.[3] Ellis says there were numerous fishermen's gods, of whom the most important were Tamai or Tahaura and Teraimatiti.[4] Moerenhout supplies the names of five of these gods, including Tahaura and Parai mavete (probably the same as Teraimatiti).[5] The deity of those who made nets was Matatini or Auta, and the first wetting of a new net was the occasion for prayers and offerings to him.[6] There were gods of the air, the chief of which were, according to Ellis, Veromatautoru and Tairibu, brother and sister to the children of Tangaroa, and dwelling near the great rock forming the foundation of the world. Hurricanes and tempests were supposed to be sent by them to punish such as neglected the worship of the gods. In stormy weather their compassion was sought by the tempest-driven mariners at sea and their friends on shore. It was believed that liberal presents would purchase a calm, and if a first attempt failed renewed offerings were made. The same gods were appealed to for the production of storms, and in case of invasion by a hostile fleet large offerings were made to them with prayers for its destruction.[7] It is stated that Tiipa, who was a god of the Pomare family, was also a god of winds.[8] Moerenhout says that the gods and goddesses of the valleys presided over agriculture, and he gives the names of thirteen of them.[9] Both Ellis and Moerenhout give the names of gods who were invoked by the *tahua faatiri*, or expelling priests, being supposed to be

[1] Corney, *Tahiti*, vol. II, p. 259. [2] Ellis, vol. I, pp. 328 *sq.*
[3] Moerenhout, vol. I, p. 452. [4] Ellis, vol. I, pp. 140, 329.
[5] Moerenhout, vol. I, p. 453.
[6] Ellis, vol. I, pp. 140, 142; cf. Moerenhout, vol. I, p. 453.
[7] Ellis, vol. I, pp. 329 *sq.* [8] L.M.S. *Trans.* vol. IV, p. 433.
[9] Moerenhout, vol. I, p. 452.

able to counteract the effects of sorcery and expel evil spirits; both writers include Ru and Temaru in their lists, and Ellis includes Tane.[1] Several doctor gods are mentioned, some apparently being connected with physic, and others with surgery, the help of the latter being invoked for righting dislocations, healing fractures, and so on.[2] Heva was the god of ghosts and apparitions.[3]

Turning now to departmental gods connected with crafts and occupations, we are told of a god of husbandry, and a god of carpenters, builders, canoe-wrights and all who worked in wood.[4] As regards canoes, it is stated that their construction was the subject of religious performances, the priests engaging in ceremonies, and numerous and costly offerings being made to the gods of the chief and of the profession of the craftsmen when the keel was laid, when the canoe was finished, and when it was launched. Even valuable canoes were often included in national offerings and were afterwards regarded as sacred to the service of the god.[5] There were also gods of thatchers, and especially of those who finished the angles where the thatch on each side was joined;[6] there were the patron gods of actors, singers, and the like, these deities presiding over the scenic performances, with their singing, music and dancing at festivals.[7] There was even a god of hairdressers and combers, whose help was invoked at toilet;[8] and there was, as we have seen, Hiro, the god of thieves.

On the question of the god of the dead, G. Forster and J. R. Forster say that Maui was the being with whom the souls of the departed lived and feasted.[9] Another belief was that Tangaroa was the god of the dead.[10]

Each family had its own gods;[11] and every father of a family might have a temple near his dwelling.[12] Temeharo, for example, was the principal god of the Pomare family, and extended his protection to the whole of Tahiti.[13] He was said to have been the son of Tane. Other gods of the Pomare family were Terii-

[1] Ellis, vol. I, p. 333; Moerenhout, vol. I, p. 453.
[2] Ellis, vol. I, p. 333; cf. Moerenhout, vol. I, pp. 445, 453.
[3] Ellis, vol. I, p. 333.   [4] Ibid.   [5] Ibid. p. 164.
[6] Ibid. p. 333; cf. Moerenhout, vol. I, p. 453.
[7] Moerenhout, vol. I, p. 453; cf. Ellis, vol. I, p. 332.
[8] Ellis, vol. I, p. 136.
[9] G. Forster, Voy. vol. II, p. 151; J. R. Forster, Obs. p. 553.
[10] J.P.S. vol. II, p. 58; vol. X, p. 51.
[11] Lesson, Voy. vol. I, p. 399; cf. Tyerman, vol. I, p. 247.
[12] Moerenhout, vol. I, p. 283.
[13] Lesson, Voy. vol. I, p. 400; cf. L.M.S. Trans. vol. IV, p. 433.

taputura and Tiipa.[1] No doubt the family god of a great chief would become a powerful god of his subjects, or perhaps an important god would be selected as his family god. The *oromatua* and *tii* would probably be primarily family supernatural beings; though the more important and powerful of them would acquire a wider influence.[2]

MARQUESAS

Atea (light) and his wife Atanua (the dawn), the great beings whose names are so prominent in the Marquesan poem of creation, and to the former of whom was credited the lifting-up of the sky from the earth in another legend, were recognized gods of the group. Writers refer to a god Oataia, who must probably be identified with Atea. According to Mathias, Atea or Akea was the god or father of stones,[3] and Atanua, also called Mou-mouou, was the mother of the waters of the ocean.[4] Christian says that Atea was the god of husbandry, the patron saint of agriculture and planting, who brought good seasons with re-freshing rain. He does not mention Atea's wife, Atanua, but speaks of a wife Vene, who bore the kava plant in the land of Ahu-Take, whence it was brought across the seas to the Marquesas. Another wife of Atea was Puoo, who brought forth Mako, the shark. His progeny also included Kiva, the smooth rocks, and Kakaho, the reed-grass.[5]

Mathias refers to a tradition, of which he had not himself heard when in the Marquesas, though he does not dispute its existence, that Atea and Atanua had arrived at a distant period from another island bringing with them breadfruit, sugarcane, and other plants, and settled down and had forty children, who scattered over the country, and multiplied exceedingly.[6] Porter is evidently referring to the same matter when he says that Gattenewa (the most powerful chief of the valley of the Tieuhoy) traced his ancestry back eighty-eight generations, reaching the period when the island was first peopled—to the arrival of Oataia, or daylight, and Anaoona his wife, from Vavao. He says it is certain that this chief drew his greatest consideration from inheriting the honours of the great Otaia, and an alliance with

[1] L.M.S. *Trans.* vol. IV, p. 433.   [2] *Ibid.*
[3] On a similar being called Ata, cf. Tautain, *L'Anthro.* vol. VIII, pp. 538 *sq.*   [4] Mathias, p. 44.
[5] Christian, *J.P.S.* vol. IV, p. 189; cf. p. 187.
[6] Mathias, p. 6.

him was sought by every family of considerable rank in the island of Nukuhiva.[1]

There is very little information concerning the other island gods of the Marquesas. Tohe Tika was a thunder god, and he and Ao-mei (or Hau-mei) and Haka-nau are referred to as gods who ate human flesh, the latter having a special partiality for his victims' eyes.[2] Tohe Tika is also referred to as a much dreaded god of thunder, violent rain, and war, by Christian.[3] He was the patron saint of the Haapa valleys.[4] Haamata-Kee was a goddess who had come overseas from the magic land of Aitua, and taught the people to make the great stone tiki or images.[5] Hanau was a god of fish.[6] Te-anu-ti-ananua, also called Kee-moana, was the Marquesan god of the sea;[7] the second of these names is probably only descriptive, iki moana meaning "god of the sea". Moe-Hakaava was the god of fishermen.[8] There were two wicked gods, called Tuivivi and Potoro fiti who chained men.[9] Oupu was their goddess of paradise; but Tiki and Hina were the gods of the underworld.[10]

Christian gives a long list of Marquesan gods, which refers to departmental gods among others, including gods of thieves, of lust and prostitution, of marriage and concubinage, of childbirth, of fishermen, of songs and poetry, of dances, of housebuilding and carpentry, of feasts and kava-drinking; also gods of certain specific trees, plants and animals.[11] They also evidently had district and family gods.[12] Handy provides additional information on the gods of the Marquesas.[13]

PAUMOTU

As we have seen, Atea was known in the Paumotu islands. He is probably also the Gambier Island god Tea, who was credited with having created the water, the wind, and the sun.[14] The Society Island god Oro was also known in that island.[15] They had a god Tairi, who was supposed to make the thunder

[1] Porter, vol. II, p. 30; cf. d'Urville, Voy. pitt. vol. I, p. 501.
[2] Mathias, pp. 42 sq.
[3] Christian, J.P.S. vol. IV, pp. 188, 190.   [4] Ibid. p. 190.
[5] Ibid. p. 189.   [6] Mathias, p. 44.
[7] Christian, J.P.S. vol. IV, p. 189.   [8] Ibid. p. 190.
[9] Mathias, p. 43.   [10] Christian, J.P.S. vol. IV, p. 190.
[11] Ibid. pp. 189 sq.
[12] Cf. Tautain, L'Anthro. vol. VIII, pp. 540 n. 1, 677; Christian, J.P.S. vol. IV, pp. 188, 190, 202; Shillibeer, p. 39.
[13] Handy, N.C.M. pp. 244 sqq.; M.L. passim.
[14] A.P.F. vol. XIV, p. 332.   [15] Moerenhout, vol. I, p. 110.

roar,[1] and who may be identical with the Tahitian god Teiri and the Tahitian Eri-t-era, spoken of as the king of sun or light,[2] may have been the same god. Arikitenou was king of the ocean, saw to the preservation of the various sorts of fish, and gave success to the fishermen who invoked him. A-nghi directed storms and caused famine by his burning breath or devastating fury. Mapitoiti, the most malevolent of their deities, was the god of death.[3] There were evidently family gods, for it is said that everyone had his peculiar deity.[4]

Henry says that Tangaroa, Tu, Tane, and Atea were the chief gods of the Tuamotus, and after them came Ti'i.[5] She also mentions the names of several other beings connected with the cosmogony in her account of the Tuamotuan creation.[6]

Recent field researches in the Tuamotus by Stimson suggest that there existed an esoteric cult of a supreme being called Kiho, who might be equated to the Maori Io. In spite of the vast mass of textual material collected by Stimson, the conditions under which his information was obtained must lead us to regard his conclusions with caution.[7]

ROTUMA

Rahou was the chief island god of Rotuma,[8] and the legend as to his creation of the island by throwing a basket of sand into the sea has already been told;[9] Gardiner says that Tangaroa had a son Toirangoni, personified in the turtle, to whom in the sea were ascribed the same attributes as those of his father on land; but Gardiner could not find that any acts of worship were offered to him.[10] Ngarangsau ruled over *Li'mara*, the abode of ghosts in the sea.[11] There were also hundreds of lesser gods, incarnate in fish, birds, and the like, and also deified chiefs.[12] There were also tutelar gods of the different *hoang* or family groups.[13]

FOTUNA

There is no reference to any prominent island god in Fotuna. Grézel mentions a god Taofialiki, but tells us nothing about

[1] *A.P.F.* vol. XIV, p. 322. [2] Bougainville, p. 255.
[3] *A.P.F.* vol. XIV, p. 332.
[4] Beechey, vol. I, p. 243; cf. d'Urville, *Voy. pitt.* vol. I, p. 250.
[5] Henry, *A.T.* p. 109. [6] *Ibid.* pp. 347 sqq.
[7] Stimson, *T.R.* and *Kiho-Tumu*, passim.
[8] *A.P.F.* vol. XX, p. 363. [9] *Beliefs*, vol. I, pp. 70–1.
[10] Gardiner, *J.R.A.I.* vol. XXVII, p. 467. [11] Hocart, *Man*, No. 75, p. 130.
[12] *A.P.F.* vol. XX, p. 363.
[13] Gardiner, *J.R.A.I.* vol. XXVII, p. 466.

him.[1] Percy Smith says the principal gods were Faka-Veli-Kele, Songia and Fitu, but tells us nothing specific of the two latter. He says that all evils were attributed to these gods, who persecuted the people with sickness and death. Invocations and offerings were made to them on several occasions; each god had a separate house, and each was supposed to have power over a different part of the body, and was the recipient of offerings in case of sickness or disease affecting the part under his control, the illness always being attributed to his eating it.[2] Below these gods there was a swarm of inferior spirits called *atua mouri*, who abode in living men or women and their descendants in hereditary succession, and from whom also, it was said, all ills came.[3] It seems clear that these *atua mouri* were family gods;[4] probably they were dead relations.

MANIHIKI AND RAKAHANGA

There is little information as to the island gods of Manihiki, beyond the bare reference by Turner to three deities, Hikasora, Tupua Lenga, and Leulu Leunga, each of whom had a separate *marae*.[5] Dr Buck refers to the two "stolen gods", Te Puarenga and Te Uru-renga, and to a third god Hika-hara, who was stated to have "drifted ashore". The latter statement is of some interest. According to Dr Buck, what really drifted ashore was a log from foreign lands. This log was taken and placed outside the chief's house, and in the morning objects which had been placed on and against it were found scattered. This apparent power to repel objects led to the conclusion that it possessed *mana* and it was subsequently deified as the god Hika-hara.[6]

EASTER ISLAND

As we have seen above the chief gods of Easter Island were, according to Geiseler, Make-make and Haua, to whom first-fruits of all the productions of the soil were offered.[7] He tells us nothing more about Haua, but we know a little about Make-make. He was represented by the eggs of the sea birds of Motu-nui islet, on the south-west side of the Rana Kao crater,

[1] Grézel, p. 256. [2] Smith, *J.P.S.* vol. I, pp. 44 *sq.*
[3] *A.P.F.* vol. xv, p. 39; cf. Smith, *J.P.S.* vol. I, p. 44.
[4] Cf. Bourdin, p. 442. [5] Turner, p. 279.
[6] Te Rangi Hiroa, *M. & R.* pp. 205–7. This sanctification of objects washed ashore is paralleled in Tikopia, where certain rusty nails in a piece of driftwood were taken by the natives and incorporated into their ritual scheme, becoming objects of superlative sanctity. [7] Geiseler, p. 31.

and these eggs might only be collected in the months of July, August, and September, being taboo at all other times. He was also worshipped in the form of a carving or painting of a sea bird.[1] Thomson, in discussing the Easter Island rock-carvings, says the most common figure was a mythical animal, half human in form, with bowed back and long claw-like legs and arms, representing the god Make-make (he spells it Meke-meke), the great spirit of the sea, and he illustrates some of these carvings.[2] In three of these illustrations the bird-like forms of the head and beak are obvious; the fourth does not seem to suggest a bird at all. Though the ideas of the people on the subject of creation seem to have been dim and devoid of special legends, it was believed that Make-make had created the earth, sun, moon, stars, and everything else.[3] The people believed in one spirit god, Make-make, who made man grow from the ground.[4] He was their most dreaded god, and it was believed that, though he protected the souls of the good, who might sleep on the island under his protection after death, he killed and ate the souls of those whose lives had been evil.[5] According to Geiseler, the god was never directly worshipped, but only through his images;[6] on the other hand, Thomson is apparently referring to Make-make when he says that in performing ceremonies necessary on declaration of war, the warriors first made obeisance to the sky, each one repeating the prayer, "May we be killed in battle if we neglect to worship the Great Spirit!"[7] The importance of Make-make and his sea birds' eggs is illustrated by the annual egg-gathering performances. It should be noted that the festival took place, when the sea birds were beginning to nest, at the edge of the great volcano Kao, which forms the south promontory of the island, and near which was, as we have seen, the islet the eggs of whose sea birds were sacred to Make-make; and that the winner of the competition was he who was able to climb the rocks of the islet and bring back the first egg, and that in the following ceremony everyone had one of these eggs in his hand.[8] Thomson refers to the idea that the successful competitor was such because he had won the approval of the great spirit Make-make.[9]

[1] Geiseler, p. 31.
[2] W. J. Thomson, pp. 481 sq. and Fig. 8, and Plates 15, 17, 18.
[3] Geiseler, p. 33.
[4] Palmer, *J.E.S.* N.S. vol. I, p. 372.   [5] Geiseler, p. 31.
[6] *Ibid.*   [7] W. J. Thomson, p. 519.
[8] Lapelin, *R.M.C.* vol. xxv, pp. 109 sq.; cf. W. J. Thomson, pp. 482 sq.
[9] W. J. Thomson, pp. 482 sq.

There is a little information as to a few more Easter Island gods. Mea Ika was a fish god. Thomson in describing the stone representing him says these gods were never common, being possessed by communities or clans.[1] He may be referring to the same god when he says that fishermen were always provided with the stone god that was supposed to be emblematic of the spirit having cognizance of the fish.[2] Mea Kahi—the bonito—[3] may have been the same god. There was as we have seen a tradition connected with the substitution of bone for stone fish-hooks, of a fisherman spending the whole night worshipping Mea Kahi.[4] Moi-mare was apparently the god of bananas, who was worshipped at the time of their ripening.[5] Medicine was produced by the god Aoevai and the goddess Kava Kohekoe.[6] There was a god of thieves under whose patronage successful operations were believed to be accomplished, and it was only when these were not sanctioned by him that thefts were detected.[7]

We are told of a god whose image was the figure of a lizard, while that of another represented an eel;[8] and a god of dancing, whose image was only brought to special feasts, its appearance causing great excitement.[9] Lapelin says priests spoke in the names of many gods, including gods of good, evil, theft, war, harvest, lust, and so on.[10] Reference has already been made to Thomson's long list of gods and goddesses whose marriages produced all sorts of natural phenomena.[11]

AUSTRAL ISLANDS

The chief feature of interest concerning the island gods of the Austral group is that in the island of Rurutu they had a *marae* of the Society Island god Oro.[12] Williams refers to a god Aa as their national deity, being a deified ancestor by whom the island had been peopled.[13] Ellis says the principal god of the island of Rapa (near the Austral group) was Paparua, immanent in a coconut husk cylinder;[14] and it is stated that this god was appealed to for victory in war, recovery from sickness and abundance of turtle.[15] Another god of Rapa was Poere, represented by a stone in the ground, who was supposed to control the supply of water in the

[1] W. J. Thomson, p. 537. [2] *Ibid.* p. 470. [3] *Ibid.* p. 537.
[4] *Ibid.* p. 533. [5] *Ibid.* p. 53. [6] *Ibid.* p. 521. [7] *Ibid.* p. 465.
[8] Geiseler, p. 32. [9] *Ibid.* p. 48.
[10] Lapelin, *R.M.C.* vol. xxxv, p. 111. [11] See above, p. 33.
[12] Ellis, vol. III, p. 397. [13] Williams, pp. 43 *sq.*
[14] Ellis, vol. III, p. 364. [15] *Ibid.*

springs, and was invoked on the launching of a canoe and the opening of a newly built house.[1] It is said that the Rurutu people had family gods.[2] Aitken says that Taio Aia was the supreme god of Rurutu, and mentions two lesser "presumably local" gods, Terii Rerehiti and Rua Paauri.[3]

TOKELAU

Lister refers to two gods of the island of Fakaofo. One of these, called Fakafotu, was the god of storms and hurricanes; and thunder was called his anger; the other was Semoana, whose stone stood beside that of Tui-tokelau, but was smaller.[4]

WALLIS ISLAND

The French missionaries refer to Kakau and Finas as the two powerful deities of Wallis Island, and say there was an annual feast in their honour.[5] There seem to have been a number of other gods, though we are not told their names. One of them was king over the others who were his ministers. One of these looked after the sick; another saw to the observance of taboo; there was a god who decided upon peace or war; another had charge of the winds and waves, and protected the crops. There were also a great number of minor deities.[6]

ELLICE ISLANDS

According to Murray the people of the island of Nanomea (Ellice group) had ten principal gods, but he does not name them.[7] Turner says the chief gods of this island were Maumau, Laukiti, Folaha and Telahi, each of whom had a temple and priests, and strangers arriving at the island were not allowed to communicate with the people until they had been taken to each of these four temples and prayers had been offered to the god to drive away any disease or treachery which the strangers might have brought with them.[8] He says the principal gods of Nanomanga were Foelangi and Maumau, each of whom had a temple;[9] that the chief gods of Nukufetau were Foilape and Tevae;[10] that in Vaitupu (Oaitupu) Moumousia, Tapufatu, Terupe, and Moekilaipuka were regarded as the four gods who ruled the earth

[1] Ellis, vol. III, pp. 364 sq.
[2] Tyerman, vol. I, p. 508.
[3] Aitken, Tubuai, p. 115.
[4] Lister, J.R.A.I. vol. XXI, p. 51.
[5] A.P.F. vol. XIII, p. 15.
[6] Ibid. pp. 12 sq.
[7] Murray, 40 years, p. 408.
[8] Turner, p. 291.
[9] Ibid. p. 289.
[10] Ibid. p. 285.

(Taatamaofa being the king of heaven) and that at death these four tried to keep the soul with them on earth, but if persuasion failed, sent it on to the heavens.[1] Kennedy, however, states that the chief guardian spirits of Vaitupu were Tinai (or Teinati) a female, and her two brothers Te Moloti and Foilape, and he also refers to an unnamed deity who dwelt in the sky.[2]

Perhaps the chief feature of interest in the Ellice Island gods is the connection with Samoa which the presence of some of them suggests. Le Folasa, for instance, was, as we have seen, a Samoan god. Murray, after mentioning the ten principal gods of Nanomea, says there were various objects which the people held sacred, the chief of which seemed to be the skull of one of their ancestors whom they called Folasa.[3] Folaha, mentioned by Turner, was evidently the same god, and Foilape may have been.

Tinilau was the hero of a Funafuti story of the seduction of Sina.[4]

The god Kulu was the principal deity of the island of Niutao, where prayers were offered to him at the evening meal for rain, coconuts, fish and freedom from disease;[5] he was also one of the gods of Vaitupu and Nanomanga.[6] Tufakoula, incarnate in a sea bird, was one of the early gods worshipped in Funafuti;[7] and Tafakula, presumably the same god, was worshipped in Vaitupu and Nanomanga.[8] It is stated that both these gods, Kulu and Tafakula, were deified Samoan chiefs, as also were the deities Foelangi, Foilape, Laukiti, and Maumau mentioned above.[9]

[1] Turner, p. 283.
[2] Kennedy, *C.V.* p. 147; cf. Wilkes, vol. v, p. 43; Hale, p. 166; Turner, p. 281; Powell, *A.A.A.S.* vol. vi, pp. 609 *sq.*; Hedley, pp. 46 *sq.*
[3] Murray, 40 *years*, p. 408. [4] Mrs David, pp. 93 *sqq.*
[5] Turner, p. 288. [6] Powell, *A.A.A.S.* vol. vi, p. 609.
[7] Hedley, p. 46. [8] Powell, *A.A.A.S.* vol. vi, p. 609.
[9] *Ibid.* pp. 609 *sq.*; cf. Gill, *Jottings*, p. 21.

CHAPTER IV

THE WORSHIP OF THE GODS

FOR convenience of classification we have separated religious ideology from religious practices, and have so far been concerned with the former. It must, however, be emphasized that these two aspects of religious institutions are closely interconnected, and that it is impossible to assign any phenomenon connected with Polynesian religion to one or other of these categories exclusively. For example, in dealing with the gods, we have had occasion to mention their worship, and the purposes for which they were invoked, a subject which is perhaps more closely connected with religious practices than with religious beliefs. However, the actual category in which we place these subjects does not matter very much, so long as we bear in mind the fact that every rite is related to some system of religious belief, and, conversely, that every religious belief of any importance is correlated directly or indirectly with human behaviour.

INDIVIDUAL AND FAMILY PRAYERS

In regard to prayers offered to the gods by individuals, we are told very little. Moerenhout says the Society islanders repeated their prayers on getting up in the morning, before meals, before going to sleep, and, indeed, before every act of their lives;[1] and Ellis says prayer was offered by these people before eating, tilling the ground, planting gardens, building houses, launching canoes, casting nets, and at the beginnings and ends of journeys.[2] In addition to the family prayers offered up at the domestic *marae* by the head of the household, any member of the family might go there to present petitions to the gods.[3]

The following is a translation by Moerenhout of a Society Island evening prayer:

> Save me! save me!
> It is evening;
> It is evening of the gods.
> Watch near me, O my God!
> Near me, O my Lord!

[1] Moerenhout, vol. I, p. 391 *n.*   [2] Ellis, vol. I, p. 350.
[3] Henry, *A.T.* p. 143.

Keep me from enchantment;
From sudden death;
From evil conduct;
From wishing evil (cursing) or from being cursed;
From secret practices (plots)
And from quarrels over boundary-marks.
Let peace reign far and wide round us, O my God!
Preserve me from the furious warrior,
From him who roams about furious (delights to terrify)
Whose hair is always standing on end.
Let me and my spirit live
And rest in peace this night, O my God![1]

In the Hervey Islands there were prayers for everything; for success in battle; for change of wind (to overwhelm an adversary fishing alone in his canoe, or that an intended voyage of the worshipper might be propitious); for the growth of coconuts; for the success of a thieving expedition; that the hook or net might catch fish; that the worshipper's kite might outfly the others; or that a strong tooth might take the place of his child's first tooth.[2] Few middle-aged men in the Hervey Islands were without a number of these prayers, which, indeed, formed an important part of a man's equipment in life. Some of them were of a hostile character, and were uttered in an inaudible way, lest they should be heard by a stranger, who would thereby become armed with a dangerous weapon of offence. If a plantation was to be robbed the appropriate prayer, to be fully effective, had to be uttered near it; if a man was to be clubbed in his sleep the prayer was not spoken until the hut was in sight. It is said that they generally had one or two prayers reserved for the event of a premonition of death in sickness or battle; for if a man's last bit of "wisdom" had been exhausted he would die.[3]

Gill gives an example of a Hervey Island prayer uttered on reaching the house of the victim of a thieving or murdering expedition. It was the prayer of a party, led by their chief, and not of a solitary individual; but it illustrates the nature of these buccaneering prayers.

Here is our sure helper.
Arise on our behalf;
Stand at the door of this house,
Oh thou divine Omataianuku!
Oh thou divine Outuutu-the-tall,
And Avaava-the-tall!

[1] Moerenhout, vol. II, pp. 81 *sqq.* [2] Gill, *S.P.N.G.* pp. 21 *sq.*
[3] *Ibid.* p. 22.

We are on a thieving (or murdering) expedition.
Be close to our left side to give aid.
Let all be wrapped in sleep.
Be as a lofty coconut tree to support us.
Oh house, thou art doomed by our God!
Cause all things to sleep.
Let profound sleep overspread this dwelling.
Owner of the house, sleep on!
Threshold of this house, sleep on!
Ye tiny insects inhabiting this house, sleep on!

This last line was then repeated many times, except that in each line the things addressed were different—these being first the beetles in the house, then the earwigs in it, then the ants, then the dry grass spread over it, then, in succession, the different parts of the house, the central post, ridge pole, main rafters, cross-beams, little rafters, minor posts, covering of the ridge pole, reed sides and thatch; after which the prayer concluded thus:

The first of its inmates unluckily awaking
Put soundly to sleep again.
If the divinity so please, man's spirit must yield.
Oh Rongo, grant thou complete success![1]

Loeb gives the following translation of a prayer addressed to Tagaloa by a *tika* (dart) player in Niue:

Tagaloa, bend down from the sky, bless me.
Bring and turn thy *tika*, bless me.
The *hega* fly together coming from Tonga, bless me.
They come and separate near the coast, bless me.
To bring and turn thy *tika*, bless me.
The *tika* comes and stops before the mark, bless me.
Leave my *tika* so that no one will beat it, bless me.
Atuvave (a good thrower) is lined up, bless me.
Leave my *tika* so that no one will beat it, bless me.[2]

Loeb also gives a number of other invocations from Niue, pointing out the close inter-relationship between prayers, charms and curses; and he also indicates the way in which these shade off into purely "magical" formulae.[3]

Very little information seems to be available as to the character of daily family prayer; but it may almost be assumed that it would be somewhat similar to that of individual prayer, but probably longer and more formal. As we have seen, in the Society Islands the head of the family officiated as its priest and

[1] Gill, *Myths*, pp. 150 *sq.*
[2] Loeb, *Niue*, p. 181; cf. Firth, "A Dart Match in Tikopia", *Oceania*, vol. i, pp. 74 *sqq.*   [3] Loeb, *Niue*, pp. 180–4.

they had their domestic temples. As regards Samoa, we are told that the father of the family was the high priest, and usually offered a short prayer at the evening meal that they might be preserved from fires, sickness, war and death. He, also, would occasionally direct a family feast in honour of their household gods; and on these occasions a cup of kava was poured out as a drink-offering. All this was done in the family house in which they assembled, under the belief that the gods had a spiritual presence there.[1] In the Marquesas the same tone and order were observed at a family gathering for prayer and religious feasting as at a national one, the only difference being that the number of worshippers was smaller.[2]

PUBLIC PRAYER

Society Islands

In regard to the character of public prayers, Moerenhout says the liturgy of the Society Islands was composed of a multitude of long prayers, containing catalogues of the gods, and innumerable legends and traditions, all expressed in metaphorical and obscure language, and requiring long practice and prodigious memory.[3] He thinks that even the priests who recited these traditions hardly understood even their literal meaning.[4] Ellis describes these prayers as abounding in expressions and images of licentiousness and crime.[5] He gives an example of a morning prayer, called "the awakening of the gods". This began "Awake Ru; awake Tane; awake unnumbered progeny of Tane; awake Tu; awake Tuaratai...", and so on, about twenty gods being called upon by name, and directed to the birds, and to Roo, the god of morning, and parent of clouds, to the formation and increase of clouds, to the blue cloud, the red cloud, the low hungry cloud and the horned or pointed cloud. The gods were then directed to mark the progress of Roo, the property or offerings of Roo, his plaited coconut leaf, through which his power was conveyed to his image, or through which he received the spirit of the offerings. All the gods were then invoked to enter their *tapu*, or coconut leaves, and open their mouths wide. Each one was then addressed by name, as food was offered to him; after which they were invoked to take off the sacredness or restriction,

---

[1] Turner, p. 18.   [2] Mathias, p. 63.
[3] Moerenhout, vol. I, p. 504; cf. Ellis, vol. I, pp. 342 sq.
[4] Moerenhout, vol. I, p. 443.   [5] Ellis, vol. I, p. 343.

and to hold it fast, apparently so that men might attend to their avocations with safety.[1] Moerenhout distinguishes between *ouhou* (prayers), *tarotaro* (invocations) and *hamori* (adoration and praise);[2] Ellis says that *pure* was the designation of prayer, *tarotaro* was the invocation preparatory to prayer, and *hamori* was praise or worship.[3]

Turning to the ceremonies themselves we must mention in connection with the Society Islands the importance of exact accuracy in the repetition of prayers by the priests; the slightest mistake was fatal, and necessitated, not merely the cessation of the invocation, but a suspension of the service which was being held, however important the occasion might be; for a mistake was the worst of omens. These priests, therefore, had to be practising continually, as repeated errors would immediately bring them into disrepute.[4] They had, however, aids to memory, not, it would seem, as to the details of each prayer, but as to the sequence in rotation of the prayers. Moerenhout says that they had for guides, in order of their exercises, bundles of little sticks of different thicknesses and dimensions, one of which they drew out and put aside as they finished each prayer.[5] Ellis says that small pieces of coconut leaf were suspended in different parts of the temple, to remind the priests of the order to be observed.[6] Bligh gives an account, which seems to be another version of the same thing. He found, collected together at the temple, a number of people, among whom were sixteen priests, engaged in prayer. These priests were all sitting on their heels; in front of them was a pole, covered with a plaited coconut branch; and before each of them were a number of small pieces of coconut leaf, also plaited, and each of them had a similar piece round his wrist. When one of them had uttered a short sentence he was answered by all the rest together; and, when a few of these sentences and responses had been repeated, they all rose and placed their pieces of coconut leaf at the foot of the pole, afterwards returning and repeating other prayers, in the same way, until all the pieces of coconut leaf were exhausted, on which the ceremony ended.[7] Bligh assumed that the first repeater of the prayers was the chief priest and those who responded were inferior;[8] but possibly the former was only acting as leader for the time being, for Moerenhout says that, the prayers being so excessively long, the priests,

[1] Ellis, vol. I, pp. 343 sq.
[3] Ellis, vol. I, p. 343.
[5] *Ibid.* p. 504.
[7] Bligh, pp. 105 sq.
[2] Moerenhout, vol. I, p. 504.
[4] Moerenhout, vol. I, pp. 504 sq.
[6] Ellis, vol. I, p. 343.
[8] *Ibid.* p. 106.

of whom there were many, used to relieve one another from time to time.[1] Forster, in describing public prayer by the high priest, says the beneficent gods were addressed in prayers, which were not pronounced aloud, but only distinguished and made known by the motion of the lips;[2] a statement which, unless applicable only to a special ceremony, seems hardly compatible with the evidence of the other witnesses.

A Society Island priest prayed at the temple with one knee on the ground or sitting cross-legged on a large stone, near the middle of the enclosure, leaning against a pillar from four to five feet high, placed there for the purpose.[3] According to Moerenhout, he faced the pyramid, on the top of which were the images of the gods, and sometimes looked in that direction; but generally he kept his head inclined.[4] Forster, on the other hand, still speaking of the high priest, says that he looked up to the skies, and the god was supposed to come down, unseen by all the people, and hold converse with him, which he alone could hear.[5] The priests usually addressed the god in an unpleasant, shrill, or chanting tone of voice, though at times the worship was extremely boisterous—especially in the northern islands of the group.[6]

MARQUESAS

The sacred songs of the Marquesas were evidently introduced into, and formed part of, their public prayers.[7] They also contained metaphorical and obscure expressions,[8] and many of them were intelligible only to the priests.[9] They were various; and in them were embodied all the traditions of the people—the story of the origin of their islands, the names of other islands in whose existence they believed, the genealogies of the chiefs, carried back to their first origin, the feats of their heroes and histories of wars and of all other events of which they professed any knowledge.[10]

The mode of addressing public prayers to the gods of the Marquesans has elements of similarity to that of the Society Islands. Only the priests took part in the chanting; and their method was for one only of these priests to repeat a few words,

[1] Moerenhout, vol. I, p. 504.   [2] Forster, *Voy.* vol. II, pp. 152 *sq.*
[3] Moerenhout, vol. I, pp. 507 *sq.*; cf. Ellis, vol. I, p. 343.
[4] Moerenhout, vol. I, p. 508.   [5] Forster, *Voy.* vol. II, p. 153.
[6] Ellis, vol. I, p. 343.   [7] See Mathias, p. 63.
[8] Mathias, p. 65.   [9] Stewart, vol. I, p. 249.
[10] *Ibid.*; cf. Mathias, p. 65.

which were afterwards taken up by the others; and the attitude of prayer was one of sitting cross-legged.[1] According to Mathias, however, the prayers were not, as in the Society Islands, ancient forms, carefully learnt. They were generally improvised to suit the occasion, very varied in character, monotonous and long, and chanted with much reverence. He draws a picture of a group of at least ten priests, old and young, ranged in a circle or semicircle, one chanting, and others responding, all acting with the utmost gravity, and two or three men beating time with their hands on large drums; whilst the general assembly (other than the priests), also sitting cross-legged, listened in reverent silence; and he says that whole nights were spent in these ceremonies, and sometimes a part of the day also; and that on special occasions, when some matter of great importance was impending, the praying might continue for a week or longer.[2] Stewart, who confirms Mathias in one or two particulars, describes this chanting prayer as being spoken in much prolonged notes, at the close of which the voice was shaken in a hoarse undulation; but he tells of another prayer, a sort of recitative, in which the priest declaimed with the utmost violence of voice and action, concluding with a sharp sound like the bark of a dog, directed towards the audience, who returned a suitable response in a general chorus resembling a low growl.[3]

MANGAIA

In Mangaia all the prayers were metrical, and were handed down with the utmost care from generation to generation.[4] The prayers offered to the gods worshipped at the national or tribal temples were called *karakia*, whilst those offered on minor occasions to lesser gods were called *pure*.[5] Offerings to the gods were accompanied by appropriate words, the length of the formula varying with the occasion.[6]

ELLICE ISLANDS

Kennedy gives the following translation of a pre-Christian Ellice Island prayer, which was delivered at a gathering in a meeting house for the purpose of supplicating divine aid in entertaining a band of visitors:

[1] Mathias, pp. 64 *sq.*
[2] *Ibid.* pp. 63 *sqq.*
[3] Stewart, vol. I, p. 249.
[4] Gill, *S.P.N.G.* p. 21.
[5] *Ibid.*
[6] Te Rangi Hiroa, *M.S.* p. 183.

PRIEST

O Thou who dwellest on high.
Look down on all your people
Bring up the vegetation on shore
That it may come up
To be your gift
To this congregation,
And dost thou look down on us with favour from above?

CONGREGATION

Favour!

PRIEST

And chase down from above
A school of whales
As your gift
To this congregation.
And dost thou look down on us with favour from above?

CONGREGATION

Favour!

PRIEST

Bring up a crowd of turtle,
A shoal of flying-fish,
A shoal of bonito,
As your gift
To this congregation.
And dost thou look down on us with favour from above?

CONGREGATION

Favour!

PRIEST

Chase hither from the south-east
A school of whales
As your gift
To this congregation.
And dost thou look down on us with favour from above?

CONGREGATION

Favour![1]

There are one or two points of general interest about this prayer. In the first place we know a little of the sociological context in which it was uttered, and in view of this its general intention becomes more significant. The importance of hospitality for all Polynesian peoples is well known. The entertainment of guests had important social implications—it was a means of establishing friendly relations and of making arrangements for political co-operation, marriages and other inter-tribal activities. It was governed by elaborate rules of etiquette, and generosity

[1] Kennedy, *C.V.* pp. 148–9.

was commended, just as meanness was despised. In view of all this the earnest plea for plenty, concretely expressed in the prayer under consideration, becomes significant in terms of a real social situation.

Another point of interest relates to the word translated "favour". In the original text this word is *mana*. The concept of *mana*, both in Melanesia and Polynesia, has been the subject of much discussion,[1] and to deal with the meaning of the word at all adequately would entail a digression on the general theory of primitive language. One or two points may, however, be mentioned.

In the first place there are a number of words by which the term *mana* may be translated—thus Handy[2] mentions power, might, influence, authority, strength, energy, skill, cleverness, intelligence, prestige, glory, majesty, effectual, and effective as various translations of *mana*. The multiplicity of the possible translations derives, of course, from the fact that there is no exact English equivalent of the term, and also from the number of different situations in which it was used. Its primary meaning seems to have been "effective" with the general implication that the efficacy so imputed went beyond that encountered in every-day life. But the different contexts in which the word was uttered gave to it a variety of shades of meaning. For example, in the text cited, the word *mana* seems to have had two distinct meanings when uttered by the priest and by the congregation respectively. In the line "And dost thou look down on us with favour from above"[3] it would perhaps be better translated by "grace", this word having the implication of specifically *divine* favour. On the other hand, when uttered by the congregation, it seems to be more closely equivalent to "amen"—a ritual affirmation of the fact that the worshippers in general associate themselves with the request uttered by the priest to the god.

Two points, then, emerge from the study of this prayer: Firstly, that native texts can only be understood in terms of their institutional setting—it is the urgent need to supply adequate hospitality which gives this prayer its meaning in terms of native life. And secondly, that native words cannot be "translated"

[1] See in particular F. R. Lehmann, *Mana, Der Begriff des "ausserordentlich Wirkungsvollen" bei Südseevölkern* (Leipzig, 1922), and Handy, *P.R.* pp. 26–34.
[2] *Loc. cit.*
[3] From the general context it would appear more probable that this line was uttered as a request or supplication rather than as a question, as suggested by the mark of interrogation in Kennedy's text.

by single English equivalents, though a rough approximation is necessary as a first step towards the understanding of their meaning. This must, however, be supplemented by a detailed study of the context of utterance, including the whole body of belief and practice which surrounds their use in actual speech.

POSSESSION AND INSPIRATION

Under these headings we shall include the phenomena of the supposed entry of the god into the body of the man, his consequent acquaintance with the wishes of the gods, or knowledge of coming events, and his exposition of these things to the people. This close association of humanity with the gods does not appear to have been nearly so close a monopoly of the priests as were invocation and intercession.

SOCIETY ISLANDS

Ellis says that in the Society Islands every island had its oracle, and divination in various forms was almost universally practised by the priests, Oro being the god who was supposed to inspire them, and Opoa, his reputed birth-place, being therefore the most celebrated oracle of the group.[1] He tells us that people, other than priests, had from time to time foretold events which were to happen at remote periods;[2] but it is clear that in this he is only referring to very occasional cases of distant prophecy.

Moerenhout says that the Society Island priests had allowed themselves to be supplanted as regards powers of divination, the role of the inspired generally being played by other people, and only occasionally by the priests.[3] He also says that the social rank of the person inspired was apparently immaterial—that anyone might be inspired.[4]

According to the missionaries of the *Duff*, some of the inspired priests were only visited each by one god, whilst others had many divine patrons; some, claiming acquaintance with the superior gods, were the most consequential and were treated with the greatest reverence.[5] Insane people were believed to be possessed or inspired by gods who had entered their bodies; therefore they were treated with the highest respect, and, though avoided, were not controlled.[6]

[1] Ellis, vol. I, pp. 370 sq. [2] *Ibid.* p. 382.
[3] Moerenhout, vol. I, p. 482. [4] *Ibid.* p. 479.
[5] Wilson, p. 337. [6] Ellis, vol. III, p. 40.

TONGA

In Tonga the priests were the people who were commonly inspired by the gods and were thus able to divine.[1] But this power was not confined to them; anyone, however low his rank, might be inspired.[2] Also, though the priests were seldom or never great chiefs,[3] the latter, and, we are told, King Finau, were sometimes inspired.[4] If the prophecy of a priest did not come true, no reflection seems to have fallen upon him; the belief being that the god, for some wise purpose, had misled the priest, or that the god had changed his mind, or spoken prematurely without consulting the other gods.[5]

SAMOA

In Samoa it was the priests who not only claimed to be the means of communication with the gods, but were believed to be possessed by them in all communications made to the worshippers; they also predicted events.[6] But here, as in the groups already considered, the official priesthood were not the only people blessed with these powers; for it was often believed that at times of family worship the god came among them, and spoke, not necessarily through the father, who was the family priest, but possibly through some other member of the family, telling them what to do in order to remove a present evil, or to avert a threatened one.[7] Lunatics also were supposed to be possessed;[8] and powers of inspiration were possessed by the *alataua*, the great orator-chiefs.[9]

HERVEY ISLANDS

The power of divination in Mangaia (Hervey Islands) is by the local legends traced back to their god Motoro, whose priests were the most powerful order in the island. This god, having been thrown by his brothers into the sea and drowned, was devoured as to his body by sharks, but his soul floated on a piece of hibiscus till it reached Mangaia, where it inhabited or possessed Papaaunuku, the first original priest of Motoro, thus making him deliver oracles.[10]

[1] Mariner, vol. II, pp. 87, 128.
[2] D'Urville, *Astro.* vol. IV, p. 84; cf. Mariner, vol. I, pp. 102 *sq.*
[3] Mariner, vol. II, pp. 87, 128.   [4] *Ibid.* p. 87.
[5] *Ibid.* p. 128.   [6] Brown, p. 228.
[7] Turner, p. 18; cf. Brown, p. 224.   [8] Brown, p. 181.
[9] *Systems*, vol. I, p. 82.   [10] Gill, *Myths*, p. 27.

When it was desired that the will of the gods should be known, the first step was to take a present to the priest, the present consisting of food and a bowl of kava, and its value depending upon the rank and means of the enquirer; the present might be carried by male slaves to the outskirts of the temple, but it was the enquirer whose duty it was to carry it to the priest within the sacred place.[1] The priest then retired alone, to a little distance away in the most sacred place,[2] and there threw himself into a frenzy, delivering a response in language only intelligible to the initiated.[3]

Dr Buck says that the Mangaian priests were the *pi'a* (receptacles) which their gods entered when required. In connection with matters of tribal importance, they consulted the gods, who spoke through them. "Unswerving obedience to the god's commands gave the priests great power and made them the last court of appeal in deciding knotty problems with regard to war and tribal politics. The priests, who were the scholars and men of learning, were wise enough to follow the feelings and desires of their group when making known the wishes of the gods."[4]

VISIBLE SIGNS OF POSSESSION AND INSPIRATION

The possession or inspiration of a human being by a spiritual agency was generally accompanied by abnormal physical manifestations. Thus the first visible sign that the god had entered into a Society Island priest was, according to the *Duff* missionaries, that he began to yawn, and rub his arms, legs, thighs and body, which began to be inflated, as if the skin of the abdomen would burst.[5] Ellis says the priest became violently agitated, and worked himself up to the highest pitch of apparent frenzy; the muscles of the limbs seemed convulsed, the body swelled, the countenance became terrific, the features distorted, and the eyes wild and strained. In this state he often rolled on the earth, foaming at the mouth, and in shrill cries and violent, and often indistinct, sounds revealed the will of the god; and the other priests in attendance, versed in the mysteries, received and reported to the people the statements he had made.[6] The

---

[1] Gill, *S.P.N.G.* p. 20.   [2] *Ibid.*
[3] Gill, *Myths*, p. 35.   [4] Te Rangi Hiroa, *M.S.* p. 119.
[5] Wilson, p. 337.
[6] Ellis, vol. I, pp. 373 *sq.*; cf. Wilson, p. 337; Moerenhout, vol. I, p. 482.

response to the enquiry being completed, and the god having left the priest, he remained on the ground, motionless and exhausted, and finally with a loud shriek came to himself, awaking as it were from a profound sleep, and unconscious of everything that had occurred.[1] Sometimes, however, the god did not immediately leave the priest, but continued to possess him for two or three days; in that case he wore a piece of native cloth, of a peculiar kind, round one arm, as an indication of his continued inspiration, or the indwelling of the god; his acts during that period were regarded as the acts of the god, and hence the greatest attention was paid to his expressions, and the whole of his deportment.[2]

Moerenhout says that the state of ecstasy, real or counterfeit, into which inspired people were thrown, really seemed to have a powerful influence on their intellectual faculties and powers of expression. Men who had previously shown neither talent nor eloquence suddenly, in their convulsive delirium, uttered the most apt and weighty observations, using the figurative language —distinct from the common one—which only chiefs and orators understood, having learnt it from childhood; and they dealt with the most subtle and difficult questions, which one would have imagined to be utterly strange to them. These powers apparently faded away with the frenzy which had produced them.[3]

A solemn consultation of the gods by a priest in Tonga is described by Mariner. On the night previous to the ceremony a chief caused a pig to be killed and prepared, and a basket of yams and two bunches of plantains provided. On the following day these were taken to the priest, and a kava ring was formed, the priest being seated in the central place of honour and the *matabule* ranging themselves on either side of him; the chiefs sat indiscriminately among the people, under the belief that such modest demeanour would be pleasing to the gods. As soon as they were all seated the priest was considered as inspired, the god being supposed to exist within him from that moment. He remained for a considerable time in silence and motionless, with his hands clasped before him and his eyes cast down. During this time the victuals were being shared out and the kava prepared, and the *matabule* began to consult him. Sometimes he

[1] Wilson, p. 338; cf. Ellis, vol. I, p. 374.
[2] Ellis, vol. I, p. 374; cf. Moerenhout, vol. I, p. 482.
[3] Moerenhout, vol. I, pp. 483 *sq.*

answered them; at other times not; often he would not utter a word until the repast and the kava were finished. When he spoke, he generally began in a low and very altered tone of voice, which gradually rose to nearly its natural pitch, and sometimes went a little above it. All that he said was supposed to be the declaration of the god, and so he spoke in the first person, as though he were the god. All this was generally done without any apparent inward emotion or outward agitation; but on some occasions his countenance became fierce, and, as it were, inflamed, and his whole frame agitated with inward feeling. He was seized with a universal trembling; the perspiration broke out on his forehead; and his lips, turning black, were convulsed; at length tears started in floods from his eyes, his breast heaved with great emotion, and his utterance was choked. These symptoms then gradually subsided. Before the paroxysm came on, and after it was over, he often ate as much as four hungry men could devour under other circumstances. The fit having passed off, he remained for some time calm; and then he took up a club, which had been placed by him for the purpose, turned it over, and regarded it attentively. He then looked up earnestly, now to the right, and now to the left, and so on several times. At length he suddenly raised the club, and after a moment's pause, struck the ground or the adjacent part of the house with considerable force. Immediately the god left him, and he rose up and retired to the back of the ring of people.[1]

Mariner describes possessed people, other than priests, as being low-spirited and thoughtful, as if some heavy misfortune had befallen them. As the symptom increased, they generally shed a profusion of tears, and sometimes swooned away for a few minutes. The height of the paroxysm generally lasted from a quarter to half an hour. These were regarded as fits of inspiration, and were firmly believed to be visitations from some god, who accused the party of neglect of religious duty, not by any apparent audible warning, but by an inward compunction of conscience. Some of the people could bring on a fit of inspiration whenever they wished.[2] He does not say that these people revealed the future or the wishes of the gods.

In Samoa the approach or presence of the god was indicated by the priest commencing to gape, yawn, and clear his throat; after which his body underwent violent contortions; and then, in loud, unearthly tones, the god was heard announcing his

---

[1] Mariner, vol. I, pp. 101 *sq.*   [2] *Ibid.* pp. 102 *sq.*

approach, and the terrified people sat silent and trembling at a respectful distance from the priest.[1]

In the Marquesas inspired priests became convulsed and glared fiercely, their hands trembled, and they ran about, talking in a squeaking voice, and prophesying death to their enemies, sometimes demanding human victims for the gods by whom they were possessed. They often cried out at night with a shrill voice, and in wild unnatural tones, and gave answer in their own usual voices, thus pretending to be conversing with the gods within them; and sometimes they would make a rustling in the leaves with their fingers, and aver that they had been miraculously taken through the thatch of the house and brought in again by the door.[2] The belief of the people was that, when a priest was inspired, the god had entered into his stomach, the seat of the soul.[3] Mathias describes the inspiration of the Marquesan high priest. He says the visitation generally occurred at night, in a sacred place, whilst the priest was resting, with his head against the head of a coconut tree, near the place sacred to the god. Then came a cry from the priest that the god was coming; and a sound was heard, sometimes loud, sometimes soft, but always curious, such as might be made by a ventriloquist. Then the priest called out, "There he is! There he is! I have him!" and closed his hand.[4] If the idea here suggested is that the priest had caught the god, it differs somewhat from the more usual and natural idea that the god had entered the priest.

NATURAL OMENS AND EXPERIMENTAL AUGURY

These two topics may conveniently be considered together, since they both depend on the same procedure, namely the observation of natural phenomena in order to ascertain the future course of events. Comprehensive lists of things observed in this way are given by various writers,[5] and we shall here content ourselves with giving a series of examples, selected at random, in order to illustrate, in the first place the kinds of activities in connection with which omens and auguries were consulted, and in the second place the kinds of phenomena observed.

---

[1] Stair, p. 223; cf. Brown, p. 224.   [2] Stewart, vol. I, p. 246.
[3] Mathias, p. 46.   [4] *Ibid.*
[5] See Henry, *A.T.* pp. 225–8; Kennedy, *C.V.* pp. 150–2; Loeb, *Niue,* pp. 178–80.

The omens in which the Polynesians believed were of various types; but most of them seem to have been associated with the important question of war. There were a great number of such omens in Samoa. In one district before going to war they watched the movements of a fish, in which their god was incarnate; if it swam briskly all was well; but if it turned round occasionally on its back, the omen was bad.[1] In another district before starting on an expedition, the priest prayed to the cuttle-fish god Fe'e for help; and if he stuttered in the enunciation of a single word of his prayer the omen was bad. In this same district they would watch the movements of the cuttle-fish; if seen near the shore, the omen was good; if far off it was the reverse.[2] In another district, whose war god was immanent in a coconut-leaf basket, the finding, whilst on the war path, of a newly plaited basket turned upside down was a bad omen, and they returned; but if the basket was an old one, and lying, not across the road, but on one side of it, lengthwise in the direction of the road, the omen was good and they proceeded.[3] In another district the war gods were represented by two teeth of the sperm whale. These were kept in a cave; and when the people went off to fight, a priest remained behind to pray for success, and to watch and report upon the position of the teeth; if they lay east and west, it was a good omen; but, if they turned over and lay north and south, it was a sign of defeat.[4] In another district, a number of fancy stones were kept in the temple, and appealed to in time of war. The priest, in consulting them, built them up in the form of a wall, and watched their collapse; if they fell to the westward the omen was good; if to the eastward, it was bad.[5] In another district the war god was incarnate in a dog. If the animal wagged his tail, barked, and dashed ahead in sight of the troops of the enemy, it was a good sign; but if he retreated or howled, it was a bad one.[6] In another district the god was present in a bundle of shark's teeth which was consulted before going to war; if it felt heavy, the omen was bad; but if light, the omen was good, and they started off.[7] In another district the war god was incarnate in the rail; peace or war depended on the bird's appearance; if reddish and glossy, they fought; but if dark and dingy, the omen was bad and they kept back.[8]

The movements of birds in time of war appear to have been

---

[1] Turner, p. 27. [2] Ibid. pp. 28 sq. [3] Ibid. pp. 32 sq.
[4] Ibid. p. 35. [5] Ibid. p. 46. [6] Ibid. p. 49.
[7] Ibid. p. 55. [8] Ibid. p. 61.

the form of omen, pointing to assurance of success, or the desirability of abandoning an operation, most commonly recognized in Samoa. Turner gives eleven examples of this;[1] and each of the birds mentioned by him was the incarnation of the god of the people whom it directed, and they included owls, rails, herons, and kingfishers, and also bats and flying-foxes, which, though not birds, must be included among them here. In almost every case if the bird flew in front of the troops (in the direction in which they were going) it was a good omen, and the action which was regarded as a bad omen was sometimes a flight backwards or sometimes a flight across the path of the troops. There are several other references to the flight of birds being observed as war omens in Samoa, the interpretations of their movements presenting a certain amount of variation.[2]

In a district of Samoa the cuttle-fish god Fe'e was believed to be immanent in the conch shell; a string of them was hung in the house of the god's priest, and it was supposed to murmur or cry when war was determined on. The colour of these shells was then watched; if it was a clear white, the colour loved by the god, the omen was good; but if dark and dingy, the omen was bad.[3] In another district a war god was supposed to be present in the shell; and when about to go to war the shell was blown by the priest, whilst all listened; if it blew rough or hollow, it was a bad sign; but if the note was clear and euphonic, the party started off encouraged and confident.[4]

Turning to Polynesian omens in general we may present, for purposes of comparison, a brief list based upon statements of earlier observers. It should be noted that the list includes the Samoan war omens already mentioned.

Omen and implication	Locality	References
Appearance of new moon: war omen	Society	Cook, vol. VI, p. 152; Ellis, vol. I, p. 378
Dim moon: death of chief	Samoa	Wilkes, vol. II, p. 132
Planets above horizon at sunset: two chiefs plotting against each other	Society	Ellis, loc. cit.
Bright starlit night: death of a chief	Samoa	Wilkes, loc. cit.
Spiral clouds at sunset: division of councils	Society	Ellis, loc. cit.
Conspicuous cloud at sunset: death of chief	Society	Ellis, loc. cit.
Cloud ahead when going into battle: success; cloud behind: defeat	Samoa	Turner, p. 27
Shooting-star: birth of great prince	Society	Ellis, vol. III, p. 171
Comet: death of chief	Samoa	Wilkes, loc. cit.

[1] Turner, chap. IV.
[2] Pritchard, p. 111; Krämer, S.I. vol. I, p. 151; Wilkes, vol. II, p. 132; Turner, pp. 25 sq., 64.
[3] Turner, pp. 28 sq.   [4] Ibid. p. 54.

Omen and implication	Locality	References
Meteor falling across course of war party at sea: failure; meteor falling in line with course: success	Samoa	Pritchard, p. 111
Rainbow: sign of war	Samoa	Wilkes, *loc. cit.*; Turner, pp. 35, 43
Thunder in hills: failure in war; thunder towards sea: success	Samoa	Krämer, *S.I.* vol. I, pp. 151, 229
Lightning: success or failure in war	Samoa	Turner, pp. 59 *sq.*
Red sky at sunset: war	Society	Ellis, vol. I, p. 378
Sudden swoop by bird: failure in war	Tonga	Mariner, vol. II, pp. 189 *sq.*
Birds as messengers of gods: impending danger	Mangaia	Gill, *Myths*, pp. 35, 205 n. 1; *Jottings*, p. 99; *S.L.P.* pp. 162 *sq.*
Lizard running ahead of troops: success; lizard running across path of troops: failure	Samoa	Turner, p. 44
Lizard running straight down centre pole of house: success in war; lizard running zig-zag course: failure	Samoa	Turner, *loc. cit.*
Lizard running about in bundle of spears— running towards points of spears: success in war; running towards centre of bundle: failure	Samoa	Turner, pp. 46 *sq.*
Sea-eel driven ashore: evil	Samoa	Turner, p. 32
Squeaking of rats: bad luck	Samoa	Wilkes, vol. II, p. 132
Movements of fish: war omen	Samoa	Turner, p. 27
Priest stuttering in prayer: failure in war	Samoa	Turner, pp. 28 *sq.*
Movements of cuttle-fish: war omen	Samoa	Turner, *loc. cit.*
Finding of plaited basket: war omen	Samoa	Turner, pp. 32 *sq.*
Position of sperm whale's teeth: war omen	Samoa	Turner, p. 35
Collapse of stones: war omen	Samoa	Turner, p. 46
Behaviour of dog: war omen	Samoa	Turner, p. 49
Weight of bundle of shark's teeth: war omen	Samoa	Turner, p. 55
Appearance of rail: war omen	Samoa	Turner, p. 61
Movements of birds: war omens	Samoa	Turner, chap. IV; Pritchard, p. 111; Krämer, *S.I.* vol. I, p. 151; Wilkes, vol. II, p. 132
Colour or sound of conch shell: war omen	Samoa	Turner, pp. 28 *sq.*, 54

So far we have been concerned entirely with omens (as opposed to augury), that is, with fortuitous events believed to foretell the future. We may conclude our treatment by a brief reference to augury, that is, cases in which the situation observed was deliberately produced. It must be emphasized that there is no hard and fast line between the two, for example the Samoan beliefs connected with the conch shells of Fe'e might be regarded as belonging to the category of auguries rather than omens, and the reverse might be said of certain Hervey Island beliefs connected with fishing, which we shall mention presently.

The Hervey Islanders engaged, on the eve of battle, in a form of augury called *ka-pa-te-vai*, or "enclose the water". The experiment was made by the warrior chief himself. He arranged the cut stems of a banana in a square on the ground, and in the hollow so formed he placed a leaf of *Alocasia*, filled with water, of which it held about half a bucket full. Into this water were dropped a number of centipedes, green lizards, and dragonflies; some of these would, perhaps, escape, but some might be drowned, and the total number drowned prefigured the number of warriors doomed to perish in the next day's battle. There was a special prayer in connection with the ceremony.[1] Gill describes the performance of this ceremony in Mangaia on one occasion; only one insect was drowned, and afterwards only one of their combatants was killed.[2]

Another Mangaian form of augury on the eve of battle was effected by fish-catching. Three or four large fish of a certain species would be seen in the shallow waters of the reef, and it was known that these, if chased, would not escape out to sea, but would always make for the shore, or some hiding-place in the reef, taking refuge, perhaps, in some large hole in the coral. They hunted the fish, and the number caught represented the number of the doomed.[3] If this hunt was usually limited to three or four fish, it would seem that the casualty list in one of their battles was hardly likely to be a long one.

There was a Rarotongan belief as to fishing, the idea being that if on a special ceremonial fishing expedition a warrior was bitten by a conger-eel, or his legs were caught by an octopus, this presaged for him a violent death. If, also, he caught a really fine fish, he was destined to conquer and kill some person of distinction, and so enhance the fame of his tribe; whilst if his catch was only some insignificant fish, he could only hope to kill some very unimportant person—not a chief or a warrior.[4]

Sometimes, in the Hervey Islands, a warrior chief would deposit two shells, intended to represent the two hostile armies, in his own temple in the evening, uttering an appropriate prayer. No general information is given as to what events were looked for; but we are told of a specific occasion on which the chief, on the following morning, found the enemy shell upside down— this foreboding destruction, which accordingly occurred.[5]

The Society Islanders had one or two modes of augury by use

[1] Gill, *S.P.N.G.* p. 21.
[2] Gill, *S.L.P.* p. 194.
[3] *Ibid.* p. 194 *n.* 1.
[4] Gill, *S.P.N.G.* p. 16.
[5] *Ibid.* p. 21.

of a coconut. One of these was effected by cutting open the coconut and examining its parts.[1] Another, called *patu*, was quite different; a ripe coconut was divided into two equal parts, and the half opposite to that to which the stalk was attached was taken in a canoe out to sea; here the priest offered his prayers, and then placing the coconut in the water, and still continuing his prayers, watched it as it sank; from the result of these observations he foretold the result of the proposed measures as to which he had been consulted. This form of augury was often resorted to when negotiations for peace were proceeding between belligerent parties.[2]

In the Hervey Islands the coconut seems to have had some significance as representing the human head; and, whilst ordinary people drank the milk out of it through its eye, a priest must have the opposite end knocked off, so that he could quaff freely, and so symbolize the doctrine that the power of life and death lay with him. We are told that the coconut was used for purposes of augury by splitting it open; but no further information is given.[3]

In Funafuti (Ellice Group) they read the future by spinning a coconut before the altar; if it came to rest in a particular position, success was assured; they did not, it seems, rest satisfied if the result of the experiment was not to their liking; but coaxed and fondled the nut and then spun it again.[4]

OFFERINGS AND SACRIFICE

The dedication of material wealth to the gods was an outstanding element in Polynesian religion. The nature and occasions of such offerings varied very greatly. There are many references to regular offerings at meal times, a portion of the food eaten being dedicated to the gods. The periodic offering of first-fruits, generally connected with the seasonal festivals so widespread through Polynesia, is also reported from most of the islands. Special ceremonial occasions, such as births, marriages and deaths, were accompanied by offerings to the gods. After fishing, it was frequently the custom to offer a share of the catch to the gods, and other important activities such as house-building, the launching of large canoes, and warfare were likewise occasions for the making of sacrifices.

---

[1] Ellis, vol. I, p. 377.   [2] *Ibid.* pp. 377 *sq.*
[3] Gill, *L.S.I.* p. 350.   [4] Hedley, p. 48.

The offerings made consisted mainly of food, particularly of highly prized varieties such as turtle and large fish. It should be noted that in the vast majority of cases the foodstuffs so offered were not wasted, but were actually consumed after their dedication by the worshippers. The idea underlying this practice was that the gods abstracted the spiritual essence of the food, leaving only the crude material remains for consumption by the people. Kava roots, or libations of the beverage made from them, were also common forms of offering.

HUMAN SACRIFICE

Owing to its spectacular and (to the European mind) revolting character, human sacrifice is the type of offering about which we have the greatest amount of information. It was common in Polynesia in pre-Christian times, and served to mark occasions of great religious importance. For this reason we may deal with the subject in some detail, though we must emphasize the fact that, in spite of their importance to the natives and their spectacular character, human sacrifices were comparatively rare, compared with the far more common offerings of ordinary foodstuffs.

As we have said, the practice of offering human beings in sacrifice to the gods was widely spread in Polynesia; and though it has not been found, and the custom was denied by the natives, in some of the islands, it must not be assumed that they were and always had been innocent. We may begin our discussion by considering the basis of selection of individuals for human sacrifice.

SELECTION OF THE VICTIM

A marked feature in the choice of victims for human sacrifice in the Society Islands was the selection of undesirable characters for this purpose. Thus writers speak of various types of people who were chosen: men who had been guilty of blasphemy, or some enormous crime; a stranger who had fled to the district for shelter from some other part on account of his ill conduct; a prisoner of war or a person obnoxious to the chief or priest.[1] According to Moerenhout very old men were always chosen in preference to all others, as being nearer the end of life in any case; but he evidently regards the private enemies of the chiefs

[1] Cook, vol. III, pp. 168 sq.; vol. VI, p. 36; Wilson, pp. 338 sq.; Ellis, vol. I, p. 346; cf. pp. 95 sq., 317.

as the presumed victims, and says that when there was an
insufficiency of these, resort was had to common people, the
first seen being seized.[1] The *Duff* missionaries say that no
woman was liable to be offered in the Society Islands;[2] but there
is a missionary statement to the contrary,[3] and this is supported
by Lesson's report that it was only on rare occasions that
pregnant women were sacrificed.[4] Children were liable.[5] Henry
states that the victims might be of three kinds: prisoners of war,
manahune (commoners of the lowest class), and people of the
middle classes who had made themselves obnoxious.[6] It seems
clear from a number of statements[7] that the priests acted in
concert with the chiefs, the former demanding, and the latter
selecting, the victims required.

In Mangaia women were sacrificed as well as men, but less
often.[8] The selection of the victim lay with the sacred and
secular kings.[9] It will be noticed that this in effect involved
co-operation between head priest and head chief, as in Tahiti.

In Tonga, according to the *Duff* missionaries, women appeared
to be the principal victims;[10] but probably they are referring
to the strangling of the widows of important chiefs.[11]

In the Marquesas persons of either sex were sacrificed.[12] The
victims were generally adults; but children were sometimes
offered.[13] Apparently the victim was never a member of the
social group whose priest demanded it, but had to be taken from
a neighbouring people. This is said to be so as regards a sacrifice
required on the death of a high priest,[14] or of a chief,[15] or, it would
seem, on any other event.[16] Indeed, in the case of the death of
a priest, at all events, hostilities would be commenced against
neighbours simply for the purpose of procuring the necessary
sacrificial victims.[17] The demand for victims came from the
taua or chief priest, to whom it was revealed, in a dream, who
should be the victim.[18] Stewart says the priest became convulsed,

---

[1] Moerenhout, vol. I, p. 510. [2] Wilson, p. 339.
[3] L.M.S. *Q.C.* vol. I, p. 478; cf. Ellis, vol. I, p. 309. On this point see below,
p. 266 n. [4] Lesson, *Voy.* vol. I, p. 402.
[5] L.M.S. *Q.C.* vol. I, p. 478. [6] Henry, *A.T.* p. 196.
[7] Cook, vol. III, pp. 168 sq.; vol. IV, p. 36; Moerenhout, vol. I, p. 510; Ari'i
Taimai, p. 14; Wilson, pp. 338 sq.; Henry, *A.T.* p. 197.
[8] Gill, *S.L.P.* p. 80. [9] *Ibid.* p. 105.
[10] Wilson, p. 339. [11] Cf. Gifford, *Tonga*, p. 321.
[12] Mathias, p. 65. [13] *Ibid.* p. 112.
[14] Krusenstern, vol. I, p. 170; Lisiansky, p. 81; d'Urville, *Voy. pitt.* vol. I,
p. 503. [15] Vincendon-Dumoulin, *I.M.* p. 254.
[16] D'Urville, *Voy. pitt.* vol. I, p. 503. [17] *Ibid.* pp. 503 sq.
[18] Langsdorff, vol. I, p. 201; cf. *A.P.F.* vol. XIV, p. 300.

and ran about prophesying death to their enemies, and some-times demanding human victims for the god by whom he was possessed.[1]

In some islands there were groups of people—perhaps tribes, clans, or families—who were specially devoted to sacrifice. This was the case in Mangaia of the Hervey group, where the first human sacrifice was associated with the arrival from outside of a party of Tongans; they were defeated by Rangi, king of the Ngariki, and one of their number was slain by the victors ex-pressly for sacrifice to Rongo, this being the first human sacrifice ever offered in Mangaia.[2] After this the Tongan people (especially the Teipe branch of the group), though allowed to remain on the island, were devoted by the Ngariki to the furnishing of victims for sacrifice.[3] But victims were also obtained from other groups when defeated in war, only one of the Mangaian tribes, the Ngariki, being always immune from providing human sacrifices.[4] The liability to be sacrificed also attached itself to families; if any one member of a family had been selected as a victim, all the other male members of it were looked upon as devoted to the same purpose.[5]

Williams says that in Rarotonga the district of Arorangi was the weakest, and its chief is spoken of by him as "the conquered chief". This district had to supply the human victims for sacrifice in the island.[6]

Practically the same custom prevailed in the Society Islands. There the practice of devoting groups of people to sacrifice applied to families and districts,[7] and there are examples of chiefs whose duty it was to provide victims demanded by the king.[8]

As regards families, Ellis says that in Tahiti, when an indi-vidual had been taken in sacrifice, the family to which he belonged was regarded as taboo or devoted, and when another

[1] Stewart, vol. I, p. 246; cf. Langsdorff, vol. I, p. 202; Stevenson, S.S. p. 98.
[2] Gill, Myths, p. 289.
[3] Gill, S.L.P. p. 105; cf. Te Rangi Hiroa, M.S. pp. 179–80.
[4] Te Rangi Hiroa, loc. cit.
[5] Williams, p. 554; cf. Gill, Myths, pp. 309–12, 312 n. 1.
[6] Williams, p. 171.
[7] Ellis, vol. I, p. 346; Moerenhout, vol. I, pp. 510 sq., gives details of the pro-cedure of sending stones as a requisition for a victim, and this practice is referred to by other writers (Ellis, loc. cit.; Rovings, vol. I, p. 229). Moerenhout tells us that the districts devoted to sacrifice were those which had been conquered. On the procedure adopted see also Williams (p. 553) who refers to the chief's habit of selecting victims who had offended him.
[8] Tyerman, vol. I, p. 165; Williams, p. 552.

victim was required, he was more frequently taken from that family than any other. Hence when it was known that any ceremony at which human sacrifices were usually offered was near, the members of these devoted families fled to the mountains, and hid themselves till the ceremony was over.[1]

West says that in Tonga the sacrificial victim was usually selected from a certain tribe;[2] and Sarah Farmer refers to a family, the servants of a great chief, the members of which were always liable to be offered in sacrifice.[3]

PROCEDURE

The procedure adopted in human sacrifice varied considerably. In the Society Islands the usual method seems to have been a blow on the head with a stone or club,[4] though other methods, some of them of great cruelty, are also described.[5] Several special observances connected with human sacrifice are mentioned by writers. The Society Islanders were always very careful not to allow the wife or daughter or any female relative to touch the corpse, for the pollution of a woman's touch, or even breath, would have rendered it unfit for offering to the gods;[6] indeed a man who had in his lifetime been bitten and disfigured by a woman became permanently unclean, and could never be offered in sacrifice.[7] The *Duff* missionaries say that in killing the man they tried to prevent any disfigurement of the body; not a bone might be broken and the corpse might not be mangled or mutilated.[8] On the other hand, the more bloody the sacrifice was, the more pleasing to the gods was it thought to be.[9]

In Mangaia the sacrifice having been decided upon, and the victim selected, by the sacred and secular kings, the executioner was invested with the "sacred girdle", as a sign that he was commissioned by the gods.[10] Victims were knocked on the head;[11] but care was requisite in slaying them not to batter them too much, as Rongo would thereby be insulted.[12]

In the Marquesas, the priest having demanded human sacrifice

[1] Ellis, vol. I, p. 347; cf. Moerenhout, vol. I, p. 510.
[2] West, p. 257. [3] S. Farmer, pp. 140 *sq.*
[4] See and compare Cook, vol. VI, p. 36; Wilson, p. 338; Williams, pp. 365, 553; Ellis, vol. I, p. 347; Tyerman, vol. I, p. 165.
[5] L.M.S. *Q.C.* vol. I, p. 479; Williams, pp. 553 *sq.*; Lesson, *Voy.* vol. I, p. 403. Cf. L.M.S. *Q.C.* vol. I, p. 478; Lesson, *Voy.* vol. I, pp. 403 *sq.*
[6] Williams, pp. 550 *sq.* [7] Wilson, pp. 338 *sq.*
[8] *Ibid.* p. 338; cf. Moerenhout, vol. I, pp. 508, 512.
[9] Moerenhout, vol. I, pp. 508, 512; cf. Ellis, vol. I, p. 227; Cook, vol. VI, p. 36.
[10] Gill, *L.S.I.* pp. 40, 42. [11] *Ibid.* pp. 39, 43.
[12] Gill, *Jottings*, p. 233.

and specified the victim, those present went off and hid themselves in a likely place, and caught anyone they found who had some resemblance to the person described by the priest as having been seen in his dream.[1] So also, on the very day of the death of a chief, warriors set out and fell on the victims, who were speared or strangled.[2]

All the references to the killing of children on the illness of a Tongan chief say that they were strangled;[3] as was done in the case of atonement for the desecration of a sacred place.[4]

The method of disposal of the remains, again, varied to a considerable extent. In the Society Islands the general procedure seems to have been to leave the bodies of victims, either exposed, buried, or hung on trees, within the precincts of the *marae*.[5] This applies to the victims of human sacrifice in general, but there are other statements relating specially to the bodies of enemies. In Tahiti on the day following a battle they collected the bodies of the slain enemies, and offered them to the god, Oro, with prayers for a continuance of his help;[6] but the evidence as to what was done with them is conflicting. Cook says they were carried to the *marae*, where a hole was dug with much ceremony, and the bodies buried in it.[7] Wilkes says they were consumed in a fire made on a thick part of the *marae* wall.[8] Ellis says that parts of the bodies were eaten by the priests, and the rest piled on the sea coast and left there till decomposed.[9] The bodies of females were offered to two daughters of Tangaroa and subjected to barbarous treatment.[10]

Mariner gives an account of fighting in Tonga in which the victors divided the bodies of the slain enemies between a number

---

[1] Langsdorff, vol. I, p. 201.

[2] Vincendon-Dumoulin, *I.M.* p. 254; cf. Mathias, pp. 67 *sq.*, 81. In this connection we should refer to the Marquesan custom of treating victims taken alive in war for subsequent sacrifice with extraordinary consideration in the meantime. If they were women, all the impositions of the sex taboos were removed. An example is given in the case of the capture of five women of a valley with whom the captors were at war. The women, whose ages varied from fifty or sixty to twelve or fifteen were fêted with banquets and orgies (Mathias, pp. 67 *sq.*).

[3] Wilson, p. 235; Mariner, vol. I, p. 300; vol. II, p. 21.

[4] Mariner, vol. I, pp. 190 *sq.*

[5] Wilson, pp. 320 *sq.*, 378; Cook, vol. VI, pp. 32, 38; Moerenhout, vol. I, pp. 509, 512; Wilkes, vol. II, p. 32; Ellis, vol. I, pp. 347 *sq.*; L.M.S. *Q.C.* vol. I, p. 478; Tyerman, vol. I, pp. 121, 165, 271.

[6] Ellis, vol. I, p. 308; cf. Moerenhout, vol. I, p. 524.

[7] Cook, vol. VI, p. 40.

[8] Wilkes, vol. II, p. 32.

[9] Ellis, vol. I, p. 317; cf. p. 358; cf. Moerenhout, vol. II, p. 188.

[10] Ellis, vol. I, p. 309.

of gods, and the share of each god was placed in front of his house, and left there for a few hours. The bodies were afterwards removed, and some were given to relatives for burial, whilst the rest were disposed of in different ways, some being burnt, others hung up on trees, and others again cooked and eaten.[1]

There are several statements as to the disposal of the body of the victim in the Hervey Islands. Gill says that in Mangaia the whole body of the victim was laid on the altar, but that in Rarotonga only the head was offered to Tangaroa.[2] In Mangaia it was the altars of their two great gods Rongo and Mororo which received the bodies; and afterwards the decaying corpses were thrown into the bush for Papa, Rongo's mother, to feast upon.[3] The latter practice was, he tells us, based upon a myth, as to a dispute between Vatea and Papa, the parents of their twin children Tangaroa and Rongo, as to which of these sons was to be lord of Mangaia.[4] In Rarotonga the heads of the slain were offered to Tangaroa; they were piled in heaps in the *marae*, and the bodies furnished a cannibal feast.[5]

In the Marquesas the bodies of human victims were sometimes eaten, and sometimes hung up on trees until the flesh wasted away, after which the bones were buried or burned. Portions of the bodies were dedicated to the gods.[6] Apparently they allowed relatives of the enemy dead to take away the bodies and bury them,[7] but this can hardly have referred to all of them; for we are told that the bones of the enemies killed in battle were used for making harpoons, ornaments, images, and the like.[8] Ellis says that the bodies of such enemies were made the subject of a regular banquet.[9] Mathias and Langsdorff refer to the chiefs, priests, and warriors as the people who participated in the feast,[10] though Melville thinks it was only the chiefs and priests.[11] Stewart says only the priests might eat anything offered to the gods,[12] and Ellis says the victims were eaten within the *marae* by the priests.[13]

---

[1] Mariner, vol. I, p. 172. [2] Gill, *Myths*, p. 11 *n.*
[3] *Ibid.* p. 305. [4] *Ibid.* p. 11.
[5] Ellis, vol. I, p. 359; cf. Gill, *Myths*, p. 11, and *Jottings*, p. 118.
[6] Krusenstern, vol. I, p. 170; Lisiansky, p. 81; d'Urville, *Voy. pitt.* vol. I, p. 494.
[7] See Porter, vol. II, p. 41.
[8] Krusenstern, vol. I, p. 162; Porter, vol. II, p. 46; d'Urville, *Voy. pitt.* vol. I, p. 505.
[9] Ellis, vol. I, p. 309; cf. Mathias, pp. 68 *sq.*
[10] Mathias, pp. 58, 81; Langsdorff, vol. I, p. 180.
[11] Melville, p. 261.
[12] Stewart, vol. I, p. 252. [13] Ellis, vol. III, pp. 313 *sq.*

Occasions of Human Sacrifice

The occasions for the offering of human sacrifices were generally connected with important institutional activities, particularly war, the victims in this case being generally enemies captured or slain in battle.

In Tonga human sacrifices were offered to propitiate the gods, when anything calculated to offend them had been done. We are told that a child of a chief by an inferior female attendant was always selected for the purpose, thus presenting the god with a victim who had chiefs' blood in him, whilst avoiding the sacrifice of one who, if his mother were of chiefly rank, would be a chief. Mariner gives an example of a sacrifice of this sort after the desecration of a consecrated place by killing a man in war within its sacred precincts.[1] Perhaps the proposal, prevented by the missionaries, of Tongans to cut off fingers, or even take the lives, of a number of children, on the occasion of an earthquake shock[2] was based on the belief that the phenomenon betokened anger of the gods for something.

Another type of situation in which human sacrifices were offered was the illness or death of an important person. In Tonga effort was made to avert the illness of a great chief by human sacrifice.[3] In Nukuhiva (Marquesas), on the illness of a priest, victims secured from a hostile valley had to be offered.[4] In the Society Islands a symbolic sacrifice was resorted to upon the illness of an important chief, his family and friends presenting themselves at the temples with ropes round their necks.[5]

Related to the subject of human sacrifice is the custom of killing a man's widow and burying her with him which has been reported from Tonga and the Marquesas. The custom of sacrificing other people on the death of a great chief or priest prevailed in the Marquesas, where an enemy victim had to be secured for the purpose; and a similar custom on the death of a great chief was observed in Rotuma and the Paumotu group.

In dealing with the Society Islands we shall have occasion to

---

[1] Mariner, vol. I, pp. 189 sq. Cf. the statement of Turner that in Samoa, though people would not kill or eat the animal in which their god was incarnate, a visitor might do so, and in such a case a member of the family had to propitiate the offended god by being placed in a cold oven, ready for cooking, which may be regarded as an act of symbolic sacrifice. (Turner, pp. 31 sq., 38.)

[2] A.P.F. vol. XVII, p. 26.

[3] Gifford, Tonga, p. 321.

[4] Langsdorff, vol. I, p. 202.

[5] Moerenhout, vol. I, p. 545; cf. Ellis, vol. I, pp. 349 sq.

refer to human sacrifices connected with important building operations, whether of *marae*, chiefs' houses, or canoes[1], and also to those associated with the *rites de passage* of high chiefs.[2] Important events in the lives of chiefs were similarly celebrated elsewhere in Central Polynesia. In Mangaia the ceremony of making peace, which involved the inauguration of the victor as secular king, was also an occasion for human sacrifice. Gill tells of the sacrifice of a human victim on the birth of the first-born son of the king of Rarotonga,[3] and Williams says two victims were needed.[4] In the Marquesas a victim was sacrificed when the daughter of a chief of high rank was about to have her ears pierced and receive her first ear-rings.[5]

[1] See below, p. 218; Ellis, vol. I, p. 346; Tyerman, vol. I, p. 242; vol. II, pp. 14, 38 *sq.*; Wilson, p. 388.
[2] See below, pp. 260 *sqq.* Also cf. Ellis, vol. III, p. 109; Moerenhout, vol. II, p. 23.   [3] Gill, *Myths*, p. 37.
[4] Williams, p. 554.   [5] Mathias, pp. 66 *sq.*, 130.

CHAPTER V

TABOO

IN considering the question of the taboo, we shall try to confine ourselves to matters in which the restriction which it involves rests on a religious or magical basis, though it is not always clear whether a particular form of prohibition was associated with a magico-religious sanction or not. It will become clear, however, that restrictions based upon fear of supernatural punishments played an important part in Polynesian life.

The underlying conceptions upon which all taboos were based were similar in character, but the evils for the avoidance of which the taboos were established, the magical methods by which those evils might operate, and the precautions to be taken to avoid that operation, varied. We shall deal first with the taboos affecting persons.

We may first refer to the taboos necessitated by the infectious sanctity of great chiefs, illustrations of which have been given elsewhere[1] in discussing the sanctity of chiefs. This sanctity infected any person who touched or came into contact, direct or indirect, with the chief, and any object which he had touched; and if any person touched that object the infection was retransmitted to him.[2] A similar taboo resulted from contact with the body of a dead man; and it can hardly be doubted that the idea upon which it was based was similar, though not identical.[3]

Again, it was believed that persons who were not permanently taboo by reason of sanctity or uncleanness might become so temporarily under certain conditions. Such was in some islands the condition of a woman during pregnancy and after childbirth. Though there are not actual statements as to her danger to others, there were customs of placing her in seclusion from other people, from which it may possibly be inferred.[4] In the Marquesas a girl beginning to show signs of maturity was kept apart in a remote hut, built specially for the purpose,[5] and a possible reason of this may have been the idea of impurity during menstruation.

---

[1] *Systems*, vol. III, chap. XXXI.
[2] For a general discussion of this subject see Frazer, *G.B.* vol. III, pp. 132-4
[3] Cf. Frazer, *B.I.* vol. I, p. 28; *G.B.* vol. III, p. 139.
[4] Cf. Frazer, *G.B.* vol. III, p. 147.   [5] Langsdorff, vol. I, p. 173.

though there is no evidence of general seclusion of women at these periods. Then again there are cases in which a newly born child was itself taboo. Its seclusion with the mother and certain prohibitions during the period of that seclusion might be based upon beliefs as to the impurity of the mother; but some of the evidence introduces customs which can only be associated with the child. Thus there are statements that a person who has touched the child may not feed himself, as to introducing into the house the food of the mother and of the child by separate windows, and as to the effect upon a tree of accidental contact with a newly born child's body, especially its head.

In connection with the period of transition from boyhood to manhood there are statements indicating customs of seclusion as well as certain food taboos, and taboos against self-feeding in connection with incision; of seclusion and food taboos at the time of tattooing, and during a period in the life of a young chief, and of preparation for the priesthood and, as regards the aspirant for priesthood, of sexual abstinence. Again we must refer to the taboo on warriors who had killed an enemy in battle, and to their seclusion and abstention from marital intercourse while the taboo lasted; this may be associated with the fact that they had been in contact with a dead man,[1] or with the idea that they were specially in danger of the angry revengeful ghost of the victim.[2]

A person who was taboo in the sense of being either sacred or unclean was in consequence subject to dangers, as also were other people who had become taboo through contact with him. We have seen, in discussing the sanctity of great chiefs, that in some islands this was such that it was not safe for them to feed themselves, so they had to be fed by other people; also that similar precautions had to be taken by other persons who by contact with a great chief had become infected with this sanctity, and that dire and fatal internal troubles would befall an unhappy man who neglected these precautions. In one or other of the islands the taboo against self-feeding arose after contact with the dead; it applied to the mother during her seclusion with her child, and to anyone who had touched the child; and it applied to a youth after his incision.

We may next mention the deliberate placing upon an object of a taboo for the purpose of preventing other people from entering into or interfering with it. This might be done by a chief or priest in order to prevent intrusion into a sacred place or to

---

[1] Cf. Frazer, *G.B.* vol. III, p. 169.   [2] *Ibid.* pp. 165, 186.

reserve the tabooed article for the needs of the community or a special ceremony, or sometimes perhaps for purposes of his own; or by anyone for the protection of his own property.

TABOO PLACES

We may now turn to a consideration of certain aspects of taboo in greater detail. Dealing first with the places regarded as taboo, these were primarily temples and places for the interment of the dead—often identical. In the Society Islands there were very seldom any houses in the vicinity of a *marae*. Except on feast days and during religious ceremonies, there always reigned an impressive silence, which even the priests and guardians of the *marae* dared not interrupt. No one entered the *marae* unless obliged to, and everyone maintained the strictest silence when passing, and uncovered to the waist long before approaching it.[1] Moerenhout says the priests alone might enter the *marae* at all times, eat the flesh of animals offered in sacrifice, and the fruits of trees enclosed in the limits of the sacred enclosure.[2] We are also told that the priests lived near the *marae*, which was under their guardianship; they allowed no persons to come near the precincts—the spirits of the dead would come and torment them if they permitted such a thing.[3] There are several general statements that all *marae* were permanently taboo to women,[4] but these must be taken subject to certain reservations. In the first place we know that in the Society Islands a woman could be a chieftainess—the head of a social group—in her own right; and such a woman had her seat or throne in the *marae*, even though her husband might be excluded,[5] the exclusion of the husband arising from the fact that he was not a member of the social group to whom the *marae* belonged. Then, again, we shall see in a subsequent chapter that there were certain ceremonies at a *marae* which women had to attend. Such cases, however, were in the nature of exceptions to the general rule excluding women from the *marae*.

The *faleaitu* or spirit-houses of Samoa were always regarded with reverence, and even with dread, and for a long time after the arrival of Europeans the natives resented any intrusion into

---

[1] Moerenhout, vol. I, p. 469; cf. pp. 507, 519; Corney, *Tahiti*, vol. II, pp. 40 *sq.*, 57, 260 *sq.*; Cook, vol. I, p. 224; G. Forster, *Voy.* vol. I, p. 324; J. R. Forster, *Obs.* p. 547; Wilson, p. 335; Ellis, vol. III, p. 105.
[2] Moerenhout, vol. I, p. 478. [3] Corney, *Tahiti*, vol. II, pp. 260 *sq.*
[4] Moerenhout, vol. I, p. 469; Wilson, p. 329; Tyerman, vol. I, p. 268.
[5] Ari'i Taimai, p. 10.

their sacred precincts.[1] Only the priests entered these houses, the worshippers remaining outside.[2] In Tonga all the spirit-houses were taboo, except to certain persons in charge of them.[3] It was sacrilege for anyone to go within the enclosure, and death for anyone but the priests to touch the god.[4] Women were never allowed to enter the sacred precincts, as their presence would desecrate and pollute them even more than would the entry of pigs.[5] So also anyone would avoid, if possible, passing a *faitoka*, or burying-place, during the twenty days following an inter-ment; and if he did so, he had to walk slowly with bowed head and hands clasped before him, any burden he was carrying being lowered from his shoulders and carried in his hands or in his bent arms. At all times this sign of respect had to be shown on passing the *faitoka* of a great chief.[6] It may be mentioned, as regards the Society Islands, Samoa and Tonga, that in each of these groups they had what writers call priestesses,[7] but it is not clear whether and to what extent restrictions excluding women would apply to them. In Mangaia, of the Hervey group, only great men might assemble at the famous *marae* and take part in the worship there. Common people, after depositing presents of food to their gods in the name of the chiefs, retired to a distance, and waited till the ceremonies were concluded. All women and children were excluded.[8] Taboos on temples and burial places are reported from the Marquesas,[9] and it is stated that the penalty for their infringement was death, though it is not clear whether this referred to killing by the people (which perhaps it often did), or whether what was feared was death at the hands of the gods. But Mathias, telling of a visit by him and his colleagues, guided by two boys, to a secluded temple, says the boys were much surprised that they came back alive.[10] And Bennett visited a secluded place of interment where there was a corpse of a man who was related to a family living in a village; but none of the dead man's kindred would go with him because they said the spot was taboo, and if they approached it they would die.[11] These

[1] Stair, *J.P.S.* vol. III, p. 240.
[2] Murray, 40 *years*, p. 172; Brown, p. 225.
[3] D'Urville, *Astro.* vol. IV, p. 83.   [4] Young, *S.W.* p. 225.
[5] Williams, p. 319 *n.*   [6] Mariner, vol. I, p. 321.
[7] Cf. *Systems*, vol. II, chap. XXVII.   [8] Gill, *L.S.I.* pp. 148 *sq.*
[9] On the subject of Marquesan taboo places see Mathias, pp. 59 *sq.*; Vincendon-Dumoulin, *I.M.* p. 262; Radiguet, vol. XXII, p. 449; *A.P.F.* vol. XII, p. 580; Lambert, p. 138; Shillibeer, p. 40; Stevenson, *S.S.* p. 100; Langsdorff, vol. I, pp. 180, 209; Christian, *J.P.S.* vol. IV, p. 202; Krusenstern, vol. I, p. 173; cf. Melville, pp. 99 *sq.*; Tautain, *L'Anthro.* vol. VIII, pp. 669 *sq.*
[10] *A.P.F.* vol. XII, p. 580.   [11] Bennett, vol. I, p. 328.

statements suggest death at the hands of the gods, or the ghost of the dead man, which would be in accord with Polynesian beliefs and customs generally.

In the Paumotu Islands no one might approach a *marae* in the absence of the priest, and the gods punished with death those who infringed this law.[1] There seems to have been a stone which marked the point at which women had to stop. Percy Smith mentions a sacred enclosure on the island of Niue[2] and similar sacred places are reported from Fotuna (Horne Island),[3] Penrhyn Island[4] and Niutao in the Ellice group.[5] In Easter Island burial places were taboo.[6]

TEMPORARY TABOOS

So far we have been referring to such places as temples and places of interment which were inherently sacred. We may now turn to objects not necessarily sacred in themselves, but which were made taboo for the purpose of protecting them from interference. These taboos were of two sorts: one was a general taboo placed by a chief, priest or head of a social group over a specific food or foods extending over the area within his jurisdiction; and the other was a private taboo placed by a man over his own property.

Ella, speaking of Samoa, says the taboo system was employed chiefly for the purpose of protecting plantations and fruit trees from thieves. Each individual was supposed to have the power of tabooing his property by means of a significant symbol, without the aid of a priest, and bringing punishment on those who disregarded the taboo.[7] And when a man was ill a priest would attribute the illness to some curse hanging over him, or some transgression of a taboo.[8] A taboo ordained by a family would, it is said, place the object tabooed under the protection of the family *aitu*, who would punish the man who tampered with it.[9] Turner gives examples of beliefs connected with taboo signs used in Samoa. One of these, intended to protect, say, a man's breadfruit trees, was a representation of a sea pike, made with plaited coconut leaflets, and hung from one or more trees;

[1] Seurat, *L'Anthro.* vol. XVI, p. 477; cf. Beechey, vol. I, p. 168; Smith, *J.P.S.* vol. XXVII, pp. 122, 125; d'Urville, *V.P.S.* vol. II, Part I, p. 393. Cf. *A.P.F.* vol. X, p. 164; vol. XIV, p. 333. [2] Smith, *J.P.S.* vol. XI, p. 201.
[3] Bourdin, p. 445. [4] Lamont, pp. 120 *sq.*; cf. p. 275.
[5] Gill, *Jottings*, p. 14. [6] Geiseler, p. 28.
[7] Ella, *A.A.A.S.* vol. IV, p. 638. [8] *Ibid.* p. 639.
[9] Krämer, *S.I.* vol. II, p. 98.

the idea involved was that a sea pike should run into the body of a thief, and anyone proposing to steal would be prevented by a fear that, if he did so, a sea pike would actually dart up and wound him mortally, the next time he went out to sea. Another form adopted was a representation in plaited coconut fibre of a shark, the belief as to which was similar. A stick hung horizontally from a tree threatened the would-be thief with a disease which would run right across his body, and remain fixed there till he died. The ulcer taboo was effected by burying in the ground some pieces of clam shell, and erecting over them three or four reeds tied together at the top in a bunch like the head of a man; and the threat involved was that the thief might be laid down with ulcerous sores all over his body. A man who had stolen, in spite of the taboo sign, and afterwards had swellings or sores, would attribute them to his act; he would therefore confess, and send a propitiatory gift to the person he had robbed, who in return would send back some native herb as a medicine and pledge of forgiveness. A spear fixed in the ground threatened the robber with the agonies of facial neuralgia. The death taboo was made by pouring oil into a small calabash and burying it near a tree. A small coconut-leaf basket, filled with ashes from a cooking-house and two or three stones, and suspended from a tree, indicated a threat that rats would eat holes in the fine mats of the thief, and destroy any cloth or other property he might value. The plaiting of some coconut leaflets in the form of a small square mat, hanging the mat on a tree, and adding to it some streamers of white cloth threatened a thief or his children with death by lightning.[1]

In Tonga it was thought that if anyone infringed a taboo, or committed an act of sacrilege his liver, or some other viscus would be liable to become enlarged or scirrhous; and they often opened dead bodies out of curiosity to see if men had been sacrilegious in their lifetime.[2] Thomson illustrates this in a curious way, though his example does not refer to the idea of taboo which we are now considering. He says the people thought a man would die if he infringed the taboo, and that, after the introduction of Christianity, they believed this fate would fall on a man who swore falsely on his Bible. He refers to a case of suspected arson in which, before the courts could interfere, the people, taking no interest in the judicial enquiry, met for trial

[1] Turner, pp. 185 sqq. Cf. Krämer, S.I. vol. II, p. 98; Friedlaender, Z.f.E. vol. XXXI, p. 46.   [2] Mariner, vol. I, p. 172.

by ordeal. Each person took the oath of innocence, and it was assumed that the guilty person who did this would die in a few weeks; surely enough an elderly woman began to sicken, grew worse, confessed to the crime, and died.[1] Another idea was that the curse which followed disregard of a taboo sign would cause the culprit's child to die within a year.[2] The visible sign of a taboo over fruits and flowers was generally a piece of white *tapa* or a piece of plait in the shape of a lizard or shark; but Mariner says that the people would not refuse to pluck and eat such things if he or any foreigner would first remove the sign.[3]

In the Society Islands members of all classes of society had power to place a taboo on their own land or any particular sort of provision.[4] Infringement of the taboo was punished by the gods, by death or illness; goitre (not a common illness) was a form of disease likely to be incurred, and anyone suffering from this was an object of horror.[5] Tyerman and Bennet saw coconut trees with bunches of leaves tied round them, and were told that they were taboo to all but their owners; and anyone disregarding the sign would be banished to a desolate island.[6] It may be noticed that the punishment involved was, so far as the statement goes, only at human hands; but there is no doubt that the people feared, or had previously feared, supernatural punishment.[7] Shell-fish on the reef could be tabooed by erecting at its extremities two tree branches, to which a white cloth was attached, and the sign was also a prohibition of taking fish there.[8] We are told of two marks, looking like beacons, set up on an extensive rocky flat at Papeete (in Tahiti), which were taboo marks to keep people from picking up shells or fishing upon the queen's preserves.[9]

In the Hervey Islands the infringement of taboo laws of all kinds caused death.[10] In Rarotonga it was stated that if a native cut down an ironwood tree which had been tabooed by the queen he would suffer a glance from the evil eye and die.[11] In this island all taboo restrictions were indicated by pinning to the soil or hanging on a tree an entire coconut leaf plaited after a fashion supposed to represent the proprietor clutching it.[12] The idea involved was that if the midrib of the emblem was injured, the

[1] Thomson, *D.P.M.* p. 309 and *note*.   [2] Hedley, p. 27.
[3] Mariner, vol. II, p. 187.   [4] Wilson, p. 323.
[5] Moerenhout, vol. I, p. 529.   [6] Tyerman, vol. I, p. 83.
[7] Cf. Wilkes, vol. II, p. 33.   [8] Wilson, pp. 83 *sq.*, 323.
[9] Fitzroy, vol. II, p. 514.   [10] Gill, *S.P.N.G.* p. 23.
[11] Wragge, p. 144.   [12] Gill, *Jottings*, p. 205.

owner would consider that his spine was figuratively broken, a mortal injury only to be atoned for by the blood of the offender.[1] This curious conception of the mode of operation of the power of the taboo is shown in greater detail by the method adopted by the owner of the soil in Mangaia to eject a tenant from his holding. He would put on the soil the sign of a *rahui* or taboo, this being simply a green coconut frond, plaited in three places on either side of the midrib as a rough representation of human form; the symbol was secured by pegs driven into the ground, and represented the proprietor taking possession of the land with his hands and legs, and if the taboo were disputed and the symbol chopped up, the lord declared that his spine, represented by the midrib of the coconut frond, had been chopped in two, and only death could atone for such an insult.[2]

In the Marquesas any man could, according to von Krusenstern, place a taboo on his property, such as a breadfruit or coconut tree, a house or plantation, by declaring that the spirit of his father or of some king, or indeed of any other person, reposed in the tree or house, which thereupon bore that person's name, and no one dare attack it.[3] Taking this statement by itself one might assume that von Krusenstern referred to the soul of a dead person; but a further illustration of the matter by von Langsdorff shows that it might be the spirit of a living person. He says that if, say, a pig had been stolen, and the owner guessed who was the thief, he would give to the pigs or trees of the suspected person his own or another man's name, whereby, according to native ideas, those articles became possessed or bewitched; for they believed that the spirit of a dead or living man was in the things, and sometimes this belief was sufficient to impel the thief to abandon his property and settle down elsewhere; pigs which were *nateta* or possessed might not be killed. All people could cause the fruits of their trees to be possessed, and thus make them taboo.[4] Christian refers to the use, as a sanction to enforce a taboo, of the name of Tana-Manaoa, a deified mortal, the god of a tribe, and worshipped in one district as a household god.[5] No one, not even a king, would venture to infringe a taboo; but if anyone were so irreligious as to do so, and were convicted of the offence he was called *kikino*, and it was believed that in war he would be the first to be devoured by the enemy.[6]

[1] Hedley, p. 207.
[2] Gill, *S.L.P.* p. 67.
[3] Krusenstern, vol. I, p. 172.
[4] Langsdorff, vol. I, p. 182.
[5] Christian, *J.P.S.* vol. IV, p. 190.
[6] Krusenstern, vol. I, p. 172.

According to other writers his penalty would be illness or sudden death.[1] Stevenson says the coconut and breadfruit taboos worked more quickly than the fish taboo, producing swelling and discoloration of neck and face during the night after the offence and death in two days, unless a cure was applied. He gives illustrations of the magical character of cures for one who had violated a taboo. The illness caused by eating a tabooed fish could only be cured with the bones of the same fish, burnt with due mysteries; and that caused by eating tabooed fruit was cured by means of a preparation from the rubbed leaves of the tree which the patient had robbed, so that he could not be cured without confessing to the person he had wronged.[2]

REMOVAL OF TABOO

We shall include under this heading two matters which are more or less distinct. The first is the supernatural means by which a taboo of sanctity or uncleanness by which a person was afflicted could be cured, and the other is the visible sign by which a taboo deliberately placed upon an object, not necessarily sacred in itself, could be raised.

The widely spread method of curing a taboo of sanctity or uncleanness was that of bathing or of anointing with water or coconut-water, and with these may be associated practices of anointing with oil—probably the oil used was generally derived from the coconut. An interesting feature disclosed by the evidence is that these media appear to have been used to impart sanctity, as well as to remove it.

In addition to this very general method of removing taboo, there were certain specific procedures which were adopted. One of the most interesting of these is the *moe-moe* ceremony of Tonga. Anyone who had become taboo by contact with a chief removed it by performing the *moe-moe* ceremony of touching with his hands the soles of the feet of a superior chief; and if in the meantime he had already inadvertently placed himself in the deadly peril induced by feeding himself, he had to perform the *fota* ceremony—he had to press the chief's foot against his own abdomen, so that the food that was in him might not cause him to swell up and die. If the chief by whom he had originally been infected was the *tuitonga* the difficulty caused by the lack of any

[1] Langsdorff, vol. I, p. 186; Mathias, p. 228; Stewart, vol. I, p. 229; du Petit-Thouars, vol. II, p. 356; Stevenson, *S.S.* p. 51.
[2] Stevenson, *S.S.* pp. 51 *sq.*

chief of superior rank was overcome by touching a bowl belonging to him.[1]

As to the raising of a taboo, the removal of the taboo sign was
probably the usual method, as we have very little evidence of any
other.[2] Sometimes the removal of a general taboo, laid by a
competent authority, was the occasion for a feast. Thus in Tahiti
a feast was held when a chief took off a *rahui* from a whole district; and when a middle-class landowner removed a general
taboo placed by him on his own land, an offering of a hog and
fish was made, the place was again free, and there was a general
feast.[3] Mariner describes the festal ceremony which took place
in Tonga on the removal of the general taboo placed upon the
food supply, to remove the shortage of food caused by the funeral
feast of a *tuitonga*.[4] In Samoa, according to Pratt's *Dictionary*,
the word *soli* means to tread or trample on, and *soli aitu* was a
large gathering of people for wrestling and games on removing
a prohibition from places made sacred to the gods. There are
one or two examples of the removal of a taboo by touching the
object with a stick or wand, such as the Samoan *vaipa* rite,
mentioned in Pratt's *Dictionary*, of striking a body or house with
a piece of banana stalk. A similar idea, though somewhat
differently applied, is reported from the Marquesas, the imple-
ment used being a wand.[5] So in Fotuna (Horne Island) the
taboo on the turtle as a food was removed by the king striking
each morsel with a strip of bamboo;[6] and somewhat similar to
this is the custom, reported from Napuka, of the Paumotuan
Islands, of consecrating the first turtle caught in the season by
placing on it a small stick.[7]

FOOD TABOOS

Many Polynesian taboos were connected with food and eating.
Of these we may mention first those which depended on a
division between the sexes. It is not always possible to state
definitely that customary restrictions of this kind were taboos,
in the sense in which we are using the term—sometimes, no
doubt, they depended mainly upon convenience or the economic
division of labour, rather than upon any idea of contamination.

[1] Mariner, vol. II, pp. 187 *sq.*
[2] For an example of this see Mariner, vol. II, p. 187.
[3] Wilson, pp. 323 *sq.*   [4] Mariner, vol. I, pp. 110 *sq.*, 117–21.
[5] Tautain, *L'Anthro.* vol. VII, p. 449.
[6] Smith, *J.P.S.* vol. I, p. 41.   [7] *J.P.S.* vol. XXVII, p. 135.

But in certain cases the latter conception was very definitely present.

SEPARATION OF THE SEXES AT MEALS

Practices of sexual separation at meal times were widely spread; but there are discrepancies in the evidence which probably arise through abandonment of restrictions that had prevailed previously, and through more or less local differences at any one period in the customs even of neighbouring islands or districts. There is a good deal of evidence on this subject from the Society group. The authorities are unanimous in saying that women ate apart from the men; some of them refer to the application of the rule as between husband and wife, and three of them (Cook, Ellis and Moerenhout) say that it applied as between children. Several methods of separation are mentioned. One is that of sitting in different parts of the house (Cook, *Duff* missionaries, J. R. Forster). Ellis, after asserting the general rule, refers to the use by the men of their own eating-house, while the women ate in little huts. He also says that a wife not only might not eat with her husband, but that her daughters' food might not be cooked at the fire at which the men's food was cooked, and had to be placed in separate baskets. Cook also refers to the use of separate baskets, and tells of brothers and sisters visiting his party with their baskets, and sitting down to eat, evidently in two groups, two or three yards away from each other, each facing away from the other, there being no interchange of a word during the meal between the two groups.[1] According to one writer a husband had to eat with his servants, being excluded from the companionship, not only of women, but of the unmarried men; and he ascribes to this restriction the unwillingness of men to marry early and the formation of liaisons instead.[2] The explanation of the general custom given by Ellis is that the men were considered *ra* or sacred, while the women were only *noa* or common;[3] and it is said that if a woman broke the taboo the god would punish her by making her one-eyed, withered-armed, or deformed.[4]

In Samoa, according to Turner, men, women, and children,

[1] Cook, vol. I, pp. 102, 190; vol. VI, p. 142; G. Forster, *Voy.* vol. I, pp. 284, 337; vol. II, p. 80; J. R. Forster, *Obs.* p. 405; Ellis, vol. I, pp. 129 *sq.*; Hawkesworth, vol. I, p. 471; Bougainville, p. 270; Wilson, pp. 347, 351; Turnbull, p. 338; Hamilton, p. 51; Moerenhout, vol. II, pp. 58 *sqq.*; Corney, *Tahiti*, vol. II, pp. 55, 215, 258, 471. [2] Parkinson (2), p. 47.
[3] Ellis, vol. I, p. 129; cf. Corney, *Tahiti*, vol. II, pp. 258, 471.
[4] Corney, *Tahiti*, vol. II, p. 471.

all ate together at the evening meal;[1] and Ella apparently confirms this.[2] Von Bülow says that when the women and girls had finished making the *lega* (yellow colouring matter made from turmeric) the young men, having prepared food, brought it to the women, and they all ate together.[3] Stair on the other hand says that though some chiefs of inferior rank allowed their wives to eat with them, speaking generally, women and children took their meals alone, not being allowed to eat with men, though in his time this restriction had been swept completely away.[4] In Tonga women were not, according to Cook, excluded from eating with men,[5] and a statement by Mariner seems to imply this;[6] if there had been a change of custom in this respect, Cook's evidence shows that it must have occurred some time ago. In the Hervey Islands women had to eat their meals at a distance from the men;[7] even husband and wife did not eat together.[8] The evidence from the Marquesas is conflicting, some writers saying that men and women did not eat together[9] and others that they did.[10] Perhaps the true interpretation is to be found in the statements of von Krusenstern and Lisiansky who say that women might not appear in the men's dining-houses, but that men and women ate together in their own homes.[11] In Rotuma, according to Lesson, the women and children only began their meal after the men had finished;[12] this custom continued to comparatively recent times, and indeed it is stated that the women had, even then, to retire to another house for their meal.[13] In Wallis Island it was taboo to the women and children to eat with the husbands and fathers.[14] In Fotuna (Horne Island) at a public feast the women took their meals apart in another house.[15] In Rurutu, of the Austral Islands, a joint meal of converted men, women and children was engaged in as a test of the falsity of the old gods, and the fact that none of them became convulsed or suddenly stricken with death was accepted as evidence of this.[16]

[1] Turner, p. 115.
[2] Ella, *A.A.A.S.* vol. IV, p. 656.
[3] Von Bülow, *I.A.E.* vol. XII, p. 72; cf. Brown, pp. 139 *sq.*
[4] Stair, p. 122.   [5] Cook, vol. V, p. 417.
[6] Mariner, vol. II, p. 134.   [7] Williams, p. 212.
[8] Gill, *L.S.I.* p. 94.
[9] La Rochefoucauld-Liancourt, vol. III, p. 22; Vincendon-Dumoulin, *I.M.* p. 262; Bennett, vol. I, pp. 317 *sq.*
[10] Porter, vol. II, p. 116; Marchand, vol. I, p. 130.
[11] Krusenstern, vol. I, p. 261; Lisiansky, p. 87.
[12] Lesson, *Voy.* vol. II, p. 438.
[13] Gardiner, *J.R.A.I.* vol. XXVII, pp. 421 *sq.*
[14] *A.P.F.* vol. XIII, p. 19.   [15] *Ibid.* vol. XV, p. 33.
[16] Ellis, vol. III, p. 399.

Cooking by Opposite Sex

In addition to the separation of the sexes at meals, there were also restrictions preventing people from cooking food for members of the opposite sex, though some of these, again, may have been a matter of convenience rather than of taboo. In Tahiti women might not cook for men.[1] Similarly women did not eat anything that men had cooked, believing that serious ill would befall them if they did so;[2] the work was done for them by their maids, if they had any, or if not, by themselves;[3] or it was done by boys employed for the purpose who attended them at meals,[4] and who presumably were not regarded as having attained to manhood; or by the "feminine male associates who waited on and lived with them",[5] by which is no doubt meant the *mahu*, who were regarded as being women. In more modern times common men cooked for both sexes; but there were restrictions as to the way they did it. The food of the two sexes had to be cooked at different fires; the cooks might not touch the dishes destined for the women; even in gathering breadfruit and taro for the women, they had to carry them under their arms, and not on their shoulders.[6] In Samoa, according to Wilkes, women prepared the food for cooking, and men cooked it;[7] Pritchard also says the men did the cooking.[8] There are a few more modern statements that cooking was done by both sexes, though according to some of them the women only helped the men, who seem to have been the real cooks;[9] this, however, involves the assumption that both men and women handled the food, and there is no suggestion that people only cooked for their own sex. Mariner in his list of the various crafts and occupations of Tonga, in which he discriminates between those of men and women, includes cooking among the duties performed by men;[10] but he probably does not mean to imply that women might not do it, or help in it, for there is no mention of any taboo affecting the matter. In most of the islands of the Hervey group women did the cooking, and it is stated that a woman cooked her husband's

[1] Corney, *Tahiti*, vol. II, pp. 258, 279.　　[2] *Ibid.* p. 258.
[3] *Ibid.* p. 279.　　　　　　　　　　　　　[4] Cook, vol. I, p. 190.
[5] Wilson, p. 347.　　　　　　　　　　　　[6] Moerenhout, vol. II, p. 92.
[7] Wilkes, vol. III, p. 148.　　　　　　　　[8] Pritchard, p. 127.
[9] Churchward, p. 320; Ella, *A.A.A.S.* vol. IV, p. 636; Krämer, *S.I.* vol. II, p. 57.
[10] Mariner, vol. II, pp. 197–201.

meal;[1] but in Rarotonga the men cooked.[2] The reference to the woman cooking for her husband is inconsistent with any inter-sex taboo; but the evidence is all comparatively recent. In the Marquesas women only cooked for themselves;[3] and the statement that it was taboo to women to eat *popoi* prepared by a man[4] implies that men only cooked for themselves, unless we are to believe that it only refers to the particular food mentioned, which seems improbable. In Rotuma the men, and not the women, cooked the food; but the latter served it to the men.[5] This does not seem to involve any taboo, and in any case the evidence is recent. Men did the cooking in Wallis Island[6] and in Fotuna (Horne Island);[7] but here again there is no evidence of any taboo affecting the matter. Apparently cooking was in modern times done in Funafuti, of the Ellice group, by both men and women without any question of taboo arising.[8]

SEPARATION OF DIFFERENT RANKS

There were also taboos against feeding in the presence of other people, based upon relative rank, and not on difference of sex. The extent to which this taboo might sometimes be carried is illustrated in Cook's account of the ceremony of the public recognition of the son and successor apparent of the *tuitonga*, at which, when the young man was about to eat for the first time with his father, the whole company had to turn round and sit with their backs to them.[9] Cook says that he never saw in Tonga a large company sit down to what we should call a sociable meal by eating from the same dish, and that there were certain ranks or orders that could neither eat nor drink together, this distinction beginning with the king, though he could not say where it ended.[10] Ellis (of Cook's party) says there was a custom which forbade, at particular times, a person of inferior rank to eat in the presence of his superiors; even the *tuitonga* was not exempt from it, for, on the sudden appearance, while he was eating, of his father's sister and her son and daughter, he had immediately desisted, and put the victuals on one side, apparently a good deal confused.[11] Mariner says, "it is tabooed also to eat when a superior relation is present, unless the back is turned towards

[1] Gill, *A.A.A.S.* vol. II, p. 332; Gill, *Jottings*, p. 94 n. 2.
[2] Gill, *Jottings*, p. 94 n. 2.   [3] Shillibeer, p. 45.
[4] Du Petit-Thouars, vol. II, p. 357.   [5] Gardiner, *J.R.A.I.* vol. XXVII, p. 421.
[6] Mangeret, vol. I, p. 99.   [7] *A.P.F.* vol. XV, p. 32.
[8] Mrs David, pp. 154 *sq.*, 203.   [9] Cook, vol. V, p. 374.
[10] *Ibid.* p. 417.   [11] Ellis (Cook), p. 97.

him; for when a person's back is turned towards another, that other may be said, in one sense, not to be in his presence".[1]

In Samoa it was a crime to eat in the presence of a chief, the young people in particular not eating while the chief was having his meal.[2] At the evening meal the master of the house ate first and alone, and it was afterwards that the others did so.[3] Stair only refers to the custom as applying to chiefs of rank (sacred chiefs), who always partook of their meals separately.[4] Probably a somewhat similar custom prevailed in Tahiti, at all events as regards the great chiefs or kings, though the evidence is only presumptive. Cook says that the *eowas* and *whannoes* were allowed to eat with the king; but he did not know whether anyone was prevented from doing this except the *toutous* (common people) and women.[5] The *eowas* and *whannoes*, to whom he refers, were the principal persons about the king forming his court, being generally his relations.[6]

EATING WITH STRANGERS OR VISITORS

There are records that point to practices of not eating in the presence of strangers or visitors, or not expecting the latter to eat in the presence of their hosts. This evidence is difficult to evaluate with any approach to exactitude, partly for lack of exact information, and partly because of the difficulty of defining the term "stranger", and of finding any clear differentiation in customs on the arrival of, say, a ship of white men, who were absolute strangers, and that of native visitors, who may have been known to, and perhaps relations of, their hosts; the evidence, however, shows that customs of this kind were widespread. In Samoa, when a party of visitors arrived at a village they were entertained at the *faletele*, where food was brought to them and a feast began, in which only the visitors took part.[7] After presenting the food, the hosts either disappeared, or seated themselves in a cluster some distance from the house.[8] So also in Tonga when Cook's party were being entertained by the brother of the *tuitonga*, the food having been prepared, and handed to the guests to be disposed of at will, the Englishmen wanted the

[1] Mariner, vol. II, p. 188; cf. Cook, vol. III, p. 185; vol. v, pp. 309, 318, 338; Forster, *Voy.* vol. I, p. 464; Labillardière, vol. II, pp. 118 sq., 129; Thomson, *D.P.M.* pp. 46 sq.
[2] Krämer, *S.I.* vol. II, p. 102; cf. Stuebel, p. 91.
[3] Krämer, *S.I.* vol. II, pp. 89, 132. [4] Stair, p. 121.
[5] Cook, vol. III, p. 323.
[6] *Ibid.*; cf. J. R. Forster, *Obs.* p. 357 n.; G. Forster, *Voy.* vol. I, p. 328.
[7] Pritchard, pp. 132 sq. [8] Churchward, p. 364; cf. pp. 100 sq.

Tongans to share in and eat it then; they, however, had great scruples about this, and it was only when they were assured that it was in accordance with white men's customs that they complied, and even then some of them carried their food off; it was with the greatest difficulty that the *tuitonga* was prevailed upon to eat a small bit.[1]

Similar customs prevailed in the Society Islands[2] and in the Hervey group,[3] but it is extremely doubtful whether they can be described as taboos, since there is no evidence of any supernatural sanction associated with them. On the contrary, it appears that they merely formed a part of the elaborate code of etiquette and formality which governed Polynesian commensal ceremonies.

FASTING

There are a few records of restrictions on eating after a death. In the Marquesas from the time of death till the priests had finished the songs chanted on such occasions, the people all fasted, no one touching provisions, and no fire was allowed to be kindled within sight; when the songs had been chanted, the funeral feast began.[4] In Samoa while a dead body was in the house, no food was eaten under the same roof, the family eating their meals outside, or in another house.[5] In Tahiti it was forbidden to make a fire or eat before night-time for three days after the death of a chief.[6] There are some examples of taboos being placed upon certain foods after deaths, in which the motive appears to have been merely to provide food for a subsequent feast, but these are not relevant at the moment. Restrictions against eating are recorded in connection with a few other matters also. In the Society Islands, if a great chief was ill, and the disease made progress in spite of the prayers of the priests, there were fast days for all the people and general prayers;[7] and in Tonga, when anyone, especially a chief, was ill, the people tabooed themselves from certain kinds of food.[8] In Nukuhiva (Marquesas) a sorcerer preparing a charm to produce sickness had for three days to refrain from eating and to drink only sparingly.[9] So also in Ra'iatea, of the Society group, a sorcerer,

[1] Cook, vol. v, pp. 350 *sq.*
[2] Bligh, p. 120; Tyerman, vol. I, p. 115; Wilson, pp. 186 *sq.*, 359; Mrs Hort, p. 261; Wheeler, p. 84.
[3] Gill, *Jottings*, pp. 42, 58; *L.S.I.* p. 56; *S.L.P.* p. 153.
[4] Stewart, vol. I, p. 265.   [5] Turner, p. 145.
[6] Moerenhout, vol. I, p. 550.   [7] *Ibid.* p. 545; cf. p. 464.
[8] Wilson, p. 273.   [9] Langsdorff, vol. I, p. 210.

trying to secure the death of a victim, would continue praying to a god day and night for at least five days to kill him, and fasted the whole of that time.[1] It has been said that in the Marquesas an inspired priest who was to announce the number of victims required for a ceremony of human sacrifice had, after lying for a stated time in his house like one dead, to run for three days through the territory of the clan, naked and starving, and that it was death for anyone to encounter him on his rounds.[2] In Mangareva, of the Paumotu group, the principal part of the ceremony of the inauguration of young priests was, according to Percy Smith, that called *touma*, which he translates "to consecrate". The chief priest took part of the food which the young men had brought, held up the hand containing it to heaven, and consecrated it by addressing the great god Tu in a low voice. He then chewed the consecrated food, and afterwards took it out of his mouth and put it into the mouths of the young men, saying to each of them that they were to receive it; it was Tu; it was various other gods whom he named in succession. He then told them to rest five days without eating, so that it might not be necessary to attend to a call of nature before Tu and his subordinates had taken root in them.[3]

TABOOS ON SELF-FEEDING

Reference has been made elsewhere to the taboos against self-feeding to which sacred chiefs were subject, and which also had to be observed by persons who had come in direct or indirect contact with them. Similar taboos arose in some islands in the case of people who had been in contact—direct or sometimes indirect—with the bodies of the dead, and in cases of mothers after childbirth and boys undergoing initiation, and even perhaps of a woman whose hands were taboo because she had woven a state-mat.

TABOO FOODS

There are numerous references to certain kinds of food being taboo to special classes of people. Reference has been made elsewhere[4] to beliefs that certain animals, which were taboo as food to the general body of the people, might be eaten by chiefs or priests. There is also evidence that in some of the islands

---

[1] Tyerman, vol. I, p. 545.
[2] Stevenson, *S.S.* p. 98. The author says that he was only told of this by one priest, and that though the latter was a good authority, the fact that he (Stevenson) had not heard of the practice elsewhere makes him report it with diffidence.
[3] Smith, *J.P.S.* vol. XXVII, pp. 122 *sq.*   [4] *Systems*, vol. III, chap. XXXI.

women were not allowed to eat the better sorts of food. In the Society Islands the men, who were regarded as *ra* or sacred, might eat the flesh of pig and fowls and certain varieties of fish, coconuts and plantains, and whatever was presented as an offering to the gods; but the women, being *noa* or "common", were forbidden on pain of death to touch these things, as it was supposed that they would pollute them.[1] Turtle also is mentioned as a food forbidden to them.[2] In the Marquesas women and lower-class men were interdicted from the better kinds of food, both vegetable and animal, these being eaten by the men on the sacred pavements.[3] According to Stewart, breadfruit, coconut, yam, and most kinds of fish were free to everyone; but bananas, pigs, turtle, cuttle-fish, bonito and albicore were taboo to women and lower-class men; while Christian says that women were prohibited from eating bananas, fresh breadfruit and coconuts, many kinds of fish, brown pigs, goats and fowls.[4] Women eating the better kinds of food, reserved for men, would be put to death.[5] In Rarotonga certain kinds of food were reserved for men and gods.[6] In Mangaia women might not taste eels, but this restriction appears to have been based on a legend concerning eels.[7] In Bow Island, of the Paumotu group, women seem only to have eaten inferior sorts of food.[8] In Penrhyn Island turtles and porpoises were eaten only by men, and if a woman ate a porpoise her children would have porpoise faces;[9] women were also not allowed to eat flying fish.[10] In Rimitara, of the Austral group, women were not allowed the choicest food.[11] We have referred (in connection with the subject of separation of the sexes at meals) to a joint meal by converted men, women, and children, of Rurutu of the same group, as a test of the falsity of the old gods; another feature of this test was that women and children ate turtle, pork and other kinds of prohibited food. The priests had declared that they would instantly be destroyed by the gods of their ancestors, and the fact that this was not so was accepted by the rest of the people as evidence.[12]

[1] Ellis, vol. I, p. 129; cf. Cook, vol. VI, p. 142; Moerenhout, vol. II, p. 94; Wilson, p. 347.   [2] Cook, vol. VI, p. 142.
[3] Mathias, pp. 51, 143; cf. Vincendon-Dumoulin, *I.M.* p. 262; Bennett, vol. I, p. 315.
[4] Stewart, vol. I, p. 217; Christian, *J.P.S.* vol. IV, p. 202; cf. Wilson, p. 143; Shillibeer, p. 45.   [5] Mathias, p. 52.
[6] Williams, p. 212.   [7] Gill, *L.S.I.* pp. 278 sq.
[8] Beechey, vol. I, p. 242; cf. Moerenhout, vol. II, p. 71.
[9] Gill, *Jottings*, p. 147.   [10] Lamont, p. 218.
[11] Ellis, vol. III, p. 389.
[12] *Ibid.* p. 399; cf. L.M.S. *Q.C.* vol. II, p. 242.

CHAPTER VI

TEMPLES AND BURIAL PLACES

HAVING dealt with some of the religious beliefs and practices of the Polynesians, we may now turn our attention to a very vital aspect of their religious institutions, namely the material equipment associated with worship, using these terms in a very broad sense. We shall deal first with temples and other religious structures, and after that with sacred objects in general. In discussing temples we shall also include some material bearing upon burial places, since the two were very often identical. Thus burial places were sometimes the centre of an ancestral cult, while temples were frequently the repositories of human remains, particularly those of people of high rank. It should also be mentioned that such places often served purposes other than religious, being assembly grounds and meeting places, but these more secular functions will only be mentioned incidentally.

SOCIETY ISLANDS

Concerning the Society Islands, we shall have occasion to refer to the significance of their *marae* or temples. As regards these Ellis says that they were either national, local or domestic. The former were depositories of their principal idols, and the scenes of all great festivals; the second were those belonging to the several districts; and the third such as were appropriated to the worship of family gods. All were uncovered, and resembled oratories rather than temples.[1] According to Moerenhout, each district, or each principal chief, had at least one important temple where the *atua* were adored; and these public *marae* were generally near the shore and isolated. The domestic *marae*, though smaller, were all made on the same plan as the large *marae* and were very numerous; those of the chiefs, though private, were always imposing places, and were respected and venerated by the people.[2]

The general construction of the larger *marae* was, according

---

[1] Ellis, vol. I, pp. 339 *sq.*; cf. vol. III, p. 6.
[2] Moerenhout, vol. I, pp. 467 *sqq.*

to Ellis, as follows. The whole structure was included in one large stone enclosure of considerable extent, the form of the interior frequently being that of a square or parallelogram, the sides of which were forty or fifty feet long. The front of this area was bounded by a low fence, and the two sides were enclosed by a high wall; whilst at the back was raised a solid pyramidal structure, often of immense size. Several of these temples contained smaller inner courts, within which the gods were kept. Inside the enclosure were the houses of the priests and keepers of the idols, the sacred dormitories and altars, and the little buildings in which the "idols" or images were kept. These temples were erected on the extremity of a point of land projecting into the sea, or in the recesses of an extensive and overshadowing grove. The sacred trees growing within the walls, and around the temples, excluded the rays of the sun and produced a sombre gloom.[1] Similar descriptions, varying only in minor details, are given by Moerenhout[2] and by J. R. Forster.[3] Other writers give accounts of individual *marae* which add some detail to the general descriptions, and seem to suggest a certain amount of diversity of structure.[4]

A comparison of these descriptions of the larger *marae* shows that in one or two cases the pyramidal structure (sometimes truncated) which is described as being built in steps or stages was absent, whilst as regards others the enclosed open space had not been identified by observers.

It is quite possible that the general designs of these structures have varied in these respects in different places and at different times; but it seems that the combination of the enclosed space and the pyramid was probably the usual form; and in view of the dilapidated condition in which many of the *marae* were found it is very possible that they had often originally included features which had not survived. We may believe that the general forms of the local or district *marae* were similar, though they would be on a humbler scale.

We may now pass to the domestic *marae*, in which the family gods were worshipped. Moerenhout's statement, that the domestic *marae* were made on the same plan as the large *marae*, and that those of the chiefs, though private, were always

[1] Ellis, vol. I, pp. 340 *sq.* [2] Moerenhout, vol. I, pp. 466 *sq.*
[3] Forster, *Obs.* pp. 543 *sqq.*; cf. Corney, *Tahiti*, vol. II, pp. 327 *sq.*
[4] Cook, vol. I, pp. 158 *sq.*; Wilson, pp. 204 *sq.*; Bennett, vol. I, pp. 134 *sq.*; vol. II, p. 41; Wilkes, vol. II, p. 31; Forster, *Voy.* vol. I, p. 267; Tyerman, vol. I, pp. 239–42, 265 *sq.*, 282 *sqq.*; d'Urville, *Voy. pitt.* vol. I, p. 539.

imposing places, justifies a belief that the latter, at all events, would be somewhat similar to the public *marae*. It also implies that people other than chiefs had their domestic *marae*, and these would probably be the middle classes.

The material bearing on family *marae* is somewhat meagre in quantity and quality, but descriptions are given by Forster,[1] Tyerman and Bennet,[2] and d'Urville.[3]

As regards all the houses containing images of the gods, and occupied by priests, it seems clear that they were merely wooden and thatched structures, formed more or less like ordinary houses or open sheds. According to a Ra'iatean belief concerning the transformation of Tangaroa into a canoe, his skeleton, after his career on earth had ended, was laid upon the ground, the backbone upwards, and the ribs resting on the land. This became a home for all the gods, and thenceforth the "temples" in Ra'iatea were open sheds, consisting of thatched roofs, supported on posts, according to the cage-like model of Tangaroa's remains.[4]

Several writers give descriptions of Society Island altars. Ellis says the food-offerings to the gods were deposited on the *fata* or altars, of which those in the public temples were made of wood, and of large size, usually eight or ten feet high. The surface of an altar was supported by a number of wooden pillars, often curiously carved and polished. The altars were covered with sacred boughs and ornamented with a border or fringe of rich yellow plantain leaves. There were also, connected with the temples, altars resembling small round tables supported by a single post fixed in the ground. Occasionally the body of a sacrificial pig was placed on the larger altar, whilst the heart and internal organs were put on the smaller one, called a *fata aiai*.[5]

The *marae* of the Society Islands were used as repositories, temporary or permanent, for the remains of the dead, the procedure varying with the rank of the deceased. The bodies of chiefs and members of the upper classes were temporarily placed in vaults in the *marae*—in times of peace for a year or

[1] Forster, *Voy.* vol. I, pp. 293 sq.   [2] Tyerman, vol. I, pp. 270, 280 sq.
[3] D'Urville, *Voy. pitt.* vol. I, p. 539; cf. Corney, *Tahiti*, vol. II, pp. 209 sq., 260, 470, 482.   [4] Tyerman, vol. II, pp. 310 sq.
[5] Ellis, vol. I, pp. 344 sq., 351; cf. Moerenhout, vol. I, pp. 257, 470; Forster, *Obs.* p. 543. For descriptions of the altars of specific *marae*, see Cook, vol. I, p. 159. Cf. Wilkes, vol. II, p. 32; Wilson, pp. 205, 208; Tyerman, vol. I, p. 282; d'Urville, *Voy. pitt.* vol. I, p. 539; Corney, *Tahiti*, vol. II, pp. 209 sq.

two, in times of disquietude for a very much shorter period—
after which they were removed to their final resting places in
hidden mountain caves.[1] People of lower rank either interred
their dead in the *marae* or placed them in a cave, but the
temporary period during which the corpse rested at the family
marae seems to have been universal.[2]

SAMOA

Murray refers to a Samoan temple as being a great curiosity;
he says that the people of the group were famed among other
islands of Polynesia as being a godless lot, having neither
temples nor idols and admits that this was so substantially,
though the people had *some* temples.[3]

Turner, however, after stating that each village had its
village god, says there was a small house or temple consecrated
to that god; or if there was no formal temple, the great house of
the village, where the chiefs were in the habit of assembling,
was the temple for the time being, as occasion required. Some
settlements had a sacred grove, as well as a temple, where
prayers and offerings were presented. He refers to objects
regarded with religious veneration found in these temples, such
as a conch shell, suspended from the roof in a basket of sinnet
network, which the god was supposed to blow when he wished
the people to go to war; a couple of stones; an object resembling
the head of a man, with white streamers flying, raised at the
door of the temple on the usual day of worship; a coconut-shell
drinking cup suspended from the roof and before which prayers
were addressed and offerings presented. He does not mention
any images.[4] He also refers to Si'uleo as a village god in the
island of Savai'i, where he was a fisherman's god, and had a
fisherman's hut erected for him on the seashore.[5] Stair, in
referring to the building of a house for a chief on his marriage
with a lady of rank, says that it was erected on a raised terrace
of stones from fifty to seventy feet square, and often many feet
in height. He says that the adoption of this form of structure
was a widespread custom throughout the whole Samoan group,
not only in the case of dwelling-houses, but also in that of
sacred buildings, the *fale-aitu*, or houses of the gods, which
were always built on *fanua-tanu*, or paved grounds, by the

---

[1] Henry, *A.T.* pp. 135, 295.   [2] *Ibid.* p. 292.
[3] Murray, 40 *years*, p. 171; cf. Brown, p. 225; Hood, p. 141.
[4] Turner, pp. 18 *sq.*   [5] *Ibid.* p. 52.

people of the district. He adds that in some remarkable instances these raised stone terraces or platforms were of very massive construction; but here he is only referring to the platforms and makes no mention of pyramidal structures.[1] He afterwards says that some *aitu*, principally but not only war gods, had *fale-aitu*, these being similar in form to ordinary dwelling-houses, or sometimes mere huts. They were usually placed in the principal *malae* of the village, surrounded with a low fence, built of materials similar to those used in ordinary buildings and almost always placed on *fanua-tanu*, or raised platforms of stones.[2]

Pritchard distinguishes between small towns, as he calls them, in which the *faletele* was used for the worship of the town god, larger towns which had temples, and still larger towns, which had, dedicated to the service of the god, a sacred grove as well as a temple.[3] In this, it will be noticed, he supports Turner. He also says that the family god was spiritually present in the house occupied by the head of the family,[4] a statement which was probably true for Polynesia generally. Krämer refers to an *aitu* house in Tuamasanga village in which there was, hung under the ridge beam, a basket, the abiding place of the *aitu*;[5] this may be compared with the basket of sinnet network referred to by Turner.

Murray describes a temple in the village of Sailele in the island of Tutuila. It was a house made of the wood of the breadfruit tree, and thatched, as were other Samoan houses, with sugarcane leaf. It was about ten feet in length and six in breadth, and so low that a man of middle height could not stand upright in it. Within it were deposited three stones, and he illustrates the importance attached to these stones by saying that a missionary having chipped bits off some of them, the next time the temple was visited the stones had been buried to avoid further desecration. Close by was a small coconut grove, the offspring apparently of one original tree, whose sanctity and association with the god of the temple were such that it might not be touched, nor its fallen fruits picked up. Only the priest might enter the building, the worshippers remaining outside.[6] This was probably the temple of what had been an important village, for Murray says that worshippers

[1] Stair, pp. 111 *sq.*; cf. Te Rangi Hiroa, *S.M.C.* p. 70.
[2] Stair, pp. 225–8; cf. Ella, *J.P.S.* vol. VIII, p. 234 *n.* 3.
[3] Pritchard, p. 110.   [4] *Ibid.* p. 108.
[5] Krämer, *S.I.* vol. I, p. 226.   [6] Murray, 40 *years*, pp. 171 *sq.*

used to resort to it from all parts of the island,[1] and, according to Krämer, the village of Sailele was the place of government of the worshippers in Tutuila of that important group of goddesses, Nafanua, Tilafainga, and Taema.

Turning now to the question of burial places, Turner refers to the absence of village burying grounds, and to the desire of people to lay their dead with their ancestors in their own particular burying ground.[2] He says that the grave, which was often close by the house, was marked by a little heap of stones a foot or two high, and that the grave of a chief was neatly built up in an oblong slanting form, about three feet high at the foot and four at the head.[3] According to Dr Buck, the size of memorial cairns varied with the importance of the deceased, from loose heaps of stones in the case of children and commoners to large stepped rectangular structures in the case of high chiefs. Some of the smaller cairns were merely extensions of the stone house platforms, the Samoans preferring to bury their dead near their houses rather than in detached cemeteries.[4] There are several other descriptions of Samoan graves, but they are too lengthy to quote here.[5]

Before concluding our treatment of Samoan religious structures, we should refer briefly to two sets of remains which have been described by writers. One of these, reported by Sterndale,[6] is said to have been an extremely large truncated conical structure. The description at once suggests similarities with similar stone structures elsewhere in Polynesia, but unfortunately subsequent attempts to locate the remains have been unsuccessful, and Dr Buck suggests reasons for discounting the accuracy of Sterndale's account.[7]

The other structure to which we must refer is *Le Fale-o-le-Fe'e* (the House of the Octopus), the famous stone platform some miles inland from Apia, in Upolu. Here again there are contradictions and misunderstandings in the reports of early

[1] Murray, 40 *years*, p. 172; cf. Krämer, *S.I.* vol. I, p. 342.
[2] Turner, p. 147.   [3] *Ibid.* pp. 147 *sq.*
[4] Te Rangi Hiroa, *S.M.C.* p. 322.
[5] Pritchard, p. 151; Stair, pp. 178 *sq.*; cf. Brown, p. 404; Churchward, p. 370; Wilkes, vol. II, p. 76; Ella, *A.A.A.S.* vol. IV, p. 641; Hood, p. 95. Krämer refers in several places to the positions of graves and their forms, his descriptions of the latter being more or less in accord with one or another of those of other writers (Krämer, *S.I.* vol. I, p. 282; vol. II, pp. 103 *sqq.*, 107); but a special feature of interest is his illustration of a Malietoa tomb in Apia, an oblong structure, made of stones, rising in three step-like tiers, and apparently rather higher at one end than the other (*ibid.* vol. II, p. 106, Fig. 38).
[6] *J.P.S.* vol. I, pp. 62–4.   [7] Te Rangi Hiroa, *S.M.C.* pp. 328–9.

observers.[1] The available evidence has been summarized and digested by Dr Buck[2] who himself examined the site in 1928. Nothing definite is known of the part which these two structures played in the religious life of Samoa in the days before the arrival of the white man.

TONGA

Mariner, who divides the Tongan gods into classes, says that several of the original gods had houses dedicated to them; these houses were built in the usual style; but generally rather more care was taken both in building them and in keeping them in good order and decorating their enclosures. About twenty of these gods had houses thus consecrated to them, some having five or six, and others only one or two.[3] These houses were clearly temples; and in them were kept images of the gods. At the time of the illness of the daughter of Finau, the girl was removed from her father's house to another, inside a fencing, consecrated to the tutelar god of the *hau* or secular kings, and pigs were killed almost every morning for about a fortnight, and presented before the house, as an offering to the god, to whom prayers for her recovery were offered several times a day. On this proving unavailing the girl was taken to the "fencing" of another god, where the same ceremony was performed; and again, on this failing, to others in succession.[4] Shortly after the girl's death, Finau himself was taken ill; and he was taken in the same way, first to one place and then to another, some of these places being what we have called temples, and others *faitoka* (burial places), until he died.[5] The gods were approached at their temples in a similar way with regard to matters other than illness; Mariner tells how, after a sacred place had been violated in war, a child was sacrificed to appease the anger of the gods;[6] and again in describing the sacrifice after war of the dead bodies of the enemy, he tells how they were laid before the houses of these gods and left there for three or four hours, after which they were taken away.[7]

There are several other references to these temples. D'Urville saw several of them, each being in the midst of a grove,

[1] Turner, p. 31; Stair, p. 228; *J.P.S.* vol. III, pp. 241 *sqq.*; Pritchard, pp. 119 *sqq.*; Churchward, pp. 173–81.
[2] Te Rangi Hiroa, *S.M.C.* pp. 324–8.   [3] Mariner, vol. II, pp. 103 *sq.*
[4] *Ibid.* vol. I, pp. 288–95.   [5] *Ibid.* pp. 299 *sq.*
[6] *Ibid.* pp. 189 *sqq.*   [7] *Ibid.* p. 172.

enclosed in pretty palisades, and quite bare and undecorated outside; and in one of them he saw a wooden image rudely carved in the shape of a human head. He says that they were dedicated to different "spirits", and that the sick were brought to them.[1] The *Duff* missionaries describe an enclosure of three or four acres of ground, surrounded by a fence of reeds six feet high, and containing five houses one of which was sacred to the "God of Pretane", and it was here that the old chief Mumui slept when indisposed, in the hope of obtaining a cure. On its floor were four large conch shells, and on the rafters were spears, clubs, and bows and arrows, placed there to receive from the god the supernatural power to render them successful. The missionaries were told that there were several enclosures of this kind.[2] Meinicke distinguishes between gods of the first class—the great gods—who had special temples, and those of the second class—souls of men—who were worshipped at the graves.[3] This brings us to the question of burial places, or *faitoka*.

As the chiefs were deified at death, it follows that the *faitoka* in which they were buried would in a sense become temples, as probably was the case in other islands of the Pacific. Their use for this purpose is illustrated by Mariner, as for instance when Finau (being about to engage in war against his old opponents in Tongatabu) proceeded with several of his chiefs and *matabule* to the *faitoka* of his father, where the whole party engaged in the usual performances betokening their humility. After this the principal *matabule* addressed the soul of Finau's father, reminding him of his son's attention to religious duties, and beseeching his protection in the fighting, this being followed by offerings of kava.[4] The use of these *faitoka* as temples is also referred to by Cook;[5] and Sarah Farmer says that when the people desired great blessings, such as health, children, success in war, or the removal of a great evil, they would go to the burial grounds of their great chiefs, clean them up thoroughly, sprinkle the floor with sand, and lay down their offerings.[6] When Finau was dying, after carrying him to certain temples, they took him to the grave of a female chief, and invoked her for his recovery.[7]

[1] D'Urville, *Astro.* vol. IV, p. 83.
[2] Wilson, p. 102; cf. Williams, pp. 318 *sq.*; Young, *S.W.* p. 225.
[3] Meinicke, vol. II, p. 80. [4] Mariner, vol. I, pp. 93 *sq.*
[5] Cook, vol. III, p. 206; vol. V, p. 424.
[6] S. Farmer, p. 127. [7] Mariner, vol. I, p. 301.

Cook apparently distinguishes between the *faitoka* of the chiefs and those of other people, the former being temples as well as burial grounds, and the latter only burial grounds.[1] This would almost follow from the fact that only chiefs were deified after death; but probably the graves of middle-class people would be temples in the sense that the people would offer prayers there to the souls of their departed relatives. We are told that the practice of praying to their dead prevailed among the *matabule*,[2] and the natural place for supplication would be at the dead man's grave. Several writers[3] give detailed accounts of Tongan *faitoka*, and there are a number of miscellaneous references to them.[4] From a consideration of these it seems clear that the two most usual forms of the *faitoka* of the chiefs were an enclosed grassy space rising upwards in the centre, and a pyramidal structure of one or more steps, and that in either case a wooden house was erected in the centre of it. None of the authorities cited refers to a house of this sort on the top of a pyramidal structure; but it seems probable that it would be there, as in the case of the other form of *faitoka*, and the illustration by the *Duff* missionaries shows the house on the top of the pyramid. The pyramidal form was evidently a special one, only used for great chiefs; indeed it would almost seem that it was confined to the case of the *tuitonga*, as apparently it was not the form adopted in the case of the *tuikanokubolu*. This, however, is not clear. The body was evidently buried in the centre of the structure, and the house was apparently erected over it. D'Urville's statement that in the case of a pyramid the number of the steps of the erection related to the number of persons interred in it is not confirmed by any other writer; but there seems to be no reason for doubting its accuracy. Mariner confirms the suggestion that two or more bodies might be placed in the same grave.[5] The other two forms referred to by writers are the square spaces enclosed by stone walls with high stone uprights at the corners, referred to by the *Duff* mission-

[1] Cook, vol. III, p. 206; vol. v, pp. 421, 424.

[2] Mariner, vol. II, p. 109.

[3] Thomson, *J.R.A.I.* vol. XXXII, pp. 86 *sqq.*; Cook, vol. III, pp. 182 *sqq.*; vol. v, pp. 342 *sq.*; Wilson, pp. 278 *sq.*; Young, *S.W.* pp. 224 *sq.*; G. Forster, *Voy.* vol. I, p. 451; cf. J. R. Forster, *Obs.* p. 566; Wilson, p. 236; d'Urville, *Astro.* vol. IV, p. 82.

[4] Cook, vol. III, p. 206; vol. v, pp. 421, 424; d'Urville, *Astro.* vol. IV, pp. 101, 106 *sq.*, 361 *sq.*; *Voy. pitt.* vol. II, p. 31; Ellis (Cook), vol. I, pp. 110 *sq.*; Veeson, p. 79; West, pp. 268 *sq.*; *A.P.F.* vol. XVII, pp. 12 *sq.*; Mariner, vol. I, pp. 135, 309; vol. II, p. 181; Wilson, p. 247; Thomson, *D.P.M.* p. 379.

[5] Mariner, vol. I, p. 317 and *note*.

aries, and the oval forms of which d'Urville speaks; but as no one else mentions either of these it seems improbable that they were common. Sometimes, apparently, there were two or more mounds, each with its house, within one common walled enclosure. Though there is no actual description of the burial places of the middle classes, it seems probable that these would be enclosed spaces with a small house in the centre. The description by the French missionaries of graves placed near the houses of the parents of the dead would probably refer to the graves of commoners, as well as those of the general body of chiefs, though it may be assumed that in the case of commoners the enclosed spaces would only be small.

There were two structures in Tonga, the purposes of which have never been definitely determined. One of these was the celebrated trilith of Haamonga, at the eastern end of the island of Tongatabu, in the district of the *tuihaatakalaua*. This has been discussed or referred to by several writers.[1]

The other unexplained structure is described by Thomson. It was an artificial hill about fifteen feet high near Holeva, among the mangroves on the western side of the Mua lagoon. Thomson says that he questioned the local native repositories of ancient lore, but they could tell him nothing about it. He was afterwards, however, informed that the mound was attributed to a *tuitonga* of a very remote period who ordered his people to build it, and that numerous other mounds in the district belonged to the daughter of that *tuitonga*, and were ascribed to a feast that in olden times was celebrated by the chiefs.[2]

MARQUESAS

The information concerning the temples and places of interment of the Marquesas is somewhat confusing. Mathias says that the people of the Marquesas had temples, altars, sacred pavements, statues and public places equally sacred, in the form of immense arenas, having houses symmetrically ranged round them, for national feasts.[3] Some temples were dedicated entirely to cannibal rites; these were in secret places, and were hidden

---

[1] Thomson, *D.P.M.* pp. 380 *sqq.* and in *J.R.A.I.* vol. XXXII, pp. 81–4; Pritchard, p. 398; Monfat, *Tonga*, p. 4; Meade, pp. 300 *sq.*; Mackenzie, *Anthrop. Review*, 1866, vol. IV, pp. cxcviii *sq.*; Smith, pp. 157 *sq.*; Brenchley, pp. 132 *sq.*; Foljambe, p. 168.
[2] Thomson, *J.R.A.I.* vol. XXXII, pp. 84 *sq.*
[3] Mathias, p. 54.

in the recesses of thickets near the tops of the mountains.[1]
There were only a few of these remote cannibal temples; but
there were on the roads and cross-roads, and near some houses,
a great number of altars, ornamented with offerings of food,
and surrounded with long clusters of white wands, on which
were rags of stuff of all colours; they were often surrounded by
little walls of dry stones protecting them, or raised on a heap of
stones, and in them were found figures of Tiki.[2] According to
the *Duff* missionaries there was a *marae* in each district, where
the dead were buried beneath a pavement of large stones.[3]
Langsdorff says that every native had a burial place by his
house; and on it, or not far from it, was the *popoi-tabu* or taboo
eating-house, where men consumed their pigs. The *marae* of
the *taua* (priests) of districts were quite apart from all dwellings,
and slain enemies were generally eaten there.[4] It is stated in
Rovings in the Pacific that their burial places or *marae* were
close to their dwellings, and the remains of any great chief were
ultimately deposited beneath heaps of massive boulders, arranged with unusual strength and care. He saw several of these
tumuli, and owing to a recent great mortality many bodies had
been covered under one stony barrow, and much human hair
lay scattered about, and appeared between the interstices of the
stones.[5] Porter refers to the practice of keeping some of the
remains of the dead in the *marae*.[6] According to Shillibeer a
marae, or burial place, consisted merely of a large heap of
stones, very irregularly piled, having on the top a small house,
for the purpose of receiving the remains of the king, and of his
family, or those of the principal chiefs; it was in it that sacrifices
were made.[7] It is obvious that this writer is describing the
marae of a person of high rank. Lisiansky was told of the
leaving of the bones of two victims to decay, at the death of a
priest, on the *marae*, after which they were burnt.[8] Stewart
says that all the temples contained three images, one at each
end, opposite and facing each other, and one in the middle
against the thatch behind.[9]

Tautain gives both general observations and a detailed
description of a Nukuhivan *marae*. He says that most of the
principal *marae* of tribes or valleys were so ruined that it was

[1] Mathias, p. 57.
[2] *Ibid.* p. 59.
[3] Wilson, p. 143.
[4] Langsdorff, vol. I, p. 180.
[5] *Rovings*, vol. II, pp. 197 sq.
[6] Porter, vol. II, p. 123.
[7] Shillibeer, p. 41.
[8] Lisiansky, p. 81.
[9] Stewart, vol. I, p. 267.

often impossible to reconstruct the old arrangement. They were shaded by large ancient trees, which had fallen and broken the structures by their weight, whilst young trees shooting up between the interstices of the pavements had disjointed and burst the walls. Of the individual *marae*, the sacred places peculiar to families, nothing was left but a shapeless cairn. He then goes on to describe the principal *marae* of the Tekea branch of the Hapaa group,[1] and he illustrates his description by a ground plan and two sectional plans. Tautain's account is too long to give here, but it is important to refer to it, because he says that the description of the *marae* in question gives some idea of what all these *marae* (he sometimes calls them "altars", but is evidently using the term with the same meaning) were like and what was requisite in them.[2] Other writers give descriptions, often fragmentary, of specific Marquesan *marae* and burial places.[3]

The material supplied by Handy suggests that some of the confusion in the descriptions of earlier writers may be due to local variations, and to differences in mortuary customs depending on the rank or position of the deceased. As regards burial the body was often dismembered, and sometimes special treatment was accorded to the head. The usual procedure seems to have been either to wrap the remains in *tapa* and suspend the bundle from the side of the house, or to put them in a coffin which was placed in a cave or in a banyan tree, or hung up inside the dwelling house or in a house specially constructed for the purpose. The skulls of chiefs were generally placed in the temple, the rest of the body being hidden away in a cave. Inspirational priests were buried in a vault within the temple.

The places of sepulture of the families of Hiva Oa were domestic shrines, but were not referred to as *me'ae*, a term reserved for the places where the bodies of chiefs and priests were placed, these being centres of tribal ceremonial. The mortuary and religious functions of these *me'ae* were interrelated, for the ancestor cult centred around the sacred remains of the dead.

The *me'ae* were groups of platforms, made of a stone casing

---

[1] Cf. *Systems*, vol. I, chap. VIII.
[2] Tautain, *L'Anthro.* vol. VIII, pp. 667 *sqq.*
[3] D'Urville, *Voy. pitt.* vol. I, pp. 490, 491, 494; cf. Vincendon-Dumoulin, *I.M.* pp. 243 *sq.*; Porter, vol. II, pp. 110 *sq.*; Melville, pp. 100 *sq.*; Stevenson, *S.S.* p. 99; Mathias, pp. 57 *sq.*; Stewart, vol. I, pp. 266 *sq.*; Wilson, pp. 132 *sq.*; Radiguet, vol. XXII, pp. 466 *sq.*, 449–54; Krusenstern, vol. I, p. 127; *A.P.F.* vol. XII, pp. 579 *sq.*; Bennett, vol. I, pp. 322, 329 *sqq.*; Lambert, pp. 137 *sq.*

filled with earth, broken stones and rubble. The most important of these platforms was the one which held the images, while others were surmounted by houses used for various religious purposes. Beneath some of the *me'ae* were vaults for the burial of ceremonial priests. According to Handy, the *me'ae* had no enclosing wall, the limits of the sacred precincts being well enough known to the people, but they were always associated with sacred trees or groves, as in the Society Islands.[1]

In addition to the family burial places and public *me'ae*, there were other religious structures of less importance—places where hair and other sacred things were placed or where offerings were made to the evil spirits which caused women to die in childbirth,[2] as well as certain temporary structures erected in connection with religious ceremonies[3] and sacred precincts associated with industry.[4]

HERVEY ISLANDS

As regards the Hervey Islands there is a certain amount of information from Rarotonga and Mangaia. Arai-te-tonga was the principal *marae* of Rarotonga where the sacrifices to the gods were made, and the *takurua*, or annual feast at the presentation of the first-fruits, was held, accompanied by many ceremonies and much rejoicing; with it were associated several other structures, stone seats and a long seven-roomed house, called *are-kariei* or "house of amusement", the term *kariei* (sometimes spelt *karioi*) being, as Smith points out, the Rarotongan equivalent of the Tahitian *arioi* and Marquesan *ka-ioi*; and when the *mataiapo*, or minor chiefs, visited the *ariki* they lodged in the seven-roomed house, and occupied the stone seats. Near the *marae* was also a house called *are-vananga*, used by the *ariki*, probably as chief pontiff, during great functions.[5]

There are one or two references to religious structures in Mangaia by Gill,[6] and more recently by Dr Buck. According to Buck, the Mangaian god-house was distinct from the *marae*. The former was of simple construction, and in it were kept the images of the gods, which were tended by a special caretaker. These images, he thinks, were never taken to the *marae* for religious worship.

[1] Handy, *N.C.M.* pp. 113–20.   [2] *Ibid.* p. 115.
[3] *Ibid.* pp. 231 *sqq.*   [4] *Ibid.* pp. 146, 164.
[5] Smith, *J.P.S.* vol. XII, pp. 218 *sqq.*; cf. Savage, *J.P.S.* vol. XX, p. 218.
[6] Gill, *L.S.I.* pp. 15, 95, 100; *Jottings*, pp. 23 *sq.*

The *marae* themselves were important in worship and also in establishing titles to land. They were rectangular courts surrounded by walls of coral rocks embedded in the ground, the interior being filled in with earth and stones to form a level terrace. There are no traces of raised stone platforms, though platforms of wood or slabs of stone were employed in connection with human sacrifice. "The maraes were used for purposes other than religious, and some of them were entirely secular."[1] Buck gives a list of forty Mangaian *marae*, together with the gods and tribes to which they belonged.

Special miniature houses were built upon the *marae* when peace was declared. No images were kept in them but the god was believed to take up his spiritual residence in them as an alternative to the god-house.

On public occasions the priests officiated at the *marae*, but such ceremonies were occasional and for ordinary purposes they screened off a portion of their dwellings as private shrines.[2]

PAUMOTU

Systematic descriptions of Paumotuan *marae* are provided by Seurat. The *marae* of Katipa in the island of Fakahina (Akahaina) was, he says, the largest of those in that island, and the only one where human sacrifices were offered, the victims being strangers who landed on the island. It was near the slope leading to the outside reef. There was a large rectangular enclosure, surrounded by slabs of limestone coral. Back to back (*adossées*) with the external wall of the enclosure were objects resembling praying desks on which the priests knelt. The heads of victims offered at this *marae* were deposited in a large hole near another *marae* adjoining it, on the bank of the lagoon; but the bodies were buried in the large *marae* itself.

Seurat also describes the *marae* of Tahitinui, also in the island of Fakahina. It was less complicated in structure than that of Katipa. Seurat says that human sacrifices were not made on this Tahitinui *marae*. It was the place where men came to eat turtle—a sacred animal—women and children not being allowed to be present. The god of the *marae* informed the priest of the presence of a turtle on the reef, and the latter ordered men to go and seek it. On their return the priest, aided by two assistants, cut off the animal's head, and kneeling before

---

[1] Te Rangi Hiroa, *M.S.* p. 174.   [2] *Ibid.* pp. 172–7.

a large stone of the *marae* with the head of the turtle in his hand, offered it to the god. Then those present ate the turtle, after which the bones and entrails were not thrown away, but were put in a space, called *pafata*, surrounded by stones. The head was strung on a pandanus branch, and the shell was put on a wooden screen. Seurat also describes *marae* similar in essentials to the other two in the islands of Fagatau (Angatau?) and Napuka.[1] There are a number of references by other writers to Paumotuan *marae*,[2] though most of them are only fragmentary in character.

As regards burial of the dead in the *marae*, we have only Seurat's statement quoted above, which refers specifically to the victims of human sacrifice, but we may well believe that certain small grave-like *marae* referred to by writers were used for interment. It may be mentioned that Seurat states that altars (by which he means *marae*) were numerous in Fakahina, and that each family seemed to have its own.[3]

OTHER ISLANDS

The material bearing upon temples and burial places in other parts of Central Polynesia is fragmentary in character. As regards Rotuma, Gardiner does not refer to temples, though he describes stone structures associated with burial places, which are also mentioned by other writers.[4]

Percy Smith refers to chiefs' seats and coronation stones in Niue and to sacred places of worship, though these do not appear to have been temples, with the possible exception of an enclosure in the village of Paluki, near the centre of the island. The dead were buried in caves, though the bodies of chiefs were first exposed for some days on a heap of stones in the bush.[5]

---

[1] Seurat, *L'Anthro.* vol. XVI, pp. 475 *sqq.* It should be noted that the three islands mentioned above are near the extreme north-eastern limit of the Paumotuan group, and Seurat says the *marae* of these north-eastern islands were of a type quite different from those in the islands of Temoe and Marutea, close to Mangareva.

[2] Beechey, vol. I, pp. 167 *sqq.*; d'Urville, *V.P.S.* vol. II, Part I, p. 393; Moerenhout, vol. I, pp. 97 *sq.*; *A.P.F.* vol. VIII, p. 48; vol. IX, pp. 16, 161; vol. X, p. 189; vol. XIV, p. 330; cf. Waitz-Gerland, vol. V, pp. 223 *sq.*; Smith, *J.P.S.* vol. XXVII, pp. 119 *sqq.*; *Rovings*, vol. I, pp. 242 *sq.*, 336; *J.P.S.* vol. XXVII, pp. 134 *sq.*; Quiros, vol. I, p. 200; vol. II, pp. 418 *sq.*; Hawkesworth, vol. I, pp. 102 *sq.*; Courteaud, *Rev. d'Eth.* vol. III, pp. 548–9.

[3] Seurat, *L'Anthro.* vol. XVI, p. 476.

[4] Gardiner, *J.R.A.I.* vol. XXVII, pp. 431 *sq.*, 464 *sq.*, 483, 503 *sqq.*, 515; Lesson *Voy.* vol. II, pp. 433, 437; *A.P.F.* vol. XX, p. 363; *Rovings*, vol. I, p. 166; Allen *A.A.A.S.* vol. VI, p. 577; Wood, *J.R.A.I.* vol. VI, p. 6.

[5] Smith, *J.P.S.* vol. XI, pp. 100, 174 *sq.*, 198, 201, 207; vol. XII, pp. 90, 219 Thomson, *S.I.* pp. 95 *sq.*; *J.R.A.I.* vol. XXXI, pp. 139, 142; Turner, p. 306 Loeb, *Niue*, p. 87.

Both Wilkes and Hale describe a *marae* (apparently not built of stone) in the island of Fakaafo (Bowditch Island) of the Tokelau group, sacred to the great Tui Tokelau,[1] and Hamilton, speaking of the island of Atafu (Duke of York Island), refers to a place of venerable aspect, formed entirely by the hand of nature, and resembling a druidical temple.[2] As regards burial places, Lister describes a grave as a mound of coral shingle, with a vertical slab of stone at the head, and other slabs laid on the top and sides of the mound.[3]

In the interior of the island of Fotuna (Horne Island) there was a thick forest which had, from time immemorial, borne the name of the "sacred wood"; in the centre of this wood was a vast enclosure, where the king, his ministers, and all the notables of the country gathered together for great deliberations. Here and there in this enclosure human heads and bones were hanging on trees; it was there that old men, women, and children were slain in honour of the god; it was there that, the night before war, the people came to sing war hymns, and again, after the battle, to devour the corpses collected on the battlefield; and, most often of all, the people came there in crowds to fêtes, which began with dancing and games and ended in all sorts of orgies.[4] We are not told anything of the character of this enclosure, or whether there were any stone or other structures associated with it. The Fotuna people buried their dead near their houses.[5]

There was in each village in Wallis Island a kind of cell, destined solely for the lodging of the god of the place, when, coming back from the "night" (the abode of the gods), he wanted to have some rest during the day.[6] Every village had a house of the dead; it was generally on a hillock, surrounded by walls and a hedge of shrubs, and was a common sepulchre.[7]

Lamont describes the *marae* of Tongareva, which, he says, were used for the burial of warriors and chiefs, and a quantity of additional information, mainly archaeological, is provided by Dr Buck.[8] The principal ceremonies carried out at the *marae* were the appointment of priests, invoking the gods, the ceremonial eating of turtle and the drinking of coconut milk.[9]

[1] Wilkes, vol. v, pp. 14 *sq.*; Hale, pp. 157 *sq.*
[2] Hamilton, pp. 74 *sq.*   [3] Lister, *J.R.A.I.* vol. XXI, p. 55.
[4] Bourdin, p. 445.   [5] *Ibid.* p. 449 *n.* 1.
[6] *A.P.F.* vol. XIII, p. 7; cf. Mangeret, vol. I, pp. 158 *sq.*
[7] *A.P.F.* vol. XIII, p. 8.
[8] Lamont, pp. 111, 159, 209, 235 *sq.*; Te Rangi Hiroa, *E.T.* pp. 148 *sqq.*
[9] Te Rangi Hiroa, *op. cit.* p. 177.

There are some scraps of information concerning the temples and burial places of the Ellice Islands. There was evidently a stone enclosure with images of the gods in Niutao and it can hardly be doubted that the *fale atua* of Funafuti was in the form of a house; apparently the temples and the burial grounds were distinct, though Turner speaks of the skulls of departed chiefs and people being laid out in rows in the temples.[1]

[1] Turner, pp. 281, 285, 289 *sq.*; Hedley, p. 52; Newell, *A.A.A.S.* vol. VI, pp. 607 *sq.*; Gill, *Jottings*, pp. 12, 14.

CHAPTER VII

SACRED OBJECTS

IN dealing with temples we have had occasion to mention certain sacred objects associated with Polynesian worship. Of these the most important were the images of the gods, found in certain groups, around which were centred the religious ceremonies of the people. In addition to these, everything within the precincts of the temple was sacred. The houses used for preserving the images, the altars, posts and pillars as well as various other structures were invested with sanctity either through their association with the temple, or by virtue of specific beliefs connected with them.

In many of the islands there were rocks or blocks or fragments of stone, either standing by themselves or preserved within the sacred precincts, which had a peculiar sanctity attached to them. Again certain natural objects such as conch shells, or manufactured articles such as canoes, often played an important part in religious worship. Coconuts, and more particularly coconut leaves, were often used for ceremonial purposes.

SAMOA

As regards Samoa, neither Turner nor Stair mentions any images, and the absence of images of any sort is asserted by both Williams and Brown.[1] Krämer, however, refers to an alleged Samoan wooden image, and to a statement that some of the people had roughly carved idols as representations of deceased chiefs, to whom they paid religious homage.[2] Wilkes also says that the Samoans had carved blocks of wood and stone erected in memory of deified chiefs.[3] But in spite of the lack of carved images in Samoa, there were a number of sacred objects, particularly stones. Thus the belief prevailed that certain natural stone formations ("*tupua* rocks") were of human origin, while others were believed to be legendary seats or kava bowls.[4] Smaller sacred stones were deposited in the temples.

[1] Williams, p. 436; Brown, p. 225.   [2] Krämer, *S.I.* vol. II, p. 207.
[3] Wilkes, vol. II, p. 132; cf. Murray, 40 *years*, p. 172.
[4] Cf. Pratt, *s.v. tupua*; Fraser, *J.P.S.* vol. v, p. 182 *n.*; Stair, *J.P.S.* vol. v, p. 34; Te Rangi Hiroa, *S.M.C.* p. 329.

The supposed human origin of the *tupua* rocks is illustrated by the legends; thus there was a tale of a man and his wife living at Falealupo (in Savai'i); their daughter Tapuitea married the king of Fiji, lived in Fiji, and had two sons Toiva and Tasi. She developed such alarming cannibalistic habits that they fled, but she pursued, and followed them to Falealupo. Toiva, at the request of Tasi, in order to save him from his mother, buried him alive, and he was represented by a stone there.[1] Two stones at Aopo (in Savai'i) were identified with a descendant of Pili who slew a nine-headed pigeon, and was himself afterwards killed, he and the pigeon being changed into stones.[2] There are a great number of other Samoan legends of this type.[3]

In addition to the *tupua* rocks, there were other stones connected with gods without any reference to human origin. There was in Tutuila a god Nave represented by a stone.[4] Turner mentions twin gods called the lizard and the stone which were worshipped at certain villages in time of war, famine, and pestilence, the month of May being a time specially fixed for prayers and food offerings.[5] Two unchiselled smooth stones of the stream spoken of by Turner were kept in a temple at one of the villages and guarded with great care, no stranger or over-curious person being allowed to approach; one of them was credited with providing yams, breadfruit and coconuts and the other sent fish to the nets. A stone, carefully housed in another village, was the representative of a rain-making god. When there was too much rain, the stone was laid by a fire and kept heated till fine weather returned; but in time of drought the priest and his followers went in procession to the stream, dipped the stone into it and prayed for rain.[6]

Brown tells us of a Samoan temple in which were deposited three sacred stones,[7] and in the Manu'an island of Tau there was a large standing stone, said to have been the net stone of a legendary person called Sa'u-mani, a great fisherman, and here offerings were made to him.[8] In the house of Tuitele in Leone (in the island of Tutuila) there was an *aitu* stone called *ma'a o*

---

[1] Turner, pp. 260 *sq.*; cf. Krämer, *S.I.* vol. I, pp. 80, 100.
[2] Krämer, *S.I.* vol. I, pp. 63 *sq.*
[3] Powell, *R.S.N.S.W.* vol. xxv, pp. 125, 246 *sq.*; Krämer, *S.I.* vol. I, pp. 282, 286, 370, 451 *sq.*; Fraser, *J.P.S.* vol. VI, pp. 113 *sq.*; Turner, pp. 25, 31, 45.
[4] Turner, p. 40.   [5] *Ibid.* p. 44.   [6] *Ibid.* pp. 44 *sq.*
[7] Brown, p. 225; cf. Murray, 40 *years*, p. 172.
[8] Pratt, *R.S.N.S.W.* vol. xxv, pp. 70 *sqq.*; cf. Krämer, *S.I.* vol. I, p. 369.

Taema, indicating that Taema (one of the twin goddesses of Samoa) landed there.[1]

Special mention should be made of sacred shell trumpets in Samoa, and their special connection with war. Stair refers to an inner chamber in a Samoan mountain burial place, in the centre of which was a small stone cromlech, upon which was a great conch shell, white with age and encrusted with moss and dead animalculae.[2] He says it was used in Samoa for parade and show in times of peace, and for signals or triumphs in war;[3] and tells us that the *songa*, or trumpeter, would walk before the chief, when the latter was journeying, and announce his approach by continually blowing the conch shell.[4] Turner says that shell trumpets were among the insignia of royalty in Samoa, and that the canoe of an important chief had on board one or two of them, which were blown every now and then as it passed the villages.[5] Turner gives a number of examples of various gods supposed to be immanent in or represented by conch shells. In one case the shell was consulted in time of war and by its magical manifestations the decision to fight or not was made.

There are also several references to sacred drums in Samoa. In the small, but important, island of Manono, among the objects that were supposed to be inspired by the district war gods was, according to Stair, the *limulimu-ta*, a sort of drum, and this drum was one of the symbols which accompanied the fleets of the island.[6] Stair also tells us of a Samoan drum, the use of which was formerly restricted to seven families.[7] According to von Bülow drum-beating was one of several methods of making a noise in order to keep off the *aitu* on the death of a man.[8] Churchward says that every town of any respectable size had its drum for summoning the inhabitants at the chief's will, or to give warning that something unusual was happening.[9] There is some evidence as to the sanctity of the coconut in Samoa, and the connection of this with its use as a taboo sign. Thus the great Samoan war goddess Nafanua was specially associated with coconut leaflets; and to this

[1] Krämer, *S.I.* vol. I, p. 326.   [2] Stair, p. 222.
[3] *Ibid.* p. 135.   [4] *Ibid.* p. 123.
[5] Turner, 19 *years*, pp. 351 *sq.*; cf. Erskine, p. 43; Steubel, p. 99; Churchward, p. 262; Stair, p. 221; Turner, pp. 19, 23; cf. pp. 26 *sq.*, 28 *sq.*, 54.
[6] Stair, p. 221.
[7] *Ibid.* p. 135; cf. Krämer, *S.I.* vol. II, p. 221.
[8] Von Bülow, *Globus*, vol. LXVIII, p. 267.
[9] Churchward, p. 262.

connection was attributed the use of these as taboo marks tied round trees,[1] and as tokens, laid between hostile war parties, of a temporary truce.[2] It is said that in Samoa generally the use of the coconut leaf as a taboo sign was connected with the family god.[3]

TONGA

The material bearing on the images of Tonga is interesting, because of the references to the lack of respect with which some of them were treated. G. Forster reports the finding in Tonga of two pieces of wood a foot long, carved with some resemblance of the human figure, apparently in the building on a *faitoka* or burial place, or a neighbouring house, but they were trodden on and kicked about and treated without respect.[4] Possibly J. R. Forster is referring to the same images when he says that he asked if they were *eatooa* (*atua*) and was told that they were not so—they were *teeghee*.[5] He also refers to the lack of respect shown to the images. Cook refers to images in the house on the *faitoka*, and says that the natives dared not enter the house, but told him that the images were merely memorials of chiefs who had been buried there, and not representations of any deity.[6] There are other references to rudely carved logs of wood or images and the lack of respect paid to them.[7] Meinicke refers to the little wooden images, often very old, found in the Tongan temples, which he thinks were representations of the gods of the second class (souls of men).[8] It is said that they buried figurines of wood, representing people of both sexes, with the corpse, a few inches deep.[9]

The images referred to above seem all to have merely represented *ti'i*; but Williams refers to images of gods.[10] There are several references to whale's tooth images, which appear to have represented gods. One of these was given to the missionaries by a *tamaha*, and she called it her grandparent.[11] The god Fakatomafi was represented by a large necklace of whales' teeth,[12]

[1] Turner, p. 39. [2] Brown, p. 267.
[3] Krämer, *S.I.* vol. II, p. 98.
[4] G. Forster, *Voy.* vol. I, pp. 451 *sq.*
[5] J. R. Forster, *Obs.* p. 566.
[6] Cook, vol. V, p. 342; cf. vol. III, pp. 182 *sq.*
[7] Wilson, pp. 247, 252; d'Urville, *Astro.* vol. IV, pp. 83, 106, 279 *sq.*
[8] Meinicke, vol. II, p. 81. [9] D'Urville, *Astro.* vol. IV, p. 362.
[10] Williams, pp. 318 *sq.*; cf. Thomson, *D.P.M.* p. 347.
[11] Lawry, *F.F.I.* (1), Appendix, p. 246.
[12] Lawry, *F.F.I.* (2), p. 37.

and there are several other statements[1] concerning gods associated with whales' teeth.

Turning to sacred objects of a more general character, the
stones of Topukulu and Nafanua were worshipped in "Tonga
and the other islands". When there was a drought the people
asked the two goddesses for rain; in time of dearth they were
asked for abundance; in case of tempest they were appealed
to for a calm; and generally they were entreated for abundance
of fish and fruits and all other foods. These were, however, the
only matters concerning which they were approached, and in
particular the people did not do so in cases of illness.[2]

As regards the use of conch shells in war, the *Duff* missionaries refer to a sacred house where there were four large
conch shells which were used to alarm the country in time of
danger,[3] which suggests some sanctity in the shells and their
use in time of war, though in Mariner's accounts of military
operations there is not a single reference to a conch shell.
However, he describes their use in connection with the *inaji*
ceremonies and with the mortuary rites of the *tuitonga*.[4]

SOCIETY ISLANDS

The material bearing on the images of the Society Islands
presents a certain amount of diversity, perhaps owing to local
variations. Ellis says that the idols of Tahiti were generally
shapeless pieces of wood, from one to four feet long, covered
with sinnet of coconut fibres, ornamented with yellow and
scarlet feathers. Oro was a straight log of hard casuarina wood,
six feet long, uncarved, but decorated with feathers. The gods
of some of the adjacent islands exhibited a greater variety of
form and structure.[5] He gives illustrations of some of these
images.[6] Elsewhere Ellis describes the wooden idols as having
been generally hollow, with sacred red feathers inside them,
though others were solid pieces of wood, bound or covered with
finely braided fibres of coconut husk, to which the feathers
were attached. He refers to these images as *too* and it is evident
that the important ones were kept in the big *marae* or temples,
and those of families in their private temples.[7] On another page
Ellis distinguishes between images called *too*, representing the

---

[1] Lawry, *F.F.I.* (2), pp. 34–5; Young, *S.W.* pp. 225, 251.
[2] Reiter, *Anthrop.* vol. II, p. 754.   [3] Wilson, p. 101.
[4] Mariner, vol. II, pp. 169–72, 182 *sqq.*; cf. Veeson, p. 79.
[5] Ellis, vol. I, p. 354; cf. vol. II, p. 112.
[6] *Ibid.* vol. I, p. 356; vol. II, p. 111.   [7] *Ibid.* vol. I, pp. 338 *sqq.*

national or family gods, and those called *ti'i*, representing the spirits.[1] All these images were kept under cover.[2] The preparations for war included the building in a canoe of the house of Manaha, or host of gods, designed to be the abode during the fighting of the gods and spirits; and into this house were placed the *too*, or "images of the spirits", or feathers taken from them.[3] There was a funeral ceremony of chiefs intended to bury the sins of the dead man; a hole was dug in the earth near the bier, and in it was planted the pillar or post of the corpse, as it was called, "perhaps designed as a personification of the deceased, to exist after his body should have decayed", after which the earth was thrown over, as they supposed, the guilt of the departed, and the hole was filled up.[4] Ellis gives no description of this pillar; but it seems clear that it remained unprotected out of doors. In describing the ravages of warfare, Ellis speaks of the way in which the enemy demolished the temples, destroyed the idols, broke down the altars and used as fuel the *unu*, or curiously carved pieces of wood marking the sacred places of interment, and emblematic of *ti'i* or spirits, and he refers to the reinstatement of these after the war, in a way which seems to make it clear that these *unu* were regarded by him as being distinct objects, and not the images; but he does not describe the *unu* or say where they were.[5] In describing the great sanctity attributed to the kings and their property, Ellis says that the ground for a considerable space on both sides of a king's house was sacred, and a *ti'i* or carved image, fixed on a high pedestal, was placed by the roadside at the boundary; travellers passing the house, whether the king was residing there or not, had on approaching one of these images to uncover their upper bodies, and so walk until they reached the image at the opposite boundary.[6]

Moerenhout, like Ellis, distinguishes between *too* and *ti'i*. He says the *too* were images of *atua*, those made of wood being hollow inside, either with hardly any shape or face, or presenting horrible features, and having monstrous legs and arms or only indications of them, whilst the stone images were usually merely a column (*colonne*) or a triangular block covered with cloth.[7] They were kept very carefully in the *marae*, special priests, called *amoi toa*, taking charge of them; the priests laid

---

[1] Ellis, vol. I, p. 337.   [2] *Ibid.* pp. 335, 340.
[3] *Ibid.* pp. 280 *sq.*   [4] *Ibid.* pp. 401 *sq.*
[5] *Ibid.* p. 348.   [6] *Ibid.* vol. III, p. 106.
[7] Moerenhout, vol. I, p. 471.

offerings before them, presented victims and prayed to them, and on very solemn occasions of ceremony at the great *marae* they were placed on the tops of the pyramids.[1] The images of the *ti'i* were worked with much more care than those of the superior *atua*, but were but little respected, being sold or broken when the people were displeased with them. Some of them were placed round or at the extremities of the temples as guardians of the sacred grounds.[2]

Cook refers to a number of sepulchral buildings, which were decorated with many carved boards, set upright, and having on their tops various figures of birds and men,[3] and he refers to an image of a bird, carved in wood, on the top of the *marae* of Amo and Purea, near which lay the broken image of a fish, carved in stone.[4] He also saw in the corner of a house four wooden images, and was told that they were gods of the *toutou* or servants, though he expresses a doubt as to these people having special gods.[5] Cook also gives descriptions of the arks or chests in which the images of the gods were carried about.[6] Banks refers to a stone image, and also describes some of the arks referred to by Cook—in fact one account is evidently taken from the other.[7] J. R. Forster says that the *ti'i* (spirits) lived mainly in the wooden figures erected near the *marae*, and were regarded as male or female according to the sex of the deceased persons with whom they were connected.[8] G. Forster describes a number of images around the burial place of a great chief.[9] The *Duff* missionaries saw in the house of a Tahitian chief many wooden gods of different names, the god of the sun, the moon and stars, and of men, women, children, and so on. Each had a sword, axe, or hammer in its hand, which, a priest said, was to kill those who offended them, unless sacrifice and atonement were offered.[10] Bougainville describes two wooden figures —the family god and goddess—which he found in the house of a Tahitian chief, both of them made of wood, about three feet high, ill made, and standing on carved hollow cylindrical pedestals about six or seven feet high.[11] He also speaks of the *ti'i* as wooden figures representing subordinate genii, and

[1] Moerenhout, vol. I, pp. 471, 478 and 461.   [2] *Ibid.* pp. 471 and 461.
[3] Cook, vol. I, p. 150.   [4] *Ibid.* p. 159.
[5] *Ibid.* vol. III, p. 342.
[6] *Ibid.* vol. I, pp. 233, 237; vol. VI, p. 35.
[7] Banks, pp. 112, 114, 120.   [8] J. R. Forster, *Obs.* pp. 543 *sqq.*
[9] G. Forster, *Voy.* vol. I, p. 267.   [10] Wilson, p. 165; cf. p. 208.
[11] Bougainville, pp. 221 *sq.*

called *ti-tane* or *ti-aine*, according to their masculine or feminine genders. He says the people of Tahiti had several of them in their houses and that they were employed in religious cere-monies.[1] Wilkes, speaking of the Tahitian *marae*, with their pyramids or mounds, says that whenever war broke out between two districts, each was desirous of obtaining possession of the other's *ti'i* or idol, for the loss of it was an acknowledgment that the god was less powerful than that of the other district.[2] Wallis,[3] Tyerman and Bennet,[4] and the Spanish observers[5] also give descriptions of Society Island images.

There are several references to stones associated with gods and ancestors in the Society Islands. In Eimeo there were two large stones which the people regarded as *atua*, and were said to have been a brother and sister, who had come by some supernatural means from Ra'iatea.[6]

At the *marae* of Tane in the island of Huahine there was a remarkable stone, set on end, which was said to have caught his tail when he attempted to rise from the top of it into the air on a journey of mischief;[7] and in another spot on the island, ap-parently near the *marae*, was another stone on which the image of the god was set down "that he might rest himself" after the fatigue of being carried from his *marae* on important cere-monial occasions.[8] Near Oro's *marae* in the same island were two stones, one upright and the other prostrate, remains it was said of a very ancient *marae*, but whose origin was unknown; and prayers were offered, and honours paid, to these stones.[9] In the island of Tahaa there were rocks of curious forms, to one of which was assigned the name or semblance of a red dog, and another was called a fish-hook, and was supposed to have been employed in fishing by the god Hiro.[10]

In Tahiti large conch shells were used in war to stimulate in action, by the priests in the temple, by the herald, and on board the fleets. They were blown when a procession walked to the temple, or their warriors marched to battle, or a restriction was imposed in the name of the gods.[11] According to Moerenhout a conch was blown by a priest when the will of the gods became

---

[1] Bougainville, p. 472.   [2] Wilkes, vol. II, p. 31.
[3] Hawkesworth, vol. I, p. 485.
[4] Tyerman, vol. I, pp. 243, 267; vol. II, p. 58.
[5] Corney, *Tahiti*, vol. I, pp. 296, 337; vol. II, pp. 85, 327 *sq*.; cf. *J.P.S.* vol. IV, p. 287 and *n.* 104 on p. 293.   [6] Cook, vol. VI, p. 82.
[7] Tyerman, vol. I, p. 283.   [8] *Ibid.* p. 277.
[9] *Ibid.* p. 244.   [10] Bennett, vol. I, p. 358.
[11] Ellis, vol. I, pp. 196 *sq*.; cf. vol. III, pp. 109–13; Moerenhout, vol. I, p. 519.

known to him, or he felt himself inspired.[1] Anderson says it was blown as a signal to all the king's subjects that they were to bring food of every sort to him.[2]

The Society Island drums, made of solid pieces of wood hollowed out, and having at one end a diaphragm of shark's skin, are described by Ellis, who says the large drums were called *pahu*, and the smaller ones *toere*. The *pahu ra*, or sacred drum, was particularly large, sometimes standing eight feet high. These sacred drums were beaten on every occasion of extraordinary ceremony at the *marae*, such as human sacrifice.[3] Another occasion was the ceremony of inauguration of a king, at which the big drum of the *marae* was carried about and beaten by the priests.[4] Moerenhout says that the priests beat the sacred drum before war—generally as a sign that the gods required human victims.[5] Drums were also used to animate the warriors when marching to battle,[6] as well as at dances, song recitals, and the like.[7]

There was a certain degree of sanctity attached to important canoes in the Society Islands. The *Duff* missionaries speak of Tahitian war canoes and those sacred to the *atua* as though they were not identical, which in fact they do not seem to have been. Both sorts were built by the whole community on orders from the chief. Feasts were held before cutting down the necessary tree, and afterwards at various stages in the construction of a canoe, the object of the feast being to engage the favourable help of the *atua*. The greatest festivity of all took place when the canoe was finished, and at this stage we find a differentiation, because only non-human offerings were presented to the gods in the case of a war canoe, whereas in the case of a canoe given to the *atua* a human victim was required. The sacred canoe was decorated with cloth and red feathers, and drawn up to the *marae*, where it was offered to the *atua* with prayers and sacrifices; and the body of the victim was buried in the *marae*.[8]

Moerenhout says that sacred canoes always had to be carried, as they might not touch any soil but the sacred soil of the *marae*; they might not even be laid down anywhere else in transit.[9] In time of war they laid the bodies of their slain enemies in rows

[1] Moerenhout, vol. I, p. 509. [2] Cook, vol. VI, p. 155.
[3] Ellis, vol. I, pp. 193–5; cf. Cook, vol. VI, p. 32.
[4] Ellis, vol. III, pp. 109–12. [5] Moerenhout, vol. I, p. 510.
[6] Ellis, vol. I, pp. 195, 285. [7] *Ibid.* p. 195.
[8] Wilson, pp. 377 *sq.* [9] Moerenhout, vol. I, p. 526.

on the beach, and used them as rollers, over which they dragged the war canoes in launching them and afterwards on landing.[1] The sacred canoes played an important part in the ceremonies prior to war; temporary temples with small altars were erected in them, and in these temples were deposited the sacred red feathers taken from the images of the gods, and the heads of the sacrificial pigs were placed on the altars.[2] So also it was the sacred canoes, adorned with flags, garlands and flowers, that bore the bodies of the human victims and other offerings to the gods required on the conclusion of peace,[3] and, apparently, prior to fighting.[4] G. Forster speaks of a few canoes of the *atua* which accompanied the fleet when it went out to battle, and which were to carry the bodies of the killed.[5]

According to Tyerman and Bennet the priests accompanied the naval forces to battle in a separate canoe, bearing the image of their gods. This canoe went in front of the others, and during the fighting the image was sometimes held up aloft. The fighting by these priests was carried to the most desperate extremity, for if the image fell into the hands of the enemy, the divinity of the god was lost and his adherents fled panic-stricken.[6] Moerenhout and Ellis identify the canoe that bore this image with the sacred canoe.[7] It is evident that these sacred canoes took their part in certain ceremonies, for there is an account of the use of the sacred canoe, bearing the image of Oro, on the occasion of the inauguration of a Tahitian king.[8] Apparently there was a practice for sacred canoes to be built by the chiefs; Tyerman and Bennet refer to the finding in the island of Borabora of the remains of an old canoe, built in the last war, to appease the anger of a god; and they say that these canoes were constructed entirely by the kings and chiefs themselves, no vulgar hands being allowed to aid in the sacred work.[9] So also Pomare I of Tahiti was one of the most experienced canoe-builders in the country, and for a month before the expedition into Attahuru his sole employment was building a canoe as an offering to his *atua*.[10] Sacred canoes in the Society Islands were adorned with images, some animal and some human. Hamilton

[1] Ellis, vol. I, p. 309.
[2] *Ibid.* pp. 281 *sq.*; cf. Cook, vol. VI, pp. 35 *sq.*, and vol. III, p. 316.
[3] Moerenhout, vol. I, p. 525.   [4] *Ibid.* p. 527.
[5] Forster, *Voy.* vol. II, p. 65.
[6] Tyerman, vol. I, p. 334; cf. Henry, *J.P.S.* vol. IV, pp. 257, 287, 290.
[7] Moerenhout, vol. II, p. 36; Ellis, vol. I, p. 212; cf. p. 154 and fig. on p. 153.
[8] Ellis, vol. III, pp. 110 *sq.*; cf. Moerenhout, vol. II, p. 26.
[9] Tyerman, vol. II, pp. 20 *sq.*   [10] Turnbull, p. 345.

says that in Tahiti every war canoe had "a figure head of the god Priapus, with a preposterous insignia of his order";[1] and J. R. Forster says the war canoes had at head and stern the rude figure of a man called *E-teehe* (presumably Ti'i).[2] We are also told of a Society Island custom of having little temples and altars and images on canoes other than those admittedly sacred or devoted to war.[3]

There are records of beliefs and practices connecting the coconut and coconut leaves with the gods, and of their use for supernatural purposes. In Tahiti the images of the gods were wrapped up in finely braided sinnet (coconut fibre).[4] Coconut leaves, generally three in number, called *tapaau*, played an important part in the people's ceremonies.[5] The sacred canoe of Oro was distinguished from the others by the *tapaau* or sacred wreaths of plaited coconut leaves by which it was surrounded, and which were worn by everyone on board.[6] Coconut leaves were worn by the priest when going round to announce a taboo or feast,[7] and he wore a *tapaau* of coconut leaves round his arm at an inauguration ceremony.[8] The body of a human victim was placed in a long basket of coconut leaves, in which it was carried to the *marae*.[9] The altars were decorated with coconut leaves,[10] and there are several other references to their use in ceremonial.[11]

MARQUESAS

As regards the Marquesas, Porter describes a number of images kept at the *marae*, and the religious ceremonies connected with them.[12] He says that, besides these gods at the *marae*, the people had household gods, as well as small gods, generally made of bone, which they hung round their necks. These gods were not, however, held in any estimation.[13]

Stewart says that each of the temples contained three images, one at each end, opposite and facing each other, and one in the middle against the thatch behind.[14] He draws attention to the disrespectful way in which the people treated the images.[15]

[1] Hamilton, p. 49.   [2] Forster, *Obs.* pp. 458 *sq.*
[3] Henry, *J.P.S.* vol. IV, pp. 257, 277, 285, 287, 290, 293.
[4] Ellis, vol. I, p. 337; cf. p. 344.   [5] Smith, *J.P.S.* vol. I, p. 45 *n.*
[6] Ellis, vol. III, p. 110.   [7] Moerenhout, vol. I, p. 478.
[8] Ellis, vol. I, p. 109.   [9] *Ibid.* p. 347.
[10] *Ibid.* p. 349.
[11] Cook, vol. I, pp. 215, 218; cf. Bligh, p. 131; Ellis, vol. I, p. 371.
[12] Porter, vol. II, pp. 110 *sq.*   [13] *Ibid.* p. 114.
[14] Stewart, vol. I, p. 267.   [15] *Ibid.* pp. 262, 296, 298.

Sometimes a bundle, called a "clothed god", consisting of a wooden log, wrapped in cloth, with four conch shells fastened to it, was lifted up and carefully laid down again by the priests, all the people standing and making responses to an unintelligible jargon during its elevation.[1] Frequent use was made in religious ceremonies of a piece of wood, with another fastened across the top of it; also of a small canoe decorated with human hair. At times, too, a *hami* or girdle, or other article was held up, and the name of the god invoked in a loud and bold manner.[2]

D'Urville saw at a *marae* in Nukuhiva an image, coarsely carved from a huge block of wood, and almost buried under offerings of coconuts, breadfruits, and the like; and at another *marae* he saw, inside the enclosure, three images coarsely carved. He noticed that the people did not treat the images with great respect.[3] Several other writers provide additional information concerning Marquesan images.[4]

As in other groups, the conch shell was used for various ceremonial purposes[5] as well as in war,[6] while sacred drums were prominent in the *marae* ritual and other ceremonies.[7] In this group all canoes were taboo to women, who were not allowed to sail in them.[8]

There are a few references bearing on the sanctity of the coconut in the Marquesas. The coconut palm had its own god, Uuhoa;[9] and a head priest (*taua*), awaiting inspiration from the gods, would lean his head against the trunk of a coconut tree near the *marae*, and this, apparently, always induced visitation by the god, whom the priest caught in his hand;[10] and certain priests always wore a hat of coconut leaves and a collar made

---

[1] Stewart, vol. I, pp. 250 *sq.*   [2] *Ibid.* p. 251.

[3] D'Urville, *Voy. pitt.* vol. I, p. 491; cf. p. 494.

[4] *A.P.F.* vol. XII, p. 580; Mathias, pp. 42, 51, 55, 58, 59, 127; Radiguet, vol. XXII, pp. 443, 449, 454; vol. XXIII, p. 610; Shillibeer, pp. 39 *sq.*; Krusenstern, vol. I, p. 127; Quiros, vol. I, pp. 27 *sq.*; Vincendon-Dumoulin, *I.M.* p. 243; Melville, pp. 99 *sq.*, 190 *sq.*, 194–7, 198 *sq.*; Tautain, *L'Anthro.* vol. VIII, pp. 672, 675 *sqq.*; Christian, *J.P.S.* vol. IV, p. 189.

[5] Shillibeer, p. 51; Wilson, p. 135; Bennett, vol. I, pp. 332 *sq.*, 329.

[6] Shillibeer, p. 39; cf. p. 56; Langsdorff, vol. I, p. 222; Quiros, vol. I, p. 18; Coulter, p. 192; Fanning, p. 212; Bennett, vol. I, p. 332; Coulter, p. 193; Langsdorff, vol. I, p. 223.

[7] Tautain, *L'Anthro.* vol. VIII, p. 668 and *n.* 1; cf. pp. 552, 670; Melville, pp. 184 *sqq.*; Langsdorff, vol. I, p. 222.

[8] Stewart, vol. I, p. 216; Lisiansky, p. 75; d'Urville, *Voy. pitt.* vol. I, p. 485, and *V.P.S.* vol. IV, p. 300; Vincendon-Dumoulin, *I.M.* p. 262; du Petit-Thouars, vol. II, p. 357; Christian, *J.P.S.* vol. IV, p. 202; Melville, pp. 146 *sq.*; cf. Tautain, *L'Anthro.* vol. VI, p. 640.

[9] Christian, *J.P.S.* vol. IV, p. 190.   [10] Mathias, p. 46.

from a coconut branch, the wearing of which was absolutely necessary in the exercise of their office.[1]

PAUMOTU

In the Paumotu islands *tiki* was the term for a statue, a carved object or a doll.[2] In Gambier Island there were houses in the midst of reeds, on the slopes of the mountains, or at extremities of settlements, in which were hidden gods at which the people were not allowed to look;[3] these are probably referred to in the statement that the idols in the temples were long beams (*poutres*), the extremities of which represented very indecent human figures,[4] and in the reference to a temple, decorated with human figures, rudely carved, whose names indicated that they were the gods worshipped by the people.[5] Beechey describes a hut, in the centre of which was an idol three feet high, neatly carved and polished, with the eyebrows sculptured, but not the eyes, and muscles well defined. It was placed in an upright position, and beneath it were several paddles, mats, and pieces of cloth that had been offered to the god, and a calabash of *avy* (kava?) water.[6]

Seurat mentions stone images, or *tiki*, connected with the Paumotuan *marae*[7] and Moerenhout describes a *marae* of Gambier Island, formed like a house, with a paved forecourt, at one of the extremities of which stood an image three feet high, fairly well sculptured, and in good proportion, except that the arms were too small; he was told that this was a *ti'i*, a second-class deity, placed there to mark the limits of the sacred place.[8]

In Mangareva they had what is spoken of as an "observatory", consisting of stones, set from distance to distance, which indicated by their shadows the points of the rising of the sun, its course, and even the return of the seasons, which were occasions for celebration. A man had charge of observations of this kind.[9] Perhaps the people realized the fact that during a portion of December the shadow fell northward, instead of southward.[10]

---

[1] D'Urville, *Voy. pitt.* vol. I, p. 504. [2] Tregear, *J.P.S.* vol. IV, p. 80.
[3] *A.P.F.* vol. X, p. 189. [4] *Ibid.* vol. IX, pp. 166 *sqq.*
[5] *Ibid.* p. 16. [6] Beechey, vol. I, pp. 167 *sq.*
[7] Seurat, *L'Anthro.* vol. XVI, pp. 476 *sqq.*
[8] Moerenhout, vol. I, pp. 97 *sq.*
[9] D'Urville, *V.P.S.* vol. II, Part II, p. 436; cf. p. 437.
[10] Young, *J.P.S.* vol. VIII, p. 268.

HERVEY ISLANDS

In Mangaia there were carved images of the more important deities, those of Rongo being of stone and those of the other gods of wood. All these were kept in the national god-house, but the priests also had extra images in their houses.[1] Gill refers to Rongo being represented by a trumpet shell.[2] Sacred drums were beaten in connection with peace-making ceremonies,[3] and among some of the Mangaians the big drum used at dances was called "the voice of Tane", and was evidently regarded as sacred to that god, as the tutelary deity of dancing;[4] and one of the songs, repeated by Gill, suggests that the sound of it brought beings from spirit-land to join in the dance.[5]

Coconuts and coconut leaves were ritually employed in the Hervey Islands. In Mangaia sinnet was used for the ornamentation of the images of their gods, and that of Mokoiro, their god of fishermen, was entirely made of sinnet.[6] No fisherman would venture out in his canoe to fish unless he took with him the extremity of a coconut leaf bound up with sinnet by the "priest of all food".[7] After the beating of the drum of peace, and the inauguration of a secular king, coconut trees were planted all over the island to mark the duration of peace.[8] In Mangaia, the extremity of a coconut leaf was placed on the stomach of a dead man, and served as a charm or safe conduct on entering the invisible world.[9] In Aitutaki, the kernel of a coconut was so placed to save the ghost from having to eat the bowl of live centipedes offered to it by Miru of the underworld.[10]

ELLICE ISLANDS

As regards the Ellice Islands, Gill describes a temple in the island of Niutao, the central side post of which, stouter than the rest, and crooked, was identified with the god, and was the object of daily worship.[11] The Ellice Islanders also had stone gods.[12] There was a tale of a famous and powerful priest who, instructed in a dream by seven spirits, made a god of a red

---

[1] Te Rangi Hiroa, *M.S.* p. 170.   [2] Gill, *S.L.P.* p. 229; cf. *Myths*, p. 28.
[3] Gill, *Myths*, pp. 294 *sqq.*; cf. Te Rangi Hiroa, *M.S.* p. 185.
[4] Gill, *Myths*, pp. 219 *sq.* and *note*.
[5] *Ibid.* pp. 259–64. (See also comments on this, March, *J.R.A.I.* vol. XXII, pp. 327 *sq.*)   [6] Gill, *Jottings*, p. 206.
[7] Gill, *Myths*, p. 79.   [8] *Ibid.* p. 300.
[9] *Ibid.* pp. 170 *sq.*, 269.   [10] *Ibid.* pp. 170, 173 *sq.*
[11] Gill, *Jottings*, pp. 15 *sq.*
[12] Turner, p. 281; cf. pp. 289, 291; Murray, 40 *years*, p. 408.

stone which was wrapped in pandanus leaves, and placed in a case, *fe'ou*, like a hencoop; and if anyone fell sick the stone was taken out of the case and implored to relieve or cure the sufferer.[1] In Niutao, Tangaloa, the god of heaven, was represented by an upright slab, not unlike a headstone in an English graveyard;[2] and in an "idol-house" Gill saw on a swinging tray a smooth round pebble, worshipped as a god, near which lay offerings of green coconuts, with the sacred leaflet;[3] during the worship of the central post of the image-house, each new act of worship involved the tying of a fresh coconut leaf round the post, and another round the arm of the worshipper, and three green coconuts and a sacred leaflet were offered morning and evening.[4]

NIUE

Thomson says there were no images in Niue;[5] but according to Turner, the people worshipped the spirits of their ancestors, and once, long ago, they paid religious homage to an image with legs like a man; but at a time of a great epidemic they broke up the image and threw it away, believing it to be the cause of the sickness.[6] Again, they had a legend concerning Huanaki, the god of the north end of the island, that a "likeness" of him was made of stone on the coast of his district.[7] They had a sort of feather head-dress, identified with Tangaloa, which seems to have been possessed with some power of the character of *mana*, and gave prosperity to the island.[8]

OTHER ISLANDS

In Fotuna (Horne Island) the presence of ancestors and dead relations was indicated at the domestic hearth by a pillar, called the divine pillar; in the field by a stone of conical shape, and in the forests by a little basket hung on a tree.[9] According to Smith there was, before the house of each principal chief of a valley, a sacred stone, which the natives dared not touch for fear of their great god Faka-veli-kele,[10] and there are other references to sacred stones connected with religious

[1] Hedley, p. 47.
[2] Gill, *Jottings*, p. 12.
[3] *Ibid.* p. 16.
[4] *Ibid.* pp. 15 sq.
[5] Thomson, *J.R.A.I.* vol. XXXI, p. 139.
[6] Turner, p. 306.
[7] Smith, *J.P.S.* vol. XI, p. 196; vol. XII, pp. 22–4.
[8] *Ibid.* vol. XI, pp. 175 sq.
[9] Bourdin, p. 442; Mangeret, vol. I, p. 269.
[10] Smith, *J.P.S.* vol. I, p. 47.

ceremonies.[1] As in Tahiti, the *tapaau* of coconut leaves (generally three) played an important part in ritual.[2]

In Fakaofo (Bowditch Island) of the Tokelau group, there were, according to Wilkes, images, of which the largest was fourteen feet high and eighteen inches in diameter. It was covered with mats, and over all a narrow mat was passed, shawl fashion, and tied in a knot in front, with the ends hanging down. He also speaks of a smaller idol of stone, four feet high, only partly covered with mats.[3] Tui Tokelau, the great god of this island, was supposed to be embodied in a stone, which was carefully wrapped up in fine mats, and never seen by anyone but the king, and even by him only once a year when the decayed mats were stripped off and thrown away.[4] Sick people were washed with coconut water, some of which had previously been sprinkled on the stone; and if a person wished to die he would crawl to the foot of the stone, and his belief that he would die generally accomplished the wish to do so in two or three days. The stone was apparently not carved.[5]

In Fakaofo two coconut leaves were laid across the chest of a dead man,[6] and coconut leaves were used as taboo signs on trees.[7]

INSIGNIA OF RANK AND OFFICE

Having considered the more important of the material objects held as sacred, there is one more matter with which we must deal, namely the distinguishing insignia of chiefs and other important persons. Though this subject might be regarded as belonging more properly to political and social organization rather than to religion, the general sanctity of chieftainship throughout Central Polynesia justifies us in mentioning it here.

Prominent among the artefacts which formed the insignia of rank and office in Polynesia were objects made partly or entirely of coconut leaves, a fact which may be considered in relation to the ritual use of coconut leaves in other contexts, as well as certain more general material bearing on the sanctity of the coconut.

Among the ceremonial articles made of coconut leaves were the sacred head-dresses worn by chiefs and priests in the

[1] *A.P.F.* vol. XVI, p. 365; Bourdin, pp. 444 *sq.*, 471.
[2] Smith, *J.P.S.* vol. I, p. 45.   [3] Wilkes, vol. V, p. 15.
[4] Turner, p. 268.   [5] Lister, *J.R.A.I.* vol. XXI, p. 50.
[6] *Ibid.* p. 54.   [7] Hedley, p. 26.

Society Islands[1] and the Marquesas;[2] other coconut-leaf decorations were worn upon ceremonial occasions in Fotuna,[3] in the Tokelau[4] and Ellice[5] groups, and in Tikopia.

Apart from their use as decorations, coconut leaves were used for other ceremonial purposes. Thus Ellis says that throughout the Society group a coconut leaf was the emblem of authority; and requisitions for labour or property, preparations for war, or the convocation of a national assembly, were made by sending a coconut leaf to those whose service or attendance was required. Refusal of the symbol was an insult to the king and a sign of resistance to his authority.[6]

In Mangaia also a coconut frond was a symbol of authority,[7] and was apparently used for a somewhat similar purpose. The extremity of a great coconut leaf, called the *iku kikau*, was used in inviting great chiefs to a feast.[8]

In addition to coconut leaves, feathers, and particularly red feathers, were extensively used in Polynesia in the making of the decorations and insignia of rank. Though we cannot examine the evidence in detail there were two feather ornaments of pre-eminent importance, namely the sacred red belt and the feather head-dress which may be considered here.

The *maro ura*, or belt of red feathers, was one of the most sacred objects in the Society Islands. In this group, whilst the term for a chief was *ari'i*, a head chief was called *ari'i rahi*; a few head chiefs, however, were entitled to the still more glorious title of *ari'i maro ura*, "the chief who wore the *maro ura*".[9] Cook saw the *maro ura* used at a sacrificial ceremony held in anticipation of war at the great *marae*, Maraetaata in Attahuru, of the young King Pomare, and he describes the *maro* as follows: It was a girdle about five yards long and fifteen inches broad, ornamented with red and yellow feathers, mostly the latter. One end was bordered with eight pieces, each about the size and shape of a horseshoe, having their edges fringed with black feathers; the other end was forked, and the points were

[1] Moerenhout, vol. II, pp. 22 *sq.*; L.M.S. *Trans.* vol. IV, p. 433.
[2] Porter, vol. II, p. 11; Bennett, vol. I, p. 311; Stewart, vol. I, p. 248; d'Urville, *Voy. pitt.* vol. I, p. 504, and *V.P.S.* vol. IV, pp. 28, 281; Mathias, p. 60; Lesson, *Poly.* vol. II, p. 197; cf. *A.P.F.* vol. XII, p. 572.
[3] Smith, *J.P.S.* vol. I, pp. 41 *sq.*
[4] Lister, *J.R.A.I.* vol. XXI, pp. 53 *sq.*   [5] Gill, *Jottings*, p. 22; cf. p. 12.
[6] Ellis, vol. III, p. 122; cf. Moerenhout, vol. II, p. 32; Tyerman, vol. I, pp. 349 *sq.*   [7] Gill, *S.L.P.* pp. 67, 152.
[8] Gill, *Myths*, p. 79.
[9] Williams, p. 549; Ari'i Taimai, pp. 7, 109; cf. Moerenhout, vol. I, p. 142.

of different lengths. The feathers were in square compartments, ranged in two rows, and otherwise disposed. These feathers had first been fixed on some of their own native cloth, and then sewn to the upper end of a pennant left by Wallis. About six or eight inches square of the *maro* was practically unornamented.[1]

An interesting fact connected with the *maro ura* was that additions were made to it upon ceremonial occasions, for example at the inauguration of every sovereign.[2] Cook says feathers were added at the ceremony after making peace.[3] Tyerman and Bennet, in describing a Tahitian *maro ura*, say it had two lappets attached, signifying that two monarchs had been arrayed in it;[4] and they say of the long *maro ura* of Ra'iatea that almost every handbreadth of the patchwork that composed it represented a separate reign and reminded the national chroniclers of the prince's name, character, achievements, and the main incidents of his time; so that the robe might be regarded as a hieroglyphic tablet of the annals of Ra'iatea.[5] So sacred was this royal garment that human victims were required during its making and subsequent lengthenings.[6]

The ideas of the people concerning the *maro ura* are illustrated by the following observations. It was sacred, even as the persons of the gods, the feathers being supposed to retain all the dreadful attributes of power and vengeance which the images of the gods possessed, and with which it was designed to endow the king, whom it raised to the highest earthly station, identifying him with the gods.[7] The sacrifice of the victims not only invested the belt itself with a high measure of solemn importance, but also rendered the chiefs who wore it most noble in public estimation.[8] The belt was more sacred than the images of the gods and its wearer was inviolable and sacred, and almost equal to the gods.[9] It was the symbol of divinity and fire.[10] The donning of the belt was, of course, an essential feature at an inauguration ceremony; but it was also worn on other solemn occasions.[11] Cook says that it was worn by King Pomare when making peace with Eimeo;[12] and that it was in

---

[1] Cook, vol. VI, p. 34. For other descriptions see Ellis, vol. III, p. 108; Williams, p. 549; Moerenhout, vol. I, p. 472; Tyerman, vol. I, p. 527; Henry, *A.T.* p. 189; cf. below, p. 262. [2] Williams, p. 549.
[3] Cook, vol. VI, p. 62. [4] Tyerman, vol. II, p. 56.
[5] *Ibid.* vol. I, p. 527.
[6] Williams, pp. 549 *sq.*; cf. Moerenhout, vol. II, p. 28; Ellis, vol. III, pp. 108 *sq.*; Tyerman, vol. II, p. 56. [7] Ellis, vol. III, p. 108.
[8] Williams, p. 550. [9] Moerenhout, vol. I, pp. 471 *sq.*
[10] *Ibid.* p. 448. [11] *Ibid.* p. 472. [12] Cook, vol. VI, pp. 61 *sq.*

evidence at an offering of human victims prior to war, though on that occasion the king did not wear it, but held it in his hand.[1]

As we have said, only a few of the *ari'i rahi* or head chiefs of the Society Islands were entitled to wear the *maro ura*, and to be called also *ari'i maro ura*, and the importance of this privilege in the political history of Tahiti has already been indicated elsewhere.[2] Moerenhout says the twelve head members or grand-masters of the *arioi* might wear it.[3] References to the *maro ura* are found in several of the songs or legends about the gods.

Moerenhout says that in the Marquesas the priests wore the *maro ura* at the great feast in October (spring) celebrating the return of Maui;[4] at that feast they used it to kindle the fire for the sacrifices at the *marae*.[5]

We may also mention a sacred belt used upon ceremonial occasions in Mangaia, though we are not told of what it was made nor whether it was red.[6]

As regards feather head-dresses, Krämer says that one of the items of the festal attire of the Samoan nobility was the *tuinga* or head-dress, which included an ornament made almost entirely from the red feathers of the *senga*, a bird referred to in the legends and regarded as sacred.[7] In Tonga they had much-valued head ornaments made or decorated with the red feathers of the tropic bird.[8] Moerenhout, in describing Tahitian funeral ceremonies, refers to the *parai*, a kind of tiara, worn by the *hiva tupapau*, or sacred mourner, and says that it was also worn on solemn occasions by chiefs. It was made of feathers of different colours, divided into rays (*rayons*) like the rainbow, which it imitated, and was covered with shells. He says it was one of the most imposing ornaments which adorned the chiefs and authorities of the country;[9] it was also worn by the inferior chiefs as a war dress.[10] Probably he is referring to the same thing when he speaks of diadems, covered with feathers and very rare shells, worn by the priests.[11] No mention is made of the kinds of feathers so worn; but Fitzroy speaks of headpieces

[1] Cook, vol. VI, p. 34.
[2] See *Systems*, vol. I, chap. V.
[3] Moerenhout, vol. I, p. 472.
[4] *Ibid.* p. 561.
[5] *Ibid.* pp. 516, 561 n.
[6] Gill, *L.S.I.* pp. 39 *sq.*, 54; *Myths*, p. 128.
[7] Krämer, *S.I.* vol. II, pp. 285–8.
[8] Cook, vol. V, pp. 303, 408.
[9] Moerenhout, vol. I, p. 548.
[10] *Ibid.* vol. II, p. 34.
[11] *Ibid.* pp. 24 *sq.*

surmounted by feathers of the tropic bird, which, he fancied, were worn by priests when sacrificing a victim.[1] Cook says that in Atiu, of the Hervey group, only chiefs and dancing women wore red feathers; and he describes a chief who, when receiving the English, had in his ears large red feathers, pointing forward.[2] A distinctive decoration of a Marquesan chief was the *tavaha* or diadem of cocks' feathers, only worn on great occasions.[3] Bennett refers to a head-dress of black tail-feathers of a cock worn by warriors.[4] Radiguet says that at the funeral feast held six months after the death of a high priest warriors wore the *tavaha*, which he describes as a fan of dark green feathers with a crescent-shaped object below it studded with red berries and decorated with tufts of old men's beards.[5] There are numerous other references to Marquesan feather head-dresses,[6] and as regards the Paumotu Islands there are several allusions to chiefs wearing head ornaments of black or white feathers.[7] We are told of a king of the island of Fotuna and his son who wore crowns made of white feathers, adorned with green and red feathers of parakeets and pigeons.[8] Geiseler and several other observers give descriptions of feather head ornaments worn on Easter Island.[9]

In conclusion we must mention several references to the carrying of staves or sticks by people of high rank. There are also one or two allusions to their use of fans or fly-flaps, the latter being of particular importance in Samoa. The carrying of staves or sticks was of course a common thing in Polynesia, but there were certain objects of this character which had a definite official or symbolical meaning.

The orator's staff of Samoa is well known to all students of Polynesian ethnography. It is referred to in legends, quoted elsewhere,[10] of the distribution made by Pili among his sons, in which he gave the orator's staff and fly-flap to his son Sanga.

---

[1] Fitzroy, vol. II, p. 522. [2] Cook, vol. v, pp. 232, 239.
[3] Mathias, p. 88; cf. du Petit-Thouars, vol. II, p. 346; d'Urville, *Voy. pitt.* vol. I, p. 486; *A.P.F.* vol. XIX, p. 28.; cf. Mathias, pp. 135 sq.
[4] Bennett, vol. I, p. 310. [5] Radiguet, vol. XXIII, p. 620.
[6] Lesson, *Poly.* vol. II, p. 197; d'Urville, *Voy. pitt.* vol. I, pp. 482, 492 sq.; Fanning, p. 179; *A.P.F.* vol. XIX, p. 28; Shillibeer, p. 47.
[7] Quiros, vol. I, p. 202; vol. II, pp. 339 sq.; Beechey, vol. I, pp. 171 sq., 209; d'Urville, *Voy. pitt.* vol. I, p. 517.
[8] Dalrymple, vol. II, p. 46.
[9] Geiseler, pp. 34 sq., 51 sq.; de Brosses, vol. II, p. 236; Behrens, pp. 88 sqq.; W. J. Thomson, pp. 535 sq.; Forster, *Voy.* vol. I, p. 589; Chamisso, vol. II, p. 257; Corney, *Easter*, p. 143; Geiseler, pp. 51 sq., and 35.
[10] *Systems*, vol. I, p. 58.

Its use by orators in the *fono* has also been described.[1] It is said that these staves were handed down from generation to generation as valuable heirlooms, and often bore the names of the great orators of the respective families.[2] The son or other representative of a political head, when sent on any important message to another district, took with him his father's staff and fly-flap, as evidence that his message was brought with the sanction of the person to whom they belonged and carried his authority.[3] Apparently the staves sometimes fulfilled the functions of policemen's batons and were used by their owners for restoring order;[4] and there are references to spears being used instead,[5] especially in time of war.[6] Apparently a similar badge of office was carried in Tonga, for Waldegrave refers to a "staff-bearer" sitting on the left of the *tuitonga*, and presiding over the kava-making at a feast.[7] G. Forster refers to Tahitian priests, each having a long wand.[8] As regards the Marquesas, Fanning, in describing a procession at his reception by a young Nukuhivan king, refers to a row of eight chiefs, bearing long black and yellow rods or canes, made of hard wood, and having at one end bunches of human hair.[9] Bennett refers to fans as having been peculiarly characteristic of the aristocracy of the island of Tahuata (Marquesan group); he says they had wooden handles, curiously carved with grotesque images, were semi-circular, and made with coconut ribs, the surface being either blackened with candlenut or whitened with coral lime.[10]

In the Paumotu group Wallis saw natives with sticks, which seemed to be ensigns of authority, as the people who carried them kept the rest back.[11] When the Spaniards were at Gente Hermosa of thè Tokelau group, among the natives who tried to drag their launch ashore was "a very audacious old man",

[1] *Systems*, vol. II, p. 460; cf. Erskine, p. 73; Hood, pp. 67 sq.; Monfat, *M.S.* p. 18; Whitmee, *J.R.A.I.* vol. VIII, p. 271.
[2] Whitmee, *J.R.A.I.* vol. VIII, p. 271.
[3] Turner, 19 *years*, pp. 349 sq.
[4] La Pérouse, vol. III, pp. 234, 280.
[5] Monfat, *M.S.* p. 183; Krämer, *S.I.* vol. II, p. 209.
[6] Turner, 19 *years*, p. 341.
[7] Waldegrave, *J.R.G.S.* vol. III, p. 187.
[8] Forster, *Voy.* vol. I, pp. 272 sq.; cf. Fitzroy, vol. II, p. 523.
[9] Fanning, p. 179; cf. Vincendon-Dumoulin, *I.M.* pp. 283 sq., who also mentions fans.
[10] Bennett, vol. I, p. 312. There are many other references to ceremonial rods and fans in the Marquesas: d'Urville, *V.P.S.* vol. IV, p. 281; Radiguet, vol. XXII, pp. 434, 461, 466; vol. XXIII, p. 621; Porter, vol. II, p. 10; *A.P.F.* vol. XIX, p. 28; Belcher, vol. II, p. 318.
[11] Hawkesworth, vol. I, p. 431; cf. *A.P.F.* vol. X, pp. 414 sq.

who carried a long and thick lance of palm wood;[1] and when they approached an island of the *Duff* group, its chief, who came to meet them, bore a staff in his hand.[2]

It cannot be contended that every occasion upon which someone in authority was seen carrying a staff must be taken as evidence that it was a symbol; but the cumulative effect of all the evidence seems to leave no doubt that it was so pretty generally in Polynesia, staffs being carried by chiefs or their high officials.

[1] Quiros, vol. I, p. 211.   [2] *Ibid.* vol. II, p. 459.

Part II

THE PLACE OF
RELIGION IN THE CULTURES OF
CENTRAL POLYNESIA

CHAPTER VIII

THE STUDY OF PRIMITIVE RELIGION

WE have, in the preceding sections, reviewed a certain amount of ethnographic material bearing on the religious systems of Central Polynesia, their background of belief, their ceremonial observances, and the material substratum of sacred objects associated with them. It now remains for us to attempt to place this material in its social context by indicating its relation to other aspects of native culture, in this way seeking to gain an understanding of its significance in the lives of the Polynesians. But before doing this it seems desirable to consider certain theoretical points relating to the study of primitive religion in general, in order to clarify the point of view from which we intend to approach the problem.

No phase of primitive life has, in the past, attracted so much attention as that which is concerned with the savage's relation to the supernatural, his religion and his magic. The motives for this interest in primitive religion and magic have been of various kinds. In the first place nothing about primitive man so readily fires the popular imagination as his bizarre ceremonies and exotic beliefs, for these constitute at the same time the most striking and the most inexplicable phase of his life. Elsewhere we can always detect immediately something which the native shares with ourselves: his kinship organization may appear unnecessarily complicated and bewildering, but its *fons et origo*, the individual family, provides some basis for understanding; his methods of production in the economic sphere may appear to us as crude, but we recognize as entirely rational the ends which they are designed to attain; and though we may not understand the complicated mechanism of a political institution such as chieftainship, we comprehend it as founded upon the need for socially recognized authority. But the religions of primitive societies are so alien to our own culture—in the nature of their beliefs, in the forms of their ritual, and in the character of their ethical standards—that they cannot readily be understood in terms of anything familiar to us in everyday life. Many of the early missionaries attempted to explain them as manifestations of the powers of darkness,[1] but apart from this primitive religion was dismissed as the quaint and irrational expression of a childish, illogical superstition, unworthy of the serious attention of civilized man.

THEORETICAL APPROACH TO PRIMITIVE RELIGION

The development of scientific anthropology brought with it a new kind of interest in primitive religion, and led to an attempt to explain the facts rather than to ignore or condemn them. The earliest treatments of primitive cults regarded them as prototypes of more advanced religions, and the chief object in studying them was to gain an understanding of the *origin* of human religion, and of the psychological processes whereby man first arrived at a belief in the supernatural. The first of these attempts to explain the origin of religion was the animistic theory propounded by E. B. Tylor, and subsequently adopted by Herbert Spencer. According to this view the idea of the soul was the essential fact in the development of religion, which was held to have been due to a process of reasoning carried out by primitive man.

The steps in the intellectual process whereby man arrived at a belief in the soul were, according to the animistic theory, as follows: The idea of the soul was derived originally from the experiences of dreams when, apparently, a part of the sleeper leaves his body and wanders abroad as a separate entity, from which was inferred an essential dualism in the nature of man. Fainting and other similar conditions provided further examples of a temporary separation between the body and the soul, while at death a further separation took place, this time of a permanent character. The soul, which left the body permanently at death, was held still to influence the lives of the survivors for good or ill, and this led to prayers and sacrifices designed to secure blessings and avert evil. The first religion was thus the cult of ancestors, which subsequently gave rise to other forms.

Among the most important of these later religious forms was the worship of nature, based upon the belief in the supernatural qualities of animals, plants and material objects. This

[1] Thus Ellis thought it not impossible " that communities, so wholly given to idolatry of the most murderous and diabolical kinds, should be considered corporeally, as well as spiritually, to be lying in 'the wicked one'" (vol. I, p. 362).

cult Tylor and Spencer derived from the worship of ancestors, though in different ways. According to Tylor the extension of religious interest from the souls of ancestors to the phenomena of nature was due to the peculiar mentality of the primitive, who, like the very young child, did not distinguish between the animate and the inanimate, and thus came to endow the phenomena of nature with a spiritual quality analogous to his own. The manner in which Herbert Spencer derives the worship of nature from that of ancestors is rather different. For him, the transition was due to linguistic errors: Men are frequently known by the names of animals, plants or other natural objects, and Spencer suggested that, after such a man had been dead for some time, his descendants would mistake his name for a descriptive title—if he had been called "Tiger", his descendants would, in time, come to believe that he really was a tiger, and since the ghost is often believed to re-visit its old home, the divinity of the ancestor would eventually come to be regarded as incarnate in the animal. He offers similar explanations of other aspects of nature worship.[1]

As we have seen, the animistic theory gives primacy to the worship of the soul, and derives the worship of nature from it. But another school of thought, associated particularly with the name of Max Müller, reverses the order, and derives the belief in supernatural beings from the sensations aroused in man by the overwhelming and at times cataclysmic manifestations of nature. These, far from being "natural", were calculated to make the human mind aware of "the overwhelming pressure of the infinite". Such sensations were the germ of religious experience, which grew into religion proper through a disease of language. Müller holds that man first called the striking phenomena of nature by terms which denoted their activities—"a thunderbolt was called *something* that tears up the soil or that spreads fire; the wind *something* that sighs and whistles",[2] and so on. This description of the phenomena of nature in terms of human or quasi-human activities led to an interpretation of them in anthropomorphic terms, and divine personalities were invented to account for the activities of natural phenomena. The origin of religion thus lay in a disease of thought and of language—since the words used to describe the awe-inspiring phenomena of nature were terms denoting human activities,

[1] *Principles of Sociology*, vol. I, chaps. XXII–XXIV.
[2] Quoted by Durkheim, *Elementary Forms of the Religious Life*, p. 77.

these terms were taken to imply the existence of personal agencies operative in the natural phenomena themselves.

The theories which we have so far mentioned derive religion essentially from the supposed primordial speculations of man concerning phenomena with which he came in contact, whether spiritual or material, religious beliefs arising from the impressions, intellectual or emotional, produced by a contemplation of these phenomena. They assumed a certain abstract philosophical curiosity concerning the phenomena of human life and of nature, which drove man to a series of inferences, the end-product of which was religion. It was Sir James Frazer who first introduced the pragmatic element into the study of primitive religion by attributing its growth to an active desire for effective control of the phenomena of nature, rather than to passive impressions derived from the contemplation of them. The source of primitive religion he finds in the failure of magic to effect the desired results. Magic he believes to be a mistaken application of principles of association which, properly employed, lead to science:

> The fatal flaw of magic lies not in its general assumption of a sequence of events determined by law, but in its total misconception of the particular laws which govern that sequence.... The principles of association are excellent in themselves, and indeed absolutely essential to the working of the human mind. Legitimately applied they yield science; illegitimately applied they yield magic, the bastard sister of science.[1]

Magic, then, seeks directly to influence the natural sequence of cause and effect, and shares with science the fundamental belief that this sequence is absolute and invariable. But religion rests upon a different assumption, namely the belief in the existence of "powers superior to man which are believed to direct and control the course of nature and of human life".[2] This stage of belief, which is a step beyond that of faith in magic, is reached when man realizes the futility of his magical practices, and instead offers supplications to powers higher than himself, who can, he believes, alter the normal sequence of cause and effect at his behest. This theory goes far beyond those which we have mentioned previously, in stressing the part played by human needs in the genesis of religion, as well as philosophical speculation. Such speculation is held to be carried out under the stimulus of man's desire to control life

[1] Frazer, *The Golden Bough* (abridged edition), pp. 49–50.
[2] *Ibid.*

and nature in accordance with his own wishes, a desire whose first manifestation is found in magic. But like the other theories, that of Frazer is orientated from a specific methodological point of view, based upon a desire to discover the origin of religion in the history of mankind, rather than to understand the reality of existing religions, and the part which they play in living human communities.

This specific orientation of early theories of religion was due to the hypothesis of evolution, which had, at the time when they were conceived, revolutionized biological science, and it seems not unnatural that the first attempts at a scientific study of religion should have regarded present-day phenomena mainly as a means of understanding the past. The most striking example of this tendency is, as one would expect, the sociological system of Herbert Spencer who sought, in every phase of social life, a progression from simple to more complex forms comparable to that which is observable in biological evolution. Based upon this common *motif*, each theory developed along particular lines, understandable in terms of the context in which it was conceived. It seems natural that Tylor, reviewing for the first time the range, of primitive religious beliefs, should be struck by the active part which ghosts and spirits of the dead play in many primitive communities, as opposed to their nebulous character and the apathy towards the concerns of the living which they exhibit in a civilized European community. In view of this it is not surprising that he should find the origin of religion in the cult of ancestors. Again Max Müller, studying the history of religion as a philologist, quite naturally found its beginnings in linguistic usage. Finally Sir James Frazer, bringing to the study of primitive society a wealth of classical scholarship, emphasizes just those facts which were important in the religion of ancient Greece, namely on the one hand the active influence of the gods on human affairs, and on the other that intellectual curiosity which led to the birth of philosophy. His theory may perhaps be regarded as a synthesis of these two conceptions.

The work of Émile Durkheim, the French sociologist, for the first time shifted the emphasis in the study of primitive religion from the past to the present. He criticizes in detail the earlier theories,[1] the main point of his argument being that they all regard religion as a survival of some elementary

---

[1] See *Elementary Forms of the Religious Life*, Book I, chaps. II and III.

intellectual blunder, some primordial process of muddled thinking. Any such theory, he holds, fails to explain why religion, founded upon a great illusion, should have survived so long, and should play the part which it does in human communities. If, on the other hand, we regard religion as corresponding to *some* reality, as meeting some actual human requirement, this problem does not arise. The reality upon which religion is founded is, for Durkheim, essentially social, and is based upon the solidarity and spiritual communion which the individual feels with the fellow-members of his social group, and he proceeds to elaborate this theory in relation to Australian totemism.

The defect of Durkheim's view is that he regards social solidarity, which is nowhere adequately defined, as an end in itself, and does not attempt to relate it to other aspects of native life, nor to individual urges considered apart from "collective representations" superimposed upon the individual by society. Undoubtedly a sense of solidarity or community feeling exists in all social co-operation, but such co-operation depends upon individual needs attaining their ends through social institutions. Religion has an effect in expressing and maintaining social cohesion, but it cannot be considered apart from other social activities of a non-religious character. Concretely, for example, Australian totemic increase ceremonies do undoubtedly serve the function which Durkheim attributes to them, namely that of increasing the sense of the individual's participation in the life of his social group. But they do far more than this; in the first place they possess a marked economic function;[1] they imply organized co-operation in productive activities, and they are very definitely related to the practical pursuits of a hunting and collecting people; their control by the old men emphasizes the political organization of the tribe, and their associated mythology is closely related to family life through the totemic theory of death and reproduction. The social solidarity which they express can therefore only be understood by considering it in concrete terms, that is, in relation to the extraneous institutional activities to which they are so closely related. Can we then, in approaching Polynesian religion, so orientate our study that we shall on the one hand describe the specific function which religion serves in native life, and on the other

[1] Cf. Malinowski, "The Economic Aspect of the Intichiuma Ceremonies", in *Festskrift tillegnad Edvard Westermarck, i anledning av Hans Femtioarsdag.*

hand gain an understanding of its functional relations to other aspects of culture?

It seems desirable to embody such an approach in a definition. Our aim will be *an analytical study of the existing reality of Polynesian religion in its cultural context.* But before attempting this let us split up this definition into its component parts in order to gain a clearer understanding of its significance.

In the first place we have insisted upon an *analytical* study. In dealing with any religious system, all its aspects must be taken into account, its dogma, ritual, and ethics, as well as the individuals and social groups involved, and the material equipment which they employ in worship. All of these are important elements, and only by recognizing the significance of each of them, and their relation to each other, can we understand the totality of primitive religion. A failure to recognize this has in the past led to one-sided treatments of the problem, both in actual field-work and in theoretical speculation. Field records of primitive religions too often consist of lengthy accounts of native religious dogma, in the form of legends, cosmogonies and the like, without the slightest hint of how these affect the lives of the people in relation to their ethical conduct, nor how they influence religious ritual. Equally one-sided are the prolix descriptions of religious ceremonies, many of which tell us nothing of the effect of these ceremonies in maintaining moral codes, nor of their effect on social life generally. On the theoretical side also, one aspect of religion is often stressed at the expense of the others. The theories of Tylor and Frazer, for example, lay undue emphasis upon dogma, and derive ritual exclusively from a pre-existing belief. Such a view obscures the fact that a large part of the function of dogma is to provide a justification, a mythological charter, for ritual. Again religious ceremonies often appear as bizarre, absurd and fantastic unless they are considered in relation to the body of significant belief upon which they are founded. In view of these considerations we shall endeavour to give due weight to all aspects of Polynesian religious systems, and to define as far as possible the relations between them.

Returning to our definition, we have set as our aim a study of *existing* religious institutions. This term is here used somewhat equivocally owing to the difficulties presented by the material. Almost all Polynesian communities have been under the influence of European civilization for many years, and the influence of traders, missionaries and government officials has produced far-reaching changes in the native mode of life. This is more or less true of native communities the world over, and for this reason the modern anthropologist is faced with an initial problem of profound significance. Shall he study the culture-contact situation as it exists to-day, taking into account only those elements of the original culture which survive in an active way, and continue to play a part in the social life of the natives? Or shall he attempt to reconstruct, partly from actual observation, partly from the records of early observers (travellers, missionaries and the like) and partly from accounts given from memory by the older inhabitants, the native culture as it was before the arrival of the white man? To illustrate this we may cite, in reference to a specifically Polynesian problem— the social organization of Samoa—Dr Felix Keesing's work *Changing Samoa* as an example of the first, and Dr Margaret Mead's *Social Organization of Manua*, of the second method. There is much to be said for each of these lines of approach. The former has a very definite value, particularly in relation to problems of administration and assimilation. But from the point of view of comparative social anthropology it can only be of value if the elements of a mixed culture which are indigenous are carefully distinguished from those which are due to European influence. From this point of view the former approach presupposes the latter, and demands that we should know as much as possible of the native culture as it was before the arrival of the white man. It is with the latter problem that we shall be concerned in the present work, namely an examination of the native religion as it was at the time of the arrival of the white man. But we would still further define it by limiting it to the phenomena existing at that time. By this we mean that we shall not be concerned with the origins of Polynesian religious institutions, their history, evolution, or diffusion, but simply with their place in the contemporary native culture. The theoretical grounds for such an approach will be discussed elsewhere.

In defining the scope of our study, we have insisted that it is with the *reality* of native religion that we are concerned. This qualification is necessary because of the character of the information at our disposal. It is only in recent years that a scientific technique of anthropological field-work has been evolved, and most of the information on Polynesian religion was collected before scientific discipline was introduced into ethnographic observation. In the first place, the earlier observers often placed their own interpretations on beliefs and customs which they recorded, and it is at times difficult to distinguish between the custom as it actually existed and the observer's interpretation of it. This is particularly true in connection with the motives lying behind customs, which are rarely described in relation to the ideology of the people. Thus we often find practical and rationalistic interpretations of customs which were clearly of a magico-religious character, and *vice versa*. For example, attention has been drawn, in regard to taboos, to the difficulty of distinguishing between those prohibitions which were enforced by a supernatural sanction and those which depended upon etiquette, the economic division of labour, and other non-religious forms of customary behaviour.

Secondly, much of the early information was collected by the "question and answer" method of interrogating natives, rather than by direct observation. In matters in which the native is not emotionally concerned (in the details of technology, for example) this method is valuable enough, but in other fields it is apt to give a distorted impression of the reality of native life. In the investigation of religion, magic, morals and personal relationships, native statements are notoriously misleading. The reasons for this are various, but they may all be reduced to the fundamental fact that the native informant is a human being, and his account of matters which concern him vitally is bound to be distorted by his own emotional bias. Such factors as reticence, shame, egotism, or the fear of ridicule may lead him to give misleading information. If he is partially Europeanized, he may deny or distort his original creed, or he may gloss over those facts which appear to the white man as repugnant or absurd;[1] if he is still mainly under the influence of his own culture he may seek to present it in a favourable light, or to put up a barrier of reserve at the point where criticism might be incurred. Again, the questioning of exceptionally intelligent and well-informed natives may lead to a too elaborate and intellectualized view of the culture, derived from the reflection and criticism of its more intelligent members. Finally the method of direct enquiry must necessarily be orientated from the point of view of the enquirer's interests, for the native will naturally dwell at length on those aspects of

[1] Cf. Te Rangi Hiroa, *S.M.C.* p. 613; Stimson, *T.R.* pp. 3-4.

culture which the white man finds interesting to the exclusion of those which, in spite of their importance to the native, do not attract the attention of the European. It is for this reason that anthropological field-work in the past has been obsessed with the strange, the bizarre, the exotic and the spectacular in native life. Many ethnographic records contain lengthy and startling descriptions of religious ceremonies, but not a word on methods of agriculture; elaborate and more or less accurate accounts of native relationship terminology, without any allusion to the obligations which kinship entails; and descriptions of birth and puberty ritual (there is no tribe about which we do not know what is done with the umbilical cord) without the slightest scrap of information about family life. This selective tendency can only be overcome by exact observations in the field, and if the available information is deficient, it is important to indicate the omissions in it.

The final condition of our study is perhaps the most important of all. We have set ourselves to study Polynesian religion in its *cultural context.* By this we mean that religion does not occur *in vacuo*—it invariably forms part of a social system, of a living culture, to every other aspect of which it is closely related. This makes necessary a short digression, in order to clarify the concept of culture.[1]

THE FUNCTIONAL STUDY OF HUMAN CULTURE

The concept of culture is a very general one, and may be defined in several ways, according to the particular angle from which it is considered. From the point of view of biology, culture is the specifically human form of adaptation, the means by which man, as distinct from other animal species, ensures his own survival. The vital requirements of nutrition, reproduction and self-defence are satisfied in the human species by cultural institutions, which are radically different from anything found in the animal kingdom, even among the so-called "social" animals. Sociologically, culture is the body of material and spiritual wealth which is passed on, in the form of artefacts and verbal traditions, from one generation to another, and which gives to human society its continuity and its cohesion. Psycho-

[1] For a fuller treatment of the subject, see Malinowski's article *s.v.* "Culture" in the *Encyclopaedia of the Social Sciences,* edited by E. R. A. Seligman and Alvin Johnson.

logically, culture may be regarded as the sum of the influences which members of a human group exert upon one another, influences which produce patterns of behaviour conforming to generally accepted norms. A comprehensive view of culture must take these three factors—biological, sociological, and psychological—into account.

Starting with the biological approach, we are struck by the fact that man satisfies his psycho-physiological requirements through forms of social co-operation determined by culture. This means that in addition to individual physiological needs and psychological wants man possesses other requirements depending on the fact that his life is lived in organized co-operation with other individuals. The *universal human needs* arising on the one hand from the nature of the human organism and on the other from the constitution of human society have been classified by Professor Malinowski into primary, derived and integrative. *Primary needs* arise out of the biological constitution of the human organism, for example the need for food or for sexual satisfaction. Another primary need of equal importance derives from the prolonged dependence of the human, as opposed to the animal, infant upon its parents, and the length of time which the human individual takes to reach physical and mental maturity. This in turn is related to the predominance of acquired as opposed to instinctive modes of behaviour in the human species and, on the neurological side, to the development of the cerebral cortex. Thus it is that the requirement of protection, care and education of the immature individual is a universal primary need of human society. Other primary needs 'are those of shelter and clothing, of drinking water, of care for the sick, and of protection against wild beasts and hostile communities. Even the bodily functions of excretion may become significant elements in human behaviour when woven into the complex pattern of culture.

But the specifically human ways of satisfying these primary needs involve the development of further or *derived needs*. Such activities as agriculture, hunting, and fishing necessitate the use of tools or implements, which in turn must be manufactured according to a standardized technology. The organization of family life requires some form of communal shelter, as well as domestic utensils. Thus it is that every society has a material substratum of manufactured articles which are employed in the satisfaction of the primary needs of its members.

Finally, the organization of society involves the satisfaction of other less tangible needs. The relation of individuals to one another, their behaviour in social situations, the entry of a new individual into society at birth, and his exit at death, as well as the various changes which take place in his social status throughout life, must all be organized. The cultural forms designed to meet such problems satisfy the various *integrative needs* of society. They regulate the behaviour of individuals towards one another in social situations and take various forms, such as political systems, moral rules, principles of etiquette, legal institutions, mortuary ritual and belief, initiation rites, as well as such specialized institutions as age grades, secret societies and other groupings for ceremonial purposes.

Turning to the sociological view of culture, we find that the requirements which have been listed find expression in systems of social activity, which, since they depend upon universal human needs, will be found in every culture, however greatly their form may vary from one community to another. Like the needs upon which they are founded, these *universal aspects of culture* will be found in every human society.

Firstly, the material needs of man involve the development of an *economic system*, designed to organize the production and distribution of material goods. Within this system food is produced, tools, weapons and implements manufactured, and shelter provided for the members of the community. Once produced, these material goods may change hands according to the socially recognized pattern which forms the basis of distribution, of the mechanism of exchange and of the rights and privileges of ownership.

Every human community possesses some form of *political organization*, some means whereby the power of the community is mobilized when collective action is required. This, again, is closely related to the *legal* aspect of culture, which is concerned with the application of effective sanctions when the traditional mechanisms of customary behaviour prove inadequate to inhibit violent insurrectionism or to overcome obstinate refusal to co-operate on the part of individuals.

The human infant, as we have seen, is at first weak and helpless, and needs to learn the means by which it can adapt itself to its environment. Thus it is that every society has some form of *education*, using the term in a very wide sense to embrace, not only formal instruction, but the whole system of forces which is brought to bear on the growing individual in order to transform him from a helpless animal into a competent and well-behaved member of society. Again every society organizes the behaviour of its members in relation to the supernatural. This *magico-religious* aspect of culture is the main subject of our study, and presents specific problems to which we shall return presently. In considering any culture, its aspects of *art* and *recreation* must also be taken into account. They serve to organize man's sensitivity to pleasant sense impressions and his enjoyment of human companionship along socially defined lines and also provide relief from the dull monotony of the crude struggle for existence.

In addition to the specific aspects of culture which have been listed, there are four very general characteristics of all forms of social activity. These general aspects enter into all the others, and are essential to social co-operation. In the first place there is the *material substratum* to which we have already referred. Though most obvious in the economic sphere, the material equipment of man shapes to a very large extent his social behaviour and his attitude towards life. Even in the most spiritual of all his activities—religious worship—material objects play an essential part. Spiritual reality is always equated to something physical, whether it be an idol, a ritually consecrated sacrifice, the Bible, or God as immanent in Nature.

The second general aspect of culture depends upon man's power of speech. Co-ordinated procedure in the course of any human activity necessitates some form of communication between the individuals engaged in it, as well as some method of storing and perpetuating an accumulated body of traditional knowledge and belief. These objects are attained by the use of language, either in the form of the ordinary pragmatic speech of everyday life, or, when necessary, by a standardized and specialized terminology. This constitutes the *linguistic aspect* of culture and embodies those rules, moral, legal and technical, by which human life is governed and regulated as well as the mechanism whereby social activity is mobilized.

Thirdly, every culture has a *normative aspect*. This is, of course, most apparent in the sphere of law, where there exist formulated rules of conduct, backed by definite sanctions in cases of breach. But these legal rules cannot, as we shall see, be considered apart from the general body of custom and the manifold forces which ensure conformity with social dictates. This body of custom enters into every phase of social life— into religion, kinship, political organization and even into economic life, where there exist definite and clearly defined rules of technology. These rules or social norms of culture are various in character, and are supported by a variety of sanctions, positive and negative; but they all imply one thing, namely that in any cultural activity there is a right and a wrong way of behaving. Of course the clarity with which this is defined and the strength with which the rules are enforced vary enormously; social sanctions range from complete social ostracism and banishment to mild ridicule or reproof. But this does not affect the general principle that every phase of social life is governed by culturally defined rules of conduct, and that there exist in every society forces which make these rules effective.

Finally, every cultural activity depends upon some form of *social organization*, some traditionally defined alignment of the members of society. In this way the place of each individual in society is fixed, his rights and obligations defined, and his patterns of behaviour determined. The forms of social grouping are of many kinds. They may depend upon physiological differences, for example between men and women or between children and adults, and this may determine important differences in economic and social function. Societies are organized territorially, and differences in rank between their component members are recognized. The inter-relations of these groups, and of their component individuals, constitute the problem of social organization.

Turning now to the psychological approach to culture, we are driven to consider how this vast mass of cultural tradition becomes impressed upon the individual. In mentioning education as an aspect of culture, we have touched upon this problem. But the process of adaptation does not cease when the individual reaches maturity and attains a mastery of his cultural tradition. The wider question of the part played by culture in the *life cycle of the individual* and the manner in which his fundamental attitudes are defined must also be considered, since it is essential to the study of human culture in general and, as we shall see, of religion in particular.

We have so far been dealing with the theoretical analysis of culture, and with a description of its general characteristics. Some such general scheme, based upon a clearly defined conception of human culture in general, is methodologically necessary in approaching any particular anthropological problem, for example the description of a given culture, or the part played by religion or economics in it. But the terms in which we have been discussing the matter correspond to general theoretical concepts, to abstractions from the realities of native life. In actual observation, whether in field-work or in the examination of ethnographic records, we are not directly concerned with these general concepts. We do not observe a "magico-religious aspect"—we see individuals or groups worshipping their gods or trying to kill one another by sorcery; we do not see an "economic system", but a number of people engaged in fishing or agriculture. On the other hand a mere catalogue of native activities would tell us nothing about the integral reality of culture, and the complicated warp and woof of social life. For this reason it is necessary to define the elements of culture with which we are concerned in ethnographic observation.

The answer to this problem is to be found in the manner in which the universal needs of man are satisfied in social life. The "individual search for food" is supplanted by organized co-operation in production—in fishing, hunting or agriculture; sex, deeply rooted as it is in the biological constitution of the organism, is not satisfied directly and instinctively, but finds expression through culturally regulated channels.[1] Human propensities, biologically determined in the first place, are organized into coherent systems of human activity, or *institutions*. The term "institution", somewhat loosely used in ordinary speech, has been given a very specific meaning in social anthropology by Professor Malinowski: "An institution could be defined as a group of people united in a common task or tasks, bound to a determined portion of the environment, wielding together some technical apparatus, and obeying a body of rules."[2] The function of institutions is so to organize human activities that various individual and social needs are satisfied. Thus economic institutions, broadly speaking, satisfy the need for food, clothing and shelter. Kinship institutions organize and satisfy the sexual and procreative needs of men and women, while the need for the training of the immature

---

[1] Cf. Malinowski, *The Sexual Life of Savages*, *passim*, and, in particular, the Special Foreword to the third edition.
[2] Introduction to Hogbin, *L.O.P.* p. xxxiii.

individual is met by the rules of family life, as well as by more specifically orientated educational institutions.

The pleasure derived from companionship is not obtained by an amorphous aggregation of human beings, but is provided by culturally defined collective activity—feasting, dancing, communal worship and the like. Again the hostile or self-assertive tendencies of man are likewise culturally defined. Vanity, pugnacity and other egotistical drives find expression through brawling, gossip, warfare, or litigation, the form and scope of which depend upon cultural tradition. It is for this reason that the concept of "instinct" must be re-defined sociologically, but with a due regard to the emotional drives which give validity to cultural institutions. In human behaviour there is no such thing as "purely" instinctive hunger or sex, and least of all is there any "herd instinct". On the contrary, the individual urges corresponding to these terms always find expression through institutions, which satisfy them in some measure, while at the same time curbing them in the interests of social life.

The considerations set forth in this section will govern our approach to the religious institutions of Central Polynesia. We shall see that these institutions have many aspects, and that economic, political, and legal elements enter into them, and so link them up with the integral reality of the culture in which they occur. Such an approach will make clear the specific functions served by magic and religion in social life. But before going on to the actual material in hand, it seems desirable to define the terms which we are using, and to examine in some detail the concept of the "magico-religious" aspect of culture. In doing this we shall have to consider the relation of magic to religion, and also the relation of these two cultural facts to those practical activities with which they are so closely related.

RELIGION, MAGIC AND PRACTICAL KNOWLEDGE

The problem of definition is a specially difficult one in the social sciences, partly because they employ to a large extent the terms of everyday speech rather than a specialized terminology. In anthropology an additional problem is presented by the fact that terms used in everyday European speech do not correspond precisely to similar concepts in primitive cultures. Specifically, the problem of defining "magic" and "religion" is complicated by the fact that in no primitive culture are there categories which correspond exactly with these terms, though there may be an approximation. The problem of definition, then, is not to say what *is* magic or religion, but to state the general classes of ethnographic facts which are to be considered under these headings. Moreover there is something inherent in the problem of definition which is far more important than merely limiting the scope of the discussion. This is the fact that a definition embodies a theoretical point of view, and should define not only the classes of facts which are to be examined, but also the methodological approach to them. When, therefore, we use the terms "magic" and "religion" in a very specific sense, we are not concerned with attaching labels to groups of phenomena; on the contrary we are firstly delimiting the scope of our study, and secondly defining our theoretical point of view towards the problems in hand.

Many attempts have been made to differentiate between religion and magic. The theories of Frazer, Durkheim and Malinowski all point out important and relevant facts connected with the native's relation to the supernatural. But none of them is able to effect a perfect dichotomy because the ethnographic material will not fit perfectly into any classification; whatever the view adopted, religion is seen to shade off into magic. And no classification is adequate when a very large proportion of the phenomena can only be classified as "borderline cases". To illustrate this, let us take Professor Malinowski's well-known statement of the difference between magic and religion since his view will in general form the basis of our methodological approach.

Compare [he says] a rite carried out to prevent death in childbed with another typical custom, a ceremony in celebration of a birth. The first rite is carried out as a means to an end, it has a definite practical purpose which is known to all who practise it and can be easily elicited from any native informant. The post-natal ceremony, say a presentation of a new-born or a feast of rejoicing in the event, has no purpose; it is not a means to an end but is an end in itself. It expresses the feelings of the mother, the father, the relatives, the whole community, but there is no future event which this ceremony foreshadows, which it is meant to bring about or to prevent. This difference will serve us as a *prima facie* distinction between magic and religion. While in the magical act the aim is always clear, straightforward, and definite, in the religious ceremony there is no purpose directed towards a subsequent event.[1]

The objection to this as a basis of classification is that it

[1] Malinowski, "Magic, Science and Religion", in *Science, Religion and Reality*, ed. Joseph Needham, p. 38.

leaves many of the phenomena unclassified. Most religious systems include ceremonies with a definite and clearly formulated objective—the provision of rain, the aversion of public calamities, or success in war. On the other hand many acts usually classified as magical lack entirely a "clear, straightforward, and definite" aim, as in the many minor observances which have only a very vague objective of avoiding "bad luck", which is probably not by any means always envisaged during their performance. Again, many religious ceremonies have an objective which, though not as specific as it might be, is none the less present, such as pleasing a deity, or removing sin from a congregation. Further, even such predominantly self-contained ceremonies as Professor Malinowski cites have a general, if not a specific, objective. For example initiation ceremonies are aimed at "making the boy into a man". This fact comes out very clearly in the beliefs concerning the results of non-performance, for in many religious ceremonies there exists a specific fear of evil consequences if the ritual is omitted or negligently carried out. Thus though we may agree with Professor Malinowski's formulation as representing a general tendency, we must not lose sight of the fact that religious ceremonies cannot be considered apart from subsequent events supposed to follow from their performance on the one hand or from failure to carry them out on the other.

Arguments of this sort might be brought against any attempt to force the phenomena into the European dichotomy between religion and magic. It seems better to think in terms of a *magico-religious system*, composed of a unitary group of cultural facts which define the native's relation to the supernatural. Every phenomenon in this system exhibits two aspects, the *religious* and the *magical*. But although we insist upon the essential unity of the magico-religious system we may for the sake of convenience in dealing with ethnographic material continue to speak of magic and religion, implying thereby that the phenomena described are predominantly either magical or religious, as the case may be. This, however, must not obscure the fact that in every magical act, spell or belief there is a religious element, and in every religious prayer, sacrifice or dogma there is something corresponding to magic. It seems desirable, taking Professor Malinowski's theory as our starting point, to formulate this view in general terms.

We have seen in the preceding section that the institutions

which satisfy human needs include a body of practical knowledge and technique which is transmitted from one generation
to another. But, because of the limitation of human potentialities, this knowledge is never thoroughly adequate to meet
the problems with which human beings are faced. However
thorough the technique of agriculture, such unpredictable
catastrophes as droughts, floods and hurricanes must always
represent a possible annihilation of the fruits of man's most
strenuous efforts. Medical knowledge may mitigate illness but
cannot eliminate it entirely—it can prolong human life but
cannot in the long run prevent death. Thus there is a need for
some body of beliefs and practices designed to supplement the
gaps in practical knowledge, and so to make life bearable in the
face of danger and tragedy, to provide a categorical denial of
human inadequacy or futility. This need is met by certain
beliefs which make life more pleasant and death less horrible,
and by practices which, either directly or through the intervention of supernatural beings, are thought to control the
incalculable course of fate in a manner more in keeping with
the infinite longings of man's spirit. This organization of
beliefs and practices, in any society, makes up its *magico-
religious system*.[1] The ubiquity of such systems testifies to their
correspondence to some fundamental human need, while they
cover a vast range of phenomena ranging from the spell (for
example, in love magic) recited by a single individual and
believed directly to affect the feelings of its object, to large
gatherings for collective worship, in which there is no explicitly
defined objective. Magico-religious systems arise in response
to the needs which we have outlined, and so serve a very
specific function in social life; and their magical aspect is to be
found in the manner in which they meet problems with which
ordinary knowledge and technique are unable to cope.

If, then, this is the specifically magical function of magico-
religious beliefs and practices, where does religion enter into

---

[1] It should be noted that magico-religious observances are not the only
cultural responses to situations of risk, though they are by far the most common.
Socially determined bravado, with its conscious recognition of danger and its
affirmation of courage, is often a substitute for magico-religious precautions,
particularly where standards of honour are concerned. "Pistols for two and
coffee for one" is akin to a magical formula, in that it expresses a morally integrated attitude towards danger. Further, the specific situations in which risk
is recognized are to some extent culturally determined, for example, the many
pathological phobias connected with sex in modern civilization, which are closely
related to its religious and ethical standards.

them? We have discussed the need for some form of knowledge designed to make up for the deficiency of practical techniques, but in order to answer the question just formulated, we must emphasize the fact that this must be conceived as *effective* knowledge, as embodying power, over and above that which is demonstrably wielded in the application of practical knowledge to human problems. For example, magical practices rest, as Sir James Frazer recognized at the outset, very largely upon associations of similarity and contiguity. But such associations are not, generally speaking, made *ad hoc* by single individuals —on the contrary, they are embodied in and validated by the cultural tradition, being taken over from it by the individual. They must have the sanction of faith, derived from social tradition. This process of validation makes up the religious aspect of culture. The function of religion is to create faith, to reinforce it by dogma, and to demonstrate it through the miracle, using this term in a very wide sense to cover any intrusion of the supernatural into the ordinary sequence of cause and effect. The manner in which this vital function is carried out demands analysis.

Professor Malinowski has shown that, in predominantly religious acts, certain psycho-physical results are produced upon the individual, through what he terms "the contagiousness of faith, the dignity of unanimous consent, and the impressiveness of collective behaviour", in addition to the satisfaction of physiological appetites, the stimulation of the dance, and similar influences. It is important to recognize that this process, to which we shall revert presently, is being brought to bear upon the individual almost continuously from the time when he first takes the nipple between his lips until he breathes his last breath in the arms of relative or friend. It is of course accentuated upon public occasions, when it is more spectacular, more impressive and probably more effective. But even the most private thoughts of the individual depend to a large extent upon language, a cultural creation *par excellence*. Thus those instances of meditation, trances, possessions, and seclusion, which according to Malinowski indicate that "in primitive societies religion arises to a great extent from purely individual sources", are to a very great extent culturally determined, as is demonstrably the case in the behaviour which follows them. What a medicine man thinks, feels, or does when he is away in seclusion in a cave may or may not be "purely individual", but when he returns to society his esoteric experiences produce patterns of behaviour which are just as much culturally determined as anything else.

Society, then, is constantly influencing the experience and behaviour of the individual, and thereby impressing its power upon him. The punishment of anti-social acts, the rewards of virtue, the actual success of recognized experts, as well as the demonstrable efficacy of practical traditional knowledge and technique all combine to impress upon the individual the fact that what tradition says, goes. The metaphor in this colloquialism expresses the putative effectiveness of any knowledge generally recognized as true. This fundamental principle underlies magic, religion and practical techniques alike, and the latter derive from tradition just as much as the others. Thus though the phenomena of magic are generally more secret and less spectacular than those of religion, the magical technique is always learned from a reputed expert, whose capacity is vouched for by his reputation, and is generally validated by a complex ideology, including ready-made excuses for failure.

The burden of the above argument is that all phenomena of magic and of religion depend upon the existence of this source of putative superhuman power generated, as it were, by the community in the course of its integrative activities, which for the sake of convenience we may term *the supernatural*. Moreover, they all involve some objective, general or specific, individual or social, implicit or explicit, and this is always an objective which cannot be attained by the practical techniques of everyday life. This is our fundamental reason for insisting upon the unitary nature of magico-religious phenomena. But granting that all such phenomena draw upon the supernatural in order to solve problems before which practical knowledge is impotent, we must distinguish their religious from their magical aspect. Following Professor Malinowski we may suggest that the religious aspect is concerned with the generation, expression, validation, and transmission of the power believed to reside in the supernatural, while the magical aspect is concerned with the use of this power towards various objectives. This point of view may be embodied in two brief definitions: The *religious aspect* of culture is concerned with the validation of the supernatural, with the generation of faith in the existence and efficacy of forces beyond those which depend upon the normal sequence of cause and effect. On the other hand, the *magical aspect* may be defined as covering those phases of social life in which the inadequacy of practical knowledge to meet individual or social problems is made good by the employment of the supernatural.

We are now in a position to clarify the intimate relationship between magic and religion, and to justify our view that the magico-religious system of any people constitutes a unitary group of phenomena which can only be isolated from one another conceptually. We have seen that religion is essentially integrative social activity. Now, as we have mentioned, all such activities produce a unique effect upon the human individual. This somewhat intangible effect (which is no less real because it is not susceptible to exact definition) lies in the subjective state which has been variously termed "community feeling", "a sense of social solidarity", or "social euphoria". This feeling is one of the most difficult subjective states which the psychologist is called upon to describe. In the first place it is pleasurable, but it is more than this. It involves a sense of power, an increase in the feeling that the problems of life can be coped with, and that all is for the best in the best of all possible worlds. A brief mention of certain integrative activities will make this conception more concrete.

Let us consider in the first place dancing. Professor Radcliffe-Brown has discussed at length the role of the dance in Andamanese society.[1] He points out that the rhythmical character of the movements allows of the maximum amount of motion with the minimum expenditure of effort. This fact, taken together with the stimulation of individual vanity, leads to just that sense of power and self-assurance of which we have spoken. Again commensal rites, by the satisfaction of the individual appetite, lead to a general sense of well-being and a feeling that things are just as they should be. An interesting study of the effects of stimulants and narcotics, communally consumed, might be made along similar lines. Finally the social functions of such reactions as weeping and laughter are determined by the psycho-physical effects which they produce upon the human organism.[2]

We have seen that integrative social activities, of which religious phenomena form one group, induce in the individual a sense of power or effectiveness greater than that which he

[1] A. R. Brown, *The Andaman Islanders*, chap. v.
[2] Cf. Piddington, *The Psychology of Laughter*, chaps. II–VII.

normally possesses. But we have also seen that magic implies recourse to some source of power beyond that which is embodied in the ordinary practical experience of the individual. We can now understand the intimate relation between religious and magical phenomena. In view of the gaps in his practical knowledge, and his lack of effectiveness along certain lines, the human individual has need of some extraneous source of power. This he finds in the practices associated with the integrative activities of his social group, and his belief in their efficacy (without which "association by similarity" is of no practical significance) is derived from the very real sense of efficacy which is induced in him by participation in such activities. Thus it is that every religious act has a magical aspect and *vice versa*. The body of supplementary knowledge which is drawn upon by magic must be validated by a belief in its efficacy, and this validation depends upon the very real super-individual efficacy of society and the feeling of dependence upon ulterior powers which this induces in the individual.

The general trend of our discussion, then, is to show that magico-religious phenomena form one group, and that, though we cannot speak of magic as opposed to religion, we can isolate the religious from the magical aspect of any phenomenon in this group. Though insisting that the distinction between magic and religion involves an abstraction rather than a classification, this theory is, broadly speaking, in line with previous analyses which have concentrated upon drawing a hard and fast line between magic and religion. The hypothesis here presented arises out of Professor Malinowski's discussion of the problem, but our reformulation of his position is designed to harmonize it with certain other views, and to show that once the principles enunciated above are recognized there is no real opposition between the various theories—they merely draw attention to different aspects of a unitary group of phenomena.

Let us consider first Frazer's distinction between magic and religion. He recognizes that both imply the exercise of power over events, but he considers that in magic the effect is produced directly, whereas in religion it is attained by the intervention of supernatural beings. This distinction cannot be pressed too far and, in fact, must be regarded as a false one if our insistence on the unitary nature of magico-religious phenomena is justified. Thus in the Roman Catholic religion the ritual of making the sign of the cross might theoretically be regarded as a plea for divine intervention, but is probably in the vast majority of cases a purely magical act, in Frazer's sense. Such borderline cases which might be multiplied indefinitely render invalid Frazer's distinction, though, on the view which we have put forward, it is not altogether irrelevant. We have seen that predominantly religious activities presuppose some source of superhuman power, and this is demonstrably associated, in the vast majority of cases, with the postulation of quasi-human beings such as ghosts, spirits, and gods. The social group, in emphasizing its own power and solidarity, tends to project these abstract conceptions in an anthropomorphic form into superhuman beings, and in this way to regulate the social sentiments of its members in terms of real human social relationships, particularly those of kinship. The existence of a sentiment presupposes its object, and if religious sentiments of dependence and veneration are to be developed, it is natural that their objects should in some measure resemble the real human objects of such sentiments, for example a father or a king.

On the other hand, the magical aspect of the phenomena which we are considering lies in the effective use of supernatural power, and though this must in the last analysis derive from society, the emphasis is primarily upon the manner in which magical practices influence events in accordance with social or individual wishes. The personal intervention of spiritual beings is not essential, though it is one of the ways in which the supernatural may be employed. And the supernatural as a part of tradition is, as we have seen, validated by religious beliefs.

Frazer's view, then, draws attention to the validation of tradition by beliefs in spiritual beings, and to the fact that beliefs in direct magical powers derive their efficacy from tradition. In some cases the two functions merge in the direct appeal to a deity for practical benefits. But there are many lazy gods, as well as cases in which the magician employs anthropomorphic spiritual forces directly under his control.

We have suggested a reformulation of Frazer's theory based on the recognition of the essential unity of magico-religious phenomena. A similar treatment might be accorded to Durkheim's view that religion is essentially social, and magic individual. We should prefer to say that the *source* from which magico-religious knowledge is drawn is essentially social, and that worship and other religious activities are predominantly collective in character. But the magical aspect of magico-religious knowledge or power is centred in the *employment* of such knowledge to influence events, and this is always done in relation to hopes, desires, and fears which are in the last analysis individual, though they may be felt in common with others.

Before going on to a study of Polynesian religion, there is one more theoretical problem to be discussed, namely the relation of magico-religious beliefs and ritual to practical knowledge and techniques. This is a most important anthropological question, and has implications bearing both upon actual observation in the field and upon the theoretical discussion of primitive cultures.

Professor Malinowski has insisted that the native distinguishes between practical and magical knowledge and technique, but this view requires careful formulation. It cannot be accepted if it is held to imply that the distinction which the native draws is similar in character to our own. We distinguish between magic and religion on an extra-cultural basis; in other words, broadly speaking, practical knowledge is that which is true, whereas "magical" beliefs are those which are erroneous and which we stigmatize as "superstition". But to the native no such distinction exists; the magical practices and technical procedures are, for him, both equally important parts of a unitary institutional activity. It is impossible to dispute Malinowski's contention that the native draws a distinction between magic and technique, in that he does not consider that one will be effective without the other. He draws this distinction, however, on the same basis as that on which he distinguishes between various aspects of practical procedure. Both magic and technique are essential elements in the attainment of a definite objective.

Is it, then, impossible to draw a distinction, in making actual ethnographic observations in the field, between magical and practical knowledge? In view of what we have said, this is a problem of some difficulty, but this difficulty is not as great as might be imagined, because items of both magical and practical knowledge never occur in an isolated form. They are always a part either of the magico-religious system or of the body of practical rules which govern institutional activities, and these two bodies of beliefs and practices are on the whole quite easy to distinguish one from the other. We may indicate briefly the basis upon which such a distinction may be drawn.

We have seen that the function of magical knowledge is to produce or prevent certain effects in situations in which practical knowledge is inadequate. Magical knowledge is then *ex hypothesi* erroneous knowledge, which means that *broadly speaking* the practices founded upon it are not followed by the effects attributed to them. But this criterion of objective validity—whether the procedures are or are not followed by the desired results—is in itself inadequate for several reasons. In the first place it frequently happens that the context ensures that the avowed objective of magic shall follow its performance. For example the totemic increase ceremonies of the Australian aborigines are regularly performed at centres near which the natural species is usually abundant, and at times of the year when the species is about to become plentiful. It so happens that in the vast majority of cases the increase of the species does in fact follow upon the performance of the rite. Secondly there is the well-known tendency of magicians to "make sure" of the efficacy of their practices by supplementing them by very practical measures, for example poisoning. Thirdly, magical beliefs do, under specific circumstances, produce the effects attributed to them, for example the Society Island *marae* builders' prayers to their gods were believed to make the stones light in their hands, a result which, psychologically interpreted, probably did occur. Moreover any criterion which depends upon real effectiveness leaves out of account a group of phenomena, namely erroneous practical knowledge, which is obviously not magical but which would be classed as such if we were to adopt an index of this character. The principle may be illustrated with reference to the off-shore fishing of the Society Islanders which will be described later.[1]

The off-shore fishing of the Society Islanders was on the one hand associated with an elaborate body of practical knowledge of the weather, of navigation, and of the habits of fish and sea birds. On the other hand, there was an important magico-religious element involved in fishing. There were special sacred places where the gods were invoked, and there were small stone images of fish called *puna*, the owners of which could influence the supply of fish for good or ill. Dealing with the first body of beliefs—the practical techniques—the vast majority of these were founded upon sound principles. Some of them were effective, but for reasons obscure even to an experienced European fisherman. Thus Mr Charles Nord-

[1] See below, pp. 243 *sqq.*

hoff who fished with the natives regularly for many years was at first sceptical about their belief that the colour of the pearl shell of certain hooks had an influence on the catch of bonito, different colours being effective on different days. Experience, however, taught him that this belief was perfectly correct. On the other hand when the fish are not biting, but an odd one has been caught, it is opened and its roe inspected. It is believed that a hook which closely resembles the colour of the roe will prove effective, a view which seems to be out of line with what is apparently the only plausible explanation. Again the belief that certain days of the lunar month are propitious for the catching of various kinds of fish may or may not be correct. But one item of practical knowledge concerning which Mr Nordhoff is extremely sceptical is the belief that bilge water must not be thrown overboard during bonito fishing. It appears that even if such bilge water does frighten away the fish it is for some reason other than that given by the natives, who attribute its frightening character to the smell of the blood of dead bonito. In these instances we have beliefs and practices which definitely appear to be erroneous or futile but which we should hesitate to class as magical.

The examples just cited indicate the final, and purely practical, objection to the criterion of accuracy of belief, namely that it presupposes a knowledge on the part of the anthropologist very much more profound than that of the native, whereas in regard to the phenomena which we are discussing the reverse is generally the case.

Our statement, then, that magical knowledge is erroneous knowledge can ·be taken as true only in a very general sense, and we must differentiate magical knowledge from practical knowledge on the basis of the *cultural consequences* which follow from this tendency for magical beliefs not to square with reality. In other words the generally inaccurate character of magical beliefs gives to them a special configuration, which forms a basis upon which they may be differentiated from practical knowledge.

In the first place, we have seen that in order to fulfil their role in culture, magical beliefs must be *validated*. We must add that this may also be said of practical techniques, but whereas these are validated by the actual results which they demonstrably achieve, magical beliefs are validated by a complex *ideology of the supernatural*.

In the second place, what we have just said implies that the forces at work are better understood in the case of practical as opposed to magical procedures. In the case of the latter there are always certain *unknown factors*, such as the possibility of counter-magic, the breach of a relevant taboo, or the caprice of spiritual beings. These find expression in the *explanations given in cases of failure*, which are generally speaking more closely related to the activity itself, more specific, consistent and precise, as well as more easily verified, in the case of practical techniques as opposed to magical procedures.

Finally, we have seen that magical beliefs are validated by an ideology more complex than that underlying practical techniques. Since the latter are validated by actual experience and the former by their ideology alone, the *subsidiary beliefs must be more firmly held in the case of magical practices*—hence the elaborate excuses for failure to which we have referred. This is why practical techniques are more readily changed or dropped altogether if they fail to attain their objectives, a fact which emerges quite clearly in situations of culture contact where, as Rivers points out, technology is generally destroyed first, then social organization, and last of all the magico-religious system.

No one of these criteria can by itself provide an adequate basis of differentiation, nor can they be applied to a single isolated belief or practice. Rather do they serve as indices for the differentiation of two systems of knowledge, which are not distinguished *as such* from one another by the native, but which play different roles in his social life. Any isolated belief or practice must be placed in its context within one or other of these systems, and only on this basis is it possible to decide whether such an element of culture is magical or practical.

In this chapter we have set forth the methodological point of view from which it is proposed to study the religious institutions of Central Polynesia, in order to understand their role in a living culture. Towards this end we have attempted a theoretical analysis of culture into its component parts, in order to be able systematically to place religion in its social context. We have also defined the view which will be taken of the relation of magic to religion, and also of the complementary nature of magico-religious beliefs and ritual on the one hand and practical knowledge and techniques on the other. We may now proceed to examine the actual ethnological material from this point of view, starting with a typical Polynesian culture, that of the Society Islanders.

CHAPTER IX

RELIGION AND MAGIC IN THE SOCIETY ISLANDS[1]

RELIGIOUS OBSERVANCES

THE system of religious observances of the Society Islanders was centred around certain sacred buildings called *marae*, whose structural features have already been described.[2] We are here concerned with the religious ceremonies of which they were the venue. Although all the *marae* served very much the same functions, they were of varying degrees of importance, ranging from the large buildings at which vast congregations assembled to small local or family *marae*, used by a few people only. Each *marae* was the religious and social centre of the group, whether large or small, to which it belonged.[3]

As we have seen, the Society Island *marae* were stone structures, built upon a rectangular base and shaped in the form of a pyramid or a low platform. Around these grew groves of sacred trees. The largest (called by Teuira Henry "international *marae*") were the scenes of religious ceremonies at which large numbers of people gathered. Such was the *marae* called Taputapu-atea of the god Oro at Opoa, on the island of Ra'iatea. Here, according to tradition, were once held gatherings to which came visitors from other islands in the Society group, from Rarotonga, Rotuma, the Australs and even from New Zealand. The visitors from these distant islands came to Opoa with elaborate ceremonial, bearing gifts and sacrifices, human and otherwise, which they offered to Oro. But about 1350 (according to the calculations of Percy Smith) these vast international gatherings were brought to an end by a quarrel between a Ra'iatean priest and a visiting high chief. The former was killed, and an attempt was made on the life of his murderer. Further bloodshed would have occurred had not the visitors taken to their canoes and paddled away, never to return.

---

[1] The material embodied in this and the following chapter is derived from Teuira Henry's *Ancient Tahiti*, except where reference is specifically made to other sources.　　　　　　　　[2] See above, p. 149.

[3] Cf. *Systems*, vol. II, pp. 60 *sqq.*

This incident, which is also recorded in the folk-lore of Rarotonga and New Zealand, brought to an end these international gatherings, and thereafter the islands of Tahiti, Huahine, Ra'iatea and Maupiti entered into an alliance against invasions from Porapora and other islands, though civil war continued between members of the alliance. This state of affairs continued until the establishment of French rule in 1847, and members of the alliance used to gather at the international *marae* which were established in various islands of the group. This was accompanied, according to tradition, by a diffusion of the cult of Oro from its original centre at Opoa.

Next in importance to these international centres were the royal or national *marae* at which elaborate religious ceremonies took place. Before discussing these ceremonies we may describe briefly the procedure adopted in establishing a new national *marae*.

The preparations for the establishment of a new *marae* began about three years before the actual work of building was commenced. Restrictions were ritually placed upon the consumption of food and the use of sources of food supply, such as fishing grounds, in order that quantities of food might be available at the time of building. When the time came, further restrictions connected with the construction of the *marae* were imposed. No one was allowed to approach the site, and fires were prohibited in the neighbourhood.

Those who were to do the actual work of building retired from their families to an encampment in the woods. They worked under the direction of an expert artisan (*tahuamarae*), and it was considered a great honour to participate in the work. Stones were cut into shape, and one special corner stone was obtained from some established *marae*.[1] After a human victim had been ceremonially buried under this special stone, other stones were placed in position. These were sometimes of enormous size, but the labourers declared that they were made light in their hands by the gods.

At the summit of the pyramidal stone structure was the most holy part of the *marae*—an enclosure, about six feet by four, in which was placed the image of the tutelar god. In addition to this image other sacred objects were kept at the *marae*—memorials to dead rulers, images of legendary fish and birds,

[1] This appears to have been the universal practice, though there are legendary accounts of the establishment of "original" *marae* (cf. *Systems*, vol. II, pp. 62–3).

sacred drums, effigies of men, representing priests at prayer, and planks carved with sacred symbols. Among these objects were two stone figures, one representing a king and the other a queen, called *pu-maro-ura* (the centre for the red feather girdle of royalty) upon which a new sovereign was seated at his or her accession. In the *marae* were certain secret recesses in which the bodies of the dead of chiefly rank were temporarily buried, before being removed to hidden caves in the mountainous districts. In the front of the *marae* were altars, upon which were placed human sacrifices, as well as offerings of food for the gods, and farther in front was a large house called the *fare-ia-manaha* in which dwelt the keepers of the *marae* when on duty and in which they made and preserved the various sacred appendages used in the ceremonies. Under this house also a human victim was buried. In addition there was a sacred canoe house, in which was kept a specially constructed canoe. In this the tutelar god travelled when his image was taken from one island to another.

When the *marae* had been built, the inauguration ceremony was held. A large assembly gathered together, each district being represented by first-born young virgins of high rank, wearing *tiare* (single gardenias) as emblems of purity. The entire congregation repaired in procession to the *marae*, and the virgins marched round it, casting up their flowers upon it as high as they could reach, while the head priest called upon the gods to be present. He then sprinkled the *marae* with sea water, invoking the tutelar god to come and take possession of the structure. After this the king climbed up one side of the *marae* and descended on the other side. The *marae* was then pronounced holy and the congregation repaired to the assembly ground, where the food which had been prepared was divided. Some was consecrated to the gods, a large quantity was given to the sovereign, and the rest distributed among the other people present. The feast was most decorously conducted, and any manifestation of greed or lack of restraint was believed to lead to supernatural punishments, such as blindness or choking while eating.

The local *marae*, or *marae mataeina'a*, were constructed and inaugurated in a similar way, though not on such a grand scale, no human victim being immolated. Local chiefs carried out the mounting ceremony, unless the district happened to be subjugated to a high chief, in which case he was invited to perform it. The place of the *pu-maro-ura* was taken by two corresponding stones, termed *pu-ari'i*.

At these *marae* gathered the local groups (*va'a-mataeina'a*, "canoes of the district") for collective worship and supplication. Each *marae* was dedicated to an important god, and the people of the district were known by the deity to whom their *marae mataeina'a* was dedicated. Those whose god was Ta'aroa were called 'Ati Ta'aroa (the people of Ta'aroa), those who had Oro as their tutelar deity were called 'Ati Oro, and so on. This established links between people from distant districts whose *marae* were dedicated to the same god. When a stranger arrived in any district he would ask the people: "*E 'ati ha 'outou?*"—"Of what *'ati* are you?" If their local god was the same as his own, he would at once be received ceremonially at the *marae mataeina'a*, the local priest officiating for him. But if his god was not the same, he performed his own devotions by the seashore.

On a smaller scale again were the ancestral or family[1] *marae*, or *marae tupuna*. These varied in size, and in the degree of ceremonial connected with their inauguration, according to the wealth and rank of their owners, who sometimes prevailed upon a high chief to perform the mounting ceremony at their inauguration, this being considered a very high honour. They were dedicated to the family god, but his identity was always a family secret, as were the family genealogies associated with these *marae*. The reason for keeping secret the name of the family deity was that it was believed that if this name became known to outsiders, they might supplant the original family in his good graces. The secrecy of the family genealogies was intimately associated with land tenure and will be discussed later.

The simplest form of *marae tupuna* consisted of a paving set upon the ground, surrounded by stone slabs, each representing a member of the family, at which he or she offered up prayers. In these *marae* were hidden such sacred family relics as images, ancestral skulls, jawbones and feather amulets, as well as objects such as snails, lizards or stones representing the secret patron spirit of individual members of the family. At the back of the *marae* was a deep pit (*tiri-a-pera*) in which were deposited

---

[1] The word "family" as used in this connection is nowhere accurately defined, but it probably refers to the extended form of family grouping usual in Polynesia.

all cast-off things from the *marae* as well as the discarded clothing, mats, nail parings and the like of members of the family.

The *marae tupuna* were the ritual centres of family life. Their functions are described by Teuira Henry as follows:

> In such a *marae*, the head of the household offered family prayers at sunrise and sunset; there, confession of sins was made, and private petitions to the gods were offered by any member of the family; there, marriage ceremonies were performed; there, prayers were offered for the safe delivery of a woman in childbirth, and the child dedicated to the gods when it came into the world; there, also, invocations for the sick and dying were made. A man went into the front part to offer his prayers and gifts, but a woman offered hers at the back part; she was considered insane if she ventured forward. When a woman was about to be delivered of her child, a small house was erected for her behind the *marae*, which was thatched with the *maire* (a species of fern)...and there the child was born.[1]

But in spite of the homage which was paid them the position of ancestral gods was not completely secure. It sometimes happened that when members of a family had suffered from much illness, and had appealed to their ancestral god in vain, they would decide to cast him off, and seek protection from another deity. When this happened the priest or head of the family would go to the ancestral *marae* and address the god as follows:

> There is casting off, I am casting thee off! Do not come in to possess me again; let me not be a seat for thee again! Let me not know thee again; do thou not know me again. Go and seek some other medium for thyself in another home. Let it not be me, not at all! I am wearied of thee—I am terrified of thee! I am expelling thee. Go even to the Vai-tu-po (river of darkness), into the presence of Ta'aroa, thy father, Ta'aroa, the father of all the gods. Return not again to me. Behold the family, they are stricken with sickness; thou art taking them, thou art a terrible man-devouring god![2]

The image of the god was buried, and a new one consecrated at the next *pa'i-atua*, as described below.

For those who had no *marae tupuna*, the sea served the purpose of a *marae*. "On the seaside the wanderer or exile who owned no land worshipped his god. There he presented his son or daughter in marriage, there he offered his newborn child to his tutelar god, and there he presented himself or members of his family when sick or dying to the healing gods, and to Ta'aroa."[3]

In addition to the national, local, and family *marae*, there were certain other ones with special functions, such as the

---

[1] Henry, *A.T.* p. 143. [2] *Ibid.* p. 178. [3] *Ibid.* p. 144.

doctors', fishermen's and canoe-builders' *marae*, which will be mentioned later.

The religious cult associated with the *marae* was carried out by special functionaries, priests and *marae* attendants. Physical perfection in such dignitaries was insisted upon. Priests were called *tahu'a*, a term meaning "author" or "expert". Thus a man skilled in house building was *tahu'a-fare*, author of houses, and a doctor was *tahu'a-ra'au*, author of medicine. Similarly a priest was *tahu'a-pure* (author of prayer) and a high priest, *tahu'a-nui* (great author). Their duty was to master the ritual, prayers and incantations which were handed down from generation to generation, meticulous accuracy being insisted upon. This sacred lore they learned in special schools, built upon sacred ground, paying their teachers well for their instruction. The priesthood in each district generally descended from father to son, the elder line having preference over the younger. Priests were well provided for, and were held in great honour. Certain priests had special functions, for example the *tiri*, or god's nurse, who was chosen from the highest grades of the priesthood and was the only individual who was allowed to handle the most sacred image of the tutelar god.

In addition to the priesthood, there were certain attendants who carried out the more domestic work which was done at the *marae*. They were called *'opu-nui*, or "august stomachs" because they were privileged when on duty to cook their food with fire made from the sacred wood of the *marae* grounds and to partake of food offered to the gods. They took turns at leaving their families and taking up residence at the *marae* which they tended, keeping it clean and tidy, preserving it from rats and insects, making sacred cloth, and feeding the pigs, dogs, and fowls of the gods around the *marae*.

As we have seen, the *marae* were the centres of the religious life of the Society Islanders, and at them all religious ceremonies were carried out. One of the most important of these was the *pa'i-atua*, the assembling and uncovering of the gods. This was performed at the national *marae* upon occasions of public importance, such as the accession of a high chief, or the laying of the corner stone of a new national *marae*. It was carried out after great calamities, and also in order to produce rain in time of drought. Elaborate preparations were made for the *pa'i-atua* ceremony, everything at the *marae*, including the sacred canoe of the god, being repaired, or, if worn out, replaced. The priests consecrated themselves by observing a number of taboos. They took no active part in family life, did not eat too much, and slept apart from members of their households. They might not cut or anoint their hair nor wear flowers or sweet-scented leaves, and their food and drinking water were ritually presented to them. Two days before the ceremony the high chief issued a proclamation, which was carried throughout the land by messengers, who in a special chant enjoined the people to cook no food for two days, to burn no fires and to light no torches. The people then cooked enough food to last them for three days, and in the evening the beating of the chief's drum announced that the restrictions had come into force. Then a great hush fell upon the villages; no one roamed abroad and no light was to be seen.

The next morning the ceremony of weeding the *marae* was carried out by the high chief and other men of rank, who removed the accumulated moss from the *marae* stones, and swept and weeded the grounds; all the rubbish so collected was thrown into the pit at the back of the *marae*. The *marae* was then decorated by the '*opu-nui*. Meanwhile the priests sat apart and intoned chants in honour of the gods. At the conclusion of the weeding ceremony the high chief and his followers returned home, and the remaining preparations at the *marae* were carried out by the '*opu-nui*.

Towards evening the '*opu-nui* retired to rest, but the priests spent the whole night intoning prayers at the *marae*. One of the most important rites of the night's vigil consisted of sending away messengers to summon the gods. Images representing these messengers were uncovered and addressed in turn by the high priest, who, calling on each by name, instructed them to summon the gods. The following is an extract from Teuira Henry's translation of one of these addresses, spoken at the *marae* Taputapu-atea dedicated to Oro at Opoa:

O Ti'a-o-atea, messenger of the gods, arise and feel thy face, bathe in the water, draw on thy loin-girdle, put on thine official clothing, take a great walking stick and run to Mou'a-'ura in 'Uporu for Tane and his host of gods to come to Opoa, as gods for this ordinance.

There is prayer in this world, in the home of warrior 'Oro.

O Rei-tu, messenger of the gods, arise...and run to Tai-nuna for Tu and Te-mehara, to come to Opoa, as gods for this ordinance.

After a number of gods have been summoned in this way,[1]

---

[1] Cf. above, p. 7.

the chant concludes with a description of the supposed reception of one of the messengers by the gods. For example:

> Whose messenger is it? It is Ti'a-o-atea, the messenger for Tane. Tane welcomes him, his host of gods welcome him:
> "Welcome, Ti'a-o-atea!" Tane says: "O Ti'a-o-atea, a great errand?"
> "I have a great errand", says Ti'a-o-atea. "I have run hither to Mou'a-'ura for you all to go to Opoa; there is prayer in the world. There is exclusion and admittance of an assembly, a seeking of gods, and gods are coming to the home of Warrior 'Oro."
> "O Ti'a-o-atea, thine errand is agreeable, we shall go to the ordinance in the house of Warrior 'Oro."
> Ti'a-o-atea is returning hither to be followed by Tane and his host.

After all the messengers and gods previously mentioned had been enumerated once more, the heralding of the gods by their messengers was announced:

> A messenger is coming! It is Ro'o, the messenger. What is his errand? He is heralding Tane and the host of gods of Tane of the open tenth sky, of Tane of distant lands, who are flying to this ordinance.
> A messenger is coming! It is Rei-tu....

By the time all the gods had been invoked in this way, it was almost dawn, and the high priest ushered in the day with a chant. After this the priests in solemn procession carried the sacred images from the *fare-ia-manaha* to the *ava'a-rahi*, the great enclosure at the summit of the *marae* and its most sacred part. First came the high priest, followed by the image of the tutelar god in its little ark, carried by four specially appointed priests called *hi'i-atua* (nurses of the god). Next came images which had been gathered from the important local and ancestral *marae*, and these were followed by the doctors, canoe-builders, fishermen and sorcerers with their respective sacred images, all carefully wrapped up. When the party had arrived at the *ava'a-rahi*, the high priest ceremonially removed the many wrappings of the image of the tutelar god, to the accompaniment of chanting from the assembled priests. When the image thus exposed had been invoked the remaining images were similarly unwrapped.

Next followed a ritual exchange of presents between the minor gods and the tutelar god of the *marae*, carried out on their behalf by their respective priests, who exchanged red feather amulets and other possessions of the gods. In this way new, uninspired images were consecrated, the gods which they represented being invoked to enter them before they exchanged feathers with the tutelar deity. While the images were still exposed, a sacred male pig was cooked and offered to the god. The smoke from the fire on which it was cooked was a signal to the populace at large that the sacred ceremony was drawing to a close. The images were then wrapped up again, that of the tutelar god being left in the *ava'a-rahi* in charge of the high priest, while the less important ones were returned to the *fare-ia-manaha*. The beating of the *marae* drums then announced that the ceremony was over and that the restrictions were removed from the people, who proceeded to cook food. While this was going on the priests at the *marae*, aided by those privileged persons who had taken part in the weeding rite, brought the ceremonies to a close with chants in honour of the gods and prayers for their blessing. Teuira Henry's translation of one of the latter is as follows:

> Hearken unto us, O gods!
> Those numerous gods, those thousands of gods, turn unto us, accept of our petitions!
> Preserve the population of this land; preserve the generation; may they live in the gods. Preserve the frontiers of the people's habitations. Watch against the man with rough cheeks, the man with angry looks, against the incendiary, against him who lets fly the ends of his loin girdle.[1] Put all those things entirely away. Preserve us human beings, O host of gods![2]

This was followed by more sacrifices of sacred pigs, and the offering of a long banana shoot, called *ta'ata-o-mei'a roa* (man-long-banana) in lieu of a human sacrifice, which was never offered at these ceremonies, except in very unusual circumstances. Then, after various chants of dismissal, the image of the tutelar god was returned to the *fare-ia-manaha*, and a great feast was held, special gifts of food being presented to the priests, to the *'opu-nui*, and to the men of rank who had participated in the ceremonies, while certain portions of food were offered to the gods, and no one dared to eat until the gods had been served. The feast concluded the ceremonies of the *pa'i-atua*. Other religious ceremonies and festivals performed at the *marae* will be described later.

[1] This expression meant that the man of evil was fleet of step, causing the ends of his girdle to fly.
[2] Henry, *A.T.* p. 171.

RELIGIOUS BELIEFS

The religion of the Society Islanders was associated with an elaborate body of dogma. This was embodied in certain sacred chants taught to the priests before their induction, and so handed down by them from generation to generation. These chants told of the cosmogony, and of the doings of gods and culture heroes in the distant past. An extensive collection of them has been published by Teuira Henry.[1] We may at this point indicate briefly their content, leaving a discussion of their significance until a later section.

Ta'aroa was the ancestor of all the gods, and the origin of everything. He developed himself in solitude—he was his own parent, having neither father nor mother. He had power over all things on the earth, in the sea, and in the sky. "Ta'aroa sat in his shell in darkness for millions of ages. The shell was like an egg revolving in endless space, with no sky, no land, no sea, no moon, no sun, no stars."

But at last Ta'aroa cracked his shell, and coming out of it found himself alone. He cried out, and no voice answered him. So he took a new shell and made it the foundation of the earth, the stratum rock. And having made the substance of the land, he shook it, and it yielded not, so he cried out: "What good property I have in this land of mine!" Then he called upon Tu to come forth and be the first artisan, Tu the great artisan of Ta'aroa, who made things under his direction. By Ta'aroa was created the god Tane, who was also the first man, and all the host of gods and demigods, whose doings are recorded in other chants. These tell how all things came to be as they are to-day. In addition to these, there are a number of less specifically religious legends, which tell of the culture heroes and their doings.

Apart from the legendary history of the past, there were two groups of religious beliefs relating to contemporary events which must be mentioned. These are the beliefs in possession and inspiration on the one hand, and the observation of omens on the other. As we have seen,[2] there were times at which certain individuals manifested extraordinary behaviour which indicated that they were possessed by the gods, though we are not told the part which such trances and possessions played in native life, nor how they influenced the conduct of the people.

---

[1] *A.T.* pp. 336–632.   [2] See above, pp. 111, 113–14.

Another group of beliefs was concerned with omens and experimental augury, though these again are not given in their institutional context. A brief reference to the list provided by Henry will, however, indicate that over a very wide range of activities, natural phenomena were observed with a view to ascertaining the future course of events. This information we may condense into a table for the sake of simplicity, but such an analysis must necessarily be regarded as approximate only, since the nature of the material makes statistical accuracy impossible. Quite apart from other considerations, the mere statement that a certain event was regarded as an omen does not tell us how often it was observed, nor how much importance was attached to it; moreover it must be questioned whether the data recorded are a fair sampling. Thus an examination of the material suggests that certain omens (for example those connected with winds) have been over-emphasized at the expense of others. Again, certain statements are statistically ambiguous—for example it is impossible to translate into numerical terms: "Various other auguries were observed by the wise, such as the appearance of clouds, the cry of the birds, and the sound and direction of the wind."

But in spite of these difficulties, the following tables will give us a general picture of the kinds of events which the Society Islanders regarded as significant in this connection, and also the types of activities in connection with which they were observed. In considering this material three points should be borne in mind: In the first place, both natural omens and experimental auguries are included; these are difficult to differentiate from one another, and Henry does not draw any distinction between them. In the second place, we must not place too much faith in the statistical accuracy of the lists, for the reasons given above. Thirdly, it is sometimes difficult to decide whether a given sentence should be regarded as indicating one omen or two, for example Henry's statement that "If a woman dreamed she broke a tooth of the upper jaw, it was a sign that she was to have a daughter; if on lower jaw, she was to have a son." Such cases, including many portents of either success or failure in war, have for the purposes of this record been regarded as single omens.

ACTIVITIES IN CONNECTION WITH WHICH OMENS AND AUGURIES WERE OBSERVED

Activity	Number of related omens and auguries recorded by Henry[1]
War	29
Peace	3
Political	2
Death	3
Canoe-building	4
Fishing	1
Safety at sea	3
Pregnancy	2
Threat of sorcery	1
Human sacrifice	1
Future of new-born child	1
Sickness	3

KINDS OF PHENOMENA OBSERVED AS OMENS AND AUGURIES

Phenomena observed	Number of cases recorded by Henry
Sun and clouds	7
Celestial phenomena	3
Moon	2
Rainbow	2
Whirlwind	1
Winds	9
Mist	1
Human behaviour	5
Dreams	4
Warning by ghost	1
Behaviour of living things	6
Accidents or portents while at work	9
Miscellaneous	4

THE DYNAMICS OF RELIGION

Having described briefly certain religious observances and beliefs of the Society Islanders, we may now proceed to an analysis of the functional relationships between their various aspects. Of these aspects we may distinguish four which are of primary importance, namely: (i) religious observances, including ritual; (ii) religious beliefs; (iii) the ethical norms associated with religion; and (iv) the personnel involved in the performance of religious ritual. The relation of these to each other we may now examine.

The dogmatic beliefs associated with religious observances provide, as Professor Malinowski has shown, a traditional

---

[1] Most of the examples quoted are given in Henry's list, *A.T.* pp. 225–8; the others are to be found in other parts of the book (see Henry's index, *s.v.* "Auguries").

charter for the ritual. This statement we may exemplify with reference to an actual Society Island ceremony, namely human sacrifice. This was carried out upon a number of important occasions, particularly those associated with the *rites de passage* of individuals of high rank, and with warfare. According to legend, this custom arose at a time of serious drought in Ra'iatea. The priests unsuccessfully prayed for rain, and at length held a *pa'i-atua* ceremony, all to no effect. So the high chief, believing Ta'aroa to be angry, ordered that a human sacrifice should be offered at his *marae*. As soon as this was done, dark clouds gathered and rain fell, and in this way men discovered that human victims were pleasing to the gods.

Now several important facts should be noted in this connection. In the first place the ceremonial custom is believed to have had its origin in a human problem, namely the provision of rain, which it solved effectively. Thus is the faith in the efficacy of human sacrifice validated by the belief that on this specific occasion it did produce tangible and beneficial results.

Secondly, this legend brings up the whole problem of supernatural beings. In instances such as this, social calamities are attributed not to natural causes but to anger on the part of some hypothetical deity. Is this "animistic" tendency, so widespread throughout human society, merely the result of a universal tendency towards muddled thinking, or misuse of words? It seems more probable that the real reason for the personification of natural forces is for the purpose of controlling them. The actual causes of a drought are beyond human control, but when the occurrence of such a catastrophe is held to be due to some personal agency, it lays the way open to a possible amelioration of the situation, because it interprets an unpleasant, unusual, incalculable (and therefore uncontrollable) situation in social terms already familiar to those who are afflicted. They are already experienced in situations in which people are angry and they know that it is possible to appease the anger of human individuals by appropriate gifts. It should be noted that this belief is completely logic-tight; just as human individuals sometimes remain unmoved by peace-offerings, so do the gods sometimes remain obdurate. But not for ever, and even when the period of desolation is a long one the very activity involved in religious ceremonial, and the comforting belief that there must be some way of escape, provide psychological relief from the stress of suffering.

A third point to notice is that the original drought was attributed to Ta'aroa, the father of all the gods and the origin of everything. He became angry, sent a drought, and was appeased by human sacrifice, thus originating the social custom. This inter-relation between social custom and the cosmogony, between the natural and the social orders, is of considerable sociological importance. It is a very general feature of folk-lore, and is found in many varieties of legend, from the most important accounts of all creation, down to minor folk-tales, for example the Society Island story concerning two varieties of banana, *mei'a* and *fe'i*, which grow on the lowlands and mountains respectively. The bunches of fruit of mountain *fe'i* stand upright from the centre of the plant, but those of the lowland *mei'a* hang downwards. There is a story that the bunches of fruit of the *mei'a* once stood upright like those of the *fe'i*, until the two went to war with each other. The lowland *mei'a* were defeated, and since then they have never ceased to hang their heads in shame. This illustrates the interpretation of a simple botanical fact in terms of social values connected with the institution of warfare.

Examples of this linking together of natural and social origins might be multiplied indefinitely. It depends upon the need of giving to social beliefs on the one hand, and to social values on the other, a cogency and impressiveness great enough to overcome individual doubt or temptation. One means by which this is effected is by identifying social norms, in myths and legends, with actual realities, and so giving them a binding force over and above that which they would normally possess. Thus the account of how natural phenomena came to be as they are provides a validation for the social system, and in this way social values are, as it were, embedded in reality. This explains the various supposed manifestations of supernatural forces, which provide the human senses with tangible or visible evidence of the existence of the supernatural world.

We have already referred to the function of religious beliefs in comforting the afflicted in times of crisis. But the salutary psychological effect of religion is not confined to cases of actual calamity, for in the ordinary everyday life of human beings dangers are constantly present, dangers against which skill and knowledge are useless. For example, let us consider certain beliefs connected with gods, birds, and trees. On the one hand many birds were believed to be shadows of gods, and on the other individual varieties of birds were associated with particular trees. Thus the white sea swallow was the shadow of Tane in the light and the black sea swallow was his shadow in the dark. These birds were particularly associated with the breadfruit tree, and it was believed that if any man climbing a breadfruit tree were to slip, a white sea swallow would fly beneath him and break his fall. Thus the dangers of a hazardous occupation were thought to be minimized by the benevolent influence of a bird, and the efficacy of this belief was validated by the conception of this bird as the shadow of a god. A further illustration of this principle is found in the belief in a bird with the power of speech which warned the intended victims of human sacrifice and so enabled them to escape to the mountains.[1]

Summing up what has been said concerning the dogmatic aspect of religious beliefs, we may say that they serve as a nexus between everyday human life and that source of putative power which is generated by society in the course of its integrative activities. This source of putative power constitutes the cultural reality of the supernatural or sacred, as opposed to the profane world of everyday activity.

We have seen in the previous chapter that the existence of the supernatural, in its dynamic sense, presupposes two things. In the first place, the sacred or supernatural must be, to some extent, beyond the experience of everyday activity. If it is to embody knowledge which will be effective in meeting problems which ordinary technical and practical knowledge fails to solve, it must transcend the latter; if it is to be associated with regularized practices, these must go beyond the ordinary procedures of everyday life, which are effective up to a point through the ordinary operation of cause and effect, but which are ineffective in dealing with those problems which magico-religious phenomena are designed to meet. In the second place, the supernatural must not be altogether removed from everyday life. It must above all be *validated*, or, in other words, there must be practical means by which the power which it embodies may be wielded, as well as actually observable evidence of its effects. A moment's consideration of the character of magico-religious beliefs will show how well adapted they are to harmonize these two conflicting principles. Their content is always in some measure removed

[1] *Systems*, vol. II, p. 263.

from everyday activity, yet is related to it in some sensible way. For example, the tales of long ago describe the activities of gods and demigods who had extraordinary powers, but the fact that they are referred to the distant past places them beyond criticism or corroboration.[1] On the other hand, the occurrence of these miraculous events is substantiated by observable evidence, in the form of the world as it is to-day. This applies both to the natural and to the social order, a fact which has already been stressed. We may consider it in relation to the Society Island myth which describes how Tahiti originally broke away from Ra'iatea in the form of a fish.

The island of Tahiti did not always stand where it now does. Once it formed one land with the island of Ra'iatea, then called Havai'i, and filled the space now occupied by the straits between the islands of Ra'iatea and Tahaa. It came away from there as a huge fish and subsequently became land again, as it is at present. The story is as follows:

Once there was a time of religious restriction at Opoa, the sacred centre of Ra'iatea, and no man might walk abroad. But one day a girl called Tere-he (Wrong-errand) broke the taboo by stealing out to bathe in a river near her home. This so enraged the gods that they caused a numbness to come over her so that she drowned, and was swallowed whole by an enormous eel, which, becoming possessed by her spirit, was enraged and dived down into the earth. Its head was at Opoa (in Ra'iatea) and its tail in the neighbouring island of Tahaa. This piece of land thus became a gigantic fish which set out to sea, leaving the straits between the islands of Ra'iatea and Tahaa. Tu, the great artisan of Ta'aroa, stood upon its head and guided it eastwards to the present location of the island of Tahiti. When it had reached this position "Tahiti the fish" remained stable, but it was necessary to cut its sinews to prevent it from moving. This was eventually accomplished by the demigod Tafa'i with a charmed axe, after many other warriors had tried in vain. In doing this Tafa'i made mountains, valleys, inlets, and other geographical features of the island, which thus acquired its present configuration.

Now this legend has two aspects. On the one hand, it recounts extraordinary events which emphasize the power of the gods and demigods. But it also finds substantiation in the topo-

---

[1] The same might be said of the placing of the homes of the gods in inaccessible regions—in the sky, under the earth, or in the sea.

graphy of the Society Islands, in the separation between Ra'iatea and Tahaa, and in the configuration of the island of Tahiti itself. Further, it is related to the existing social system, and to the superior religious and political status of Ra'iatea, for we are told that when "Tahiti the fish" first arrived at its present position it had no royal family, and was called Tahiti-manahune (Plebeian Tahiti). Neither did the gods come with the fish, but migrated at a later date. Thus is the system of social values associated with the religious and political leadership of Ra'iatea, "the cradle of royalty and religion", integrated with the legendary account of the origin of the island of Tahiti.

Another equally important aspect of religion is the ethical one. Before discussing this in relation to the Society Island material it seems desirable to be quite clear as to what we mean by the term which we are using.

The ethical code of any society forms a part of its *normative system*, by which we mean the body of rules, legal, practical, aesthetic and so on, whereby the conduct of individuals is regulated. This whole body of rules is integrated into a unitary system and no aspect of it, no isolated body of norms (for example the legal code) can be considered apart from the system as a whole. At the same time it is desirable conceptually to isolate its various aspects, in other words to differentiate one group of social norms from another, because such groups differ in the social functions which they serve. The classification of rules is best effected on the basis of the sanctions which are brought to bear when an individual transgresses them—thus a rule may be called "legal" if a breach of it is punished by a legal sanction. On this basis we may differentiate moral or ethical rules as those which are sanctioned by moral indignation. It must of course be remembered that a single rule may be validated by more than one sanction. Moreover, it must still further be emphasized that the normative system as a whole is not absolutely consistent—ethical rules may run counter to other kinds of norm, and one moral rule may even be contradicted by another. This, however, applies to a greater extent to norms abstractly formulated than to their application to concrete situations, in which there is generally a fair measure of agreement as to what is socially desirable conduct and what is not. Undue emphasis has in the past been paid to the abstract and overt formulation of norms, both legal and moral, as opposed to their operation in concrete social situations.

Religion is always associated with deeply emotional feelings, and is correlated with a body of significant ethical rules, a breach of which is sanctioned by a social reaction of moral indignation. In other words one of the most important features of every religion is its *ethical aspect*—religious beliefs and practices are, as Durkheim has pointed out, obligatory. This ethical component of religion is twofold, and consists on the one hand of the ethical rules governing religious beliefs and observances themselves and on the other hand of moral rules which, though not referring directly to religious obligations, are nevertheless religious in character. Taking, for example, the Ten Commandments, the injunction not to set up graven images is an example of the former type of rule, and the commandment "Thou shalt not kill" an example of the second. These two types of correlated ethical norms are very general features of religious phenomena, but it should be emphasized that their *relative* importance may vary from one religious cult to another. Thus, in contrasting Society Island religion with that of modern European communities, we find a predominance of the former, as opposed to the latter, type of ethical rule. Thus in the list of "mortal sins" given by Henry[1] we find such offences as "violation of sanctity by doing domestic work", "irreverence in offering human victims", "clumsiness in processions or failing in religious recitals", "hurrying over prayers to serve the food", and so on. Any of these was likely to bring disaster upon the land and the people, and a priest guilty of any of them would be suspended from office. Special confessions and atonements were necessary in order to obviate the evil effects of such offences. On the other hand it would appear that such offences as theft did not tend to excite divine wrath.[2] Thieves invoked the aid of their gods, while the exploits of the notorious legendary thief Hiro were embodied in the mythology.

Broadly speaking the ethics of Society Island religion concerned primarily the reciprocal obligations between human beings and the gods. It is important to recognize this element of reciprocity, in order to avoid the popular misconception of the native as being a "slave to his idols". Far from this being the case, the gods were conceived as having very definite obligations towards mortals in return for the worship and veneration which they received from them. This is clearly seen in the case of family gods, who might actually be cast off by the ceremony

[1] *A.T.* p. 198.   [2] *Systems*, vol. III, p. 21.

described above if they failed in their duties towards the human beings under their protection.[1] Again, the status of a god varied with the fortunes of his worshippers. Thus, during the *paʻi-atua* ceremony, when the supreme moment for unwrapping the image came, it sometimes happened that a god had been stripped of most of his red feathers by an enemy, a spectacle which was believed to be most ludicrous to the gods. In such circumstances the high priest would exclaim: "The god is beaten, and perhaps his master is beaten also. Behold he has no feathers!" The congregation were forbidden by decorum to make any response, but they immediately proceeded to invest the god with new feathers.[2]

There is much information on the formal ritual of worship and the obligations of the worshippers, but very little concerning these obligations in their dynamic aspect. In other words we have descriptions of religious obligations, but we are not told to what extent these were observed in practice, nor what sanctions, supernatural or otherwise, were visited upon those who failed to discharge them. Probably those duties which were not irksome were regularly observed, but in the case of more unpleasant impositions there were presumably cases of breach, as well as attempts at evasion. Thus we are told that during the restrictions imposed before the *paʻi-atua* ceremony no one dared to stir abroad, but the myth of Tere-he suggests that this rule was not always rigidly obeyed. Again, pork, turtle, and the flesh of large white fish were officially forbidden food to women and children, but Henry states that "on favourable opportunities ...men secretly indulged their wives and children in these forbidden meats".[3]

As to punishments visited by the gods, many of these are manifestly absurd, and were obviously mere threats. Thus anyone who offended the stork, which was the shadow of the god Rua-nuʻu, was likely to have his neck twisted round so that his face looked backwards, an affliction which could only be alleviated by a humble petition to the image of the god. On the other hand some afflictions, such as blindness or choking while eating, probably did occur and when they did were attributed to the anger of the gods.

---

[1] See above, p. 221. It should be noted that it was only the family gods who were cast off in this way. This fact depends upon the difference of function between these gods and the more important deities venerated by the entire community.
[2] Henry, *A.T.* p. 167.   [3] *Ibid.* p. 177.

In regard to punishments visited upon offenders by society, we are nowhere told of their actual incidence. Thus Henry states that "so sacred was the *pa'i-atua* regarded that were a stray man to appear upon the scene, whatever his rank or station, he was immediately seized and slain as a sacrifice to the gods", but we are left completely in the dark as to how often such an event happened, if indeed it ever occurred at all.

However, in spite of the gaps in the available information, it is quite clear that religious obligations formed an important part of the lives of the Society Islanders, and that the motives which induced people to observe them were not derived from a single source, such as the "religious sentiment". On the contrary there seems to have been a complex group of forces at work. In the first place, there was the pleasure derived from collective activity, with its positive inducements, aesthetic, gastronomic and (probably) sexual. Secondly, there was the hope of bounty from the gods when religious ceremonies were properly carried out, and fear of the supernatural punishment of any dereliction from religious duty, for example failure to dedicate a portion of turtle to the deity before eating it.[1] Thirdly, there was the force of public opinion and even the fear of possible punishments inflicted by society for such an offence as the violation of a *rahui* prohibition.[2] Last, but by no means least, there was the complex ideology as expressed in myths and beliefs which gave to religious observances a compulsive and necessary force in the manner described above.

In concluding the discussion of religious institutions we must draw attention to the personnel concerned with their functioning. Every individual was to some extent *en rapport* with the gods, for as we have seen the stranger or exile might perform religious rites on the seashore, using the sea as his *marae*. But there were also special religious dignitaries, namely the priests and the *'opu-nui*, while certain special rites were carried out by chiefs and other people of rank. The latter we shall discuss in relation to political organization, and for the moment we shall concern ourselves with those functionaries whose duties were exclusively religious.

Priests might be of any rank, even *manahune*, but they officiated only for a congregation of their own class. The priesthood normally passed from father to son, but it would appear, in spite of statements to the contrary, that the office of priest was not

---

[1] *Systems*, vol II, p. 269.   [2] Cf. *ibid.* vol. I, p. 186.

hereditary *per se*, but merely from the customary practice of a father imparting to his son the necessary sacred lore.[1]

We are told very little of the economic life of the priesthood, except that they were immune from work, from which we may infer that they were supported at the public expense. Moreover, it is specifically stated that at certain distributions of food, large quantities were set aside for the priests. In return for this they carried out important reciprocal services for the community at large, the functions of which we may now examine.

In defining magico-religious phenomena we have seen that some source of extraordinary power, embodied in the supernatural, must be drawn upon. We have also pointed out that the world of the supernatural must be to some extent removed from that of everyday life, yet must be in some way related to it. Further we have drawn attention to the fact that the function of supernatural beings is to enable human individuals to meet their most serious problems in terms of a social situation already familiar to them, that is to say by a personal appeal. But the gods are necessarily removed to some extent from the everyday life of men, and there is need of an intermediary with special knowledge of and intimacy with them, who may prevail upon them to grant blessings and to mitigate suffering. This again is a familiar social situation—namely importuning through an intermediary. The priests served this function, which is clearly reflected in the customs and beliefs which expressed their sanctity—the fact that though they were patently men, they were nevertheless in close touch with the gods. This is clearly seen in their oracular powers, and in the cases in which they were believed actually to speak for the gods, for example in assuring discouraged combatants during a battle at sea.[2] The sanctity of the priestly class is well illustrated in relation to restrictions, which were sometimes made more stringent and sometimes relaxed in the case of priests. For example, we have seen that the taboos observed by the whole community immediately before the *pa'i-atua* ceremony were greatly augmented in the case of the priests. On the other hand, in the case of the official taboo upon the eating of pork, turtle, or the flesh of large white fish by women and children, the priest was allowed openly to give these dainties to the women and children of his household, whereas the laity were forced to do so furtively. These examples are illuminating. When it is a matter of *acquiring* or emphasizing

---

[1] Cf. *Systems*, vol. II, pp. 417–18.   [2] Henry, *A.T.* p. 317.

sanctity by the observation of taboos, the obligations of the priests are more stringent, but when the object of the taboo is to prevent the individual from profaning the sacred, it is relaxed in the case of the priesthood. Thus both types of custom depend upon the same social ideal, namely the superior sanctity of the priests. This was also expressed in the belief that they were able to control the gods, who would visit death on anyone who had offended them.[1]

Again, let us consider the training of the priests. They were compelled to commit to memory the traditional religious knowledge of the people, by which process they became *tahu'a*, that is "authors" or "experts". A candidate for the priesthood would withdraw from his family and go through a novitiate with the priests. During this process he was taught the sacred chants, prayers, and the lore of omens which he must be able to repeat without a single mistake. He learned in special priests' schools, built upon holy ground, his instructors being well paid for their work. The importance of this economic aspect of a priest's novitiate should be emphasized. In the first place, it indicates that priests must always have belonged to wealthy families. Secondly, it is significant because it provided a sort of licence to practise—if the qualifications of any priest were ever challenged he would reply: "I am no beggar; I am no eater of scraps! An invoker of Ta'ere[2] am I. Purau (bark) have I taken to the teachers; fish have I chopped for the teachers; finely braided cloth have I taken to the teachers; mats have I taken to the teachers..." and so on.[3]

Summing up, we may say that the whole education of a priest is designed to bring him into closer touch with the supernatural. This is effected by initiating him into the fraternity of those already sacred; socially he severs himself to some extent from the everyday world and identifies himself with them. And above all he acquires that body of esoteric knowledge which enables him better to understand and therefore to control those forces which it is the object of religion to mobilize.

SORCERY

We insisted at the outset that the magico-religious system of any people must be regarded as a unitary group of phenomena,

---

[1] *Systems*, vol. II, p. 420.
[2] Ta'ere was the god and source of all knowledge.
[3] Henry, *A.T.* p. 156.

though we pointed out that any given magico-religious pheno-menon might be predominantly either religious or magical. So far we have been examining those magico-religious customs and beliefs of the Society Islanders which belong to the former category, and we must now turn our attention to those pheno-mena in the culture which were primarily magical. These may be differentiated on purely empirical grounds as follows: In the first place, whereas religious ceremonies were exclusively carried out by men, even sacrifices (both human and animal) being necessarily male, magic was practised by men and women alike.[1] In the second place, it is broadly speaking true that the function of religion was to cope with communal problems and public calamities and that of magic to meet individual difficulties.

Magicians (*tahutahu*) of both sexes employed familiar spirits called *ti'i* which Henry translates "fetchers". These were traditionally associated with the magical practices of Ti'i, who had a white heron as a "fetcher". Magic was practised in secret, and was a remunerative pursuit. Images of the *ti'i* were kept at special *marae* or consecrated places. Magicians would adopt certain demons, who were the malevolent disembodied spirits of rulers and warriors of ancient fame. These spirits, whom the magicians addressed as sons and daughters, were believed to be ready to respond to the orders of their *metua-tahutahu* (magician parents) when the latter importuned them to enter into the *ti'i*. With each *ti'i* was kept a tunshell, which gives a soft murmuring sound when held up to the ear. This was believed to be the voice of the *ti'i* communicating messages to the magician.

One method used to convey the evil spirits to the victim was through a *tupu*, which consisted of something tangible belonging to him, such as hair or nail parings, a piece of clothing, remains of food, or saliva and other excreta. The *tupu* was placed in a special bowl and presented to the *ti'i*, who were invoked by the magician to enter the victim and destroy him. When the *ti'i*, by various means, entered their victim, he at once felt excruciating abdominal pains, followed by other manifestations of illness, and if the process were not checked immediately he died within a day or two. In view of this belief, people were careful to destroy their *tupu* lest they fall into the hands of magicians, and

---

[1] The statements of certain early observers concerning the existence of priestesses (*Systems*, vol. II, p. 425) seem to arise from a confusion between the priestly office itself and certain special rites carried out by women.

persons of high rank had special attendants whose function it was safely to dispose of their *tupu*. Another method of sorcery consisted in placing a spell over food or drinking water which was to be consumed by the victim.

A special magician's house was an appendage of every national *marae* and it was the function of the *tahutahu* in charge of this to avenge the chiefs on their enemies, to annihilate offending *tahutahu* of an inferior order, to destroy national foes, and to aid the warriors by performing hostile sorcery against their enemies. The *tahutahu* associated with a national *marae* was a person of considerable importance, and the fear of his magical powers gave him considerable influence even with chiefs of the highest rank.

An important function of magicians in the Society Islands was the detection of theft. The person robbed would go to the *tahutahu* and ask him to discover the culprit, which he did as follows: he poured some water into a black wooden trough or coconut cup, and holding over it a young banana shoot to represent the thief, he would invoke the *ti'i* to reveal the latter's identity. It was believed that when this was done the likeness of the thief became reflected on the surface of the water in the bowl, and so strong was this belief that when it became known that the victim of a theft was about to consult a *tahutahu*, the thief sometimes returned the goods stealthily to their owner, in order to avoid the ordeal. If this was not done the process of identification was carried out and the thief was captured and taken to the sorcerer, who tried by threats to extort a confession, and if this did not succeed he proceeded to torture the culprit to death as described above.

It should be noted that when a theft was premeditated, the thief would invoke his own god, whom he asked not to heed his voice if he should tell lies, and to let him become a "fool to the god". When subsequently he was accused of the theft, he would deny it, and would call his god to witness, having previously exonerated himself by becoming a "fool to the god". This also enabled the sorcerer to discount his affirmation of innocence— saying: "He has become a fool to his god."

The *ti'i* were not believed to be absolutely reliable, and it was stated that *tahutahu* were sometimes deceived by lying spirits. Moreover magicians could discontinue their association with their *ti'i* if they wished. This they did by burying them in unfrequented ground and ceremonially bidding them farewell.

Sometimes the *ti'i* so cast off would return to haunt the sorcerer and his family, in which case he concluded that they were not satisfied with their grave, and removed them to another.

In addition to the *ti'i* of professional sorcerers, there were several other varieties. There were *ti'i-pu-rahui*, which were wooden images set up at the boundaries of land in order to indicate a local restriction on food. On a much grander scale were the *ti'i-potua-ra'au*, huge wooden figures carved from logs taken from the national *marae* and erected upon the public assembly ground, in order to proclaim a general restriction upon land and sea. Another class of *ti'i*, not possessed by demons, were the *ti'i-tu'u-'ahu*, immense figures representing the high chief, and erected at the boundaries of his land. These were venerated by passers-by, who lowered their clothes to their waists as a sign of respect, while labourers and persons meanly clad gave them a wide berth. When the land was conquered, the invaders destroyed its *ti'i-tu'u-'ahu* and set up others in their places.

When an individual was the victim of a *tahutahu*, he or his family had recourse to a special priest, who by prayers and offerings to the god Ro'o-te-roro'o might cause the *ti'i* to leave their victim, and even, if the disenchanter were powerful enough, to enter into and destroy the sorcerer who had originally sent them.

CHAPTER X

RELIGIOUS ASPECTS OF SOCIAL ORGANI-
ZATION IN THE SOCIETY ISLANDS

HAVING, in the last chapter, given a brief outline of the magico-religious system of the Society Islanders, it now remains to indicate the relation of this system to other aspects of their social organization.

The term "social organization" is used to designate the various groupings of individuals found in all societies. Such groupings may be aligned on various bases—they may be based upon kinship, local or political organization, economic differentiation, religious functions, and so on. These divisions invariably cut across each other to some extent, though to a lesser degree in primitive society than in our own. The concept of social organization is an extremely valuable one, but in view of the very general nature of the term it seems desirable at the outset to emphasize the concrete and specific realities which it covers.

The reason for insisting upon this is that specific social groupings, and social organization in general, have too often in the past been conceived in a static rather than a dynamic way, to the detriment of our understanding of native life as it is actually lived. The facts of social organization, as expressed in charts of kinship systems, genealogies, maps and other demographic documents are of undisputed value to the anthropologist in indicating the broad framework of social structure. But it is essential to remember that within this framework are living human beings, and that without an account of their activities, their mutual relationships in actual social situations, their hopes, fears, attainments and failures, the bare framework must necessarily be as devoid of life as an engineer's blue-print or a mathematical formula.

We must, then, supplement a purely formal and structural account of social organization by a study of the various social groupings as they actually work—they must be studied from the dynamic as well as from the static point of view. The object of this is twofold. In the first place, by concentrating upon the *activities* of social groups rather than upon their formal definition, the anthropologist gains a deeper insight into their nature, and so avoids being misled by purely formal characteristics. In the second place, the dynamic approach brings us at once face to face with the vitally important functional relationships existing between various forms of social grouping.

From this point of view the role of social organization in culture is at once apparent. We may define the function of social organization as being to determine, organize, and control the behaviour of individuals engaged in institutional activities. From the dynamic point of view, then, the essential reality of social groupings is to be found in the institutional activities which the members of such groupings carry out. The best way, therefore, to understand the place of religion in social organization is to define the role which it plays in the functioning of institutions. We may commence this study of Society Island institutions by describing their methods of off-shore fishing, the only productive activity concerning which we have any systematic body of information. Having in this way gained a general understanding of the magico-religious aspect of economic activities we may proceed to a more abstract treatment of its role in the economic system, considered from the point of view of its various phases of production, ownership, distribution and exchange.

THE RELIGIOUS ASPECT OF ECONOMIC INSTITUTIONS

A quantity of material concerning the off-shore fishing of the Society Islanders has recently been provided by Mr Charles Nordhoff,[1] and its value is enhanced by the fact that the author is a keen and experienced fisherman who has himself participated in many of the activities which he describes. His account covers the methods of fishing for albacore, dolphin, bonito and *ruvettus*, but only the first three of these will be considered here.

The fishing season of the Society Islands lasted for about seven or eight months of the year and was associated with the appearance of the Pleiades in November and their disappearance in May. It is noteworthy that Aldebaran in Taurus, which was believed to represent Rio, the tutelar deity of albacore and bonito fishermen, is visible throughout this part of the year, being not very far removed from the Pleiades.

The albacore was a fish of considerable economic importance to the Society Islanders, who recognized and named several

---

[1] "Notes on the Off-shore Fishing of the Society Islands", *J.P.S.* vol. xxxix Nos. 2 and 3.

varieties, as well as the various stages in its growth. Moreover, they had special terms for albacore with different characteristics, those which were strong, cautious, or easy to catch. The fish were caught by three distinct methods: sometimes small albacore were caught during the course of bonito fishing, but the two methods specially designed to catch albacore were by means of a specially equipped double canoe called *tira*, and by still-fishing at considerable depths.

The *tira* was a double canoe, operated by a crew of twenty odd, both men and women, the entire outfit being owned by this company. Each important part of the canoe had its proprietor, though there is no information as to the social significance of this term—as to the "proprietor's" rights to the use of the canoe, his obligations in regard to construction and maintenance, or his claim upon the catch. The *tira* itself consisted of two canoes joined by cross-booms of such a length that the two hulls were about five feet apart. At the bow of the larger of these two canoes was a crane (*purau*) from which hung two lines with hooks at the ends, only one line being used at a time. When a fish was hooked, the crane was raised to an almost vertical position, and the fish, being thus drawn beside the hull, was clubbed to death and then taken aboard. Between the two canoes floated a basket containing live bait, the collection of which was the special function of the women. The whole equipment of the *tira*—the hooks, lines, rigging and so on—was a most elaborate affair and necessitated the use of highly specialized technological methods and a sound knowledge of elementary mechanical principles.

Albacore fishing was always conducted over limited and well-defined areas of sea, termed *apoo aahi*, or "albacore holes", which were the property of those landowners whose estates abutted that part of the sea in which they occurred. These albacore holes were few in number—according to Mr Nordhoff's estimate there were not more than a dozen of them around the whole coast of Tahiti. Why albacore should frequent these sharply defined areas of sea presents a problem. Mr Nordhoff is inclined to accept the explanation of an experienced native fisherman that *apoo aahi* are parts of the sea where conflicting currents set up a condition like the *nini*, or "cowlick", at the back of the head. The theory is that small fry are swept there by the currents, and that the albacore resort to these places in search of food. At these *apoo aahi*, *tira* fishing was carried out. The following is a *résumé* of the description of a *tira* fishing expedition which Mr Nordhoff witnessed a decade or so ago.

The double canoe having been made ready and the bait collected, the party set out in the early morning for an albacore hole off the Paea coast, a district renowned for its *apoo aahi*. When the spot in question was reached the "captain", or director of operations, sat down beside the basket containing the live bait. A few of these he threw out into the sea, and when the albacore rose to take them the hook, baited with a whole fish, was lowered and the canoe paddled slowly backwards so that the fish bait on the hook trailed through the water in a lifelike way. Although more live bait was constantly thrown out, no albacore took the hook, and the captain cried out to the man who had baited the hook: "It is useless for you to bait the hook, yes, I heard you disputing with your wife!" The man withdrew and a girl baited the hook. The moment this was lowered a large albacore took the bait and was hauled aboard. The girl continued to bait the hook throughout the morning, and fifty large fish were caught.

Tira fishing was always a collective activity, a number of people being required to navigate the double canoe and to manipulate its equipment. But there was another method (called *puraro*) of catching albacore at very much greater depths. This was carried out by one individual in a small single canoe. At each albacore hole the depth for fishing was established by custom; to fish at a depth different from the standard one was condemned, because it gave the fish bad habits and made more work for everybody.

Puraro (a word which, according to the dictionary of the London Missionary Society, was also used for "an underhand blow among boxers") was frowned upon in the old days for several reasons. In the first place, it tended to spoil the *tira* fishing; since the latter was carried out at the surface, the practice of tempting the fish to lower levels was deleterious to it. Secondly, it lacked the communal character of *tira* fishing, and being an entirely individual affair, left more room for sharp practice. Thus, when a number of small canoes were fishing at the same albacore hole, a fisherman who was short of bait might draw close to another and, without releasing "chums" himself, might profit from those released by his neighbour. Further, a single fisherman might fish an albacore hole at the wrong depth and so spoil it for others. Finally, *puraro* fishing might be done at night, which facilitated poaching. Still-fishing for albacore by night was called *mafera*, the primary meaning of which is given by the London Missionary Society's dictionary as: "to take advantage of a person of the other sex when asleep"— apparently a practice similar to that of the *moetotolo* or "sleep crawler" in Samoa[1] which is paralleled in Ontong Java.[2] In general, then, there was a distinct moral objection to *puraro* fishing, and the fact that it has now entirely superseded the *tira* as a method of catching albacore may be regarded as symptomatic of a change in native character under European influence.

Dolphin fishing was another form of economic activity which has died out in recent years. It was carried out in sailing canoes, mainly on the side of the island exposed to the prevailing easterly winds, the leeward side being devoted primarily to albacore and bonito fishing. Dolphin were caught on a line, flying fish or crayfish being used as bait. There was an interesting restriction connected with this activity; when a school of ten or a dozen dolphin was available, nine dolphin and nine only might be taken from a single school. It was believed that an infringement of this rule would bring the worst of luck.

The third kind of deep-sea fish caught by the Society Islanders was the bonito. The habits of these fish required a highly specialized type of hook,[3] which was made of pearl shell. It was believed that the colour of the hook was of profound importance—if a hook of the right shade was not used, the fish would not bite. Mr Nordhoff was at first sceptical about this, but eight years' fishing with the natives convinced him that the fish actually do differentiate between the shades of colour or "texture", and that one hook will prove satisfactory one day and another the next. He suggests that their preference is determined by the conditions of the weather, the time of day, and the small fry upon which the bonito are feeding.[4] The natives laid great stress upon the selection of the correct hook, and some-

---

[1] Mead, *C.A.S.* pp. 93 *sqq.*   [2] Hogbin, *L.O.P.* p. 228.

[3] The bonito hook is an important and highly specialized element in the material culture of Oceania. It is more properly termed a *lure* since it is not baited like an ordinary fish-hook, but is constructed to attract the bonito by its resemblance to the small fry upon which they feed.

[4] Kennedy states that bonito fishermen in Vaitupu, of the Ellice Islands, have four varieties of lure, classified according to colour. They always try to have at least one specimen of each variety with them when fishing, for the lure is made to resemble the bonito's prey and "it appears that the bonito has a predilection for variation of diet, and whereas he may be found attacking the shoals of one species of small fish to-day, next week he will probably be found only among those of another species". (Kennedy, *C.V.* p. 43.)

times, when the fishing was bad, a single fish would be hastily opened. If it were found to contain a roe, a hook matching the colour of this as nearly as possible was selected and used.

Since schools of bonito travel very fast, speed is an essential factor in obtaining a good catch. This is the reason for the attention devoted to the selection of a hook of the correct colour and shape. With regard to the latter factor Mr Nordhoff writes:

The skill of a bonito-fisherman may be judged from an inspection of his hooks. A green hand uses long points, very sharp, to insure landing every fish that strikes. The expert uses short, blunt points, just sharp enough to lift the fish out of the water before they drop out of the jaw. While the beginner is landing a dozen bonito, many of which must be disengaged from the hook by hand, the adept will have pulled out of the water fifty fish and landed forty-five of them without touching a hook. In the Society Islands, the fisherman forced to disengage his hook from a bonito's mouth is jeered at by his companions, and if a large proportion of hooked fish fall back into the sea, jeers are the result.

When fishing in the midst of a school of bonito it was forbidden to throw out bilge water, as it was believed that the blood of the bonito already caught, mixed with the bilge water, would frighten away the rest of the school. However Mr Nordhoff notes that "fully a quarter of all the bonito caught bear more or less severe wounds, oftentimes fresh and bleeding".

In regard to the magico-religious aspect of deep-sea fishing, the available material is inadequate, owing to the very early date at which the Society Islanders were subjected to missionary influence, but we possess sufficient data to enable us to see in a general way the part which magic and religion played in Society Island fishing.

The most important deities connected with fishing were Tino-rua, Rua-hatu and Rio, the latter being the special god of bonito and albacore fishermen. Tino-rua was a merman with the tail of a swordfish, created by Ta'aroa, and his messenger was a species of shark. Rua-hatu was the "Tahitian Neptune", and features in the Ra'iatean version of the myth of the deluge. The following is an abridged account of Henry's translation of this legend:[1]

There lived, long ago at Opoa, two friends named Te-aho-roa and Ro'o. It happened one day that these two were fishing for pompanos in deep water within the borders of the reef. While fishing around the islet of Toa-marama they foolishly went to the *apo'o feo* (coral hole) of the god Rua-hatu, where they

[1] Henry, *A.T.* p. 448.

lowered their lines, using as sinkers small coral stones, as is done in all deep-line fishing. One of these coral sinkers struck Rua-hatu upon the head as he lay asleep in the depths of the sea. The god awoke and as he passed his fingers through his hair he took hold of the fish-hook and stone. Te-aho-roa and Ro'o, seeing the jerking of the line, thought they had caught a fish and proceeded to draw it in. But when they drew the "catch" to the surface they saw long thick hair spreading over the sea, and realizing that they had caught a monster, cried out: "Woe be to both of us, this is a man not a fish! It is a monster of the deep! We are doomed men!"

Rua-hatu came aboard the canoe and, scowling at the two men, he asked: "Who are you two?" They answered: "We are Ro'o and Te-aho-roa."

"Aye? What are your names?"

And Te-aho-roa answered: "Assuredly we are Ro'o and Te-aho-roa! We have transgressed in coming to this sacred spot to fish, but forgive us both, O King! We will never err in coming to this place."

Rua-hatu then asked about their people, their relatives, their chiefly families and particularly about the princess Airaro, be-loved of the gods of the ocean. Then he said:

"Go and tell them all to come out here, to Toa-marama, immediately; do not delay. Because of the good princess Airaro, you shall be saved. I am vexed with you for disturbing me; you have been unkind to me. But I will not only pluck the tips of the branches, I will overthrow to the foundation! This very night will I submerge Mount Te-mehani-ave-ari'i, at Opoa, in the sea. All Ra'iatea shall certainly be destroyed. It is I, Rua-hatu, king of the mighty ocean."

Ro'o and Te-aho-roa were terrified, and returning to Opoa told everyone of their warning. The members of the family of the high chief, including his daughter Airaro, the households of the two friends, and a few other people, gave credence to the story, and resorted to Toa-marama. But the majority scoffed at the idea, and would not go.

All the birds, spiders, and insects, shadows of the gods, were caught up by their respective deities into the skies. Then, when those to be rescued were safely established at Toa-marama, the sea began to rise, finally covering all the land except the islet of Toa-marama, which was left dry because of Airaro, beloved of the sea gods. At night all the people on this islet fell into a deep

sleep and when they awoke in the morning they saw that the sea
had receded. All upon the land was devastation: trees were up-
rooted and their branches broken, and the land was strewn with
debris from the sea, coral, dead fish and shells. Those who had
been saved returned to Opoa where they lived upon fish and
red clay until the trees grew again, which they did in one night.
The living things which had been caught up into the sky were
set down, and soon the land was as it had been before the
inundation.

After this the people erected a new *marae* to Rua-hatu on the
island of Ra'iatea. Then Rua-hatu journeyed around the various
Society Islands making inlets and passages, and erecting *marae*,
for example the famous structure called Maha'i-atea in the
district of Papara, in Tahiti, which was dedicated to Ta'aroa.[1]

The following is Henry's translation of the chant of dedication
connected with the erection of *marae* to Rua-hatu:[2] "Let
sacredness reign, give praise! It is deliverance approved, deliverance made powerful, deliverance to save, great purifying
deliverance! Save thy body of priests, O Rua-hatu! Save thy
pig feeders, thy feather seekers in the atolls, thy restrictors, thy
people inhabiting the land, hearken to our prayer."

While Rua-hatu was the general god of the sea, Rio was the
special deity of albacore and bonito fishermen, one of his titles
being: *atua fa'arava'ai i te a'ahi e te atu*. The word *fa'arava'ai*
is translated in the London Missionary Society's dictionary as
"to supply a deficiency" and the phrase quoted above thus
brings out very clearly the tutelar function of this god. Rio was
the last-born son of Ta'aroa and Papa-raharaha, the first woman,
and was represented in the sky by Aldebaran in the constella-
tion of Taurus. The name of this star was Ta'i-Rio-aitu and it
played an important part in navigation. It is mentioned in a
chant connected with the legendary voyages of the Tahitians to
the Hawaiian Islands.[3]

There were special *marae* called *o-te-feia-tai'a* dedicated to
these sea deities, to whom the priests offered up *upu rava'ai*,
prayers to ensure success in fishing. At these *marae* were kept
wooden and stone images of fish. Concerning these *marae* we
have but scanty information. It is possible that they were upon
occasion used for acts of collective worship, though it is not
clear whether they or the ordinary public *marae* are referred to

[1] Henry, *A.T.* pp. 139–40.   [2] *Ibid.* p. 454.
[3] *Ibid. A.T.* p. 401; cf. Te Rangi Hiroa, *J.P.S.* vol. xxxv, p. 193.

in the following statements quoted by Handy from Moerenhout:

In Tahiti in November and December there was a time known as the "season of the outside of the sea" when the fishing season was opened by offering a sacrifice of first fish to the gods. On a certain day a canoe went out to fish; while it was out a ceremonial tapu reigned over land and sea, requiring complete inactivity and complete silence. Upon the return of the canoe in the evening, the whole of the catch was offered in the temple. Next day the procedure was the same, except that this day's catch was for the chief. Again on the third day the canoe went out, and now the fish were for the people—the tapu on the sea was lifted, the fishing season was open.[1]

Of a rather different character were the beliefs connected with small stone images of albacore, called *puna*. According to tradition there were once *puna* for all varieties of fish, but nowadays only those of albacore are used in Tahiti. Nordhoff found it difficult to obtain information concerning these images, but the following is his brief account of their functions:

Every *puna* had its owner, who had acquired it from his ancestors. It would be useless to make a *puna* now, as there would be no *mana* in it. When the fishermen return with their catch they must not forget to give the owner of the *puna* a generous share. If he is well treated and feels friendly toward the fishermen, the owner of the albacore *puna* keeps the head of his image toward the mountain (*i uta*), which causes the albacore to stay in their "hole" close to the reef. If the owner's share is skimped or forgotten, he retaliates by turning the head of the image toward the sea (*i tai*), and the fishermen are soon brought to their senses by finding that there are no more albacore in the hole—like the image, they have turned their heads away from the land. The owner of the *puna* may still be placated with gifts, and cozened into turning the image's head *i uta* (inland), when the albacore will be found in their hole once more; but if the man is deeply incensed, he will go secretly at night to where he keeps his *puna*, make sure that its head points to sea, and cover it with a thick black cloth. Not even a stray albacore will then take the hook. Once or twice in the past *puna* have been stolen by foolish men, but in each case the thief fell ill or was pursued by bad luck, and the hiding place of the image was revealed to its true owner by an appearance of blue fire, seen at night. Nothing is stranger about *puna* (the natives say) than the way they are well known to grow —increasing slowly and steadily in size as the years pass.[2]

The deep-sea fishing of the Society Islanders was regulated, in its every phase, by a number of practical rules, involving an elaborate technology and a thorough working knowledge of the elementary principles of navigation, of the weather, and of the habits of fish and sea birds. But in addition to these practical principles fishing was governed by a number of ethical rules, some of which were of a magico-religious character, for example the restrictions associated with the first fishing expedition of the season, and the obligations to the owners of *puna*. These rules

[1] Handy, *P.R.* pp. 299–300.   [2] *J.P.S.* vol. XXXIX, p. 159.

affected not only the activity of fishing itself, but also the behaviour of fishermen and their relatives when ashore. Thus if a fisherman had quarrelled with his wife before setting out, this was believed adversely to affect his fortunes. Further the sweethearts, wives and daughters of bonito fishermen were obliged to remain chaste during the absence of the canoes at sea, and a failure to observe this rule was supposed to bring bad luck or even disaster upon the expedition.

But supernatural sanctions were only one factor in the validation of this ethical system. It was a privilege to belong to the *manuoroo* or guild of fishermen and to know their jealously guarded secrets. Incompetence was jeered at, while a reputation as a skilled fisherman (*mariripurepo*) who was *tapatai*—fearless of wind and sea—was much sought after. Habitual laziness was condemned, and earned for the offender the title of *e hurupatautai*—one who shams sleep in order to avoid a fishing expedition. Further, such selfish acts as fishing for albacore at the wrong depths and profiting undeservedly by the efforts of others brought public opprobrium upon the offender. The supremely dishonest act of still-fishing for albacore by night was compared with the predatory activities of the *mafera*, who was probably an object of ridicule and contempt as was the *moetotolo* in Samoa. In addition to these negative sanctions we must add the positive inducements—the economic advantages, the enhanced reputation, the dangerous and therefore exciting character of the work, and the pleasure from co-operative effort and good-natured rivalry, which successful fishing entailed. In the ethical system governing this activity, then, rules sanctioned by magico-religious beliefs were reinforced by other forces, positive and negative, social and individual, which made for conformity to established standards.

The above discussion of the off-shore fishing of the Society Islanders has served to indicate, so far as the available material allows, the part played by magico-religious beliefs and practices in this form of economic production; and it is highly probable that other equally important activities, such as agriculture, for example, were similarly correlated with magico-religious beliefs and practices. But here the available material is so scanty as to be worthless, and the only other productive pursuit on which we have any systematic information is canoe-building, which was carried out by special artisans called *tahu'a va'a*, *va'a* meaning "a canoe".

The importance of the canoe to an island community such as that with which we are dealing can readily be understood in the light of their social organization. Apart from the regular activity of fishing which we have described, frequent voyages were made between the islands of the group for various purposes, such as participation in religious ceremonies at the "international *marae*", attendance at *arioi* performances, visits to friends and relations, and war. In addition to this the traditions of the people were rich in legends of navigation, for example the mythical adventures of Hiro, and the traditional voyages of their ancestors to the Hawaiian Islands and other distant parts of Polynesia. The canoe was thus one of the most important objects of material culture in the Society Islands, a fact which was expressed in the many ritual usages connected with the more important vessels.[1] It is therefore understandable that every phase of the construction of a large canoe was surrounded by magico-religious ritual.

When a canoe was to be built, the *tahu'a-va'a* would go to the *marae* on the evening of the last night of the moon and perform a ceremony called "putting the hatchet to sleep". This consisted of placing the axe which he intended to use in a recess in the *marae* at the same time invoking Tane, Ta'ere, Te-fatu, and Ta'aroa to sanctify the axe by giving it sharpness, strength and lightness in order to make easy the work of construction. The artisans then held a feast, a portion of which was dedicated to Tane, on the *marae* ground and then retired to rest. At dawn the next day, each artisan "awakened" his axe with a further invocation, after which the work of construction was begun.[2]

When the canoe was finished, the artisans laid out rollers over which it was to be dragged to the sea. These were placed in position with a long invocation, designed to avert dangers at sea. The canoe was decorated with pennants and garlands and, after a further feast, was dragged over the rollers to the seashore, where it was completely immersed, with an invocation to Tane to protect it from the perils of the deep.[3]

So far we have been concerned mainly with the part played by magic and religion in production. But there are indications that other phases of economic activity were also correlated with magico-religious beliefs and practices. Thus we have seen that certain exchanges made between priests on behalf of their

[1] See above, pp. 173–5.   [2] Henry, *A.T.* pp. 146–7.
[3] *Ibid.* pp. 180 *sqq.*

respective deities played an important part in the most sacred of all religious ceremonies, the *pa'i-atua*. Here an economic transaction was invested with a spiritual significance. We have also seen that during important ceremonial distributions large quantities of food were set aside for the gods, as well as for the priests. Thus at the ceremony of the first-fruits, which was held during December, large quantities of food were brought to the public assembly ground and piled into an immense heap. This was then divided between the gods, the priests and *marae* attendants, the chiefs and the commoners. In addition to this the people invoked Roma-tane, the god of Paradise, to bring the spirits of deceased friends and relatives to share in the feasting and revelry, which lasted for several days.[1]

In the native system of ownership, magic and religion played an important part in the validation of the laws of property. Information is lacking as to the precise nature of these laws and the details of their actual working, but it is nevertheless clear that they were intimately associated with the magico-religious system.

We have seen, for example, that the rules of land tenure were connected with the family *marae* and with the secrecy of the family god. The erection of *marae* was essential in establishing claims to land. "To the *marae* were attached the hereditary names of the family, without which they could give no proof of their ownership of the land."[2] Even "to this day"[3] this principle has survived the impact of European civilization, the heirs of ancient families being compelled to establish their claims to land by referring their title to "the *marae* named so-and-so, from most of which a few uneven heaps of stones still remain".

All land was owned by someone, and it sometimes happened that people claimed a portion of a neighbour's land by moving a boundary stone or erecting a *marae* upon its borders. But this procedure was stigmatized as *ai-fenua* (eating land) and was generally avoided because of the disgrace attached to it. The family *marae* was called the *vauvau i'oa* (name container), and children by adoption were made legitimate heirs to land by receiving a name from it, failure to accord them this right being regarded as an injustice.

[1] Henry, *A.T.* p. 177.   [2] *Ibid.* p. 141.
[3] Teuira Henry died in 1915, so this phrase can only be held to apply to the beginning of the twentieth century. It would be interesting to know whether any connection between *marae* sites and land tenure still exists in the Society Islands.

When the land of a household was to be divided into shares, the people who were leaving the old home took a stone from the *marae*, and made it the chief corner stone of a new *marae* upon their respective shares. This transfer of stones, together with the titles associated with them, played an essential part in the alienation of land.[1]

The association between the family name, the *marae tupuna*, the tutelar deity, and rights to property probably extended to the ownership of those well-defined areas of sea over which off-shore fishing was carried out. These, as we have seen, were the property of the people who owned estates bordering upon the part of the sea in which they occurred, and were probably associated with the titles to such lands. It will be remembered that when Rua-hatu was disturbed during his sleep in one such "hole" he first asked the intruders: "Who are you two?" (*O vai 'orua na?*), to which they replied: "We are Ro'o and Te-aho-roa." Rua-hatu then said: "Aye? What are your names?" (*Nei? O vai to 'orua i'oa?*). Probably the word *i'oa* may here be translated "titles"[2] and the question construed as a challenge to the poachers to establish their right to fish at that particular spot.

Magico-religious beliefs also safeguarded the rights of property, in a somewhat different way, by means of the magical beliefs connected with sorcery. It cannot be doubted that the fear of detection and punishment by the *tahutahu* and their *ti'i* acted as powerful deterrents in the prevention of theft.

Not only the rights of property, but also restrictions upon their free exercise were validated by magico-religious sanctions. Such religious legends as that of Te-here tended to enforce the great public restrictions imposed by high chiefs, who used to set up *ti'i-potua-ra'au* on the public assembly ground upon such occasions, while private and incidental restrictions of food were established by setting up *ti'i-pu-rahui*. Misfortune, sickness and even death were believed to follow a defiance of these *ti'i*, which were taken down when the restriction was removed.

RELIGION AND POLITICAL ORGANIZATION

The local and political organization of the Society Islanders has already been dealt with in another work.[3] For this reason the present discussion will be limited to a brief outline of this phase

[1] Henry, *A.T.* p. 142.
[2] Cf. the conception of the family *marae* as the *vauvau i'oa*.
[3] *Systems.* See, in particular, vol. I, chap. v.

of social organization, and is designed to indicate the part played by religion in its integration.

Detailed information concerning the local organization of the Society Islands is lacking, but the following statement seems to provide a satisfactory general picture:

> The people as a whole, including all classes, and the district in which they lived, constituted a *mataeinaa*. This was applied to subdistricts as well as the large districts....But it was not applied to small local units of population. Within the *mataeinaa* were more or less autonomous groups or localities under *iatoai* or *raatira* who, by hereditary right, controlled the land. The owner of such an estate, or a subdivision of a district, should perhaps be termed a sub-chief. Such a heritage was spoken of as the *ai'a* or *ai'a tupuna*; but this word seems not to have signified a locality or group as a political unit, but rather "heritage". In matters connected with tribute and service to the Arii local groups acting as units under *raatira* or *iatoai* proprietors were spoken of as *amuiraa* or *pupu*, literally "bunch" or "group".[1]

Henry distinguishes four social classes in the Society Islands:

(1) The highest class of all, the *ari'i-maro-'ura* (sovereigns of the red feather girdle) or *ari'i-nui* (great sovereigns). These were the highest chiefs of all and claimed divine descent, they alone being allowed to wear the *maro-'ura*, which was supposed to be the costume of the gods.

(2) The *ari'i-ri'i*, or petty kings and queens, descended from part royal and part plebeian stock. These exercised sway over their little dominions, much as the barons did in former times in Europe. Together with the *ari'i-maro-'ura* they made up the aristocracy (*hui-ari'i*).

(3) The *hui-ra'atira* formed a link between the aristocracy and the commoners, being free landholders holding sway over the commoners and owing obligations of support and tribute to the chiefs under whose suzerainty they lived.

(4) The *manahune*, who made up the bulk of the population, served as workers and retainers for the upper classes, though they enjoyed their own hereditary possessions.[2]

In this system we must distinguish three aspects, namely rank, local distribution, and economic function. As far as can be gathered the relation between these does not seem to have been a rigid one. Thus the sub-chief of an *ai'a tupuna* might according to Handy[3] be an *ari'i-ri'i* or a *ra'atira* according to

---

[1] Handy, *H.C.S.I.* pp. 45–6. Elsewhere (p. 42) he states that the *iatoai* were families derived from the younger branches of the *ari'i* stock.

[2] Henry, *A.T.* pp. 229–30. Handy refers to a special class of *manahune* who were marked off as the victims of human sacrifice and were called *titi* (*H.C.S.I.* p. 44).　　　　　　　　　　　　　[3] *Op. cit.* p. 46.

whether he was of noble descent or not. But it would seem that these terms applied to rank and to economic function respectively, and it may be that a single individual might be designated by either, according to whether his rank or his economic function were under discussion. It would appear, moreover, that the social stratification was not as rigid as might appear from some of the accounts, and that between the *ari'i* on the one hand and the *manahune* on the other there was a "middle class" of *ra'atira*, individual members of which might, through such events as intermarriage or conquest, merge into the class either above or below them.[1] Nevertheless, there was a very strong feeling against intermarriage between chiefs and commoners, the penalty for such an offence being exile of the *ari'i* or death for the offspring of the union. Many chiefs chose to go into exile in the Tuamotus or elsewhere rather than submit to this law,[2] which according to an informant of Handy was strictly enforced in ancient times[3] though Ellis[4] speaks of the ceremonial by which such a marriage might be validated, while Henry[5] states that differences of rank were annulled by marriage and mentions a ceremony at the *marae* whereby this might be effected.[6] Probably the stringency with which the rule was actually enforced depended upon a number of factors, such as the degree of divergence in rank, the absolute status of the party of higher rank,[7] the personal feelings and influence of the two families, as well as public opinion. But whatever were the legal sanctions which were enforced under such circumstances, this rule was supported by a strong moral feeling, which comes out very clearly in a legend given by Henry[8] in which the prospective bridegroom of a young woman of rank was done to death by the priest of her parents' *marae*; and such action to prevent loss of prestige by an unequal marriage seems not to have been unusual. Incidentally this legend is of some interest as illustrating the various evaluations—sentimental, practical, and conventional— placed upon the situation by the various partisans and by disinterested observers. There is much expression of sympathy for the two lovers which brings out very clearly the reality of the restrictions which they sought to defy.

[1] Cf. *Systems*, vol. II, p. 357. [2] Handy, *H.C.S.I.* p. 40.
[3] *Ibid.* p. 27. [4] Ellis, vol. III, p. 98.
[5] Henry, *A.T.* p. 284. [6] *Ibid.* p. 595.
[7] Thus an informant of Handy states that "on no pretext could this law be annulled by an *ari'i-nui*" (*H.C.S.I.* p. 40). It should be noted, however, that the law referred to is against *procreation* and not necessarily against *marriage*.
[8] Henry, *A.T.* pp. 592–607.

Chieftainship in the Society Islands was a highly developed institution. The territory of each chief had certain titles associated with its various features—mountains, streams, promontories, *marae*, and the public assembly ground—which were embodied in traditional chants.[1] Each chief had a special guesthouse, as well as his own residence, and various possessions and insignia. Apart from his personal attendants he was surrounded by an *entourage* of public officials—his high priest, orator, administrator, chief warrior, messenger, mariner, and *arioi* comedian.[2] His name was sacred, and he was spoken of and addressed in a special language.[3] As we have seen, the more important chiefs actually traced their ancestry back to the gods[4] and it would appear that the highest priests were sometimes chiefs,[5] and were generally the near relatives of chiefs.[6]

Chieftainship was associated with a complicated system of obligations—economic, ritual and political—between the chief and his people. On the one hand the commoners owed tribute and service in peace and war to the chief; they were obliged to show respect to his edicts, to the members of his family and to his person, particularly his head, which was the seat of the *mana ari'i*. Insults to, and offences against, the chief were among the most serious of crimes,[7] as was the withholding of food demanded as tribute.[8] In return for this there were imposed upon the chief a number of duties, both religious and secular. We have already mentioned the part played by the chief in the consecration of *marae* and in the *pa'i-atua* ceremony. His secular functions included the administration of justice, the maintenance of decorum and good behaviour, the control of major economic activities, and the direction of public affairs generally. Much of the tribute which he received was redistributed to his people and to important guests,[9] though the precise mechanism of redistribution is not clear.[10]

Some of the duties of chieftainship were formally set out in a number of *ture*, or maxims.[11] In these *ture*, some of which may be cited for purposes of illustration, are embodied the moral and intellectual qualities desirable in an *ari'i*. He must be just,

[1] Henry, *A.T.* pp. 70 *sqq.*
[2] Handy, *H.C.S.I.* p. 35.
[3] *Ibid.* p. 38.
[4] Cf. *Systems*, vol. III, pp. 66–7.
[5] *Ibid.* p. 34.
[6] *Ibid.* p. 51.
[7] *Ibid.* pp. 16–17, 20.
[8] *Ibid.* p. 354.
[9] *Ibid.* vol. I, p. 187; vol. III, pp. 343, 355–6.
[10] Cf. *Systems*, vol. III, p. 357.
[11] Handy, *H.C.S.I.* pp. 41, 47.

but he must temper justice with mercy.[1] He must be energetic and patient in the discharge of his duties.[2] He must exercise wisdom and tact in the handling of public affairs,[3] and in the choice of his *entourage*.[4] Above all he must embody the highest ideals of generosity, honour and courage in the face of difficulties,[5] and must realize that his authority depends upon conscientious and competent administration.[6]

The maxims in which these principles are embodied provide a valuable insight into the ideology of chieftainship. Their particular interest lies in the various motives, idealistic and pragmatic, to which they appeal. Thus, while revealing a very high ideal of the moral and social duties of the chief, they do not omit to mention the very practical disadvantages which may follow upon laziness or incompetence. In spite of their sanctity and temporal power, the chiefs were always compelled to consider public opinion. If a chief became despotic, the priests and other important citizens took counsel together and pronounced the following verdict upon him: "Go and eat the leg of pork seasoned with dung! Thy royalty is taken from thee, thou art put down to tread the sand, to walk like common men."[7]

The fate which overtook a legendary despot is luridly portrayed in a story of Mount Te-mahani-ave-ari'i, in Ra'iatea. This mountain has several open winding craters, and in the

---

[1] "The *ari'i* must father a subject's claim for revenge, which is brought to him." "Let not the decrees of death be too frequent, for your own bones will follow the road to death." "The heart of an *ari'i* must be as great as his power."

[2] "Your government must be a true one. It must not be left to itself, nor allowed to be overshadowed with darkness. It must be treated with justice and not pushed aside with impatience." "Never interrupt nor discuss the words of an orator while he is performing his function; avoid impatience; be attentive with open eyes, swallowing ears."

[3] "Wisdom and a gentle heart are the best spear an *ari'i* can have." "Meditate before speaking. Your words are flashes of lightning, as mighty as the clap of thunder; they cannot be recalled."

[4] "Guard yourself against courtesans, who anoint themselves with sweet-scented oils in your household." "Never give ear to the advice of a sluggard."

[5] "Your household must not be accused of food hiding. Let not your name be associated with hidden food or hidden goods. The hands of an *ari'i* must always be open; on these two things rest your prestige." "Your oath must be as sacred as your person, as true as the coming of the morning star, Taurua, as binding as the laws of Farepua." "Accept trouble as an *ari'i-nui*. It must not find you afraid or shame-faced."

[6] "When you eat the power of government, remember that the people are the slaves of many masters; that their eyes are ever open to mistakes and abuses; and that, when the food bowl is full, bundles are quickly packed and faces turned to a new master." "The people are like a crying child, easily coaxed with gentle words, easily enraged by ill treatment." "The ants may hide themselves under leaves—but there are not enough leaves in all the land to hide your name."

[7] Henry, *A.T.* p. 196.

largest of these, it is said, there once lived an enormous monster, which was never seen by men. At one time there was a high chief called Tai-e who was much hated by his people for his tyranny. He went up to the crater with several of his subjects to ascertain what sort of creature lived there. He told the men of his party to lower him into the crater at the end of a long rope, and to pull him up when he should jerk another smaller rope which he held in his hand. On this understanding they lowered him into the abyss, but when they felt a frantic jerking of the rope, they paid no attention to it. After a while the jerking ceased, and they pulled up Tai-e, whom they found with his flesh devoured from his bones.[1]

The system of reciprocity between the chiefs and the people was organized into a hierarchy composed, broadly speaking, of the chiefs, the sub-chiefs, and the commoners. In this scheme of social organization the sub-chiefs played an important part, being both a support and a check on the king,[2] who was obliged to pay attention to their representations at council meetings because of the control which they exercised over their tenants.[3] We may safely infer that this control was validated by a similar set of reciprocal obligations between sub-chiefs and commoners.

We may now refer to certain further information bearing upon the specifically magico-religious aspect of this system of local and political organization. We have already mentioned the importance of the *marae* and their associated religious tradition with land tenure on the one hand and with social status on the other. This relationship was most marked in the case of chiefly families, whose *marae* provided a charter for their titles and rank.[4] This still remained even after a defeat in war had stripped them of their power[5] and it was for this reason that defeated chiefs were sometimes able, after a time, to reassert their power and to regain control over their conquered lands.

The sanctity of the chiefs was ritually expressed in the system of ceremonial which surrounded them. The life of an *ari'i* was associated with important religious ceremonies performed at the national *marae* from before birth until after death. The first-born son (*matahiapo*) of a high chief was a person of great importance, and was called the frontal bone (*paarae*) of the people,[6]

[1] Henry, *A.T.* p. 98.
[2] *Systems*, vol. I, p. 203; vol. II, p. 483; vol. III, pp. 121, 272.
[3] *Ibid.* vol. II, p. 484.
[4] *Ibid.* pp. 40, 65, 72.   [5] *Ibid.* p. 66
[6] Handy, *H.C.S.I.* p. 47.

for the chieftainship normally passed to him.[1] The following is a brief account, based upon material provided by Henry,[2] of the ceremonial surrounding the life of an heir to the office of high chief. Sometimes it happened that the succession passed to a woman, in which case the ritual was substantially the same.[3] Similar rites were performed for the heirs of lesser chiefs, though on a less elaborate scale, no human sacrifices being offered.

When the mother was about to be delivered of the *matahiapo* a proclamation of restriction, similar to that connected with the *paʻi-atua* ceremony, was issued, and remained in force until about five or six days after the birth. A house of *maire* fern was built at the back of the chief's ancestral *marae*, and to this the mother retired for her accouchement. While awaiting the birth, those in attendance (upon whom numerous ritual restrictions were imposed) chanted prayers invoking Roʻo, the messenger of Tane, for the mother's safe delivery, and when the child was born the accoucheur exclaimed: "*Ua muhuta mai nei te atua*" (The god has flown hither). After this the cord was ceremonially cut, and wrapped around the neck of the infant, whose body was anointed with sandalwood oil. Several days later the cord was carefully placed away in a recess in the *marae*, while everything which had been used at the birth was carefully buried close by. The child was ceremonially bathed, with an incantation aimed at ensuring his greatness as a warrior. After this the father received his child, and, hailing it as a member of his house and heir to the chieftainship, he embraced its feet and conferred upon it a name which had been chosen beforehand.[4]

[1] "When there was no direct heir to the throne the sovereign had the prerogative to name his successor. Otherwise the people elected a new ruler at the demise of the former." (Henry, *A.T.* p. 195.)

[2] *Ibid.* pp. 182–96.

[3] Handy (*H.C.S.I.* p. 24) states that a first-born female could not be *matahiapo*, but that if she bore a son he would assume the title. However, Henry's account indicates that she might pass through all the ceremonial, and that the "succession" might pass to her, though to what extent this was correlated with an assumption of the actual functions of chieftainship she does not say.

[4] This ceremony is probably responsible for the statements that the son succeeded his father at birth (cf. *Systems*, vol. III, p. 195). But Henry states that "the reigning father or mother did not abdicate their power and proclaim the young heir sovereign of the realm, as some writers have stated, for inauguration ceremonies must be performed before the people recognized a new ruler". (*A.T.* p. 185; cf. *Systems*, vol. III, p. 372.) The contradiction in the information seems to be due to a confusion of thought in connection with the term "succession". In general it would appear that the situation might be summed up by considering a native belief connected with this subject. Ellis, speaking of miraculous events which were supposed to occur in connection with the succession

The infant was next received by the high priest at the national *marae*, where it was laid upon a carpet of fine mats in the same manner as was done with the image of the tutelar god during the *pa'i-atua* ceremony.

Messengers were sent out to the various districts to announce the birth and well-being of the child, taking with them flags which they set up on the assembly ground of each district visited by them. When the people were well pleased with the news they allowed the flag to stand until it was taken away by the messenger, but if the tidings were unwelcome, they tore the flag down and broke the pole to which it was attached, sending the messenger back to his master with a challenge to war. This sometimes occurred in the case of newly conquered possessions whose people still hoped to recover their liberty.

After the *marae* ceremony the mother and child retired to a specially guarded house, where they remained for a little over a year, at the end of which time a public ceremony, sanctified by the sacrifice of a human victim, was performed at the *marae*. The child was carried shoulder high before the people, who acclaimed him, lowering their clothes to their waists as a sign of respect, and offering him many gifts. After this he was taken to the abode of his father to live.

The next important event in the life of the heir apparent was the occasion of his first tour of his father's possessions. A special canoe was built, and on its arrival with the young chief at each district, a slain human being was placed upon the seashore as a roller, over which the canoe was drawn. Again, when the heir apparent was circumcized (a rite which the Society Islanders used to practise upon boys when they were aged about fifteen or sixteen) one or more human sacrifices were made at the national *marae* while the operation itself was being carried out at the ancestral *marae*. Still later, at his coming of age, another human sacrifice was offered, the occasion being celebrated by a large feast.

The inauguration of a new sovereign was a most important occasion and for months before it was timed to take place much effort was expended in preparing food, clothes and decorations.

of high chiefs, tells of "an *aoa* tree, resembling the banyan, which shot forth a new fibrous branch at his birth; and that on his taking over the rule this branch or tendril reached the ground". (*Systems*, vol. III, pp. 326–7.) If this belief expresses the native ideology of succession, we should regard the ceremonies connected with the birth of the *matahiapo* as merely the beginning of a process which would ultimately culminate in his inauguration.

In regard to the latter, particular attention was paid to the con-
catenating of a new lappet to the *maro 'ura*, the girdle of red
feathers which was the mark of the highest rank, and derived
superlative sacredness from the fact that some of the feathers in
it were actually taken from the image of the tutelar god at the
national *marae*. This girdle has already been described[1] and a
further account is given by Henry as follows:

The royal girdle was an article of very skilful workmanship, which consisted
of a close network of fine, strong threads of the *ro'a* bark (a kind of flax), and a
background of choice *ora* (banyan cloth), closely perforated. In each little
hole was set the stem of an *'ura* feather, which was caught in a lock stitch on the
opposite side with a long polished needle of human bone, and set closely
against the next one to imitate bird's plumage. Artistic patterns, mostly in
squares, were thus formed by turning the feathers in different directions,
answering nearest to hieroglyphics of anything in the handiwork of these
islands. For they symbolize to the national chronicler the name, the character,
and the acts of every monarch that reigned and the annals of the land which
were faithfully recorded in chants and songs of those times. The sacred needle
was never taken out of the work, which was intended to continue forever, a
new lappet being added for each successive reign.[2]

The *maro 'ura* was only worn upon ceremonial occasions of the
highest importance, and at all other times was kept, carefully
wrapped in *tapa*, in the *fare-ia-manaha*. The preparation of the
maro 'ura for the inauguration ceremony was marked by three
successive human sacrifices designed to sanctify the perforation
of the cloth, the first insertion of the needle and the completion
of the work.

As a preliminary to the inauguration itself a *pa'i-atua* ceremony was held, and was marked by prayers for the high chief
elect; and similar prayers were offered up by the priests at the
marae throughout the whole of the night preceding the day of
inauguration. On the day itself the *ari'i* was led in procession
to the sea, where he was immersed, to the accompaniment of an
invocation glorifying him and his *'ura* feather girdle. It was
said that while the *ari'i* was in the water he was approached by
two sharks who caressingly rubbed their bodies against his if he
were the legitimate heir, though they kept out of his way if he
were a usurper. It is not surprising to read that certain *ari'i*
told the early missionaries that they had actually experienced
this contact.

The prospective ruler was then seated by the seashore where
the high priest invested him in turn with the insignia of his

---

[1] See above, p. 181. [2] Henry, *A.T.* p. 189.

rank: a waist girdle, a red 'ura feather head-dress, a long *toa* spear, a *miro* walking stick, and finally the *maro 'ura*; he was publicly acclaimed as *ari'i*, the gods being invoked to aid him in wisely governing his people. After this he was taken and seated upon the *pu-maro-'ura*, the chief's throne within the *marae*; here the eye of a human sacrifice was offered to him, and he made a show of eating it. The object of this rite, according to Henry, was to give keen perception and far-sightedness to the recipient. The *ari'i* then received more loyal greetings from his subjects, and much feasting and revelry followed.

The daily life of a chief was surrounded by numerous restrictions designed to preserve his sanctity and to guard him from contamination by persons of inferior rank. So strong were these prohibitions that death was often the penalty for an infringement of them.[1]

On the eve of the marriage of a person of high rank the bride was escorted to the home of the bridegroom, where presents were ceremonially exchanged between the relatives of the couple. After this they repaired to the family *marae* of the bridegroom, where the ancestral skulls were displayed in honour of the occasion. In the presence of their relatives the young couple vowed not to desert each other, and a priest offered up prayers for the blessing of the gods upon their union. After this their respective parents brought forward a white sheet, upon which the couple sat, holding each other's hands, while their relatives punctured their skins with instruments of sharks' teeth. They were then covered over for a while with another white sheet, stained with the blood of their relatives. After this the whole party repaired to the home of the bride, where a similar exchange of presents took place, followed by a repetition of the *marae* ceremony.

This elaborate ceremonial was an essential feature of the marriage of people of rank, for though prolonged cohabitation and the birth of children sufficed to render a union legitimate in the case of the common people, we are told that "when a child of the royal family formed a misalliance which the parents did not wish to equalize, they refused to solemnize the marriage rites on their side, which lowered the erring one to the level of the inferior party, at whose home alone the marriage was performed".[2]

---

[1] For a discussion of the personal sanctity of chiefs, see *Systems*, vol. III, pp. 77 *sqq.*   [2] Henry, *A.T.* p. 284.

The sickness of an important chief was the occasion for elaborate ritual at the *marae*, where a number of able-bodied men presented themselves with ropes around their necks in supplication to the gods, to whom rich gifts were also offered. Finally, at death the ritual was much more elaborate than in the case of people of inferior rank—a general restriction was imposed on land and sea, dirges were composed in honour of the deceased, while frantic mourning was indulged in by the populace at large. In the case of an *ari'i-maro-'ura* or his *matahiapo*, a party of young men, led by a priest and fantastically garbed, would run amok, wounding or killing anyone who came in their way. This reign of terror sometimes lasted for several weeks, until it was brought to a close by a hand-to-hand fight with the inhabitants of neighbouring districts. Then the priest would shed his fantastic costume, indicating that tranquillity was once more restored.[1] The bodies of wealthy men of high rank were embalmed, and lay in state at the *marae* for as long as a year, where they were tended by special officials. Food, drink and other offerings were presented to the embalmed corpse, which was sometimes taken for a ceremonial tour of the countryside. When the corpse had finally decayed, it was hidden away, the skull being preserved as a relic at the *marae*.[2]

THE GODS AT WAR

The institution of warfare was well developed in the Society Islands, and conquest was a means whereby an ambitious chief might extend his authority and prestige. The "causes of war"[3] were breaches of treaties, the murder of a visitor from another district, insults offered by one chief to another, and the desire for conquest. In addition to internecine strife arising from such causes as these, there were rebellions of discontented subjects against chiefs who were mean or despotic, or who ill-treated the children of their servants. Battles were fought on land or at sea, and in both cases the whole activity was associated with religious ritual from start to finish.

When trouble was brewing the priests consulted auguries and observed omens, as they did throughout the whole proceedings. Unfortunately the existing material fails to give any adequate

[1] Henry, *A.T.* p. 294.   [2] Handy, *H.C.S.I.* pp. 30 *sq.*
[3] This phrase is placed in inverted commas because of the ambiguity of the term—it is necessary to distinguish the reasons for fighting given by the combatants from the real sociological forces and psychological motives which led to hostilities.

account of the working of divination in actual practice, or of the extent to which it really did influence important decisions. Thus Henry states that "if in starting out to seek omens, the priests met with derision from a thoughtless group, it was regarded as a sign that defeat awaited the warriors, *and that sufficed to cause abandonment of the project*".[1] But it may be doubted whether irresponsible derision of this kind would really cause the abandonment of a promising campaign, unless there was good reason to regard it as symptomatic of hostile public opinion. Again, we are not told to what extent omens, auguries and oracular utterances were adjusted to harmonize with the particular inclinations of priests, chiefs, or the populace at large.[2] It is probable that the influence of omens and auguries has been greatly exaggerated in comparison with such forces as hatreds, jealousies, fears and above all the purely rational assessment of the chances of success. It is, however, certain that the observation of omens and auguries, as well as prayers for divine guidance and support, were always associated with warfare.

When a war was contemplated the chief took council with his subordinates and with the priests, the deliberations being conducted in public, and though the common people were not allowed to take an active part in the proceedings, it is probable that their feelings played a considerable part in influencing the course adopted by those in authority. The deliberations lasted for many hours and the final decision rested with the high chief.

About three days before the commencement of hostilities, each side carried out ceremonies, accompanied by human sacrifices, at their respective *marae*. The first of these was called *matea* (awakening), and was designed to awaken the tutelar deity to give support in the forthcoming enterprise. His image was brought out by the *tiri* and exposed side by side with the high chief's *maro 'ura*, though it was not unwrapped as in the *pa'i-atua* ceremony. At this ceremony, homage was paid to the god and to the high chief. A human sacrifice was made, the eye being presented to the *ari'i* as described above, and food was offered to the god who was invoked by the high priest. At the conclusion elaborate presents were made to the priests in

---

[1] Henry, *A.T.* p. 297 (italics ours).
[2] Cf. the statement of Dr Buck concerning the inspiration of priests in Mangaia (above, p. 113) and Dr Hogbin's description of the determination of mediumistic utterances by public opinion in Ontong Java (*L.O.P.* p. 148). It seems highly probable that similar factors influenced the Society Island priests (unconsciously, no doubt) in their observation of omens.

appreciation of their work, and in anticipation of further efforts in importuning the gods.

The next day a ceremony called *pure ari'i* (prayer for the *ari'i*) was carried out. More food was offered to the gods, and another human sacrifice made, prayers being said for the high chief and for the success of the warriors. On the third and last day a similar ceremony took place, designed to sever any alliance between the two contending parties, and after this a substantial meal was eaten, the object of which was to stay the appetite for two or three days. During the hostilities themselves the image of the god was safely hidden away to prevent its discovery by the enemy in case of defeat. No religious ceremonies were performed at home during war time, lest the gods should thereby be induced to turn back and desert the army, which was believed to be under their protection.

When an invasion was expected, the priests went out to the frontiers and there prayed, or buried *'ura* amulets designed to weaken the power of the enemy. For this reason an invading army was always on the look out for disturbed ground, where such hostile charms might be buried. A vast army of gods, and particularly Oro, god of war, were supposed to accompany and to aid the warriors in war time, and women slain in battle were offered to Toi-mata, the daughter of Oro.[1]

Before opening hostilities it was customary for the opposing armies to seat themselves on the ground facing one another and to fan up hatred by means of hostile speeches, the exchange of which between two distinguished warriors of the opposing camps was a preliminary to a duel between them. The number of these individual duels increased until both armies were wholly involved, each side being exhorted by special orators called *rauti*, who sang chants glorifying war and the conquests to be attained by it.

When the first warrior fell an endeavour was made by the enemy to secure his body, which was trussed up with sinnet and dedicated to the gods. Such a fate was not only a disgrace to the warrior and to the members of his family, but also a catastrophe to his comrades, particularly if he were a man of rank. Commoners killed in battle were sometimes beaten flat with the stem of a coconut branch, a hole being made through the body.

---

[1] These offerings, and also women slain by hostile sorcery who were offered to the same goddess, were the single exception to the rule that only male sacrifices, whether human or otherwise, were acceptable to the divine powers. (Henry, *A.T.* p. 198.)

Through this hole the victorious warrior inserted his head and, wearing the dead body as a poncho, he flaunted it before the enemy. As more and more casualties occurred, the bodies of the slain were placed in two heaps and the victors subsequently laid claim to those of the vanquished.

When one side or the other felt that it was losing, the priests appealed to the gods, who were believed to be deserting them in favour of the enemy. Sometimes an attempt to bribe the gods of the other side was made in this way, and it was believed that the victorious side was the one which had offered most to the gods. Normally no quarter was given, and the vanquished party was wholly exterminated, except for men of the highest rank and a few prisoners of war, as well as the unfit and those of the wounded who had succeeded in escaping to the *fare hua*, or houses of the helpless, which had been specially built in secluded places. The old, the women and the children who had taken refuge in the *fare hua* were under the protection of Perete'i, the divine cricket, which was the shadow of Tu. For this reason the enemy never dared to molest them during the action, though after the battle this sanctity no longer existed, and they were slaughtered with great indignity. The jaw-bones of old men were torn out by the victors for the adornment of their *marae* as were the heads of men of high rank slain in battle, while skulls were sometimes taken to be used as drinking cups at triumphal war feasts.

The victors were called '*upo'o-tu* (heads erect), an expression which in its modern form (*opo'o-ti'a*) is still used in a moral sense, as meaning "justification". They laid waste the lands of the vanquished, desecrated their *marae*, killed their priests and '*opu-nui*, and stripped their gods of their feathers and other treasures. Their own dead they took home for burial, and those of the enemy they used for various ceremonial purposes, for the decoration of *marae*, as rollers for sacred canoes, and to provide the walls of heads which sometimes marked boundaries. After a victory ceremonies were performed at the *marae* to give thanks for success and to pray for permanent peace. Feasts were held, accompanied by the usual presentations of food to the gods, to the priests, and to the chief. After land had been laid waste and its *marae* desecrated it was necessary to resanctify it, which was done with elaborate religious ceremonial.

THE GODS AT PLAY

An important institution in Society Island culture was the *arioi*, an association of men and women, whose principal function was to provide entertainment. Highly organized and numerically very strong in ancient times, it decayed rapidly under the influence of the missionaries, who were from the first violently antagonistic towards the whole institution, mainly because of the sexual practices and the rule of infanticide associated with it.

The *arioi* society was organized into a hierarchy composed of eight orders, marked off from each other by the different tattoo marks and decorations of their members.[1] Initiates were first introduced into the lowest order with elaborate ceremony and passed successively through the various grades, though few reached the highest rank of all, a privilege which could only be bestowed by the king. Each transition from one grade to another was ceremonially celebrated.

Statements as to the qualifications for membership are conflicting, some observers stating that membership was restricted to people of high rank[2] and others that members of the lower classes might be admitted.[3] Probably the reconciliation of these two opinions is to be found in the statement of Moerenhout that membership of the *arioi* was an expensive matter, which would mean that, though there might not be any rigid ban upon membership for people of the lower orders, it would *de facto* be restricted to men of wealth and rank. But the essential qualifications for membership were that the initiates should be childless, and that they should be under the inspiration of the gods.[4]

Membership of the *arioi*, and particularly of its upper grades, was a high honour, and a perfect knowledge of its poems and songs made its members sacred and favourites of the gods.[5] Even after death an *arioi* could expect pleasures for which few others could hope.[6]

The principal function of the *arioi* was to provide public entertainment. They wandered about the islands presenting performances for the delectation of the populace at large, being supported at the public expense. Their entertainments consisted of songs, speeches, recitations, dramatic presentations, dancing and sports. In these they were allowed to ridicule chiefs and

[1] Henry, *A.T.* p. 234.
[2] Forster, *Voy.* vol. II, p. 128; Bligh, p. 79; Wilson, p. 172.
[3] Ellis, vol. I, p. 239; Moerenhout, vol. I, p. 491.
[4] Henry, *A.T.* p. 235; cf. Moerenhout, vol. I, p. 492; Ellis, *loc. cit.*
[5] Moerenhout, vol. I, p. 501.   [6] *Ibid.* vol. II, p. 135.

other people of high rank with impunity. Many of their performances were, from European standards, extremely obscene,
and free sexual practices were associated with their activities.

An interesting feature of the *arioi* society was its rule of infanticide. The killing of newly born children was practised
fairly generally throughout the Society Islands, but in the case
of members of the *arioi* it was obligatory, and failure to observe
the rule meant ignominious expulsion.[1]

The *arioi* was such an unusual and highly specialized institution that the interpretation of its functions is not easy.
Organized in the first place to provide public entertainment, it
seems to have been a powerful integrative force in the community. Each important district had its *arioi* house and its
arioi "comedian", and these served for the entertainment of
visitors. Their roving habits together with the freemasonry
which existed among them did much to cement bonds between
distant districts, and to promote goodwill generally, while their
right to lampoon the chiefs allowed of criticism which would
otherwise have been impossible. Moreover, the feasting, sexual
gratification and inversion of ordinary modes of life associated
with their practices probably provided a relief from the hum-
drum round of orderly existence.[2]

It seems probable that the explanation of their rule of

[1] Henry, *A.T.* p. 235; Cook, vol. I, p. 194; Ellis, vol. I, p. 239; Corney,
Tahiti, vol. II, pp. 377 *sq.*, 472; Turnbull, p. 364. There were apparently exceptions to this rule, for Henry states that "children born in the highest ranks were
regarded as descendants of the gods, and were spared to inherit their parents'
titles." (*Loc. cit.*) Moerenhout says that an *arioi* chief was allowed to preserve his
first-born son, though all his other children were killed, while the head *arioi* only
killed their first-born sons, allowing their daughters and other sons to survive.
(Moerenhout, vol. I, pp. 495 *sq.*) As regards chiefs, then, it would appear that
the rule might be waived when the matter of succession was at stake, though
Pomare I killed his first-born child, and subsequently left the *arioi* society before
the birth of his second. (Bligh, p. 78; Wilson, p. xxii; cf. p. 152.) As regards the
inversion of this rule in the case of the head *arioi*, who were compelled to kill
only their first-born sons, the relaxation may perhaps be regarded as a concession
to their importance, though they were obliged ritually to recognize the *arioi* rule
of infanticide by the killing of the most valued offspring of all, the first-born son.

[2] The wide sociological question of the function of orgies, *saturnalia*, and
periodic relaxations of customary rules generally, cannot be discussed here. One
obvious feature is the provision of an outlet for the disruptive tendencies of sex
and self-assertion, which are normally kept in check by moral rules and the norms
governing social status and good behaviour. The satisfaction of hunger in the
feast provides an incentive towards economic effort and the thrifty preservation of
its fruits. But perhaps there is a more recondite reason for these relaxations and
inversions of customary behaviour. It is possible that by providing clear-cut and
socially defined occasions of non-conformity they actually give clearer definition
to social obligations, though the exact mechanism by which this is accomplished
presents a psychological problem of considerable difficulty.

infanticide is to be found along this line, the responsibilities of parenthood being inconsistent with a life concentrated upon enjoyment, relaxation, and self-indulgence, which would provide the populace at large with entertainment as well as a sort of vicarious satisfaction for their anti-social tendencies.

In spite of its frivolous character, the *arioi* society had an important magico-religious aspect. Its patron deity was Oro, god of war. But when associated with the society he was referred to as Oro-i-te-tea-moe (Oro-of-the-spear-laid-down), and was represented by an emblem formed by three spears so placed as to form a triangle. The origin of the *arioi* is attributed to Oro in the following legend given by Henry:[1]

Oro lived with his wife and their children, three daughters and one son, in heaven, but one day he pushed his wife down to the earth, where she turned into a great heap of sand. After this he became lonely, and his two sisters volunteered to go down to earth to get for him a new wife. After visiting several islands, where they found all the girls too coarse and common, they finally went to Porapora, where they heard of a maiden of high rank and surpassing beauty, named Vai-rau-mati. As she was in every way suitable the marriage was arranged, but when Oro came down to earth to claim her, he found that he had no worldly goods to offer to her family as presents. He consulted his sisters, and procured two heavenly youths, whom he changed into two fine pigs, a boar and a sow, which he presented to his bride's family. The two hogs subsequently became patron spirits of the *arioi*.

The following night the sow produced a litter of five little male pigs which were also associated with the legendary origin of the society, which is described as follows:

A high chief called Tamatoa who was an incarnation of Oro was the first *arioi* on earth and organized the society near Opoa, in Ra'iatea. To him Oro gave the first *arioi* pig, which was marked by a ring of sacred sinnet through its nose, and thereafter members of the society regularly dedicated pigs to Oro. The relation between myth and ritual is here apparent. The *arioi* performed religious ceremonies invoking Oro, and Roma-tane, the god of paradise, who was also specially associated with the society. These ceremonies were carried out on the admission of a new member, on setting out on an expedition, upon arrival, and upon returning home again.

[1] *A.T.* pp. 231 *sqq.*

In addition to this the *arioi* appear to have served specific religious functions in perpetuating the legends of the cosmogony and of the gods, which they translated into songs and dramatic scenes;[1] and they seem on occasion to have invoked the gods to obtain fertility in times of dearth.[2] Their members, as we have seen, were specially favoured by the gods, and entered the society under their inspiration. Altogether, it cannot be doubted that, as well as its functions as an institution for public recreation, the *arioi* society possessed a profound religious significance.

RELIGION AND INDIVIDUAL LIFE

We may conclude our treatment of the magico-religious aspect of Society Island culture by an account of the part played by magic and religion in the life of the individual, particularly in regard to those more intimate phases of it associated with kinship affiliations. Unfortunately the available material on this subject is scanty, since most writers have concentrated on the spectacular aspect of religion and magic, to the exclusion of their more intimate and personal phases. In particular the part played by religion in the conditioning of the individual, and the means by which religious beliefs and sentiments were inculcated into the child and maintained in the adult, have been neglected, though it is stated that a game called *fa'aoro'a marae*, or imitating *marae* ceremonies, was practised by children, who used a piece of wood to represent a human sacrifice and a rat for a sacrificial pig.[3]

In spite of the inadequacy of the data on the more personal aspects of the life of the individual, it is clear that magico-religious beliefs and practices played an important part in it, from before birth until after death. This was, as we have seen, more marked in the case of people of high rank, but it was also true of the common people.

Birth and childhood. Before the birth of a child, a house of *maire* fern, called *fare-rau-maire*, was built behind the family *marae*; this fern, which was believed to have an auspicious influence at such times, was associated with a legend of a man called Fa'ahotu, who tried to suckle his first-born. Three times he did this and each time the child perished of starvation on his flat bosom. So Tane arranged an exchange of sexes between

---

[1] Moerenhout, vol. I, pp. 499 *sq.*   [2] *Ibid.* p. 523.
[3] Henry, *A.T.* p. 279.

Fa'ahotu and the goddess Atea, so that the former became a woman and was able to produce two sons, Ro'o and Fa'aroa. Their umbilical cords became entangled and fell down to earth, that of Fa'aroa becoming the Fara (pandanus) tree, and that of Ro'o the *maire* fern hanging from it. Thereafter the *maire* fern was always used for the construction of the house in which a woman was to be delivered of a child.

The most important event in any family was the birth of the first-born, who was ceremonially washed at the family *marae* and was thus ritually accepted as heir. Similarly the circumcision of a boy, when he was aged fifteen or sixteen, was accompanied by prayers at the family *marae*, where the father and other male relatives punctured their skins with sharks' teeth, causing the blood to flow.[1]

Marriage and daily life. We have already dealt with the ceremonial associated with the marriage of people of rank, and it would appear that the union of commoners was generally accompanied by similar ritual, though on a less elaborate scale. The importance of the family *marae* has already been mentioned[2] and it should be pointed out that the priestly functions of the head of the family were correlated with his social position.[3] Concerning the actual dynamics of marriage and family relationships and the course of everyday life, the information is scanty. However, what we have said concerning the detection of theft, and the ordinary economic activity of fishing, tends to indicate that elements of the magico-religious system played an important part in the personal lives of individuals.

Recreation. We have already mentioned the religious functions of the *arioi* society, and it seems probable that less highly institutionalized forms of recreation also had a magico-religious aspect, even though this was not so striking as the beliefs and ritual connected with the *arioi*. Dr Raymond Firth has shown the social significance of the game of darts in Tikopia,[4] and it would seem that archery played a similar part in the lives of people of high rank in the Society Islands. Special platforms were built for archery contests, and the performers offered up prayers and carried out ceremonies at the *marae* before the contest. They wore a special dress, which at other times was kept

[1] Henry, *A.T.* p. 188.
[2] See above, pp. 221, 253; cf. also *Systems*, vol. II, pp. 70 *sqq.*
[3] *Systems*, vol. III, pp. 43–4.
[4] Firth, "A Dart Match in Tikopia", *Oceania*, vol. I, pp. 64–96.

in the grounds of the *marae* of Paruatetava'e, god of archery.[1] It is probable that other recreations[2] contained magico-religious elements, and even in such a trivial amusement as the making of cats' cradles we find that mythological allusions frequently occurred in the naming of the figures,[3] for example *te fare no Oro*, the house of the god Oro. Obviously such instances cannot be taken as an indication of any deep spiritual significance attaching to trivial activities but they do indicate a general religious background in every phase of the individual's life.

Sickness and death.[4] When a person fell ill, offerings of food and *'ura* feathers were taken to the family *marae*. The relatives called in a doctor, called *tahu'a-ra'au*. Such doctors, who were of either sex, had special *marae* of their own, called *marae-tahu'a-ra'au*, dedicated to the healing deities. Near such a *marae* the doctor prepared his medicines, the secret of which he kept to himself, for it was believed that they would lose their healing power if this were not done. The sick were treated by massage, by the application of ointments, and by invocations to the gods. If these measures proved unsuccessful the relatives of the sick person went to the local *marae*, where a priest presented a pig and other offerings to the tutelar deity whom he invoked to effect a cure. The relatives appeared at the *marae* with cords around their necks, indicating that they were ready to atone for any offence which the patient might have done to the gods. This was all that could be done and the sick person either recovered or died. In the case of the illness of a person of high rank, the *marae* ceremonies were very elaborate, many rich offerings being presented to the gods. Upon recovery from an illness, the patient presented thank-offerings to the gods at the *marae*.

When a fatal illness was drawing to its termination, a priest attached *'ura* feather amulets to the little fingers of the patient in order to ward off evil spirits. It was believed that a person always died at the same hour of the day or night as he was born. The priest placed a cluster of *maire* ferns over the patient's head, from which it was believed that the soul left the body. This was called *fare maire*, the same term as that used for

---

[1] Henry, *A.T.* p. 276.
[2] A list of Society Island games is given by Henry, *A.T.* pp. 275–80.
[3] Handy, *S.F.M.S.I.* p. 7.
[4] The following account of customs connected with illness and death is based on the material provided by Henry (*A.T.* pp. 289–95). Reference should also be made to the discussion of mortuary customs given in *Beliefs*, vol. I, pp. 251–65.

the houses built behind *marae* for the delivery of pregnant women.

Immediately after death the priest invoked the spirit of the dead person to return to the body, and when no sign of life appeared, they cried out: *Ua unuhi te varua e te atua* (The spirit is drawn out by the gods). A great outburst of grief followed from the relatives, who bathed, oiled and dressed the corpse, while the priests observed omens from which they might ascertain the cause of death, whether it was from sorcery, from an offence to the gods, or simply in the natural course of events.

Beside the corpse was placed a magic branch of ti, and under its arms were placed breadfruit flower spikes and the tips of the stems of banana leaves, each representing a relative, with the following invocation: "Here is thy father; here is thy mother; here is thy wife (or husband); here is thy son; here is thy daughter; here are thy relatives (and so on). Turn thy face to Hades; look not back to this world. Let sickness end with thee."[1] The corpse was usually kept in the house for three or four days, during which time the relatives wept over it and mutilated themselves. They received visits from neighbours and friends, who brought presents and offered condolences. Dirges were intoned, and eloquent speeches made on such occasions. All this ceremonial was very much more elaborate in the case of people of high rank.

After this period was over, the corpse, saturated in oil to prevent its decomposition, was placed in a small temporary house built near the family *marae*, where it was guarded by a priest. This lasted until the grief of the mourners was *maha* (spent), when the body was wrapped in sweet-scented *tapa* and placed in a coffin hewn from the trunk of a tree. In this it was placed in a vault in the family *marae* whence it was subsequently removed to a cave in the mountains. The skull was sometimes kept as a family heirloom, while the finger nails were plucked out and worn threaded together in the hair of young girls as charms.

The beliefs of the Society Islanders concerning the soul after death have been discussed elsewhere[2] but we may add to this treatment a brief summary of the further material provided by Henry.[3] In considering all such accounts, it should be borne in mind that the beliefs as they have been recorded may have been

---

[1] Henry, *A.T.* pp. 291–2. [2] *Beliefs*, vol. I, pp. 358–99.
[3] Henry, *A.T.* pp. 200–2.

influenced by the teachings of the early missionaries, and it is possible that they are in some measure a compromise between the native ideology of the hereafter and that of the Christian religion. Moreover, the problem is still further complicated by the possible confusion arising from equating terms such as "soul" and "spirit" to native animistic concepts.[1]

The destiny of the soul after death was supposed to depend upon the manner in which the individual in question had died. The spirits of men killed in battle were believed to haunt the battlefield upon which they had died, and the souls of people who had been lost at sea were supposed to enter into sharks. Those who had committed suicide from disappointment in love or jealousy were believed to haunt the person on whose account they had died, and the spirits of children killed at birth became home guardians of their parents. The spirits of babies born prematurely went down to the lower regions, where they awaited an opportunity to slip into another body.

But in the case of ordinary deaths from natural causes the beliefs were standardized. The soul remained in the body until three days after death when, warding off evil spirits with its 'ura feather amulets, it went to a mountain in north-western Tahiti. At this point there were two stones, one of life and the other of death. If the spirit alighted on the former it might return by powerful attraction to the body, but if on the latter it went to Mo'orea, and thence to Mount Temehani in Ra'iatea where two paths branched off.[2] One of these (the one to the right) led to the upper regions (ao) and the other to the lower (po). At the point of deviation stood Tu-ta-horoa, who might under certain circumstances return the soul to life. More frequently, however, he sent it along one of the two paths. If it went to the right the spirit met Roma-tane, to whom it presented its 'ura feather amulets as peace-offerings, and was accepted into Rohutu-noanoa (fragrant Rohutu), the Tahitian paradise. But if it was directed to the left-hand path, it ultimately made its way to the crater of Temehani, and into the presence of Ta'aroa-nui-tuhi-mate (Great-Ta'aroa-whose-curse-was-death). Here the rank of mortals was annihilated and all were treated in the same way, chiefs and commoners alike acting as menial servants to the gods

---

[1] Cf. *Beliefs*, vol. I, p. 197.
[2] Professor Malinowski has shown that in the Trobriand Islands the spirits of the dead of the different islands follow different courses after death, and it is possible that a similar situation existed in the Society Islands. Henry's account seems to refer to the souls of Tahitian individuals only.

in this region of utter darkness, and sometimes the cooks of Ta'aroa would scrape the spirits into pulp as sweetening for his *pota* (taro-leaf spinach).

After the spirit had lived thus for a year, Ta'aroa would take pity upon it and ask what it desired. When it said that it wished to return to its relatives, Ta'aroa would grant leave to go for a visit. After this stage spirits became inferior gods, called *'oromatua*, which were of three classes. Some entered into their own skulls as family spirits, and exercised a benevolent influence over the lives of their relatives. Others became wandering spirits, who occasionally came to advise or warn their kin. The last class became evil spirits who strangled and devoured people, and who were invoked by sorcerers to enter their *ti'i*. People in trances were believed to be dead, and some of them even gave accounts of the regions of *po* which they claimed to have visited.

The above ideology of the hereafter was correlated with the social obligations of the bereaved, who, during the year that the soul of the dead person was believed to be with Ta'aroa, prepared much food, upon which they feasted at the conclusion of the year, invoking the spirit to return home, a custom which was supposed to secure its goodwill.

CHAPTER XI

THE SANCTITY OF CHIEFTAINSHIP

IN the preceding chapters we have presented a brief account of Society Island religion, followed by a description of the manner in which magico-religious beliefs and practices influenced other aspects of native life. Among other things we discussed the religious aspect of chieftainship, a subject which may now be considered in some detail, with special reference to the political organization of Tonga. Before doing this we must examine briefly the kinship and family organization which Gifford describes as "the key to Tongan society".[1]

The domestic unit in Tonga consisted primarily of a man and his wife, together with their own and adopted children. But this household was often augmented by polygyny, and by resident consanguine and affinal relatives; and also, in the case of chiefs, by a number of kinsmen of inferior rank, who acted as servants and attendants. Within the kinship organization rank was determined by two factors, age and sex, the latter being the more important. A woman was always superior in rank to her brother, and the same relative status obtained between their respective children. After sex, age was the important determinant of status.

The father was the head of the household, and towards him and his brothers the children preserved an attitude of respect. But they showed an even greater respect towards his sister, an attitude which was extended to her husband. This whole system depended, of course, upon the superiority in rank of the father's sister over her brother.

The attitude of restraint, respect and obedience towards the father and the father's sister contrasts in a most marked way with the attitude adopted towards the father's father and mother's father, towards whom a considerable amount of liberty was allowed—a youth might wear his grandfather's clothes or eat his food. But this free attitude found its greatest development in the relationship towards the mother's brother; this was

---

[1] For the full account of Tongan kinship, upon which the following is based, see Gifford, *Tonga*, pp. 15–29.

described by saying that the sister's son was *fahu*[1] to his mother's brother. The *fahu* relationship was expressed concretely in a freedom of restraint in behaviour towards the mother's brother, together with a number of claims to his property, and to that of his children. This arrangement was non-reciprocal, for the mother's brother had no corresponding claims upon the property of his *fahu*, his only compensation being his corresponding *fahu* rights towards his own mother's brother. Though the sister's child was the "great *fahu*", the grandchildren of a man were also *fahu* to him in a lesser degree, as were his classificatory sister's children.[2]

THE TONGAN ARISTOCRACY

This very brief reference to kinship relations in Tonga is necessary as a prelude to the discussion of chieftainship. The highest Tongan chiefs were the heads of patrilineal lineages called *haa*; Gifford records thirteen of these, but in ancient times it would appear that there were many more. The highest lineage of all was that of the Tui Tonga, which was not called *haa*, but *sinae*, a special term designed to emphasize the Tui Tonga's transcendent rank. In order to clarify the highest ranks of Tongan aristocracy, it will be well to list briefly its more important titles.

(1) *The Tui Tonga.* The higher ranks in Tongan society all centred around the "sacred king", the Tui Tonga. The most striking thing about the Tui Tonga was his extreme sanctity on the one hand and his lack of secular power on the other. The first Tui Tonga was of divine descent, being sprung from Tangaloa, and the sanctity of the office was expressed in the number of taboos and ceremonial observances surrounding it.[3]

(2) *The hau.* While sanctity resided in the Tui Tonga, administrative power was exercised by the *hau*, or secular ruler.

[1] This term has been translated "above the law". The relationship to the mother's brother which it embodies has been given a specific interpretation by Professor Radcliffe-Brown. (See A. R. Radcliffe-Brown, "The mother's brother in South Africa", *South African Journal of Science*, vol. XXI, pp. 542–55, also Gifford, *Tonga*, p. 24.)

[2] The *fahu* relationship was not a mere kinship formality; apart from socially defined ceremonial rights, the *fahu* did in fact very often exercise his rights over the property of his mother's brother, though too great an abuse of the privilege seems to have been prevented by the force of public opinion (Gifford, *Tonga*, p. 24). Perhaps the best sidelight on the *fahu* relationship in actual life is provided by the remark of a Tongan to Gifford that he was lucky in having no closely related *fahu* as he himself had no sister (*ibid.* p. 23).

[3] See *Systems*, vol. III, chap. XXXI.

According to tradition, the two functions were once merged in the Tui Tonga, until the twenty-third of the line was assassinated; his son Kauulufonua I pursued his father's murderers throughout the neighbouring islands, finally exacting vengeance upon them at Uvea.[1] After this, through fear of assassination of himself and his descendants, Kauulufonua delegated his administrative power to his younger brother, who was given the title of Tui Haa Takalaua, and who thus became the eponymous ancestor of the lineage called Haa Takalaua. The Tui Tonga still retained his exalted status, his claims to tribute and to women of high rank in marriage, while the arduous duties of administration were taken over by the Tui Haa Takalaua. This state of affairs persisted for some time, until the sixth Tui Haa Takalaua appointed his son Ngata as the first Tui Kanokupolu. Thereafter the Tui Kanokupolu tended to assume the office of *hau*, and though the line of the Tui Haa Takalaua seems still to have exercised a considerable amount of power, this passed in time mainly into the hands of the Tui Kanokupolu.

A brief reference to Gifford's suggested chronology of this traditional series of events will perhaps help to clarify the matter. The first Tui Tonga Ahoeitu, the reputed son of Tangaloa, ruled about 950, and his successors exercised both spiritual and temporal power until about 1470, when the latter was ceded by the twenty-fourth Tui Tonga to his brother, who thus became the first Tui Haa Takalaua. This title also waned after the appointment, *circa* 1610, of the first Tui Kanokupolu, who was the son of the sixth Tui Haa Takalaua. As to the ultimate fate of these titles, that of the Tui Tonga persisted until 1865, when with the death of the thirty-ninth Tui Tonga, the title was absorbed into that of the Tui Kanokupolu by the contemporary holder of the latter, George I Tupou. The title of Tui Haa Takalaua became extinct with the death of its fifteenth holder in 1799. The title of Tui Kanokupolu is the only one which survived into the present century, and was assumed by Queen Charlotte in 1918.[2]

(3) *The great royal wife of the Tui Tonga.* The Tui Tonga had a number of wives, but there was always one, referred to as *moheofo*, who was the mother of the succeeding Tui Tonga. The *moheofo* was always a woman of high rank. Several of the earlier

---

[1] There are several variants of this legend, but they are not relevant to the present discussion.
[2] Gifford, *Tonga*, pp. 48 *sqq.*

moheofo came from other islands, two of them being Samoans. But in later times there emerges what appears to be a stylization of the relationship. Of the sixteen *moheofo* listed by Gifford[1] the seventh, eighth and ninth were daughters of the Tui Haa Takalaua, the first of these marriages taking place a short time after the institution of the first Tui Haa Takalaua. Again the inauguration of the office of Tui Kanokupolu was followed by a series of marriages in which five *moheofo* were daughters of the Tui Kanokupolu, and one his son's daughter. These cases support the statements of several observers[2] that marriage between the Tui Tonga and the daughter of the Tui Kanokupolu was obligatory. The record of actual instances is of course incomplete, there being only sixteen *moheofo* recorded as against thirty-nine Tui Tonga, but it does suffice to show a tendency for the Tui Tonga to have as his *moheofo* the daughter, first of the Tui Haa Takalaua and later of the Tui Kanokupolu.[3]

(4) *The Tui Tonga Fefine.* The female Tui Tonga (Tui Tonga Fefine) was the oldest living sister of the Tui Tonga. As such, she was senior to the Tui Tonga and to his son, which will be clear from what we have said above concerning the brother to sister and brother's son to father's sister relationships.

(5) *The Tamaha.* The daughter[4] of the Tui Tonga Fefine was the Tamaha, and was the person of highest rank in all Tonga. As the great *fahu* of the Tui Tonga, she commanded his respect, which was expressed in acts of abject obeisance and in the humble presentation of offerings.

RANK AND KINSHIP

In the above brief account of the high titles of Tongan society, we can see the importance of kinship in political organization. In the first place, the high chiefly lineages of the Tui Haa Takalaua and the Tui Kanokupolu derived their sanctity from the lineage of the Tui Tonga, and ultimately from Tangaloa. Sanctity was a relative matter, and the other high lineages derived it from the fact that they were collateral branches of the dynasty of the Tui Tonga. But apart from renowned and

---

[1] Gifford, *Tonga*, p. 60.   [2] See *Systems*, vol. II, p. 185.

[3] The exact relationship between these two offices is not clear. Probably the *hau* might originally be held by either the Tui Haa Takalaua or the Tui Kanokupolu, with an increasing tendency towards the ascendancy of the latter, as suggested by Gifford.

[4] The title of Tamaha might be held by a sister's son of the Tui Tonga (cf. Gifford, *Tonga*, p. 81), but it belonged primarily to his sister's daughter, in accordance with the seniority of sisters over their brothers.

divine descent, the system just described was reinforced by affinal relationships which at the same time organized political structure on the basis of kinship, and also set a pattern of kinship relationships which ran right through Tongan society from the highest to the lowest.

The ideal scheme of affinal relationships centring around the Tui Tonga is represented by Professor Radcliffe-Brown[1] as follows:

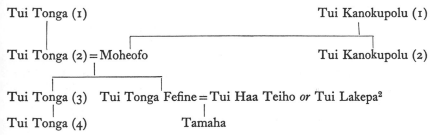

Tui Tonga (1)   Tui Kanokupolu (1)

Tui Tonga (2) = Moheofo   Tui Kanokupolu (2)

Tui Tonga (3)   Tui Tonga Fefine = Tui Haa Teiho *or* Tui Lakepa[2]

Tui Tonga (4)   Tamaha

The most important feature of this table is the marriage of the Tui Tonga to the daughter of the Tui Kanokupolu. Radcliffe-Brown states that "when the rank of Tui Kanokupolu was first established the Tui Tonga laid it down that it was the duty of the Tui Kanokupolu to give his daughter to the Tui Tonga as his wife";[3] and certainly, from the time of the thirty-fourth Tui Tonga and the fourth Tui Kanokupolu onwards, this seems to have been the general practice.[4]

[1] Unpublished notes by A. R. Radcliffe-Brown communicated to R. W. Williamson.

[2] Information provided by Gifford suggests a possible expansion of this table. According to him the Tui Tonga Fefine generally married either the Tui Haa Teiho or the Tui Lakepa, as shown above, and "it is reported that only these chiefs might beget the Tamaha" (Gifford, *Tonga*, p. 81). But it should be noted that both of these chiefs belonged to the Haa Fale Fisi, the lineage of the House of Fiji (*ibid.* p. 34). Their lineages were apparently collateral branches of the Haa Fale Fisi, both of which traced their origin back to the first Tui Lakepa, a Fijian who married the Tui Tonga Fefine Sinaitakala I, sister of the thirtieth Tui Tonga, *circa* 1643. This suggests a relationship parallel with that which Professor Radcliffe-Brown describes between the Tui Tonga and the Tui Kanokupolu. Just as the lineage of the Tui Kanokupolu provided wives for the Tui Tonga, so did the lineage of the Tui Tonga provide wives for one or other of the branches of the Haa Fale Fisi. The evidence is of course inconclusive, but the legendary origin of the Haa Fale Fisi is consistent with the view suggested here.

[3] Radcliffe-Brown, Unpublished notes.

[4] The three consecutive marriages at an earlier stage of the Tui Tonga to daughters of the Tui Haa Takalaua together with the statement of Shirley W. Baker that Kauulufonua I in establishing the Tui Haa Takalaua imposed the condition that "the Tui Tonga in office was always to have as his wife the daughter of the reigning prince" (Gifford, *Tonga*, p. 85) suggest that this was merely a continuation of the practice of giving the daughter of the secular ruler in marriage to the Tui Tonga, correlated with the rise of the dynasty of the Tui Kanokupolu.

In connection with this, Radcliffe-Brown notes several points for consideration. In the first place, there is the seniority of a sister over her brother, to which we have referred above. Though descent and inheritance were patrilineal, rank was determined to a greater extent by the mother than by the father, as is clearly seen in the custom of regarding the "half-chiefs" who were sons of women of chiefly rank and commoners more highly than those whose parents were male chiefs and female commoners.[1] For this reason the daughter of the Tui Kanokupolu would be of higher rank than his son, that is, the succeeding Tui Kano-kupolu.

Secondly, in Tonga the grandchildren occupy a very favoured position, a daughter's son ranking above a son's son. In olden days a number of respectful observances towards the daughter's son (who was a "lesser *fahu*") gave expression to this principle. This would mean that, in terms of the diagram, the Tui Kanokupolu (1) would occupy this position in relation to his daughter's son, the Tui Tonga (3). The Tui Tonga being generally either the sister's son or the daughter's son of the Tui Kanokupolu was thus entitled to the respect generally accorded to these relatives, and the whole system is thus seen to emphasize the seniority of the Tui Tonga lineage over that of the Tui Kanokupolu.

The significance of this thesis of Professor Radcliffe-Brown is that the adoption of a standard of kinship relationships between the highest members of the aristocracy served to define those relationships in a manner consistent with the political system, which was thus reinforced. The sanctity of the Tui Tonga, established in the first place by his divine origin and the legendary accounts of the illustrious deeds of his ancestors,[2] was still further emphasized by his kinship relationship to the secular ruler, to whom he was nominally senior and upon whom he exercised certain claims defined by the affinal relationship existing between them.

It is unfortunate that the information at our disposal does not allow us to extend this analysis farther, by defining in more concrete terms the sociological realities correlated with the structural pattern. Thus it would be interesting to know something of deviations from the normal scheme, for example in the marriage of the thirty-fifth Tui Tonga first to the son's daughter of the fourth Tui Kanokupolu, and subsequently to the daughter

---

[1] Gifford, *Tonga*, p. 123.   [2] See Gifford, *T.M.T.* pp. 25 *sqq.*

of the sixth Tui Kanokupolu, both of these women becoming in turn mothers of succeeding Tui Tonga. The definition of such formal kinship patterns should always be supplemented by a description of what happens when the human individuals concerned do not fit perfectly into the kinship chart, for example (in the case of "marriage with mother's brother's daughter"), when the mother's brother has no daughter, or when conquest in war or personal idiosyncrasies[1] lead to a distortion of the ideal structure. This argument of course in no way denies the existence of such a structure, nor its functional significance as a social ideal. It merely insists on the sociological relevance of the unusual adjustments which arise when conformity to the ideal structure is for one reason or another impossible.

Another principle involved in such explanations is that they cannot be consistently extended. The rigid and clearly defined patterns of behaviour founded upon kinship must necessarily be limited at a certain point. For example, we have referred to Gifford's statement that the attitude of respectful obedience towards the father's sister is extended also to her husband; while "a man marrying a woman has the same sort of social superiority to his wife's brothers that the woman herself has".[2] Yet (referring again to the diagram) it seems improbable that these principles would apply, for example, in the relation of the Tui Tonga (3) or the Tui Tonga (4) to the husband of the Tui Tonga Fefine, who was the chief of a comparatively unimportant lineage, unless the latter happened also to be a Tamaha.[3] The theoretical issue involved here may be formulated in terms of the general theory of kinship.

The social functions of kinship are twofold.[4] In the first place kinship defines the system of procreation within the individual

[1] A hint of a possible deviation of this kind is contained in Professor Radcliffe-Brown's notes. He states that "There was formerly a custom that on the death of the Tui Tonga the one of his wives whose son was to be the heir should strangle herself on the grave of her husband....Apparently if there was any dispute as to the right heir it would be settled by one of the wives thus strangling herself, which act would ensure the succession of her son." Now the Tui Tonga formerly had a number of wives, and it may be asked what would have happened if one of these who was not a daughter of the Tui Kanokupolu chose to sacrifice herself in this way. It may of course be conjectured that such a dispute would only arise as between wives who did occupy this position, but such speculations only emphasize the discrepancy between the multiplicity of the problems presented and the paucity of the material available for their solution.

[2] Gifford, *Tonga*, p. 17.

[3] Cf., for example, the case cited by Gifford, *ibid.* p. 26.

[4] Cf. Malinowski, "Parenthood, the Basis of Social Structure" in *The New Generation*, ed. Calverton and Schmalhausen.

family, the rights, obligations, and sentiments existing between father, mother and children. But these primary bonds are extended to remoter kin, and so serve to define the wider social relationships of individuals, both laterally and vertically, that is to say they lay down standardized patterns of behaviour towards contemporaries, as well as the rules of descent, succession and inheritance. But these secondary extensions are never carried out with complete logical consistency, varying both in kind and in degree from the primary relationships upon which they are patterned. Moreover, they often reach a point at which conflicting extensions intersect in such a way that one or other must be ignored.[1] It is for this reason that the limitations of extended kinship relationships are so significant and their precise definition such an important part of the empirical study of kinship systems in the field.

Again, an analysis such as that of Professor Radcliffe-Brown would be given greater point if we had a more precise account of the concrete relationships involved. Thus in descriptions of the *fahu* we have a number of elements, referred to in different contexts. In the first place, there is the mention of economic claims, the *fahu* being allowed to appropriate the goods of his mother's brother. Secondly, there is the seniority in rank of the sister's child over his mother's brother, expressed sometimes in formal acts of obeisance, for example, of the Tui Tonga towards the Tamaha. Thirdly, there is the element of authority, expressed in the statement that a man must accede to the wishes of his *fahu*. So far as the evidence goes, it would appear that the relative importance of these elements in the *fahu* relationship was rather different in the case of commoners on the one hand and of the aristocracy on the other. Taking them in turn, the economic element seems to have been of pre-eminent importance among commoners, for whom it was largely a mechanism for the transference of property, whereas we have little information as to the importance of the economic relationships existing between *fahu* relatives of high rank, though there are references to the existence of such relationships.[2] On general principles, we would expect them to be formalized to a very much greater extent than those of commoners.

Turning to the matter of respect and seniority, this appears to have been the essential thing in the royal *fahu*. The attitude

---

[1] Cf. R. Firth, "Marriage and the Classificatory System of Relationship", *J.R.A.I.* vol. xxxiii, pp. 235–68.   [2] Gifford, *Tonga*, pp. 25 *sq.*

towards the sister's children seems here to have been one of strictly formal respect, rather than friendly acquiescence in the *fahu*'s whims. This brings us to the third aspect, namely that of authority, where there is the most clearly defined contrast of all. Among commoners, compliance with the *fahu*'s wishes was an important element, but in the relationship of the Tui Tonga to the Tui Kanokupolu there is abundant evidence that this obligation was frequently ignored by the latter.[1] Though it is quite clear that the Tui Tonga exerted a considerable amount of influence, the power of making decisions rested ultimately with the Tui Kanokupolu, who was quite prepared to thwart the wishes of his *fahu*. All this tends to support the view that the *fahu* relationship took on a very different configuration in the case of commoners on the one hand and of the royal family on the other. Among the former the economic and pragmatic aspects are stressed; among the latter it is the formal expression of social superiority which appears to be the important element.

SANCTITY AND SECULAR RULE

This brings us back to the central theme, namely the sanctity of chieftainship. The Tongan material has been presented in some detail in order to indicate the elaborate mechanisms which were adopted in order to give expression to this principle. But it also raises a further problem in the marked differentiation between the religious and the secular elements in chieftainship, and in particular the contrast between the extreme sanctity and pre-eminent social position of the Tui Tonga on the one hand and his lack of temporal power on the other.

In discussing a question of this kind, confusion is apt to arise from failure to differentiate between the concepts involved. For example, to describe the Tui Tonga as the "sacred king" tells us very little about his actual functions. Or, again, the references to him as a "priest" are definitely misleading, since his sacerdotal duties were negligible. In Tonga such duties were discharged by a special class of priests, while the only religious function which can unequivocally be assigned to the Tui Tonga is to serve as an embodiment of personal sanctity. In order, then, to clarify the factors which determined the social personalities of the Tui Tonga, the secular ruler and the priests respectively, it would seem desirable to list these factors in some

---

[1] See *Systems*, vol. I, pp. 153 *sqq.*

sort of order, bearing in mind the fact that the categories employed might be still further subdivided for purposes of further analysis.

In defining the social personality of an individual of importance, such as a priest or a chief, it is necessary first of all to differentiate between his status and his functions. Broadly speaking the former is defined by the attitude adopted by others towards him, while the latter includes all the obligations which his office imposes upon him. Further, each of these categories may again be subdivided. *Status* includes on the one hand purely social rank as expressed in respectful behaviour and elaborate etiquette, and on the other personal sanctity, as expressed in divine descent and protective taboos, provided that the latter are backed by supernatural sanctions. Again the *functions* of such an individual may be subdivided into political and sacerdotal. Political functions are those related to the exercise of temporal power—to the administration of justice, to the control of communal affairs, and above all to the taking of decisions in matters of public policy. Sacerdotal functions, on the other hand, are concerned with effective communication with the gods, whether by making known their will or intentions, by invoking them, or by the offering of sacrifices.[1]

On the basis of this analysis, we may tabulate the Tongan information in such a way as to make clear the characteristics of the "secular" and "sacred" rulers, and also those of the priests.[2]

STATUS

Factors involved	Tui Tonga	Hau (Tui Kanokupolu or Tui Haa Takalaua)	Priests
Personal sanctity	Highest of all as lineal descendant of Tangaloa. All sanctity derived from his lineage	No special sanctity except as chief of an exalted lineage	Sacred only while inspired, i.e. as temporary representatives of the gods
Social pre-eminence	Second only to Tui Tonga Fefine and Tamaha	Very great, but owing deference to the Tui Tonga, and therefore to those of still higher rank	Priests generally belonged to lower orders of chiefs or *matabule*. They were not shown any particular respect except when inspired

---

[1] In Tonga as opposed to other parts of Polynesia, the priests apparently did not usually present sacrifices to the gods, this being done by the worshippers themselves (Gifford, *Tonga*, p. 320). But offerings to ancestors, as opposed to gods, were made through the priests (*ibid.* p. 319).

[2] The functions of Tongan priests will not be treated in detail; the information presented here is based upon the evidence presented in *Systems*, vol. II, pp. 409–14, and Gifford, *Tonga*, pp. 316–20.

FUNCTIONS

Factors involved	Tui Tonga	*Hau* (Tui Kanokupolu or Tui Haa Takalaua)	Priests
Political power	Nominally none, so far as Tonga as a whole was concerned, though he might exert personal influence	Politically supreme	Priests were generally not people of great political power
Sacerdotal duties	Occasional only—*inasi* festivals and incidental inspiration	None in particular	Often inspired; appealed to by people to intercede with gods

Bearing in mind this highly specialized form of religious and social organization in Tonga, let us consider the more general forms of Polynesian usage, in the island groups where there was no specially sacred official removed from the system of administration corresponding to the Tui Tonga. As regards chiefs, their personal sanctity was very great, as we have seen in dealing with the Society Islands; so also was their social pre-eminence and their political power. Their sacerdotal functions, however, were limited to participation in public ceremonies, the imposition of taboos, and the like. On the other hand we find the development of a special class of priests whose functions were primarily sacerdotal; they served as the repositories of sacred lore, they directed ritual, and they invoked the gods and were inspired by them. In the case of high priests, they were generally of high rank, but this rule was by no means universal—it seems to have been rather a matter of convenience and circumstance, arising from the influence and wealth which were associated with their rank. The functions of possession and inspiration, in particular, seem very often to have been discharged by people of the lower orders of society.

Taking the general hypothesis of Sir James Frazer, that the secular and sacerdotal functions were originally, in the history of human society, merged in a single individual,[1] Williamson has presented a theory concerning the possible historical course which the differentiation of the two offices (the sacred and the secular) has taken in Polynesia.[2] Whether we accept this historical reconstruction or not, the question still remains of the social significance of the differentiation. If, as suggested by Sir James Frazer, the sacred and secular offices were originally

[1] See Frazer, *E.H.K.* Lectures III and IV.
[2] See *Systems*, vol. III, chap. XXX.

merged in the one individual who was at the same time "king" and "magician" or "priest", why should the two functions have been differentiated? This question can only be answered by a study of the function of the differentiation in living communities.

In order to understand the general magico-religious functions of priests as opposed to chiefs, we may refer again to the two aspects of all magico-religious phenomena for which we have used the terms " religious " and " magical ". In Chapter VIII we decided to use the term " religious " to designate those social activities which serve to generate belief in the supernatural, and " magical " for the actual employment of the supernatural for social or individual purposes. Using the terms with these special connotations we may describe the religious functions of Polynesian priests as being personally to organize and reinforce the religious beliefs and sentiments of the people. They were the holders of the ancient traditions, who were well versed in the impressive legends of the gods and the creation. Ritual, too, was their province, and they directed ceremonial behaviour along lines pleasing to the gods and spectacular to the worshippers, common participation in which served to keep alive religious sentiments. When inspired by the gods they manifested abnormal or unusual forms of behaviour which provided visible evidence of their close communion with supernatural forces.[1] On the other hand, the magical function of the priests was to maintain effective communication between mankind and the supernatural. By making sacrifices and directing ritual they pleased the gods, and made them favourably inclined towards their worshippers; by prayer and intercession they sought for blessings, or the aversion of evil. And by entering into psychic *rapport* with the divine powers, they made the will of the gods known to mankind, and so provided a knowledge of the working of the supernatural which might be of practical use in human affairs. These two groups of functions were, of course, complementary, and the priests thus acted as intermediaries between men and gods, organizing the activities of each in a manner satisfactory to the other.

Chiefs, on the other hand, were primarily political officers,

---

[1] This probably explains why people of no particular social standing, who were not priests in the ordinary sense, were often inspired. It seems probable that the manifestation of abnormal behaviour depended upon a special kind of temperament, and the "neurotics" or "eccentrics" possessing this would not always occur among any special class of society.

though they had important magico-religious functions. As to the religious aspect of chieftainship, we have referred more than once to the beliefs in divine descent, the chiefs being the visible lineal descendants of the gods, whose exalted station was increased by that of their illustrious descendants. As regards the magical functions of chieftainship, it cannot be doubted that the traditional beliefs and practices associated with the sanctity of chiefs did very definitely reinforce their temporal power, and the special ceremonial surrounding their birth, inauguration and death served to give ritual expression to this principle and to draw upon the supernatural for the validation of political authority.

But we must at once add a *caveat* to what has been said concerning the religious functions of chiefs. It is probably true that, as we have suggested, the belief that the supreme political rulers were intimately associated with the supernatural did reinforce magico-religious belief. Political power, however, was never a thoroughly satisfactory validation for faith in the efficacy of the supernatural. The prestige of Polynesian chiefs was subject to abrogation by assassination, deposition or defeat in war. Such a conditional authority is inconsistent with the absolute and unquestioning faith which must characterize human attitudes towards the supernatural, and we can here discern a reason why a special class of priests should exist, a class of people whose sole function was to act as intermediaries between human beings and the gods. It is true that the priests might at times fail in their office: the gods might refuse to answer their prayers, the offerings might be insufficient, or the divine forces might be successfully invoked by hostile factions. Such incidents, however, affected merely the configuration of magico-religious beliefs, and not the beliefs themselves. But it was a different matter with the chiefs, who sometimes failed to discharge the duties of their office and whose failings and shortcomings were, in such cases, brought vividly before the notice of their people. How could a man command the gratitude of the gods by his generosity, when he was notoriously mean towards his people? How could he be regarded as the repository of wisdom and valuable esoteric knowledge if he behaved like a fool in the administration of public affairs? And finally, how could he command the gods, if he were unable to control the human beings under his jurisdiction?

Probably, if we were to pursue the matter farther, we should be able to discern other reasons why the functions of a priest are in many respects inconsistent with those of a secular ruler. Considerations of expediency in the "division of labour" would require study, particularly in the case of chiefs whose jurisdiction extended over a wide area. We should further have to examine in detail the negative cases, in which secular rulers did act as intermediaries in effective communication with the divine powers.[1] But we must now return to our main theme, namely the political and religious organization of Tonga, because this represents a specialized development of the principles which have been mentioned.

As has been said, the hazards surrounding the life of a secular ruler are to some extent inconsistent with sacerdotal duties. And the same applies, to some extent, to personal sanctity, which is diminished by the indignities which secular rulers must at times suffer. In Tonga we have an attempt to overcome this difficulty by concentrating sanctity in the person of the Tui Tonga, and at the same time removing him from the hurly-burly of administrative duties. This finds confirmation in the legend concerning the origin of the *hau* or secular rule, for it was the repeated assassinations of successive Tui Tonga which led Kauulufonua I to delegate his secular power to the Tui Haa Takalaua. But the *fiat* of an individual will (however understandable in the circumstances) is insufficient to explain sociologically a system of organization so complicated and elaborate as that which we have described. We must believe that the differentiation between the personal sanctity of the Tui Tonga and the temporal power of the *hau* represents a further elaboration of the principles set forth above. The sanctity of chieftainship was maintained by the descent of the *hau* from the divine lineage of the Tui Tonga, as well as by the affinal relationship existing between them. But it was saved from attack at its fountain head by removing the Tui Tonga from situations where his dignity might be threatened.

Unfortunately the amount of empirical information concerning the political organization of Tonga does not allow us to carry this analysis farther, and for this reason it must be

---

[1] For example in Tikopia the chiefs of the four clans of the island are also their high priests. But here there is an elaborate system of reciprocity designed to secure harmony between them, while in their supreme sacerdotal duty (that of invoking the gods for prosperity during the festival of the "Work of the Gods") they act together in a complicated system of ceremonial and economic coordination. (Firth, R., unpublished manuscript.)

regarded merely as a hypothesis for investigation in other fields. But it raises at least one general problem of method to which we must refer.

In outlining our methodological approach to the problems in hand, we suggested that social institutions serve to satisfy human needs which are universal, in that they are inherent in the psycho-physiological nature of man and in the constitution of human society. But apart from those needs which are absolutely imperative—for example hunger, procreation, or political authority—there are a number of potentialities, to some extent inconsistent with one another, which may or may not be given expression in social institutions. Thus sex is universal, and in every human society there exist norms, codes of morals, and institutions designed on the one hand to control erotic passions and on the other to give them organized expression. But the moment we go beyond such very general statements as these we are met by difficulties; for example it is true that we could, in any given community, offer a functional interpretation of love-magic, but what of those societies which have no love-magic? Or, again, we could take a custom such as the *couvade*, and show that it gives ritual expression to the relationships existing between members of a family. But what should we say of the vast majority of human societies in which the *couvade* is not practised? It is true that we should find expression given in other ways to the relationships between father, mother and children, but the problem remains why this expression should take on a specific form in some societies, and, conversely, why this specific form should not exist in others.

To reformulate this problem in terms of our discussion, we have suggested reasons why the functions of secular rule and sacerdotal duties should be differentiated, and further why in Tonga even personal sanctity should be concentrated in an individual who had little or no temporal power. But this immediately raises the problem why in other parts of Polynesia sacerdotal duties were carried out by secular rulers, and again, if our analysis is correct, why the extreme differentiation of function should have arisen in Tonga and in Tonga alone.

A partial answer to this question is to be found in the fact that every existing form of social organization has both advantages and disadvantages. We have mentioned the advantages of differentiating political authority from priestly duties. But we could also mention advantages arising from unification as opposed to differentiation. The existence of a class of priests limits the authority of the chief to secular matters, and so minimizes his prestige. Even in administration, the supernatural powers of the priests did in certain cases make them able to interfere in temporal matters. And, again, what we have said concerning the insecurity of temporal power, and its inconsistency with a conception of intimacy with the supernatural, would have to be balanced by the assertion that the actual wielding of political authority, so far as it is competent and effective, is a valuable bulwark of religious authority. Religion is never so cogent as when it is supported by political force. Throughout Polynesia generally we have various forms of compromise between these groups of opposed factors, while certain areas offer specialized developments—for example, the identification of sacred and secular offices in Tikopia, and their extreme differentiation in Tonga. The immediate task is the collection of empirical evidence which may form the basis of a more comprehensive analysis.

Such a statement will appear to some as unsatisfactory, and the suggestion may be made that the ultimate factor in determining the form of institutions is only to be found in their historical origins, the legendary account of the origin of the *hau* in Tonga being a case in point. The value of historical as opposed to functional interpretations will form part of a later study. For the present we may simply say that a partial explanation which does not go beyond the facts is preferable to a more complete one which is founded upon speculation rather than upon empirical evidence.

CHAPTER XII

RELIGION AND ECONOMICS

IN Chapter x we referred to the role played by religion in certain economic institutions of the Society Islanders. We may now examine the more general relationship between religion and economics throughout Central Polynesia. Our object in doing this is twofold: firstly, to show that, throughout this area, religion played an important part in the economic life of the people, comparable with that which we have described with reference to the Society Islands; and secondly, to demonstrate the importance in Polynesian religion of its material or economic aspect. In other words, we shall be concerned first with the religious aspect of economic institutions, and second with the economic aspect of religion.

Though the relationship between religion and economics is for various reasons an extremely important one, it has not received the attention which it deserves, mainly because of the failure of field-workers in the past to provide data concerning primitive economics. To the untrained observer, this is an aspect of the native's life which appears to be hardly worthy of study. It lacks the glamour of ceremonial, the weirdness of magic, and the piquancy of sexual customs. For this reason early observers neglected almost completely an aspect of the native's life which is of profound significance to him—the satisfaction of his material wants. On the theoretical side the economic systems of primitive peoples have been either entirely ignored or forced into the Procrustean bed of preconceived theory. In the earliest speculations concerning primitive economics, "stages" of economic life were invented *ad hoc* without the slightest empirical enquiry as to whether any primitive economic institutions do actually correspond with the supposed sequences of stages. For Adam Smith, and other exponents of the *Dreistufentheorie*, men were first hunters, then shepherds, and finally agriculturists; for Bruno Hildebrand, they passed through successive stages of exchange—barter, money, and credit; and for Lewis Morgan, the history of man's economic development was divisible into two stages of "savagery" and three of "barbarism". Again, the economics of primitive peoples were contrasted with those of civilized nations, and held up as

simple prototypes of modern forms of society, and as exempli-
fying a mode of life from which our own economic organization
has emerged. According to Karl Bücher, man's original state
was characterized by the "individual search for food" without
any social regulation; for Engels, on the other hand, it was one of
"primitive communism", a view in direct opposition to Bücher's.
None of these theories was based upon a thorough empirical
study of the realities of primitive economic life—they selected
only those aspects of it which, from a very superficial examination, seemed to fit in with the view which it was desired to
establish. Only in recent years has any attempt been made to
study the economic systems of primitive peoples in their own
right, not as stages in a hypothetical evolutionary process, but
as working mechanisms whereby man adjusts himself to his
environment. The centre of interest has shifted from anthropological fossil-hunting to an empirical study of economic institutions and their place in the contemporary life of primitive
man. By this method it has been found that economic facts
have important relationships to religion, law, political organization and family life. The functional approach to the problem
has thus revealed at the same time the social significance, as well
as the great complexity, of primitive economic systems.[1]

Although most of the accounts of Polynesian economic activities are slender, and although they confine themselves for the
most part to the matter-of-fact description of techniques and
technology, we can nevertheless gather that production, distribution and exchange in Polynesian communities were not purely
economic activities, motivated exclusively by material wants. It
is of course true that the primary function of economic institutions was to satisfy the material needs of the people—to provide
food, shelter, tools, weapons, and other "economic goods"; and
that these institutions were founded upon a sound knowledge of
certain empirical principles, which made possible the development of adequate techniques and methods of production. But
side by side with each Polynesian economic system we find a
body of beliefs, and a system of magico-religious practices,
whose functions were entirely different from those of the purely
practical activities with which they were associated. In monographs on Polynesian ethnology, we usually find the two bodies

[1] For a critical historical review of theories of primitive economics, together
with an exposition of the functional point of view, see Firth, *Maori Economics*,
chap. I.

of ethnographic data treated separately—one section on "industry" or "economics" or specific activities, such as "fishing" or "house-building", and another on "religion", in which, sometimes, we find descriptions of seasonal festivals, ritual connected with fertility and kindred subjects; but, with one or two exceptions, we never find an integrated treatment of the two aspects considered together, nor any indication of the manner in which they complement each other. For this reason we may set out certain considerations connected with the role played by religion in economic life, considerations which are vital to an understanding of these two aspects of native culture.

PRODUCTION

Considered as a general charter for existing institutions, Polynesian religious beliefs entered into every phase of economic life. As far as production was concerned, fishing, and particularly deep-sea fishing, was the activity with which religion was primarily associated. We may perhaps discern three reasons for this. In the first place, deep-sea fishing was mainly carried out by men, and there were specific taboos which debarred women from participating in it. Secondly, it was a physically dangerous pursuit, partly owing to the general perils of the sea, and partly owing to the specific risks involved in handling large sea fish. Thirdly, it was economically a speculative proceeding, and factors beyond man's control entered into it to a greater extent than in, for example, agriculture. In particular, the last two factors—personal danger and economic risk—would seem to indicate the reason for the widespread association between fishing on the one hand, and magico-religious beliefs and practices on the other. The latter brought confidence in the face of difficulties and dangers and provided at the same time explanations of failure and means which might be adopted to ensure success.

The religious background of fishing, which we have seen to be important in the Society Islands, was also prominent in the Marquesas. Professional fishermen had special precincts, which were *tapu* to women, where they kept not only their tackle, but also sacred stone images (*tiki*) connected with fishing. Within these precincts were shrines where offerings were made and where the chief fisherman performed rites and chanted invocations. There were special deities associated with particular kinds of fish, as well as general sea and fishing deities such as Tanaoa and Hahati. There were many taboos connected with fishing. Some of these were general and some specific, affecting the conduct of fishermen and their relations on shore—thus the wives of fishermen were not allowed to leave their houses, to eat, or to have sexual intercourse while their husbands were at sea. The festivals which followed fishing expeditions may have had a religious character, and Handy suggests that they were connected with the removal of *tapu*.[1]

The material on the magico-religious aspect of fishing in other parts of Central Polynesia is not sufficient to allow us to generalize, but the more detailed information from the Society Islands, from the Marquesas, and more recently from Tikopia, suggests that the scattered references to the consecration of this economic pursuit represent merely surviving fragments of what was once a complicated system of inter-relation between the material and spiritual worlds.

As far as the production of plant foods was concerned, information as to its magico-religious aspect is deficient so far as most of the island groups of Central Polynesia are concerned. But from Tikopia we have an account of an elaborate socio-religious system whereby the major sources of plant food supply were brought into ritual relation with the social system.[2] Each of the four large patrilineal groupings or clans is associated with one of the four major sources of plant food—taro, yam, breadfruit and coconut. Each of these species is said to *fakarongo*, that is to say, "obey" or "listen to" the clan with which it is associated or its chief. This does not imply an anthropomorphic conception, but is merely a metaphorical reference to the belief that the control of the plant comes within the jurisdiction of the clan chief, who carries out elaborate religious ceremonies in connection with its growth.[3] From the point of view of ideology there is a parallel association between the four plant foods and the deities of the clan to which they belong, and the whole system is validated by a legend which tells how each food was originally obtained for the Tikopia by the gods of the four clans.

Turning from the production of food to industry, we find here also that productive activity was intimately associated with magico-religious beliefs and practices. The construction of important canoes and house-building on a large scale were

[1] Handy, *N.C.M.* pp. 164–8.
[2] See R. Firth, "Totemism in Polynesia", *Oceania*, vol. I, pp. 291–321, 377–98.
[3] An exception to this statement must be made in the case of the clan associated with the coconut; a special reason for this is suggested by Dr Firth (*ibid.* p. 294).

frequently sanctified by religious beliefs and accompanied by ritual and invocation. These were often carried out by expert craftsmen, whose practical functions were correlated with their authority in matters of ritual, and sometimes by special priests. The scraps of information which we have, inadequate as they are, suffice to show the importance of religion as a correlate of economic enterprise.[1]

UTILIZATION

So far we have been concerned with the bearing of magico-religious beliefs and practices upon productive activities; we may now turn to the other phase of economic life which may be described by the general term "utilization", a broad concept embracing the facts of exchange, distribution, ownership and consumption. These facts, concerned with the manner in which man's resources are utilized, may be set against the productive phase of economic life, though the line of distinction is sometimes hard to draw. We are not, however, concerned primarily with an analysis of Polynesian institutions in terms of modern economic concepts—our object is rather empirically to describe these institutions and to show the part played in them by magico-religious beliefs and practices. We may therefore proceed at once to a concrete problem—that of land tenure—a problem so far-reaching in its sociological implications that it will bring us face to face with the various phases of economic life which we have mentioned—with exchange, distribution, ownership and consumption.

The problem of land tenure is one of great importance from the point of view both of anthropological theory and of actual field-work.[2] Moreover, in the practical sphere, a mutual mis-

---

[1] Thus in Tonga, Gifford writes: "Boat building, fishing, pigeon snaring and presumably even rat shooting were preceded by ceremonial observances." (*Tonga*, p. 345.) In the Marquesas all important work was protected by *tapu* from evil spiritual influences; the initiation and completion of house-building were marked by the intoning of a special chant, referring to the mythological origin of the craft; and other industries, such as the construction and launching of canoes, were also associated with religious ceremonial (Handy, *N.C.M.* pp. 146, 150–1, 155–6). On the ceremonial connected with Samoan house-building see Handy, *S.H.C.T.* p. 14; Mead, *Manua*, pp. 36 sq.; Te Rangi Hiroa, *S.M.C.* pp. 90 sqq. For a general survey of the subject, see Handy, *P.R.* pp. 282–96.

[2] "The study of land tenure is a somewhat difficult and very interesting problem of sociological synthesis. Nothing reveals better the constructive or creative aspect of sociological observations among a native race than an analysis of how land tenure should be studied, recorded and presented." (Malinowski, *Coral Gardens and their Magic*, vol. 1, p. 317.)

understanding of concepts relating to land ownership has probably been the most potent cause of dissension in the contact between Europeans and native peoples. Failure to study the facts of land tenure in terms of its meaning for the native has thus led, in the past, to gaps in our knowledge of the economic life of native races, as well as to clashes of interest in situations of culture contact.

The importance of the problem is now being generally recognized.[1] Specifically in regard to Polynesia, considerable attention has been devoted to it by Williamson,[2] while subsequent researches have still further emphasized both its complexity and importance.[3] It seems desirable, therefore, to formulate the problem and to treat the Polynesian data in relation to general theory, with a view to understanding the part played by magico-religious beliefs and practices in Polynesian systems of land tenure.

The difficulties which have arisen in the past in discussions of the relation of man to his material wealth have been due to attempts to superimpose upon primitive conceptions the specific ideology of European " ownership ",[4] an ideology which cannot be applied to primitive land tenure. Simple questions such as " Who owns this land?" have a meaning for the European which has no exact parallel in native thought. Research carried out by this method leads either to a mass of contradictory information, due to the complexity and diversity of claims of land, or to vague and misleading conceptions of primitive ownership as " communistic" and as lacking in any distinction between *meum* and *tuum*. It is therefore necessary to regard primitive land tenure in a very general way as *the culturally defined relationship of man to land*,[5] a relationship which can only be understood by studying its manifold sociological implications. Considered in this way land tenure is not a simple matter of legally defined claims; nor is it entirely a question of economic exploitation or usufruct.

[1] For a full statement of the problem and the type of field observations which may contribute to its solution, see Malinowski, *op. cit.* chaps. XI and XII.

[2] *Systems*, vol. III, chaps. XXXIX and XL.

[3] Cf. Firth, *Maori Economics*, chap. XI; Mead, *Manua*, pp. 70 *sqq.*; Keesing, *Modern Samoa*, chap. V; Firth, *Tikopia*, chap. XI. Several monographs by Dr P. H. Buck also contain valuable sections on land tenure. (See, in particular, Te Rangi Hiroa, *M. & R.* pp. 65–9 and *E.T.* pp. 57–9.) The importance of land tenure in the economic life of kinship groups is also recognized by Dr Hogbin. (See *L.O.P.* Index, *s.v.* "Land Tenure".)

[4] Cf. Firth, *Maori Economics*, p. 330.

[5] In considering Polynesian rights to land it is also necessary to consider fishing rights, which are frequently defined in similar terms.

Land tenure...is the relationship of man to soil in the widest sense; that is, so far as it is laid down in native law and custom and in the measure in which it controls political life, affects the performance of public ceremonies and gives access to opportunities for recreation and sports. Man's appointed and culturally defined place on his soil, his territorial citizenship, his type of residence, and those rights which underlie the various uses of his soil form an organic whole of which the economic exploitation is but a part, albeit the most important part.[1]

The most obvious question in connection with such a study is the quantitative and qualitative relationship between man as user and consumer to land, considered as a source of material wealth. The relation of the amount of land available to the population is important in defining native systems of land tenure. In the history of Polynesian groups there are several examples of an increase in the population of a given area leading to variations in the methods of organizing land tenure.[2] It would appear from the traditions of Rakahanga that the problem of land distribution did not arise until the sixth generation after settlement, when the growing population led to the establishment of a special office of "land distributor" (*tuha whenua*), apart from the ordinary political authority of the *ariki*. The word of the *tuha whenua* was final in all questions of land ownership. As the families whose lands were thus controlled developed into larger groups, authority in matters of land tenure passed from the *tuha whenua* into the hands of the heads of these groups, the *whakamaru*, who, although subordinate to the *ariki* in important religious matters, had complete control of local affairs, including the distribution of land, the settlement of disputes, the protection of property, and the control of agriculture. In this we see a progressive evolution of the system of land tenure, arising from an increase in population over a limited area of territory, and a correlated change in social and political institutions.[3]

Further, not only the total amount of available land, but also its varieties and the different purposes for which it is suitable must be taken into consideration.[4] Thus in Mangaia there were three kinds of land, firstly that on the makatea (a raised platform of coral rock running round the edge of the island) termed *rau-tuitui*; secondly the narrow upland valleys (*rau-tuanuʻe*); and thirdly the rich "taro flats" (*puna*) lying between these two

[1] Malinowski, *Coral Gardens and their Magic*, vol. I, p. 319.
[2] Cf. Te Rangi Hiroa, *E.T.* p. 58; *M. & R.* pp. 66–9.
[3] Te Rangi Hiroa, *M. & R.* pp. 65–9.
[4] Cf. *Systems*, vol. III, pp. 238, 302.

areas. Of these classes the *puna* were the most fertile, and were the prize of the victors in war. The vanquished, however, acquired a proprietary right over the inferior *rau-tuitui* and *rau-tuanuʻe*, a right which was respected by the victors.[1] Again, specific problems in the relation of human groups to their environment might lead to specific forms of ownership. Thus in Tongareva the scarcity of drinking water and the necessary substitution of coconut milk as a beverage led to the development of special rights to coconut trees, the fruit of which might be gathered by specified individuals other than the titular owners of the land. Finally, where, as in Samoa, there was a certain amount of fertile land not under cultivation, we find different rules in the case of unoccupied land on the one hand and waste land on the other.[2]

The complicated problem of primitive land tenure is generally glossed over by such statements as "the land belongs to the chief" or "the land is owned by the clan". Such bare verbal formulations are, as we have seen, inadequate, a fact which is proved by the conflicting information to which they lead. The family group, the local unit, the chief or sub-chief or some particular individual may at various times be credited with "owning" the land. This does not mean that primitive land tenure is itself based upon a jumble of conflicting ideas, but merely that it cannot be defined by a simple statement of "ownership". On the other hand such verbal formulations as we have mentioned are not by any means irrelevant to the problem. On the contrary, they define certain claims clearly recognized in native law, claims which it is the duty of the anthropologist to record. But the formulation of legal titles to land is merely the beginning of the investigation. The next step is the tabulation of the economic claims actually exercised over the produce of the land. The form of this table will necessarily vary from one area to another; it will also vary within any given area according to the various types of goods produced. So far as Central Polynesia is concerned, we can only list in a very general way the types of claims which were exercised in the economics of land tenure. No implications of priority are intended in the order in which the claims are listed.

I. *Chiefs and priests.* We have already referred to the tribute paid to chiefs in the Society Islands, and the subject has been

---

[1] Te Rangi Hiroa, *M.S.* pp. 125–6, 129–30.
[2] *Systems*, vol. III, p. 238; cf. Mead, *Manua*, p. 72.

fully dealt with in another volume.[1] Priests likewise received
liberal remuneration for their efforts, often in the form of an
exclusive claim to the food offered to the gods.

II. *Public bodies and officials.* The establishment of special
councils, public bodies, or executive offices seems to have
carried with it the institution of claims of an economic order.
Thus the Samoan *fono* imposed village levies for various purposes—the entertainment of visitors, the building of a guest
house, or the provision of a dowry for the village virgin.[2] The
claims of various official personages in Samoa are described in
even greater detail by Dr Buck. We may present here a portion
of his material, because it illustrates very well the minute detail
with which claims to material goods were defined, as well as the
manner in which these were integrated with the social structure.

For example, let us consider the division of a pig, which was
an important event in Samoan social life. Each portion of the
animal had its appointed recipient or recipients, and the following list of claims, given by Dr Buck,[3] may be cited to illustrate
the complexity of the principles governing its distribution:

Parts of pig	Recipients
Head	Young men who cook
Neck	Talking chief
Back and side (front part)	Chiefs of second grade
Shoulder	Talking chief
Loins	Chiefs of first grade
Side (below loins)	Family of chief
Rump	Women
Hind leg	Chiefs of lesser rank (*matai*)
Abdominal wall	Village virgin (*taupou*)
Heart	High chief
Cooked blood	Chiefs and young men who do the work
Liver	Talking chief (for official use)
Remainder of internal organs	Butchers and cooks

The actual carrying out of this distribution was a social event
of considerable interest. When a number of pigs were cooked
for an important ceremonial occasion, they were heaped together to make a good show. Expert carvers took pride in their
skill; sometimes a talking chief would carry out the operation,
and in any case one of them would direct the proceedings. Care
was taken to divide the portions neatly along the lines of division
laid down by custom, and to this end the first cooking of the pig
was very slight—sometimes it was only warmed through. The

---

[1] See *Systems*, vol. III, pp. 343 *sqq.*   [2] Mead, *Manua*, p. 70.
[3] Te Rangi Hiroa, *S.M.C.* pp. 120–1.

divided portions might be cooked again before eating, but the object of the very superficial cooking of the whole animal was to ensure a neat division along the boundaries between the ceremonial portions—if too well done, the flesh was apt to tear away and produce an untidy effect.

Similar ceremonial divisions were carried out in the case of turtle, bonito, shark and fowl, and were sometimes accompanied by the drinking of kava. The ceremonial divisions appear to have had important social implications. Thus in the ceremonial distribution of shark, persons of rank from neighbouring villages had certain recognized claims; for example, a talking chief of one village might send to the talking chief of another for a share of his portion, or the *taupou* to the *taupou*. Again, the part played by the talking chiefs in formulating the rules of distribution seems to have made it possible for them to obtain the best portions.[1]

III. *Productive units.* A treatment of claims arising out of participation in production must necessarily depend upon the manner in which production is organized. When, for example in agriculture, men and women belonging to local or kinship groups co-operate in production, the work which they respectively contribute gives them a claim to the products of economic effort. On the other hand, in deep-sea fishing, where men alone participate, the claims of women to a share of the catch are established through their position as dependents of the men, and reciprocal services, such as cooking, which they may carry out for them.

In connection with this we must mention the remuneration of experts, for example the elaborate payments made to members of the guild of skilled craftsmen in Samoa.[2] Another Samoan example is provided by the specific claims of the expert fisherman (*tautai*) in a bonito expedition. Upon the return of the bonito fleet the *tautai* was entitled to a levy (*aleanga*) from the catch of each canoe, the number of fish so claimed depending upon the number of fish caught. Those whose luck had been poor were exempted from this tribute, but any attempt at evasion, if detected, was severely punished, the offender's canoe

---

[1] "The part the talking chiefs play in framing the rules is seen in the allocation of shares. The high chief received the worst part of the fish in the tail, whereas the dorsal fin portion that falls to the talking chief is the best. Though the talking chief subsequently shares his portion, he has the satisfaction of demonstrating that in some things he exercises more *pule* (power) than his superior." (Te Rangi Hiroa, *op. cit.* p. 126.)   [2] Mead, *Manua*, pp. 36 *sqq.*

being broken up and his fishing tackle confiscated by the *tautai*. The fish claimed by the *tautai* as tribute were used by him to provide a feast for all the fishermen, the unsuccessful ones sharing equally with their more fortunate fellows.[1] The *aleanga* levy was thus not only a ceremonial recognition of the authority and importance of the *tautai*, but was also a practical mechanism for ensuring an equitable distribution of the catch, providing a sort of insurance against bad luck.

IV. *Magicians.* The claims of experts in practical matters leads us naturally to those of magicians. In fact, the two might coincide, as with the skilled canoe-builders of Samoa whose claims as experts were reinforced by the belief in their magical power to make a canoe unlucky, if they were not satisfied with the generosity of their employer.[2] As far as claims arising from purely magical services are concerned, we have already referred to the payments made to the owners of *puna* in the Society Islands. It would not appear, however, that the magician played such a vitally important part in Polynesian economic affairs as he does, for example, in Trobriand gardening.[3]

V. *Claims exercised through kinship.* These are of a very general character, ranging from the ordinary daily division of food within the household to the elaborate provisioning of marriages, funerals and other ceremonial occasions demanding an exchange of material goods between kin. Claims exercised through kinship may apply merely to the immediate products of the land, or to "ownership" in a wider sense, for example in the case of inheritance.[4] In connection with the latter it is important to notice that in Polynesia, a predominantly patrilineal area, claims to land were sometimes transmitted through women. Whether we regard this as a "survival" of an earlier "matrilineal" state of society is irrelevant to the present argument. The important point to recognize is the validity of claims by or through females cutting across the predominantly patrilineal structure. This principle went beyond the transmission of wealth to claims exercised among the living, for example the claims of a married daughter to coconuts from her father's land in Tongareva[5] or the immunity in Mangaia of a conquered man against eviction from his wife's land, even though he might be dispossessed of his own.[6]

---

[1] Te Rangi Hiroa, *op. cit.* p. 518. [2] *Ibid.* p. 416.
[3] Malinowski, *op. cit. passim.* [4] Cf. *Systems*, vol. III, chap. XLIII.
[5] Te Rangi Hiroa, *E.T.* p. 57. [6] Te Rangi Hiroa, *M.S.* pp. 129–30.

VI. *Gods.* The custom of making sacrifices to the gods was widespread throughout Polynesia, and mobilized the economic resources of the whole community from time to time for religious purposes. It would appear, however, that such offerings were not devoted entirely to the exclusive use of the gods. Thus in Tikopia great offerings of food are made to the gods in connection with seasonal festivals, but are subsequently consumed by the human community. The belief is that the gods abstract the *ora* or spiritual essence of the food, the material substance of which is subsequently eaten by the worshippers.

VII. *Claims arising out of specific institutions.* These depend upon particular customs pertaining in the various groups. We have already referred to tribute levied by the *areoi* society in the Society Islands. Again, in the Gilbert Islands the special development of the practice of adoption was associated with a set of economic obligations. When a child was adopted, its real parents gave to those who had adopted it a gift, usually a piece of land. Thereafter they continued to provide periodic gifts of food for the adoptive parents. In return for this the latter assumed responsibility for the rearing of the child, and in addition were expected to include the adopted child in the testamentary disposition of their lands.[1]

We have reviewed the more general types of claims to the produce of the land which were exercised by individuals or groups in various parts of Central Polynesia. But the tabulation of such claims does not complete the sociological study of land tenure. We must also enquire how the claims are validated in native law and custom, and to do this it will be necessary to consider the use and ownership of land in its cultural context, with its manifold implications, economic, political and religious.

The most obvious validation of claims to economic goods lies in their explicit linguistic formulation. As we have seen, verbal statements of claims alone are not sufficient to give us a complete picture of systems of native ownership, but they do define certain legally binding rules through the creative function of formalized speech.[2] The social acceptance of the verbal definition of a claim provides *prima facie* evidence of its validity.

But the verbal definition of legal claims is always validated by other forces, that is, by positive or negative sanctions, using

---

[1] H. C. and H. E. Maude, "Adoption in the Gilbert Islands", *J.P.S.* vol. XL, No. 4, pp. 225 *sqq.*
[2] Cf. Malinowski, *Coral Gardens and their Magic*, vol. II, p. 234.

the term in a very wide sense, to include both punishments and positive inducements arising out of the working of social institutions. The latter are by far the more important, since the study of the positive forces of social conformity lays stress upon the vast majority of cases in which custom is followed, as against the comparatively few instances in which it is defied. This is a subject to which we shall refer again at a later stage.

The most obvious claim to the products of economic effort lies in the fact of exploitation. Nominal titles to land were established[1] or reinforced[2] by occupation and use. Within the land-owning group the same principle applied. Whatever outside obligations had to be met, the individual exercised a claim on the product of his labours. The references to generosity, to communal ownership and the like have obscured this very important fact. Land might, in a sense, be owned "collectively" but each individual was expected to play his particular economic role in the work of the group. Normally this system functioned so smoothly that the existence of obligations counterbalancing rights is not easily detected. But the situation becomes clear in cases of failure to conform, that is, in the case of the lazy man. Sometimes sanctions of a very immediate material kind were brought to bear upon the offender. Thus in Ontong Java land was owned "collectively" by the joint family. But the claims of each of its members depended upon their willingness to co-operate in economic effort—thus Dr Hogbin describes the distribution of a catch of fish, in which portions were given to all members of the group, including those who had not participated in the day's fishing. To this, however, there was one exception. A man who had evaded three fishing expeditions in succession by pleading tiredness was denied any share of the catch. 'Ohuki, the man who was distributing the fish, "knew the reason for his tiredness; he was too fond of dancing on the beach at night and as a result was not fit for work in the day-time".[3] Such drastic measures were not always adopted,[4] and generally speaking the force of public opinion was sufficient to ensure energetic co-operation. The important point to recognize is that claims to the products of economic effort were counterbalanced by obligations to participate in it. Going beyond the ordinary

[1] Cf. Handy, N.C.M. pp. 57–8; Mead, Manua, p. 72.
[2] Cf. Te Rangi Hiroa, M.S. p. 129.
[3] Hogbin, L.O.P. p. 125.
[4] According to Dr Raymond Firth action such as the above would never be taken in Tikopia.

co-operating group, the services of experts and assistants gave them a claim to a reward, either in the form of payments or of reciprocal services to be rendered subsequently.

The claims of chiefs, officials, and the heads of social groups are prominent in accounts of Polynesian land tenure. In recognizing this, Williamson states that "among the important matters to be considered in connection with the subject of land tenure and control are the control of cultivation and of food supply and the imposition of restrictions on food consumption; also the payment of tribute".[1] In most of the field records we find accounts of the powers of chiefs in relation to land, of their rights of eviction, of their claims to tribute and of their privileges in regard to the exaction of labour. On the other hand, we also find references to their duties in imposing temporary restrictions upon consumption, whether for practical or ritual purposes; to their administrative duties, including the organization of tribal enterprise, participation in religious ceremonies, the provision of feasts, the offering of hospitality to visitors, and the administration of justice. But these two groups of facts are never correlated, the chief's rights being set off against his responsibilities. Yet this system of reciprocity was one of the most potent forces in the institution of chieftainship, and there were definite mechanisms which prevented, in the main, any abuse of privilege. That such abuses occasionally did occur cannot be doubted, but a check was placed upon them by various factors, particularly by the fear of deposition, which might be resorted to if the pressure of public opinion proved inadequate to ensure a recognition of the obligations of rank.

But the validation of claims goes beyond a mere system of reciprocity; it depends upon the whole cultural tradition. To understand it fully we should have to study the way in which the recognition of moral claims of an economic order is related to the normative system as a whole; how this is inculcated into children during the process of education; and how the important factor of kinship determines the claims existing between individuals. We should also have to study recreational and ceremonial activities for which the economic forces of the community are mobilized along traditional lines, and we should have to supplement a statement of verbal claims by an examination of the material objects associated with the control of ownership, boundary marks, taboo signs and the like. But it seems better

[1] *Systems*, vol. III, pp. 229, 233.

to return at once to the specific subject of our study, namely the part played by religion in the system of land tenure as it has been treated above.

In dealing with the Society Islands we have seen the importance attached to the *marae* in relation to land ownership. An instructive parallel is provided by the part played by Mangaian *marae* in native land tenure:

> The marae was not only necessary to the worship of the god, but it associated the ancestor or tribe with a particular district and, in a way, established their right to the land. If, however, the tribe was conquered, their marae became a historical landmark and could not in itself reserve the land for the tribe. The older maraes retained some prestige in denoting a more ancient occupation. This prestige, however, dwindled to a merely historical one if the temporal power of those who worshipped there was lost.[1]

This example illustrates the complementary influences of occupation and use on the one hand and religious tradition on the other in determining rights to land.

Ownership, then, was often defined in religious terms, involving a socio-religious association between the land, the human beings inhabiting it, and their ancestors or gods. But our extension of the concept of land tenure enables us to see a wider connection between magico-religious institutions and land ownership. We have seen that in addition to formal titles to land, economic claims to its produce must be considered and the integration of these claims examined. It is here that religion plays an important part in giving a validity to social institutions and so establishing the claims arising out of the functioning of these institutions. Consider, for example, the fundamental principle of Polynesian land tenure, as formulated by Williamson: "The ownership of the land of a social group, on behalf of the group, by its official head, the bearer of its name or title."[2] Subject to the detailed elaboration which we have suggested above, this may be accepted as the basis of land tenure in Central Polynesia, and we are driven at once to correlate this principle with the sacred genealogies of chiefs, with the taboos surrounding their names and titles, and with the sanctity of chiefs in general, a subject which has been discussed in the last chapter.

So far as individual claims to land or its produce were concerned, many of these were validated by magico-religious beliefs and practices. The imposition of taboos upon land and its produce together with the fear of supernatural punishments for

---

[1] Te Rangi Hiroa, *M.S.* pp. 173–4. [2] *Systems*, vol. III, p. 229.

their infringement were important factors in ensuring respect for the rights of property. Again, the use of sorcery as a means of counteracting theft, to which we have referred in dealing with the Society Islands, was widespread throughout Polynesia.

But not all claims were so directly related to the magico-religious system. As we have said, some of them arose out of the functioning of important institutions, and the connection was an indirect one, depending upon the validation of these institutions as a whole by religion. The role of religion in these cases can therefore only be seen by examining its relation to the culture as a whole and to its component institutions. Probably the most general feature of this is to be found in the part played by cosmogonies and myths of origin in establishing a spiritual link between human beings and their natural environment. This served to engender a sense of possession and even of participation in relation to the land inhabited, and so established a strong personal attachment to land, in addition to that which arose spontaneously through sentimental associations. This was more than a mere individual attachment—it was an important cultural force involving the sense of continuity expressed in the Maori proverb: "Man perishes, but the land remains." Religion thus established a spiritual relationship between man and his land over and above the pragmatic facts of habitation and use. This served to stabilize land tenure, both within the community at a given moment of time and in the process of transmission from generation to generation.[1]

THE MATERIAL ASPECT OF RELIGION

Having considered the magico-religious aspect of economic life, we may now turn to the reciprocal relationship, that is, to the material objects associated, whether permanently or temporarily, with religious beliefs. The most obvious thing to be considered here is the set of material objects which were regarded as permanently sacred. Sometimes these consisted of an elaborate paraphernalia of temples, idols, sacred precincts and the like, such as those to which we have referred in Chapters VI and VII. We have described the sort of ritual which centred around such sacred objects in one Polynesian community (Chapter IX), but sometimes the material equipment of religion was not so prominent as it was in the Society Islands. Parti-

[1] For a discussion of the importance of this principle in native sociology, see Firth, *Maori Economics*, chap. XI.

cularly in Samoa the material substratum of religion was very meagre, though no doubt this impression is enhanced by the tendentious forgetting of the ancient religion under the influence of Christianity.[1] They had, however, wooden temples constructed on the same lines as ordinary houses, where material representations of the gods, in the form of shells, bowls and the like, were kept.[2] In addition to this, certain natural features of the landscape represented historical incidents, particularly those associated with the legend of Sina, and served to link up existing social groups with their legendary history. The same might be said of the *tupua* rocks, which were believed to represent the petrified bodies of ancestors, and some of which were associated with specific taboos and observances.[3]

In connection with this subject we should also mention the incarnation of deities in animals, birds, fish, plants, and the like, a subject which has been dealt with in connection with Tikopia by Dr Raymond Firth.[4] Comparative material on this subject has been reviewed elsewhere,[5] and suffices to show that, whether we call it "totemism" or not, a profoundly significant relationship between natural species and spiritual beings did exist throughout the whole area.

The offering of sacrifices, to which reference has been made in Chapter IV, was another important element in the material aspect of Polynesian religion. Whether in the elaborate dedications of first-fruits at seasonal festivals, or humbler presentations by individuals to the lesser deities, the offering of material goods to the divine powers was an essential factor in establishing effective communication with the supernatural. Even when food or goods offered in this way were subsequently consumed by the worshippers, the formal presentation provided evidence of the devotion of mankind to the gods and a stimulus to the goodwill of the latter.

This point is of considerable theoretical importance in view of the various interpretations which have been offered of primitive religion in general and of Polynesian religion in particular. We have already dealt with the earlier theories which regarded religion as being primarily the result of intellectual speculation.[6]

---

[1] Cf. Te Rangi Hiroa, *S.M.C.* p. 613.
[2] *Ibid.* pp. 70, 613; cf. above, pp. 151 *sqq.*
[3] *Ibid.* p. 329; cf. above, pp. 165 *sqq.* ·
[4] See "Totemism in Polynesia", *Oceania*, vol. I, pp. 291–321, 377–98.
[5] *Systems*, vol. II, chapters on "Totemism", pp. 217–316.
[6] See Chapter VIII.

In the interpretation of Polynesian religion, metaphysical terms are often employed, terms which produce an impression of religious beliefs as a mere formulation of certain spiritual experiences, partly intellectual and partly emotional.[1] Such interpretations emphasize the importance of individual experiences in religion, even if the terms used do not give us any very clear conception of these experiences in terms of native ideology. But too great an emphasis upon this phase of religious life is apt to obscure its pragmatic, or even prosaic, aspects. Polynesian gods were not merely spiritual beings who had created the universe; they were active agents in the matter-of-fact affairs of everyday life. They were venerated, not only because of their spiritual characteristics, but because they played an effective part in human affairs; and, finally, the attitudes of their worshippers were not determined by intellectual speculation and spiritual hunger alone; they were embedded in a complex system of sentiments in which worldly motives of mundane acquisitiveness played an important part.[2] Neither group of factors should be stressed at the expense of the other. Beliefs in spiritual beings with human characteristics, who could be persuaded to grant blessings, and who were ready sympathetically to co-operate with man in the satisfaction of his material and spiritual wants, were important in inspiring respect and reverence. But the material context of effort on the one hand and satisfaction on the other played a vital part in validating and giving cogency to the belief in the power of the gods.

What we have said in the preceding sections leads us to two important conclusions. Firstly that, in the functional study of

[1] Cf. Handy's conception of Polynesian religion as a recognition of the "psychic dynamism" of nature (*P.R.* pp. 25 *sq.*); and the following: "The mind of Tiapu must have looked into the immensity of enfolding space; it must have seen this puny world of man bounded by the towering dome of the Kapu-ruga above the stars, by the abysmic bowl of the Kapu-raro beneath the deep gulf of the sea, margined by Havaiki-tautau-mai west of the setting sun, by Havaiki-tautau-atu east of the bursting dawn; and beyond all of these, where mind faltered in the presence of the unknown and mysterious Po, he may perchance have glimpsed in some swift flash of intuition an abiding vision of the primal cause rising like a night-mist out of the unthinkable void." (Stimson, *T.R.* p. 66.)

[2] Cf. the following statement of Dr Buck: "The significance of the laying aside of a portion of fish for the god may be interpreted through comparison with the psychological attitude toward the giving of presents in daily life. Hospitality was based on reciprocity, and giving was followed in due time by receiving. After the giving of a share of food to the god, the god would be expected to reciprocate by making future fishing operations successful. Also, the gods were angered by obvious neglect, and the failure to render a share of the fish would cause the god to render future fishing operations fruitless, and might even precipitate disaster and misfortune in other undertakings." (Te Rangi Hiroa, *E.T.* p. 88.)

economic institutions, their religious aspects must be taken into account, if we are to understand their complex organization, their spiritual as well as their material importance, and the motives which underlie them. And secondly, that the relationship between religion and economics is a reciprocal one. Just as religion sanctifies certain phases of man's workaday life, so material and economic factors enter into religion, and are, in fact, among the most important elements in its validation.

CHAPTER XIII

RELIGION AND LAW

THE analysis of land tenure, arising out of the discussion of Polynesian economics in the preceding chapter, brought us face to face with certain important facts which must be considered in relation to native systems of land ownership. One of the most significant of these was the legal aspect of the problem, for we saw that clearly formulated and concretely enforced titles to land formed one of the most important elements in land tenure. We may now deal with the legal aspect of Polynesian cultures in more general terms, discussing firstly the general problems involved in the description and interpretation of primitive legal systems and secondly their specifically magico-religious aspects in Polynesian communities.

The study of primitive law in its widest sense is perhaps the most general task of the social anthropologist. From recent contributions to the subject, to which we shall refer later, the far-reaching implications of primitive law have emerged very clearly. It has been amply demonstrated that legal institutions take on a fundamentally different form in primitive communities as opposed to modern civilizations; and that law cannot be considered apart from the whole normative system—the body of moral codes, aesthetic standards, rules of good behaviour and the like—of which institutionalized methods of legal procedure are but a part, albeit an extremely important part. This is perhaps the most important fact to be borne in mind in considering primitive law. Ethnographic observations in the field have in the past been confined almost entirely to accounts of crime and punishment, and to the procedure adopted in the settlement of disputes. The approach has been that of the lawyer rather than that of the scientist. The former, who earns his livelihood in righting the wrongs committed by others, is only interested in the comparatively few instances of breach, as against the overwhelming majority of cases of observance. Like his counterpart in the medical profession, he is only interested when things go wrong, for this is his function in society. But the sociologist who sets out to study law in its entirety is not merely interested in the one case out of a hundred in which the law is broken; he must also study the ninety-nine cases in which it is kept. He must study all the forces of conformity, including those positive inducements which ensure that, generally speaking, honesty is the best policy. But he must not be oblivious of the fact that cases of breach do occur, and that, in such instances, legal mechanisms are brought into play. Law cannot be considered apart from other forces of social conformity, but its existence as a specific element in culture must also be recognized.

An approach such as this immediately brings before us an initial difficulty—the problem of definition. In our own society law is highly institutionalized—it has its own special personnel —judges, advocates, and police; legal business is transacted in special places, is subject to highly codified rules, and is correlated with a specialized terminology. But in most primitive societies there is nothing corresponding to this elaborate body of legal institutions, with their complex and highly differentiated organization, and for this reason no purely formal definition of law, as operative in our own society, is applicable to primitive communities. The definition of primitive law is to be found ultimately in an empirical description of the way in which primitive communities cope with problems and situations comparable to those which arise in our own courts of law. Approaching the problem from this point of view we can offer a definition of law which brings out the universality in human society of mechanisms whose function is fundamentally similar to that of European legal institutions, however greatly the form of legal procedure may differ from our own.

THE DEFINITION OF PRIMITIVE LAW

As we have said, law, and particularly primitive law, cannot be considered apart from the totality of customary rules governing human behaviour. But the phrase " cannot be considered apart from " is not synonymous with " is ". In no human community do we find an undifferentiated continuum of custom which we can vaguely label " law "—on the contrary there is always a co-ordinated system of specific rules which define correct behaviour in social situations, and which are supported by various forms of sanctions. The latter term, again, must be used in a very wide sense to include not only the repressive forces which prevent breaches of custom but also the positive inducements towards social conformity. Defined in this way, sanctions are essentially *mechanisms of validation,* or forms of human behaviour which make custom effective. And the differences between various social rules within the normative system are most plainly demonstrated by a description of the sanctions by which they are enforced. By considering rules in their integral relationship to the sanctions which support them it is possible to differentiate between various aspects of custom, and in particular between legal and non-legal rules of behaviour. In speaking of primitive communities, then, what do we mean by the specifically legal aspect of their institutions? The first step in answering this question is to ask what we really mean by " law " in the context of European civilization. If we were to ask whether, in our own society, we should define law in terms of murder, theft, bigamy, and libel, or in terms of such offences as selling cigarettes after hours or parking cars in the wrong places, the answer would be fairly obvious; and it is upon the first group of functions, upon the most vitally significant aspects of law in our own society, that we must concentrate if we are to obtain a conception of law which we can extend to primitive communities. The interesting thing is that we find parallels with the above in all treatments of primitive law, with the addition of one important offence which is specific to primitive communities, namely witchcraft. Offences such as theft, adultery, incest, and murder occur with monotonous regularity in discussions of primitive law, and it is in this fact that the definition of law is to be found. All communities have rules which direct human behaviour and curb human impulses, and for the most part these are obeyed fairly generally, because it is usually easier and more profitable to conform. But certain rules have as their function the repression of deep human passions such as greed, fear, hate, jealousy, vanity and sexual desire; and the nature of these impulses is such that they are apt to sweep everything before them, to blot out from the individual consciousness all future considerations or moral restraints in the passion of their immediate appeal, and to render quite useless the usual forces of social restraint. Such cases society meets by an appeal to, or harnessing of, just those very forces which tend towards disruption. Physical violence, the confiscation of material goods, exile, abject humiliation or death are the sanctions which society employs to frustrate the more passionately disruptive forces within it. We may then define the functional significance of law as being to control the most violent, passionate and disruptive propensities of the individual by the frustration, actual or potential, of the same or similar propensities in the interests of social order. This definition applies primarily to what we usually call criminal law, but it is also applicable to civil law, because the latter depends, in the last analysis, upon a trial of physical force between the individual and the officers of the law, the result of which is a foregone conclusion.

We must not forget that legal mechanisms, as defined above, may have secondary functions. They may be extended to the correction of minor offences, to the settlement of trifling disputes, and to the regulation of administrative procedure. But we are justified in relegating these to a position of secondary importance since they might be regulated in other ways. But the primary function of law as we have defined it is something vital to the existence of every human society.

The failure to study the actual working of effective custom in primitive communities has led to a number of misconceptions concerning the forces which are operative. Of these misconceptions the most misleading is the "automatic conformity" theory, the view that the savage obeys the dictates of custom "slavishly", "unwittingly" or "automatically" without ever attempting to break through the bonds of convention or taboo. This assertion in various forms crops up over and over again in discussions of primitive law,[1] nor is it by any means limited to earlier writings or to the more academic anthropologists. Thus, in relation to our specific field, Dr P. H. Buck writes of Tongareva:

Regulations bearing upon the conduct of life, which in Western culture might be deemed to come within the province of government, were *controlled automatically* by established customs. Custom indicates appropriate procedure under the various circumstances which face the individual or the community. Children, by observing their elders or by parental instruction, are taught the correct procedure, and *no other mode of action occurs to them in life....Customs act automatically*, and there is no need for government control....What constituted right and wrong conduct had been defined by custom. *Custom was obeyed without thought of opposition* and there was little need of courts of law with police to hale malefactors to justice. Prohibitions by tapus were observed out of fear and *ingrained obedience*.[2]

The objection to such formulations as this is not merely academic. From the practical point of view there is no doubt that this idea of the automatic conformity of the savage has

[1] Cf. Malinowski, *Crime and Custom in Savage Society*, p. 10; Introduction to Hogbin, *L.O.P.* p. xxii.
[2] Te Rangi Hiroa, *E.T.* pp. 52-3 (italics ours).

created an entirely wrong impression in the minds not only of anthropologists but also of writers in general—for example, Mr Aldous Huxley speaks of the savage being "co-ordinated within a rigid framework of taboos".

It should not be necessary to refute at length the "automatic conformity" theory; in the works cited above Professor Malinowski has shown that, apart from cases of open breach of custom, there are in primitive communities organized mechanisms of evasion, due to the fact that no system of customary behaviour is ever thoroughly consistent, while human beings will always seek to gain their individual ends by defying or evading the rules laid down by their society.[1] Yet the fact remains that in the vast majority of cases human beings do conform to the traditional dictates of society, and the forces, positive and negative, which lead them to do so are the essential objects of study in considering law and custom in primitive cultures. This fact was first demonstrated for the Trobriand Islands by Professor Malinowski, and the approach in question has more recently been applied in the Polynesian field by Dr H. Ian Hogbin.[2] In dealing with Polynesian law in relation to religion it seems desirable to present a résumé of the results of Dr Hogbin's fieldwork in Ontong Java, as described in the work cited.

LAW AND CUSTOM IN ONTONG JAVA

Dr Hogbin starts with a general description of the social organization of Ontong Java. The chief sources of food supply are fish, taro and coconuts. For fish the women are exclusively dependent on the men, and the reverse is the case with taro. Coconuts are mainly collected by the men, though some women are able to supply themselves. A similar division of labour between men and women is observed in the case of house-building. After describing the individual family, he goes on to a discus-

---

[1] Thus, to quote two instances only, in the Trobriand Islands clan incest is morally condemned in explicit statement, but there is an underlying feeling that it is rather a smart thing to do. Again in Tikopia, there is a certain ceremony at which none of the participants must look at the officiating chief, being obliged to sit with bowed heads. The penalty for a breach of this rule is a handsome presentation of material goods to the offended chief. But there are instances of wealthy individuals breaking the taboo in order to be forced to make a presentation to the chief, and so make a public show of their worldly possessions. (Firth, R., unpublished manuscript.) In such instances moral rules, aesthetic standards and individual impulses such as vanity and sexual desire all co-operate in determining complex systems of human behaviour.

[2] Hogbin, L.O.P.

sion of the joint family, a group of people who trace descent from a common ancestor who generally lived about six generations ago. The leader of this joint family, or headman, is the eldest member of the group. Dr Hogbin describes the system of reciprocity within the individual and the joint families, and points out the positive incentives towards the carrying out of obligations. Thus, reverting to an instance which was cited in the last chapter, any person is normally entitled to a share of the common catch of fish, but if a man becomes known as a loafer, if he constantly shirks his share of the work, his brothers refuse to be imposed upon and deny him any fish. On the other hand a competent and energetic fisherman is honoured, and the satisfaction of vanity is thus a positive incentive. Again, members of the joint family constantly have to help one another in providing food for ceremonial exchanges, and they do this largely in the expectation of similar help for themselves in the future. Further, the authority of the headman is backed by his power to banish a member from the group, while, on the other hand, headmen might be deposed if they grossly abused their authority. Running through the whole of this system are the desire for praise and the fear of opprobrium as incentives towards social conformity.

Dr Hogbin next turns to the belief in spirits of ancestors called *kipua*, which are believed to influence the living for good or ill, particularly by visiting sickness and death upon them, or by removing it. This they may do through spite, but more often it is for some act which is socially condemned—the behaviour of the spirits is the reflection of the opinions of society. They punish such acts as failure to discharge kinship obligations, acts of violence within the joint family such as adultery, murder and displacement of the true heir, as well as incest, the breach of tapus and neglect of ceremonies. The author describes how mediums are employed to ascertain the views and intentions of the *kipua*, and he gives an account of the steps which can be taken to mitigate the illness by persuading the spirits to take up a more lenient attitude. If the *kipua* respond favourably, the patient recovers, but if they remain adamant, he dies. Dr Hogbin shows very clearly that the fear of supernatural punishment for the offences in question is an important element in social conformity.

After describing large tribal ceremonies which produce a feeling of unity within the wider group of the tribe, he goes on to deal with the legal system. Defining crime as a specific act which is punished by society, either collectively or through its officers, he tells us that there was only one crime, namely the theft of coconuts or taro from the common property, which was supervised by special officials called *polepole*. No one was allowed to go near the common property without their permission, and offenders had their heads shaved or, if they repeated the crime, they were exposed naked in the sun without food or water, or even killed. In addition to this there was private retaliation for various offences, such as adultery, or resort might be had to sorcery. In such cases society at large (as opposed to near relatives) took no part, beyond meting out praise or censure to the various parties concerned.

In this valuable contribution to the study of primitive law, Dr Hogbin has completely proved his main thesis, namely that obedience to custom and the observance of social obligations cannot be put down to any one social force—rather are they the products of the operation of a number of different factors. And he has also demonstrated the fact that forces such as those which he describes in connection with Ontong Java were also operative in other parts of Polynesia.[1] The factors of social conformity to which he draws attention may be classified in different ways, but the most convenient arrangement for our present purpose is a twofold division into those forces which depend upon self-interest, upon the hedonistic anticipation of future events on the one hand; and on the other those which depend upon tradition, upon immediate obedience to socially recognized rules of behaviour, even when these dictate lines of conduct which are not in keeping with individual desires and aspirations. Both of these groups of factors are recognized by Dr Hogbin; his description of social life illustrates very well the fact that in Ontong Java, as elsewhere, the way of the transgressor is hard. And he also refers to tradition,[2] though here his documentation is not so complete, the influence of traditional obedience being only mentioned incidentally,[3] and only in one

---

[1] Hogbin, *L.O.P.* chaps. VII–X.

[2] "We must take into account the moulding force of tradition, and the influence which results from mere membership of any given society, from sharing a common language, and a common material and spiritual culture. Participation in the life of a community inevitably creates a whole series of emotional ties. This feeling of unity itself tends to make each member respect the rights of his fellows and carry out his obligations to them. It is revived and strengthened from time to time by religious ceremonies in which the whole group takes part." (Hogbin, *L.O.P.* pp. 85–6.)

[3] For example: "Once I heard a father say: 'If you behave like this people will think you come from Malaita.'" The women gather round the well and dis-

place does he describe in detail the complementary nature of the two groups of factors to which we have referred:

Probably it is only a very small number of people who ever have thoughts of murdering a relative, or of committing adultery with his wife. But the influence of early training tends to repress any such thoughts that may arise. From childhood each man has been told that such actions are wrong, and he has heard a dozen examples of the horrible fate that overtook men who murdered their brothers or stole the wives of persons related to them. Should a sin of this kind be committed, he has an opportunity of observing the disapproval shown by his fellow tribesmen, and when the sinner dies he hears them pronounce the death as a judgment of the *kipua*. In his early days, were he to have thoughts of a similar murder or adultery, he would probably be prevented from carrying them into execution by his fear of the *kipua*. In later life his mode of thought and of action has become so habitual that it never occurs to him to commit the sin—if he is normal. The exceptional individual may be held in check by continued fear both of public disapproval and of the *kipua*.[1]

In other parts of the work he stresses the desire for public approval and the complementary impulse to avoid reproof and contempt, but when these forces are described in a context of "self-interest" motives, only half the story has been told. This is because, though vanity may be a universal human motive, the means by which it is satisfied are variously defined in different societies—in one it may be age, in another divine ancestry, and in a third prowess in war. Fully to explain its operation we should need biographical studies of the linguistic conditioning of children, comparable to those which Professor Piaget has conducted on European schoolchildren[2]—only in this way can we understand how terms of praise and blame become potent forces in opposition to individual anti-social motives. Further, we should have to ask whether there are any metaphorical linguistic usages, similar to our use of such terms as "wrong", "impossible" or, most significant of all, "unthinkable". Traditional forces possess some autonomy apart from the motives of self-interest upon which they are based; this is evidenced by the fact that in Ontong Java there exists a tendency for things to go on as they were before—a headman could abuse his authority for some time before he was deposed, and if a man were banished from his joint family by the headman, even if he were not pardoned, his children might be readmitted. This shows that even

cuss a case of adultery for hours, and "their general conclusion is that the woman is unworthy of her sex". "Few adults care to run the risk of being nicknamed '*ke moki*', sneak thief", and so on.
[1] Hogbin, *L.O.P.* p. 165.
[2] Cf. Piaget, *The Moral Judgement of the Child*.

in exile a man was still held to have some traditional bond with his joint family.

The forces of self-interest and those of tradition are, then, joint determinants of social conformity, and neither must be stressed at the expense of the other. Where one fails, the other becomes effective.[1] Human rationality is never entirely blinded by tradition, nor are ideals completely impotent in checking selfishness. Man is neither entirely a deluded Quixotic fool nor a calculating hedonist—the very nature of culture itself determines that he shall be both at the same time.

THE SUPERNATURAL AS A MORAL AND LEGAL FORCE

On the basis of the distinction which has been drawn between the sanctions of self-interest and the sanctions of tradition, we can discern the specifically magico-religious aspect of each of these groups of forces in Ontong Java. Firstly, beliefs in the supernatural provided two important mechanisms whereby self-interest was rendered socially effective. The belief in spirits and their power to cause illness acted as a powerful deterrent against certain classes of anti-social acts, while the beliefs in sorcery provided a means of redress in cases of wrong, placing an additional weapon in the hands of the aggrieved person, and providing an additional threat against the potential wrongdoer. As Dr Hogbin puts it:

> Black magic was simply the means by which justifiable vengeance was carried out, and may be compared with the dagger with which the husband killed the man who had wronged him: both were weapons by means of which property and interests were safeguarded. Sorcery was perhaps the stronger of the two because it enabled a trespasser to be punished even without his identity being discovered. Society backed both forms of retaliation in the same way, by its passive approval.[2]

Adding another analogy to that of Dr Hogbin we might compare the role of the *kipua* of Ontong Java to that of police,

---

[1] The co-ordination of self-interest and tradition in determining social conformity is perhaps best illustrated by an analogy. Comparing the activities of human communities with a steam engine, we might liken the influence of self-interest to the pressure of steam in the cylinder, the ultimate force whereby activity is generated; tradition, on the other hand, operates in a way similar to the fly-wheel; itself incapable of generating activity, it none the less possesses a certain degree of autonomy, and can ensure that the mechanism shall continue to operate for a time, even when the ultimate source of power is momentarily cut off.

[2] Hogbin, *L.O.P.* p. 221.

judges and prison authorities in our own society; they provided a very real threat of unpleasant consequences for the transgressor. The analogy is implicit in the extract quoted above from Dr P. H. Buck's reference to Tongarevan taboos, and the parallel between their role in society and that of our own legal institutions. The recognition of this pragmatic element is essential to an understanding of the part played by beliefs in the supernatural in the legal and moral systems of primitive communities. Even in Dr Buck's formulation there exists, as we have seen, the implication of "automatic conformity", which obscures the purely hedonistic appeal of tradition in general and of religious tradition in particular.[1]

But the influence of magico-religious beliefs is not confined to the provision of punishment in cases of breach of custom or rewards for its observance. They also contribute in a subtle way towards the positive maintenance of custom itself, by supporting authority and validating tradition generally. Entering as they do into all the important institutions of society, they definitely add to the efficacy of custom. In dealing with the ethics of Society Island religion, we pointed out that its moral dictates were intrinsic rather than extrinsic, the gods being more concerned with the observation of obligations towards themselves than with the behaviour of men towards one another and their moral conduct generally. To this we must now add the reservation that, though explicit rules of moral conduct do not play the same part in primitive religions as they do in our own, such religions do serve to support the institutions of society with their correlated ethical rules.[2] In terms of the Polynesian material which we have reviewed in this and the preceding chapters, it might be said that religion conduced to obedience to political authority, not by any explicit direction from the gods

---

[1] Cf. the following: "The savage...is a slave, not indeed to a visible master, but to the past, to the spirits of his dead forefathers, who haunt his steps from birth to death, and rule him with a rod of iron. What they did is a pattern of right, the unwritten law to which he yields a blind unquestioning obedience." (Frazer, *E.H.K.* p. 85.) With regard to the phrase "who haunt his steps from birth to death", compare the following: "The Ontong Javanese think no more of the *kipua* than we do of divine punishment or of criminal procedure. At times they are afraid, just as Europeans sometimes fear the arm of the law or the last judgment, but such moments are comparatively rare." (Hogbin, *L.O.P.* p. 162.)

[2] Even in Christianity the ethical influence of religion is apt to extend beyond the explicit moral dogma laid down in Holy Writ, and to influence quite extraneous modes of conduct, such as the employment of cosmetics, stimulants or tobacco.

that the chiefs should be obeyed, but by establishing their sanctity and so reinforcing their authority. In land tenure, again, there was not always an explicit religious prohibition against trespass, yet the cosmogony and the legends of tribal gods served to establish a traditional link between man and his land, and so conduced to the observance of the rights of property. Finally, in such an institution as warfare, as we have described it, in the Society Islands, the human beings concerned did not suffer injury and death because of any explicit injunction from the gods to fight; but they did live in a community whose legends were rich in tales of conflict between the gods themselves; and where these gods were believed to participate in warfare from start to finish, supporting their worshippers in battle, and being, like them, humiliated by defeat. Only by studying contextual features such as these can we appreciate fully the role of magico-religious factors in ensuring social conformity.

CHAPTER XIV

THE PLACE OF RELIGION IN CULTURE

IN this work an attempt has been made to define the cultural significance of Polynesian religion. A review of its formal characteristics—its ideology, ritual and material equipment—led us to a consideration of its relations to other aspects of native life. Dealing with the major institutional activities of a typical Polynesian community (that of the Society Islanders), we were able to show that in each of them magico-religious factors played an important part; and after this we referred to some of the problems presented by the relationship of religion to political organization, to economics, and to law. The general intention of this treatment was to show that magico-religious beliefs and practices were important integrative factors in the cultures of Polynesia; that they sanctified economic and political institutions; that they acted, together with other forces, in a very positive way towards the maintenance of law and custom; and that the real significance of religion is best understood by studying the part which it plays in the integral reality of native life. In this way Polynesian religion appears not simply as a quaint agglomeration of superstitions, nor as a collection of tedious texts and monotonous ritual, nor even as a mixture of immature philosophy and poetic phantasy. On the contrary, a study of its dynamic functions leads us to regard it as an active cultural force of profound significance, binding together social groups, co-ordinating their activities, and providing a spiritual background for every phase of social life.

ETHNOGRAPHIC *LACUNAE*

From our discussion of the relation of Polynesian religion to other aspects of native culture there emerged a number of wider problems, with which the available material does not allow us to deal in detail. In conclusion, therefore, we shall present certain generalizations concerning the place of religion in human society, some of which we have been able to document from the Polynesian material, and some of which must be regarded rather as hypotheses for further investigation. A treatment of this kind is designed to indicate not only the positive contribution of Polynesian ethnography to the study of religion, but also the gaps in the available material. In particular we are struck by the fact that the whole educational aspect of Polynesian religion has been almost completely ignored in the records of observers, although it is perhaps the most significant field of investigation in any scientific study of human society. In psychology, widely different schools of thought—the psycho-analysts and the behaviourists—have studied in detail the significance of early experiences or "conditioning" in the formation of personality; and though we may not agree with their specific interpretations, nor with the overwhelming importance which they attach to the early years of life, it is impossible to deny that the study of early childhood is significant in the understanding of human behaviour. In social anthropology a beginning has been made in the recognition of the educational aspect of social life[1]—particularly in kinship,[2] in economics,[3] and in linguistics.[4] But the empirical information concerning the manner in which culture is impressed upon the growing child is negligible in comparison with the many problems which demand investigation. Specifically in regard to the magico-religious systems of Central Polynesia, we are presented with religion as a *fait accompli* in the adult worshipper; the field records tell us of people who believe in the gods whom they worship, but there is nothing to show how faith is first instilled nor how ritual is learned; yet the *initial situation of religious experience*, the age at which the child first becomes conscious of the supernatural, is vital to an understanding of the religious sentiments and behaviour of later life.

To illustrate this statement, we may refer to certain far-reaching problems, which must ultimately be solved by a study of cultural conditioning. In the first place there is the alleged "illogicality" of primitive magico-religious beliefs, which is sometimes put down to the "pre-logical mentality" of the savage. To begin with, the terms used are unfortunate. It is not in the logical processes, in the reasoning from the premises of magico-religious beliefs, that the error of these beliefs is to be found. On the contrary, granted the premises, the inferences from them, and the behaviour based upon these inferences, are

[1] Cf. Mead, *C.A.S.* and *Growing up in New Guinea*.
[2] Malinowski, "Parenthood, the Basis of Social Structure" in *The New Generation*, ed. Calverton and Schmalhausen.
[3] Audrey I. Richards, *Hunger and Work in a Savage Tribe*.
[4] Malinowski, *Coral Gardens and their Magic*, vol. II, Part IV, Divs. V and VI.

logically beyond criticism. If, for example, it is granted that ancestral spirits are able to cause illness among the living, then the efficacy of some such system of placation as exists in Ontong Java is a logical inference from the premises. But, it may be asked, is not the very acceptance of such premises an indication of an inferior type of mentality? The answer to this question is only to be found in a study of the conditions under which the acceptance takes place, of the early conditioning which gives to culturally accepted beliefs a superlative cogency, in other words of the way in which the growing individual is led to accept the truth of magico-religious dogma. The genetic development of faith, almost entirely neglected up to the present, is perhaps the most important field of study in attempting to understand religious belief, whether primitive or civilized. And if it could be established that the forces which lead to the acceptance of dogma are universal in human society, however different may be the configuration of dogmatically held beliefs, we should have taken another step in freeing anthropological science of the incubus of "primitive mentality". In this unexplored field of scientific investigation the most that we can do is to suggest an hypothesis for investigation, the hypothesis that in all human communities there exists a certain amount of "pre-logical" thought, side by side with a great deal of rationality, but that the specific fields in which these occur vary from one community to another. In attaining his material ends, primitive man indulges in a great amount of what appears to us to be superstitious nonsense; but in his repudiation of these ends as the goal *par excellence* of all human endeavour he may be less subject to dogma than many modern communities, and is perhaps fortunate in the possession of a pre-civilized mentality.

A study of the educational aspect of magico-religious institutions might even carry us farther, and make possible historical hypotheses concerning their evolution, which is at present impossible because of the lack of empirical data. For social evolution has taken place essentially in the process of transmission. In isolated cases, perhaps, public catastrophes, migrations, or such historically significant events may have led to fundamental changes in social institutions, while the influence of exceptional individuals within any community is notoriously apt to produce or accelerate the process of social change. But historically significant events such as we have mentioned are the exception rather than the rule, while one of the principles of human society is that outstanding individuals must not be too outstanding, otherwise they are likely to find themselves in prison, on the gallows, or in the communal oven. Viewed in the broad way, social evolution has probably taken place in a far less spectacular manner, by the gradual modification of tradition in the process of its transmission, that is in the passing on of spiritual wealth from one generation to another. And an empirical study of this process as it actually works would perhaps lead us to the formulation of the general laws governing social change.[1]

Finally, a study of religious education would lead us to a very vital aspect of religion, namely its place in the life cycle of the individual from birth to death. It cannot be doubted that the implications of Polynesian religion in the life of the individual were far wider than those which we have been able to demonstrate. In Chapter XII we criticized certain metaphysical interpretations of Polynesian religion as obscuring its purely pragmatic aspect, and as going beyond the ethnographic evidence. Yet it cannot be doubted that religion, as well as serving purely practical and social ends, did exert an influence upon the individual consciousness. In such a formulation as that of Stimson, for example, attention is drawn to the importance of religion in satisfying individual spiritual needs.[2] What these needs are, what relation they bear to other more practical wants, and to what extent they are inborn or culturally determined, are matters for empirical investigation; but their universality in human societies is proved by the ubiquity of religious institutions. Our objection is not to the affirmation of their existence, but to an *a priori* definition of their nature in terms of European ideology, without any documentation by records of native statements and behaviour.

Another important aspect of Polynesian religion which has been almost completely ignored is the linguistic one. Language is important to the student of any branch of human activity in three ways. In the first place it is a purely practical tool of field-work, an expedient for obtaining reliable information; secondly, it may be studied from the purely linguistic point of view; and thirdly, it may be studied as a cultural factor *sui generis*, not merely as a verbal pattern but as a force which

---

[1] For an hypothesis as to the origins of magic, worked out along this line, see Malinowski, *Coral Gardens and their Magic*, vol. II, p. 247.
[2] See above, p. 310 *n.* 1.

influences human activity in a very definite way. The study of sociological linguistics leads to the conclusion that language is not merely a mechanism for "communicating ideas" but has far wider implications in human culture. It emerges from human activities with which it is closely correlated, and can only be understood in its integral relation to social life. Such an approach has been adopted, and its manifold implications indicated, by Professor Malinowski,[1] and it is unnecessary to repeat his arguments here. But a study of his work on the language of Trobriand garden magic, side by side with the existing material on the linguistic aspect of Polynesian religion, brings out very clearly the inadequacy of the latter. In spite of the masses of native texts which have been collected and "translated", there is yet not one single study of a comprehensive body of Polynesian religious texts with the full linguistic and sociological commentary which is necessary if translations are to reproduce the full reality of native language as a creative force in culture.[2]

THE INTER-RELATIONSHIP OF CULTURAL FACTS

In defining the relationships of religion to other aspects of culture, we have on several occasions referred to their reciprocal nature. In political organization, authority is supported by religion, which establishes the sanctity of chieftainship; but religion is itself supported by the exercise of temporal power, so far as this is effective. In economics, industry is sanctified and the laws of property supported by religious beliefs and practices; but the material equipment of temples, images and offerings provides visible, tangible, and impressive evidence of the spiritual realities with which they are associated. In law, again, we have seen that the belief in the supernatural provides definite sanctions for the enforcement of customary behaviour, while the observable influence of the spirits, in illness or death, serves to reinforce the beliefs concerning them. Thus it is that religion at the same time validates and is validated by the other aspects of culture to which it is related. This type of reciprocal relationship between social facts, which we might term the *principle of complementary validation*, runs right through all human society,

---

[1] Malinowski, *Coral Gardens and their Magic*, vol. II, *passim*.

[2] The Tikopian religious texts which have been treated in this way by Dr Raymond Firth ("Totemism in Polynesia", *Oceania*, vol. I, pp. 291–321, 377–98) indicate how greatly such an approach may contribute to an understanding of Polynesian religion.

and possesses far-reaching implications: thus, in the most general sociological problem of all—the relation of the individual to society—our analysis of culture leads us to recognize this principle. Just as social institutions derive their validity from the fact that they provide expression for the physiological and psychological potentialities of the individual, so is the unrestrained fulfilment of these potentialities limited by the very institutions which give them expression.

In insisting upon the functional unity of culture, and upon the relationship of each of its aspects to every other, we must not carry our contention too far. If we were to split a culture up into small formal elements—single sentences spoken, fragments of human behaviour, or isolated material objects—we should fail for the most part to detect functional relationships between them. This is because such a division of the integral reality of culture is artificial and unscientific, resembling the procedure of the butcher's shop rather than that of the dissecting room. It ignores the existence of organized systems of human activity— economic, political, magico-religious and the like—of which the isolated formal elements are but a part. Regarded in this way, each of the formal elements is related to every other, not directly, but through the institutionalized system of human activity of which it forms a part. As an example of this, let us refer to a specific phase of our problem, namely the relation of traditional magico-religious beliefs to Polynesian economics.

The most general function of religious beliefs in Polynesian economic life was to provide a charter for existing economic institutions. The whole system of mythology, which told of how the world came to be as it is at present, gave to contemporary institutions the binding force of long-standing authority, and invested them with the sanctity of the past. Cosmogonies served to bring man into relation with nature, firstly, by drawing natural phenomena into the scheme of social values, and secondly by justifying these values by observable evidence. Again, the legends of the gods, of their miraculous actions and supernatural powers, served to validate the belief in the supernatural, to impress upon human beings the existence of effective powers beyond themselves, powers which nevertheless played an active part in their everyday life.

The validation of social institutions by traditional belief is a general feature of all cultures, but the specific manner in which religious beliefs influence social life varies from one community to another. We may find special developments correlated with variations in social institutions, for example, the association of the guild of master craftsmen in Samoa with Tangaloa is correlated with their economic importance as a social grouping; or the association of Oro with war, and with the *arioi* society, in the Society Islands, which may be correlated with the special development of warfare and recreation in this area.

But it is, in any given culture, impossible to correlate the elements of social institutions point by point with mythology; in other words, not all elements in the social structure possess a specific mythological charter. Nor does the degree of their social importance always correspond with their validation in tradition. Sometimes we find legends associated with quite trifling details—for example, a Samoan legend connected with the manufacture of squid lures. These objects are made of pieces of dark basaltic stone, shaped like a spinning-top, trimmed with shell and bearing a trailing length of coconut root, to which are attached pieces of coconut leaflet. We are not here concerned with the detailed technology of the lure.[1] The interesting thing to note is that the completed lure is made in imitation of a rat; in action, that is to say when it is being jerked about near the bottom of the lagoon, "the lure looks ridiculously like a rat in the convulsions of drowning"; and the clicking of shell against stone is supposed to represent the squeaking of the dying animal.

The method of manufacture and the manner of use of the squid lure are associated with a legend of the rail, the rat and the hermit-crab. These three while voyaging in a half coconut shell were overtaken by a hurricane which wrecked their craft. The rail flew back to land, the hermit-crab sank to the bottom of the sea, and only the rat was left helplessly swimming about. When it cried out in despair, the octopus (*fe'e*) took pity on it and offered to carry it to land on its head. While it was saving the rat's life in this way, the rat defecated on its head without the octopus knowing it; and when they reached the land, the rat taunted the octopus with the insult which had been offered him. The octopus was furious, and, though unable to follow the rat on land, swore that if ever he caught it in the sea again, he would

---

[1] For a description of this together with its legend, see Te Rangi Hiroa, *S.M.C.* pp. 434–8. A similar association between the technology of the lure and the legendary quarrel between the squid or octopus and the rat occurs in Tonga (Gifford, *T.M.T.* p. 206) and the Ellice Islands (Kennedy, *C.V.* pp. 161–2).

avenge the insult. This explains the fascination of the squid lure for the octopus, and why men manufacture it in the form of a rat.

Here we have a fairly elaborate legend which is correlated with details of technology in a comparatively unimportant economic activity. Other examples of a similar character could be given. But our immediate interest is to contrast this instance with, for example, the inaugural rite of the Tikopian seasonal festival known as "The Work of the Gods". This festival consists of a series of ceremonies, lasting over a period of about six weeks, and performed twice a year. It is inaugurated by a rite, termed "throwing the firestick", performed by the chief of the head clan of the island. We cannot deal in detail with this ceremony here;[1] it is sufficient to note its importance in the social life of the Tikopia. It has primarily a religious significance, inaugurating a period during which men are in close *rapport* with the gods; it also marks a period of *tapu* during which both recreation and economic activities are restricted out of respect for the gods, a time at which the sacerdotal functions of chieftainship are brought to the fore, the whole system of economic, religious and political organization being closely welded in a series of profoundly significant ceremonies. Yet the inaugural ceremony has no mythological background; there is no story of how or why it was first performed—traditional precedent alone is cited as a justification for the rite.

This important ceremony, lacking as it does any validation in mythology, is cited side by side with the example of the Samoan squid lure in order to bring out the contrast between the two cases. Every field-worker is familiar with this type of contrast— on the one hand important institutional activities carried out merely because it has always been done so, and on the other trifling details of procedure in mundane activities correlated with elaborate and dramatic accounts of mythological origins. The theoretical significance of this anomaly is that it leads to two important conclusions in regard to the correlation of elements in legendary history with individual social forms, such as rites, ethical rules, or technical procedures. Firstly, that there is not always a *specific* correlation—certain social forms have no detailed validation in history, and are merely observed because things have always been done in that particular way; and

[1] The whole series of ceremonies making up "The Work of the Gods" is fully described in a book at present in preparation by Dr Raymond Firth, from the manuscript of which the following material is taken.

secondly, that the existence, or the degree of elaboration, of a legendary justification for a social form is not always directly correlated with the cultural importance of the latter. We must therefore consider the body of mythological tradition as a whole, *vis-à-vis* the entire system of existing social institutions. Mythology invests these with an aura of sanctity, by stressing particular elements and their supposed origin in the distant past, and this gives a charter to the institutions as a whole. Moreover, if we were to consider not isolated forms, but integral institutions, we should find that mythological justification enters into them at various points. Thus, to revert to our examples, the making of the squid lure is but a small element in Samoan material culture. But it forms a part of a series of vitally important institutional activities connected with the obtaining of marine creatures, the Samoans' chief source of flesh food. For this reason fishing in Samoa was associated, not only with elaborate rules of technology, but with specific economic groupings, with the division of labour between the sexes, with the privileges and obligations of the master fisherman and with the making of large sea-going canoes by the Sa Tangaloa, the guild of expert craftsmen. Again, in the Tikopian example, the "Work of the Gods" considered as a whole is associated with a body of legendary history, even though the important inaugural rite, considered by itself, has no specific justification in myth. And what we have said of the relationship of religious legends to economic activities might also be said of any other set of functional relationships within a given culture.

To illustrate this let us take two comparatively trivial social activities—cooking and recreation. Cooking is normally one of the least spectacular things which man does, and it never has, from the superficial point of view, any pronounced magico-religious significance. Yet a moment's consideration of one of its essential elements—heat, almost universally produced by fire—reminds us at once of the widespread myths concerning the origin of fire, often associated with the belief that there once was a time when men ate food raw, before they obtained fire or learned the art of making it. Nor can cooking be dissociated from the sequence of activities of which it is the penultimate stage, eating being the final one. And the economics of food production are generally associated with magico-religious beliefs and practices, determined, like the practical activities with which they are correlated, by the ultimate goal of satisfying hunger.

Again, recreation when it is highly institutionalized (as in the *arioi* performances of the Society Islands or the dart matches of Tikopia) may become associated with specific religious beliefs and ritual. But what of the apparently insignificant play of children? Here it must be remembered that children almost always play in imitation of their elders, and their games are immature reproductions of the institutional activities which they see going on around them. The games of children are institutions *in embryo*. And at the same time as they are imitating the behaviour of adults, children are hearing of the religious beliefs associated with it, and are either observing the correlated ritual or being carefully prevented from doing so. In the daytime, perhaps, they play games representing family life, while at night they may observe adults discussing the ancestor cult, making offerings to the family deities, or narrating tales of incest among the gods and culture heroes. One day they may make toy canoes, and the next witness the ceremonial consecration of a real one. Education in religious matters thus proceeds *pari passu* with training in the practical activities with which religion, in adult social life, is so closely linked.

Examples such as the above might be multiplied indefinitely, but they should suffice to show that though isolated items of culture are not always related to each other directly, there is invariably some significant link through the wider systems of human activity of which they form a part.

WEIRDNESS AND INTELLIGIBILITY
OF THE SUPERNATURAL

We must now refer again to one very general feature of magico-religious institutions, namely their special configuration when compared with other more practical activities. As we have seen, the phenomena of religion are unique in their configuration, as regards the nature of the beliefs, the character of the observances, and the form of the material substratum. Religious beliefs always contain an element of the strange, the spectacular, or the miraculous. Ritual is different, both in form and function, from the practical procedure of everyday life. And finally, religion always implies special material objects, invested with a peculiar sanctity, which is vouched for by their mythological origin, by their unusual or striking form, or by the special ritual and artistic treatment which they receive at the hands of man.

Religion, then, is essentially exotic. But it none the less contains practical and easily intelligible elements. Religious dogma makes definite assertions concerning the character of the supernatural, the operation of the superhuman forces involved, and the nature of spiritual reality. Ritual, again, is based upon beliefs in its efficacy or the need for observing it. And the material objects associated with religious cults are sacred, not because of a vague and undefined affirmation that they have *mana*, but because of the specific beliefs concerning them, and the ritual of their preparation and use. Religion is not a vague efflorescence of the mysterious, but is manifest in specific culturally defined relationships between man and his geographical and social environment.

Professor Malinowski has dealt with this matter in relation to a specific problem, namely the spells of Trobriand garden magic.[1] The language employed in these, he points out, has two important aspects, which he terms the coefficient of weirdness and the coefficient of intelligibility. Some of the words and grammatical usages of magical spells are archaic or peculiar to this particular division of native speech: on the other hand spells are for the most part made up of the words and constructions of ordinary everyday speech; so much so that the intention of the words of a magical spell is generally understandable from a general familiarity with the language, though the "meaning of meaningless words" can only be understood by an examination of their philological associations, studied in their context of cultural activity. The coefficient of weirdness he puts down to the need for removing magical speech from the language of the ordinary world, for referring it back to its historical origins in the distant past, and so increasing its specifically creative power. On the other hand all magical language defines a relationship between man and the thing to be influenced, and this is usually done in the same manner as in everyday speech. The language of the spell in this case derives its magical quality from its linguistic and cultural context, rather than from any peculiarity of form.

This view might be extended from the specific field of magical language to magico-religious phenomena in general. Some element of weirdness or mystery is essential in order to remove them from the world of everyday life, and to invest belief with its cogency, ritual with its efficacy, and sacred objects

[1] Malinowski, *Coral Gardens and their Magic*, vol. II, Part VI.

with that quality which differentiates a temple from a hut, or an idol from a doll. On the other hand, religion can never be entirely esoteric and must always bear some relationship to human affairs. Religious beliefs must have some intelligible content in spite of the tendentious *lacunae* which they impose upon the human understanding. In ritual, ordinary patterns of human behaviour are arranged in a traditionally defined sequence, designed to invest ceremonial with its impressiveness. And finally sacred objects must be made by specified techniques depending on the technological knowledge of man and the raw materials at his disposal.

This has some bearing on the discussion in Chapter VIII of the two aspects of magico-religious institutions. On the one hand their validation depends upon the generation of effective belief in the supernatural, while on the other the spiritual reality so generated must be intelligible, and its force available, to human beings engaged in magico-religious activity. This is why all systems of magic and of religion are at the same time removed to some extent from ordinary everyday life, and yet closely related to mundane affairs. The reason for this is to be found in the psychology of the individual, considered in its cultural context.

THE CREATIVE FUNCTION OF
RELIGIOUS BELIEF

Without either accepting or rejecting its many implications, we may refer at this point to Freud's opposition between the pleasure-pain principle and the reality principle, which, for the purposes of our discussion, may be formulated as follows. In every human individual there exist biologically determined urges, which seek to attain pleasure by various means—through sexual satisfaction, through vanity, and by the attainment of a feeling of security. But these potentialities must always be limited in their expression by reality, which refuses to square with the individual human being's conception of the world as it ought to be. Faced with this discrepancy between his desires and the possibility of their satisfaction, the individual seeks for some reconciliation. On the one hand, he seeks by practical and rational expedients to increase the sum of his happiness, and where this attempt is frustrated, to develop mechanisms which will attain for him an illusory satisfaction, in dreams, neurosis or harmless phantasy. The study of these purely individual phenomena[1] is a problem for psychology rather than for sociology. Their relevance for the latter study lies in the fact that human culture provides institutionalized forms of compensation for the failure of reality to satisfy man's infinite desires. Love magic provides a putative means of attaining sexual satisfaction, over and above that which can be attained by amorous advances; the ritual of economics gives confidence in cases where the satisfaction of man's hunger and vanity may be prevented by some catastrophe; and finally the ultimate frustration of all man's hopes and plans by death is made to seem less inevitable and overwhelming by beliefs in immortality and by the active affirmation of continued social existence in mortuary ceremonial. As Professor Malinowski says of magic, it is "the institutionalized expression of human optimism, of constructive hopes overcoming doubt and pessimism".[2]

It is necessary at this point to follow Malinowski in repudiating the view that magic (and, we would add, religion) can be equated at all points with the pathological phenomena of phantasy and neurosis, and that it can be fully explained in terms of the "omnipotence of thought". This view is untenable because "man never runs on the side-track of magical verbiage or of magical activities in that idle day-dreaming which stultifies action". On the contrary, magico-religious beliefs serve as a stimulus towards action, firstly, by providing a "morally integrated attitude towards the future",[3] and secondly, by organizing effective co-operation in practical pursuits. Even in the supreme protest against futility, expressed in beliefs in immortality and mortuary ritual, a number of useful practical results are attained. The individual is braced to meet the inevitable end; his friends and relatives are comforted in their bereavement; and finally the place which he filled in the social life is not left altogether empty, his status as an ancestor ensuring a continuation, for a time at least, of his social effectiveness. Religion and magic are not merely the monstrous phantasies of terrified mortals fleeing from reality; rather do they, by the organization of human activity, help to create a new

[1] To the phrase "purely individual phenomena" we must add the *caveat* that the specific configuration of these is culturally determined, as has been demonstrated in the case of dreams by Dr J. S. Lincoln (*The Dream in Primitive Cultures*, p. 23); cf. above, p. 208.
[2] Malinowski, *Coral Gardens and their Magic*, vol. II, p. 239.
[3] *Ibid.* p. 245.

reality more consonant with human needs, a reality in which economic success is in fact furthered by magic, not directly and according to the simple statement of a native informant, but indirectly, through its effects on human behaviour; and where a form of immortality is demonstrably attained by the individual through his contribution of human effort to his culture, and through the recognition by that culture of his place in its scheme of activity and co-operation.

INDEX

Aitu: Ontong Java, 36; Samoa, 10–13
Alai Valu (Tonga), 88
Alao (Samoa), 80
Alataua (Samoa), 80–1
Alo-alo: (Samoa) 82, (Tonga) 85
Ancestor worship, as origin of religion, 190
Animism, 190–1
Arioi, 268–71, 329
Art, as aspect of culture, 201
Atanua (Marquesas), 94
Atea: 56; Hervey Islands, 58–9; Marquesas, 24, 54, 57–8, 94; Paumotu, 55, 58; Society Islands, 57; Tongareva, 58
Atua: Marquesas, 23; Paumotu, 26; Rotuma, 28; Samoa, 9–13; Society Islands, 16–20; Tikopia, 35–6
Augury, *see* Omens
Austral Islands: Island Gods of, 99–100
Avatea, *see* Atea

Belief: genesis of, 324–5; role of, 228–33, 328–31, 334–6
Belief and ritual, connection between, 36, 102, 228–9
Birth, ritual of, 260–1
Buck, P. H., *see* Te Rangi Hiroa
Bulotu, 7, 14, 45, 84
Burial places: 148–64; areas: Hervey Islands, 160–1; Marquesas, 157–60; Paumotu, 161–2; Samoa, 153; Society Islands, 150–1; Tonga, 154–7; taboo, 132–4

Canoes: 42; ceremonial of building, 252; sacred (Society Islands), 173–5
Chiefs: economic claims of, 300–1; functions of, 257–9, 285–92; inauguration of, 261–3
Chieftainship: sanctity of: 257–64, 277–92; divine descent of chiefs, 19, 37, 45, 47, 69; ritual surrounding chiefs, 26, 48, 61, 71, 121–2, 130–1, 182
Childbirth, 271–2
Circumcision, 272
Coconut leaves: an insignia of rank, 180–1; sacred, 180; Hervey Islands, 178; Samoa, 167–8; Society Islands, 175
Coconuts: sacred, Ellice Islands, 179; Marquesas, 176
Conch shells: sacred, Marquesas, 176; Society Islands, 172; Tonga, 169
Context, importance of, 198, 322
Cooking: and fire myths, 331; by opposite sex, prohibition of, 142–3

Cosmogonies, 3–5, 44, 47
Culture: analysis of, 198–204, 327–32; aspects of, 200–2

Dart matches, prayers connected with, 104
Death: ritual of (Society Islands), 273–4; *see also* Immortality
Divination, *see* Possession
Drums: sacred, Hervey Islands, 178; Samoa, 167; Society Islands, 173
Durkheim, Émile: on primitive religion, 193–4; on religion and magic, 212–13

Easter Island: Island Gods of, 97–9
Economic pursuits: belief and ritual connected with, 42, 45, 57, 58, 76–7, 79, 93, 121, 129; gods and, 8, 17, 18–19, 20, 61
Economics: as aspect of culture, 200, 293–5; religion and, 243–54, 293–308, 327, 329–31, 335–6
Education: as aspect of culture, 200; religious, 271, 324, 332
Ellice Islands: Island Gods of, 100–1

Faitoka, see Burial places (Tonga)
Fakatoumafi (Tonga), 87
Faka-Veli-Kele (Fotuna), 29, 97
Fale-aitu, see Temples (Samoa)
Fanonga (Samoa), *see* Le Fanonga
Fasting, 145–6
Feaki (Tonga), 87
Feathers as emblems of rank, 181
Fe'e (Samoa), 6, 74
Fehuluni (Tonga), 87
Fenoulounga (Tonga), 87
Finau-tau-iku (Tonga), 87
Firth, Raymond: on primitive economics, 294 *n.*; (Maori) on land tenure, 298 *n.* 3, 308 *n.*; on ownership, 298 *n.* 4; (Tikopia) on chiefs as priests, 290 *n.*; on dart matches, 272; on land tenure, 298 *n.* 3; on religion, 35–6, 327 *n.* 2, 330 *n.* 1; on totemism, 296, 309
Fishing: 42, 46; ethics of, 250–1; Society Islands, 243–51; religion and, 295–6
Folaha (Ellice Islands), 100–1
Folasa, 30
Food taboos, 146–7
Fotuna: Island Gods of, 96–7
Frazer, J. G.: on force of custom, 321 *n.* 1; on religion and magic, 192–3, 211–12; on secular and sacerdotal functions, 287
Futtafaihe, 86

INDEX